The
Queer German
Cinema

Alice A. Kuzniar

**The
Queer German
Cinema**

*Stanford University Press
Stanford, California*

Stanford University Press
Stanford, California
© 2000 by the Board of Trustees of the
Leland Stanford Junior University

Printed in the United States of America
CIP data appear at the end of the book

Acknowledgments

One of the pleasures of working in cinema studies is the avid exchange of videotapes between friends and colleagues. This book would never have gotten off the ground without the support of those who helped me gather and locate films: Andy Ade, Ron Bartholomew, Susan Buie, Larry Ferber, Gerd Gemünden, Hagen Gottschalck, Sabine Hake, Tony Kaes, Larry Rickels, Jim Steakley, David Teague, and Mitch Whitchard. My immense gratitude goes out to those filmmakers discussed in this book who generously made their work available to me and especially those who didn't mind me pestering them with questions and chapters to read: Dagmar Beiersdorf, Lily Besilly, Michael Brynntrup, Jürgen Brüning, Jörg Fockele, Stefanie Jordan, Heidi Kull, Lothar Lambert, Bjørn Melhus, Matthias Müller, Nathalie Percillier, Rosa von Praunheim, Dom and Ben Reding, Hans A. Scheirl, Claudia Schillinger, Michael Stock, Lars Theuerkauff, Monika Treut, and Claudia Zoller. I also cannot thank enough a number of individuals at film archives for their pleasant and informative guidance, birgit durbahn at bildwechsel in Hamburg, Chris Horak at the Filmmuseum in Munich, Paul Seiler with his archival materials on Zarah Leander, and Rosemarie van der Zee and Wolfgang Theis at the Stiftung Deutsche Kinemathek in Berlin. I was also grateful for the opportunity to use the facilities (in the United States) at the Library of Congress, the Museum of Modern Art, Women Make Movies, and the Eastman House, and (in Berlin) at the Bundesfilmarchiv, Spinnboden, and the Schwules Museum. For their insightful comments on various chapters, I particularly want to thank Nico Beger, Eric Downing, Gerd Gemünden, Eva Geulen, Ron Gregg, Sabine Hake, Rick McCormick, Johannes von Moltke, Simon Richter, David Teague, Marc Weiner, and Christopher Wild. And I much appreciated the opportunity to discuss ideas from this book before the German Departments at Duke University, the University of Pennsylvania, the University of Rochester, Vanderbilt University, Washington University, and Whitman College.

Finally, the generous financial support of the Alexander von Humboldt Stiftung and the University of North Carolina Institute for the Arts and Humanities made it possible for me to take leave time to write this book. Klaus Scherpe and Inge Stephan kindly welcomed me at the Humboldt University in Berlin during my Humboldt fellowship. I am also indebted to the German Academic Exchange Association, the University of North Carolina Center for European Studies, and the University of North Carolina Research Council for additionally funding research in Germany. Always a noble colleague, Clayton Koelb let me tap into his research funds to help subsidize the index. Thanks to Adam Gori for compiling it.

A shorter version of Chapter 6 was published as "Comparative Gender: Rosa von Praunheim's and Monika Treut's Cross-Cultural Studies," in *Spectator: Journal of Film and Television Criticism* 15 (1994): 50–59. "Zarah Leander and Transgender Specularity" appeared in *Film Criticism* 23 (1999): 74–93.

A note on the translations: unless otherwise indicated, all translations from the German are my own.

This book is dedicated to my sister, Janet Kuzniar.

A.A.K.

Contents

**The
Queer German
Cinema**

Introduction

"New Queer Cinema" designates a swell of self-aware and openly sexualized gay, lesbian, and bisexual filmmaking from the early to mid-nineties. Its directors include Bruce la Bruce, Gregg Araki, Tom Kalin, Todd Haynes, Rose Troche, and Cheryl Dunye. "New Queer Cinema" resonates with the names of other key youthful movements, the French New Wave Cinema and the New German Cinema, thereby suggesting an equally significant revolution in technique and subject matter. But the very parallel calls into question the repeated claim to novelty: specifically, it raises the issue of whether New German Cinema itself was not already in some fashion queer. How path-breaking, then, are the New Queers? Does their German branch in particular—most saliently represented by Monika Treut—perhaps grow from a cinematic tradition that threads back at least to Fassbinder, as the leading proponent of the New German Cinema? In fact, Germany's Rosa von Praunheim, currently the most prolific maker of queer films worldwide, has been directing internationally recognized gay films even prior to Fassbinder. It is the eminence of this queer tradition that this study investigates. By drawing on theories of allegory developed by Walter Benjamin, Paul de Man, and Craig Owens, I hope to show how pervasively the Queer German Cinema—from the Weimar period to the present—represents unconventional sexualities as allegorical, ornate, and enigmatic.

Since the Weimar era German cinema has played a leading, innovative role in the annals of gay and lesbian film, with the tantalizing sexual illegibility and gender instability of figures from the 1920s screen anticipating the queer sensibilities of the 1990s.[1] For the most part, German film has eschewed or consciously parodied the stereotypes prevalent in Hollywood of the lesbian as vampire, femme fatale, or spinster or the gay man as effeminate eccentric, serial murderer, or comic transvestite (or any combination thereof). Beginning in 1919 with the educational film *Anders als die Andern* (*Different from the Rest*), Weimar cinema has been renowned for its sympa-

1

thetic portrayal of same-sex devotion, as seen in Carl Theodor Dryer's *Michael* (1924), G. W. Pabst's *Pandoras Büchse* (*Pandora's Box*) (1928), and Leontine Sagan's *Mädchen in Uniform* (1931). An insatiable demand for cross-dressing comedies, moreover, brought some of the period's most famous actors and actresses to the screen garbed as the "third sex," among them Asta Nielsen, Elisabeth Bergner, Dolly Haas, and Curt Bois. Especially as a female Hamlet with darkly made-up eyes and shapely legs in tights, Nielsen— *the* idol of the German silent screen—captured the uncanny look of androgyne. While gay and lesbian film festivals in the United States regularly screen such queer classics as *Anders als die Andern* and *Mädchen in Uniform*, their equivalent festivals in Germany have resurrected in addition Weimar's cross-dressing cinema.

Any attempt to trace a continuous history of Queer German Cinema is bound to stumble at the year 1933: clearly, the regime of National Socialism abruptly halted the heyday of 1920s trend-setting gay and lesbian culture. Notwithstanding, even the most renowned actress of the Nazi Ufa studios, Zarah Leander, openly cultivated her gay male friendships and became the most important camp icon the country has ever known, as late as the sixties and seventies performing as a diseuse to largely gay audiences. Her male impersonators still appear on cabaret stages today. Two of Leander's most famous films, *Zu neuen Ufern* (*To New Shores*) (1937) and *La Habanera* (1937)— Harry Baer notes that these were among Fassbinder's favorites (195)—were directed by Detlef Sierck, later known as Douglas Sirk. As is well known, Sirk's melodramas were Fassbinder's most influential models, and the latter's essay on the master's 1950s Hollywood films demonstrates how he (ir)reverently read them as camp. Thus it is not surprising that one finds echoes of Leander—especially her transvestitic performance of femininity—in several of Fassbinder's characters. Queer German Cinema follows a circuitous route indeed from Nazi melodrama to Fassbinder's transgendered fantasies.

Histrionic camp display, however, is not only a hallmark of the Fassbinder factory. It is even more shrill in the works of his contemporaries, Werner Schroeter and Rosa von Praunheim, who began their careers making films together. Although scholarly publication on these directors is scant,[2] they tower above many a cultural icon in Europe: Schroeter won the *pardo d'honneur* for his life work at the 1996 Lausanne film festival and, since the early 1970s, Rosa von Praunheim has epitomized gay activism in Germany as well as gay filmmaking worldwide. A landmark in the Queer German Cinema was the heated public debate about gay filmmaking that took place in 1979 between Rosa von Praunheim and Fassbinder over Schroeter's films. At issue was how openly to proclaim their gay allegiances. Another consistently productive, internationally renowned queer filmmaker of the same generation is Lothar Lambert, who has developed a style and set of actors uniquely his own.[3] In all his films, Lambert sympathetically portrays shrill, trashy characters in their Berlin milieu, and often does not shy from assuming the role of an outrageous transvestite himself.

It is from Schroeter and Praunheim, however, that the Queer German Cinema fans out. Via a frequently shared cast and team, they connect forward to Ulrike Ottinger and Monika Treut, whose films have garnered lesbian cult status worldwide.[4] For instance, Elfi Mikesch, whose own film *Macumba* (1982) explores lesbian fantasies, has worked extensively as camerawoman for Rosa von Praunheim, Werner Schroeter, and Monika Treut (with whom she codirected *Verführung: Die grausame Frau* (*Seduction: The Cruel Woman*) [1985]). And Magdalena Montezuma was a favorite actress for Mikesch, Ottinger, and Schroeter. Moreover, given that Rosa von Praunheim has been making gay films for three decades, it is no wonder that he has mentored subsequent generations of filmmakers, including Frank Ripploh (*Taxi zum Klo* [1980]) and Michael Stock (*Prinz in Hölleland* [*Prince in Hell*] [1992]). Similar constellations of friendship, production teams, and, not surprisingly, the occasional intimate tie characterize the spate of younger, predominantly experimental directors from the 1990s. Their meeting at film schools or art institutes has led to intensely creative cooperation: Ursula Pürrer and Hans Angela Scheirl form one such group, Nathalie Percillier, Lily Besilly, Claudia Zoller, and Stefanie Jordan another, while Michael Brynntrup, Matthias Müller, Claudia Schillinger, and Bjørn Melhus yet another.

Although every filmmaker is unique and each of his or her productions calls for fresh appraisal (which in their close readings the following chapters hope to accomplish), such direct links signal a trans-individual phenomenon that begs for closer analysis of its more profound stylistic, aesthetic, and thematic similarities. After the fading of the New German Cinema with Fassbinder's death in 1982, arguably the strongest movement in German filmmaking is now its New Queer Cinema. Its titles—from the directors Rosa von Praunheim, Frank Ripploh, and Wieland Speck, to Treut, Scheirl, and Pürrer—populate the gay and lesbian sections of video stores in the States (if they are not in the foreign film section). Recognizing this popularity, the Goethe Institute in New York organized in spring 1997 "Not Straight from Germany," an exhibition of eighteen queer films to run concurrently with the Fassbinder retrospective. The only contestant for this fame in recent years would be the much-touted German comedy. While drawing box office numbers at home, directors of this genre still have to gain the international reputation of an Ottinger, Treut, or von Praunheim. Especially because gay

3

stereotypes have surfaced abundantly (lesbians are absent!) in these comedies targeting a young, heterosexual audience (they include Sönke Wortmann's *Der bewegte Mann* [*Maybe, Maybe Not*] [1994], Rolf Silber's *Echte Kerle* [*Real Men*] [1996], and Rainer Kaufmann's *Stadtgespräch* [*Talk of the Town*] [1995]), there is all the more reason to recognize an innovative counterforce in Germany's New Queer Cinema, with its particular filmic heritage reaching back not only to the New German Cinema but also to Weimar. Surprisingly, even with all the scholarship on New German Cinema, not one study has isolated this important offshoot of it. And although scholarly response to the global 1990s trend in queer filmmaking has been dynamic—focusing on such topics as biographies of gays and lesbians of color, AIDS documentaries, political activism, and drag—it bypasses the conspicuous differences that characterize and comprise the tradition established in Germany. The purpose of this book, then, will be to map out the peculiarities of this queer cinematic heritage.

The book begins with an inquiry into Weimar cross-dressing films as seen through the lens of early twentieth-century German theories on gender inversion and continues with an investigation into the gay fandom and impersonation of the Nazi screen idol Zarah Leander. I then look at how Leander haunts the performance of femininity, with its transvestitic potential, in Fassbinder. The next two chapters are devoted to Fassbinder's contemporaries, Rosa von Praunheim and Werner Schroeter. As Germany's most prominent gay rights advocate, von Praunheim makes films that are engaged in queer visibility. Yet, as one can see in two of his most complex films, *Nicht der Homosexuelle ist pervers, sondern die Situation, in der er lebt* (*It's Not the Homosexual Who Is Perverse, but the Situation in Which He Lives*) (1971) and *Ich bin meine eigene Frau* (*I Am My Own Woman*) (1992), he is also aware that visibility can operate as a masquerade. Theatricality pervades Schroeter's oeuvre as well, and I examine what Michel Foucault called the "passionate evidence" of Schroeter's films—the eroticism of the gaze and voice. The chapter on Ulrike Ottinger investigates the deviant and deceptive visual splendor of her *Dorian Gray im Spiegel der Boulevardpresse* (*Dorian Gray in the Mirror of the Yellow Press*) (1984). Here a woman plays the role of Dorian, though the substitution can barely be detected.

The subsequent chapter discusses Monika Treut's work as the prime example of how nationality can be queered. She joins a host of other filmmakers that innovatively frame the issue of German identity by depicting the lesbian on foreign soil. The Queer German Cinema then culminates in the extraordinary but little-known work of such young directors as Michael Stock and the experimental filmmakers Michael Brynntrup, Matthias Müller,

Claudia Schillinger, Ursula Pürrer, and Angela Hans Scheirl. I conclude by examining a Berlin group of young lesbian animators and the noir cartoon genre they have invented.

Queer Visions

What this book aims to bring to light, then, is how in German cinema sexuality and gender have been "queered" from the Weimar era to today. The term "queer" here resists the binary sexual-orientation category as well as adherence to identity politics that "gay" or "lesbian" can all too hastily connote. From such cross-dressing Weimar films as *Der Geiger von Florenz* (*Impetuous Youth*) (1925/26) and *Viktor und Viktoria* (1933) to the bisexual dreams of Claudia Schillinger and the transgendered fantasies of Hans Scheirl, the antinormative sense for the erotic has led to novel visions of how sexualities can be expressed. Guiding this study is a belief that, if sexuality is contingently determined via word or image, the role played by an art or experimental cinema is crucial for fantasizing and promoting alternative representations. As this is a cinema where sexual identity and desires resist the containment and restraint of easy labeling, the excitement of this present endeavor lies in its quest for ways to read such intricate eroticisms.

The Queer German Cinema provocatively plays upon what the eye can and cannot see. Especially in the era of the silent film, gesture, eye contact, and dress are erotically ambivalent, suggesting sexual deviance. But the anxiety as well as *Schaulust* that sexual and gender instability arouses is toyed with by all the directors in this book. Ulrike Ottinger, for instance, in her rendition of *Dorian Gray*, casts Veruschka von Lehndorff in the lead male role, erasing all visible gender contradictions. And Michael Brynntrup repeatedly thwarts the prurient curiosity of his spectatorship via teasing mock-autobiographical revelations. Because the furtive glance can never perceive enough, queer cinema is one of baroque display and theatricality that paradoxically hides as much as it reveals. It reminds its viewer that sexual difference is not always something one can see; by disrupting and scotomizing the optic register, it challenges the accepted notion that cinema discloses and makes visible an empirical reality. Queer cinema thereby also unsettles the medicalizing discourse that still haunts homosexuality and that makes claims (rivaling those of cinema) to objective display and scientific categorization. In the works from Fassbinder, Rosa von Praunheim, Werner Schroeter, Ulrike Ottinger, and Monika Treut to Angela Hans Scheirl and Ursula Pürrer, sexual excesses—signified metonymically by the makeup, costuming, and gestures of the body—cross the boundaries between such classifications as gay and straight, male and female, normal and pathological, insisting that such transgressions cannot be entirely tamed, regulated, or closeted.

It is in this sense of boundary crossings, causing optic anamorphosis, that the word "queer" may prove illuminating and instrumental for this study (the related German word is *quer*, meaning "transverse," "oblique," or "slanting"). As gender theory has extensively rehearsed, "queer" marks an eccentricity common to gays, lesbians, bi- and transsexuals, a common protest against the hegemony and legitimacy of the normal. It challenges the institution of heteronormativity with its regulatory strictures. To echo Alexander Doty in his famous essay "There's Something Queer Here": "By using *queer*, I want to recapture and reassert a militant sense of difference that views the erotically 'marginal' as both (in bell hooks's words) a consciously chosen 'site of resistance' and a 'location of radical openness and possibility'" (73). Although "queer" does not deny that there are gays and lesbians, it recognizes variations within these constituencies and a plethora of identificatory sites. It signals difference, but not the binary difference of masculine men/ feminine women, homo/hetero, normal/pathologizing, or even gay/lesbian. Moe Meyer therein observes the advantage of "queer," for it "does not indicate the biological sex or gender of the subject" ("Introduction," 1). Insofar as it represents a deferral of decision regarding such alternatives, it participates in the dynamism of Derridean *différance*. In other words, queerness destabilizes identifications that would adhere to one pole of the binary and acknowledges that individuals often experience their subjectivity hybridly, contingently, and sequentially. Meyer goes on to address the broader implications for the concept of identity: "What 'queer' signals is an ontological challenge that displaces bourgeois notions of the Self as unique, abiding, and continuous while substituting instead a concept of the Self as performative, improvisational, discontinuous, and processually constituted by repetitive and stylized acts" ("Introduction," 2–3). Although Meyer emphasizes this deconstructive theory of "queer," another critic, Ruth Goldman, reminds one of its daily usage: "'queer' provides an acceptable alternative for the many people who wish to try to avoid essentializing identities" (171).[5]

The word "queer," imported from English, does not resonate to the same extent in the German language, where in some circles it generates ambivalent feelings as a failed rubric for joint gay and lesbian activism, hence paradoxically as the weak attempt to bridge differences coalitionally rather than, in the English-speaking context, to highlight them.[6] A German lexicon for gay and lesbian expressions lists its usage as "rare" (see Skinner, 134). Moreover, the nonconformist edge of the word, given its salvaging from its derogatory, abusive origin, does not immediately suggest itself to the nonnative speaker. The closest equivalent of "queer" in German, though without its sexual connotations, would be *schräg*. Also by way of comparison, the German word *schwul* (unlike the positive-sounding "gay") was formerly deployed to catcall homosexual men and in this sense approximates the English expression "queer." In his English version of *Nicht der Homosexuelle ist pervers*, for instance, Rosa von Praunheim translates *schwul* with "faggot" to capture this provocative edge. The term "queer" has been making inroads, however, on the academic front, having been first used by Sabine Hark in a 1993 essay entitled "Queer Interventionen." She is also coeditor of a series called "Querdenken" (Queer Thinking) for the publishing house Querverlag. A similar title, *Que(e)rdenken*, graces the cover of a 1997 collection in gay and lesbian studies from Austria. In addition, the proceedings from the 1997 conference of the Magnus-Hirschfeld Society on *Verqueere Wissenschaft* (Queered Science) are scheduled for publication.

Although "queer" may thus not be a frequent word of self-designation for German gay, lesbian, bisexual, or transgendered persons, nonetheless its range of significations can be indispensable for discussing the socially transgressive, anti-straight cultural production of gay and lesbian German cinema. For instance, it offers an *Ansatzpunkt* for reading otherwise unintelligible cross-gendered bodies, such as Erwin/Elvira in Fassbinder's *In einem Jahr mit 13 Monden* (*In a Year of 13 Moons*) (1978), the bizarre characters played by Magdalena Montezuma in several of Schroeter's works, or the androgynous Dorian Gray in Ottinger's film. The "affirmative resignification" that the word "queer" has undergone has fostered the courage "to run the risk of re-installing the abject at the site of its opposition," as Judith Butler writes in her essay "Critically Queer" (*Bodies That Matter*, 240). This reconnotation can thus act as a key to unraveling how Ottinger gives symbolic legitimacy to freaks (as in her film *Freak Orlando* [1981]) or Rosa von Praunheim and Lothar Lambert to characters socially rejected as perverse or deviant.[7] Moreover, "queer" helps characterize the uncanny, androgynous figures found in recent lesbian noir animation. And despite the theorization the expression has undergone, it still retains a rough, street quality that matches the underground feel of these animated shorts—and also characterizes films from Lothar Lambert and Rosa von Praunheim to such younger directors as Michael Stock and Jörg Fockele. In its provocation and indictment of heterosexual norms, "queer" can also serve to characterize scenarios without gay or lesbian content, such as Bärbel Neubauer's parodies of straight relations in her animation or Monika Treut's camp yet sympathetic depiction of an older man's sexuality in *My Father Is Coming* (1991). As shall be seen in the chapter

7

on lesbians abroad, in Treut's films national differences are hybridized on this model of cutting across gender divisions and traversing socially acceptable boundaries. Finally, to use the designation "queer" retroactively on directors who were prolific prior to the 1990s helps to correct any perception that "queer" merely signifies a generational difference in lifestyle and that it is solely a phenomenon of one decade.

Allegories of Sexuality

As the above examples indicate, the concept "queer" denies any transparent reading of the homosexual. The most renowned theoretician on unreadability, Paul de Man, has turned to allegory as a representational form through which such problems of illegibility can be focused for analysis. He has argued that "allegorical narratives tell the truth of the failure to read" (*Allegories of Reading*, 205) and wonders why, although "allegory is the purveyor of demanding truths, . . . is it that the furthest reaching truths about ourselves and the world have to be stated in such a lopsided, referentially indirect mode" ("Pascal's Allegory," 2). If in the twentieth century, as Foucault has posited, sexuality claims to reveal "the furthest reaching truths about ourselves," then its indecipherability in the Queer German Cinema might be illuminated by its directors' marked proclivity for allegorical discourse. Whether one thinks of the Dantesque gallery of human horrors in Ottinger's *Dorian Gray*, the Trauerspiel-like puppet theater in Michael Stock's *Prinz in Hölleland* (*Prince in Hell*) (1992), the Baroque palace setting of Brynntrup's *Narziss und Echo* (*Narcissus and Echo*) (1989), or the abstraction and theatrical exaggeration in the animation of Heidi Kull, Jenni Tiezte, or Bärbel Neubauer, allegory is omnipresent in this cinema, raising the question of its link to sexuality.

The word "allegory" is from the Greek *allo*, "other," and *agoria*, "speaking." Gordon Teskey elaborates: "If we look closely at the word *allegory* we see an oscillating movement . . . between a meaning that is other to its speaking and a speaking that is other to its meaning. An allegory means something other than what it says and says something other than it means" (6). It is this oblique signification that makes allegory unreadable: the inexpressible, mysterious truth or ideal to which it would point can only be signified through a materiality and artifice that ultimately only deflect and defer meaning. The consequence is that allegory "forces on our attention the difference between what it refers *to* and what it refers *with*" (Teskey, 11). The richness and deviance of "what it refers *with*" shall be the focus of this study, for such deflection intimates a rerouting, masquerading, and perverting of desires. The paradox of this indirect signification is that, despite its semantic obscurity (and because of it), allegory compensates with elaboration and entices with the lure of clarity: it gives the impression of hyperreality by isolating and fetishizing the image. Through its privileging of visibility, allegory pretends to open, direct statement, while actually it calls attention to the breach between sign and referent. Angus Fletcher, discussing this ambiguity at the heart of allegory, writes: "The mode seems to aim at both clarity and obscurity together, each effect depending upon the other. Enigma, and not always decipherable enigma, appears to be allegory's most cherished function" (73).

From the time of Coleridge and Goethe on, allegory has been denigrated in its comparison to symbol. Whereas the symbol gives the appearance of immediacy and a sensuous totality, allegory has been taken to indicate a dry, conventional relation between image and meaning, making its process of signification seem arbitrary and unmotivated. Its artifice, it has been charged, is extraneous to meaning and at times even clouds it. In the theoretical criticism of Walter Benjamin, Paul de Man, and Craig Owens, however, allegorical figuration has come once again into its own, its lineage connected through the stations of the Baroque, the Romantic, and the Postmodern. Its valuation resurrected; it is no longer seen as reductionist and inferior to the symbol, but as complex and ornate. Moreover, unlike the symbol with its apparent self-sufficiency, allegory calls upon the reader's involvement, indeed relies upon it in its very structure: because meaning has to be looked for, it is deferred.

Joel Fineman has observed that "historically, we can note that allegory seems regularly to surface in critical or polemical atmospheres, when for political or metaphysical reasons there is something that cannot be said" (28). In bringing allegorical illegibility to bear on sexual expression, one cannot help but note that, because homosexuality has been censored both implicitly and explicitly, internally and externally, it has had recourse to indirect representation, and hence the enigmatic, oblique signification of allegory. Yet although the allegorical indirectness in the representation of homosexuality might have its historical origins in the closet, its continued presence today suggests a different function. It is my thesis that the Queer German Cinema plays with allegory's oscillation between concealment and revelation, clarity and obscurity, sign and referent, in order to thwart the spectator's pretense of reading (for) homosexuality. The "open secret" of someone's imputed sexual being remains elusive. Instead, erotic desire becomes uncategorizable, ornate, and decidedly antihermeneutic.

Eve Sedgwick has argued that the concept of the closet structures a binary discourse derived from the epistemological assumption or presumption that the "truth" of sexuality can be reduced to the opposition between homo/

9

heterosexuality and that we can diagnose the difference in others. The dichotomy operates on the premise that we know what the opposite terms signify in relation to each other, with their very duality being deceptively clear. This single binary, then, according to Sedgwick, has generated a host of similar ones: "the now chronic modern crisis of homo/heterosexual has affected our culture through its ineffaceable marking particularly of the categories secrecy/disclosure, knowledge/ignorance, private/public, masculine/feminine, majority/minority, innocence/initiation, natural/artificial" (*Epistemology of the Closet*, 11). This dualistic structure of "secrecy/disclosure, knowledge/ignorance" evokes the dismissive assessment of allegory as dogmatically and automatically decodable once the key to unlock it has been found. According to this model, innuendoes, gestures, and even physiognomy, once perceived and translated by the self-appointed enlightened viewer, could divulge an illicit subtext; they are taken as conventional markers that expose the homosexual. Yet, as indicated, such a view of allegory deceives in its apparent simplicity, for in its ultimate failure to unveil that to which it would refer, allegory admits the impossibility of its project. In the Queer German Cinema, then, which is not aligned with the "epistemology of the closet," the sexual secret, always suspected, is *not* suddenly exposed or outed, in other words, the "signs" of homosexuality resist a simplistic, homophobic detection and decoding.[8] Instead, the estrangement of sign from referent constantly subverts the spectator's claim to master such distinctions as gay/straight or female/male, thus unsettling or queerying the spectator's own sexual desires and identity positioning.

Yet the notion of a closeted meaning for the initiated is not one that I would wish to abandon, for political reasons. It is decisive who claims the position of knowledge and in whose hands the mastery of ambiguity lies. Gerhard Kurz has observed that esoteric, allegorical speech can serve as a means to protect one's knowledge as a secret, as well as to prevent the profanation that would occur with direct utterance (39–40). A definite purpose for allegorical indeterminacy in a queer cinema would be to create texts whose ambiguity only the initiate would be able to read. Especially in animation, the absence of dialogue, the shorthand sketch, as well as the brevity of the film can give rise to uncertainty about what the "look" of a character signifies. For instance, the tall, strong woman in *Late at Night* (1997) might not be perceived by a heterosexual audience as a dyke cruising lamplit streets searching for someone like herself; with her powerful stride she might not even be registered as a woman. But lesbian spectators would certainly recognize her as one of their own and, in so doing, see the film as addressed to them. Moreover, in reading the doppelgänger figure in the film as a reflection of this very irony, they are attuned to rather than repressive of the work's signifying potential.

What an allegorical queer cinema foregrounds, then, are not immediately identifiable gays or lesbians but this scene, even pageant, of irony. Paradoxically, by virtue of its enigma, the gender or sexual sign becomes a spectacle. In other words, in the attempt to cover up the gap between image and referent, allegory turns to hyperbolic, theatrical performance; through a kind of baroque saturation it compensates for the failings of representation. In writing about the affinity between allegory and theater, Rainer Nägele observes their common "scene of show, which is constituted by pure acts of looking and nothing else" (27) and describes how allegory stages the split between signifier and signified. Beginning with Weimar's silent cinema, the body itself becomes the vehicle for allegorical indirectness and theatricality; without the voice but through the hyperbolic gestures of the hand and eye, the body here acts out its yearning, the exaggeration itself intimating sexual deviance. Later, in the work of Schroeter, the voice is cut off from the image to sing of its excessive, unnatural ardor, above all in the *Hosenrolle* parts that Schroeter cites in both *Der Tod der Maria Malibran* and his latest film *Poussières d'amour / Abfallprodukte der Liebe* (1996). It is as if the voice, separated from the image, had to overcome the gap via its emotion-laden, histrionic immediacy. The operatic stage reappears in Ottinger's *Dorian Gray*, while the torch song evokes the haunting presence of Zarah Leander in Fassbinder's works, from his play *Der Müll, die Stadt, und der Tod* (*City, Garbage, and Death*) (1975) to the films *Lili Marleen* (1980) and *Die Sehnsucht der Veronika Voss* (*Veronika Voss*) (1981), whose plots revolve around, respectively, a singer and former actress of the Third Reich. Female-to-male lesbian performance, as well as scopophilic spectatorship, take center stage in Monika Treut's *Die Jungfrauenmaschine* (*Virgin Machine*) (1988), while Lothar Lambert's characters are all searching for an audience. And if Fassbinder's or Ottinger's characters perform like marionettes emptied of soul, then the puppet theater becomes the dominant metaphor in Michael Stock's *Prinz in Hölleland* (*Prince in Hell*).

I should emphasize that the transvestism and theatricality of this cinema is not in the service of redefining selfhood through an experimental, subversive trying out of different roles, as one might hastily assume in the wake of Judith Butler's writings. These films are not exercises in the autonomy, agency, or intervention of the self, but quite the contrary: the coldness of the puppet marks a radical antisubjectivity and resistance to psychological probing, whereby Paul de Man's words come to mind: allegory "prevents the self from an illusory identification with the non-self, which is now fully, though painfully, recognized as a non-self" ("Rhetoric of Temporality," 207). Yet

11

even de Man's phrasing, in its pathos, misrepresents the distancing that characterizes the acting from Ottinger and Schroeter to the mock self-display of Brynntrup, Scheirl, and Pürrer. Their works delight in the visual spectacle and sheer indulgences of camp extravagance, while playing on the spectator's scopic fascination with gender and sexual eccentricity. The noninvolvement of the self in the aesthetic performance is further illustrated by the sado-masochistic scenes in Cléo Uebelmann's *Mano Destra* (1985), in Monika Treut's *Verführung: Die grausame Frau* and *Didn't Do It for Love* (1997), or in Stefanie Jordan's short, *Crude* (1996). Here the stylization and ritualization as well as the accouterments of the costuming deflect from the pain and psychology of bondage.

Especially in works like these, replete with fetishistic rigging, the allegorical image draws our eye to it while preventing us from looking beyond it. The result is that the surface alone attracts and is all that remains to be seen, a phenomenon that Maureen Quilligan calls the "absurdity of the surface" (28) in allegory. Sensuousness replaces sense, and the more isolated, fragmented, and textured the image is, the more tantalizing it becomes. It is at the level of the surface that artifice, which is extraneous to meaning, collects—ornamentally and immoderately. Camp thereby reveals its allegorical mode:[9] "the essence of Camp is its love of the unnatural: of artifice and exaggeration" (Sontag, 105).[10]

Thus, despite the mood of exaltation and distance that evokes a certain otherworldliness, it is this lavish attention to detail and the fragmented gestures of the body (that is, its surface) that paradoxically render the work of Schroeter and Ottinger sensually immanent. This schism between the vertical gesture toward the sacred or transcendent, on the one hand, and the profane materiality of images, on the other, traditionally characterizes allegory; but in these queer postmodern allegories, the theological dimension is absent, while appearance and artifice are spotlighted instead.[11] In Schroeter's work, in particular, a sexualized yearning takes the place of the metaphysical: "Distanced at the beginning from its source, allegory will set out on an increasingly futile search for a signifier with which to recuperate the fracture of and at its source, and with each successive signifier the fracture and the search begin again: a structure of continual yearning, the insatiable desire of allegory" (Fineman, 45). Because paratactic elements gain in relative importance in Schroeter's and Ottinger's films, their narratives, if one can even call them that, obey this structure of longing and become episodic and open. Their films read like a gallery of disparate scenes, seemingly randomly accumulated, which give the impression of surplus. The same sense of puppetlike acting, episodic structure, and refutation of the homosexual's easy legibility characterize Rosa von Praunheim's early, extremely important film for the history of the gay movement in Germany, *Nicht der Homosexuelle ist pervers.* In this work yet another aspect of allegory comes to the fore—its sententiousness and didacticism: accompanying the protagonist's stations of life is a quasi-psychologizing, relentlessly negative, self-debasing assessment of the "faggot." However disconcerting, this pretentiously authoritative voice-over is also ironized, for in this postmodernist and self-reflexive film the function of allegoresis is mocked.

The disparate, unconnected singularity of images is most evident in experimental film, which is the main reason why (apart from dwindling financial subsidies) the legacy of the Queer German Cinema is currently best represented in this short form. As in the work of Michael Brynntrup and Matthias Müller, one witnesses here an erotic signifying exaltation, a vertiginous cascade of images. The breathless montage emphasizes the discontinuity between shots. The soundtrack, rather than suturing over the cuts, either highlights them through abrupt changes in rhythm, modality, and volume, or utilizes a quick tempo to underscore the rapid succession and manipulation of the images. Experimental cinema thus particularly verifies Craig Owens's assessment: "Film composes narratives out of a succession of concrete images, which makes it particularly suited to allegory's essential pictogrammatism" (230).

The reverse side of this manic signification is a melancholic awareness of the transience of the cinematic image and the silences that lie behind allegory's abundance and accumulation. Lavishness conceals and compensates for what cannot be named, whereby the cloaking of desires deemed abnormal by society paradoxically leads to the representation and enjoyment of this very deviation. Opulent substitution also occurs in Matthias Müller's films, but here as an antidepressant, to counteract the grief caused by the loss of friends to AIDS. Likewise in Michael Stock, the pervasive theme of death and intravenous drug addiction, allegorized in the jester Firlefanz's puppet play, evokes AIDS, although the word is never uttered in the film. Gordon Teskey, who has written persuasively on violence in allegory, notes how allegory "draws on the power of what it has to repress" (68). Its cryptic signification is a way to mourn a loss too aching to be articulated directly; yet the very process of signification, inevitably insufficient, also threatens either to debase or to irreparably efface its referent. Depression over allegory's imperfection and the cruelty that gives rise to it ("its power to seize and tear" [Teskey, 18]) are thus two sides of the same coin. In *Ursprung des deutschen Trauerspiels* (*The Origin of German Tragedy*) Walter Benjamin similarly links allegory's depressive nondifferentiation of signs to its aggression: "every person, every thing, every relationship can mean a random other . . . accordingly, the profane world is both elevated in its status and demeaned" (152–53).[12] Indeed, Benjamin recognized the sadistic tendency in allegory: "Not so much revelation [Enthüllung] as the exposure of earthly things [Entblößung der sinnlichen Dinge] is the function of the baroque image-script [Bilderschrift]. The emblematician does not proffer the essence behind the image" (162). The word *sinnlich* also means "sensuous," while *Entblößung* suggests a nakedness, the abject literalness of the flesh that time and again the directors of the Queer German Cinema present on the screen in the disarming form of their own bodies—Fassbinder, Lambert, von Praunheim (in his autobiographical *Neurosia* [1996]), Stock, Schillinger, Scheirl, and Pürrer come immediately to mind. At their own risk, they present the body as fascinating in its materiality and sensuality yet ultimately opaque and strange to itself; it is not that the body is *enthüllt*, rather its vulnerability and malleability are *entblößt*.

In summary, one could say that through its oblique, disconcerting signification, allegory is always already "queer." In his essay "The Allegorical Impulse: Toward a Theory of Postmodernism," Craig Owens links it to perversion: "Allegory *is* extravagant, an expenditure of surplus value; it is always *in excess*. Croce found it 'monstrous' precisely because it encodes two contents within one form. Still, the allegorical supplement is not only an addition, but also a replacement. It takes the place of an earlier meaning, which is thereby either effaced or obscured. Because allegory usurps its object it comports within itself a danger, the possibility of perversion" (215). The Queer German Cinema, then, develops this "possibility of perversion" by indulging in an array of supplementary, scopic pleasures—the theatrical exaggeration of gestures and costume (Weimar cinema, von Praunheim, Schroeter, Ottinger), the playful allusion to pornography (Brynntrup), the imaginary anatomy of the multi/transgendered body (Fassbinder, Scheirl, and Pürrer), the supplement of the lesbian dildo (Treut, Schillinger), and the seductively androgynous look of the cartoon character (Kull, Zoller, Jordan).

In gratifying the eye, this visual immoderation positions the spectator as susceptible to queer pleasures. Gender and sexual indeterminacy suggestively proposition the viewer, encouraging him or her to imagine various "as-if" scenarios. Indeed, the allegorical sexual occult, demanding decipherment by the viewer, reframes and refines the theory and reception history of cinematic spectatorship, as we shall see in the chapters on Weimar cross-dressing comedies and on Zarah Leander. Unlike a mass-media entertainment that homogenizes gender and dulls sexuality, cinema when viewed queerly addresses the fantasy of the spectator. He or she erotically supports the film, making sensory, lived experience a part of the field of vision. The phenomenological import of this cinema goes even further. Allegorical excess disrupts the belief that perception is invariably correct and true: it avoids a recognizable representation of homosexuality and brazenly makes fun of the fear that homosexuality might go undetected and unmarked in others. Its eroticism slyly appeals to all. It thereby signals a queer resistance to the reification of sexual and gender difference and the systematic organization of desire in the optic field: these queer allegories deny that the realm of the visible must necessarily codify, inscribe, and delimit sexualities.

Queerying Master Narratives

The foregoing discussion makes clear why a number of German feature films with gay, lesbian, and bisexual characters will not be the focus of this study—those that take place in a realistic setting with the aim of portraying an accurate image of gay men and women and their problems. Prime examples would be Ulli Lommel's *Die Zärtlichkeit der Wölfe* (*The Tenderness of Wolves*) (1973), Ula Stöckl's *Erikas Leidenschaften* (*Erika's Passions*) (1976), Wolfgang Petersen's *Die Konsequenz* (*The Consequence*) (1977), Alexandra von Grote's *Novembermond* (*November Moon*) (1978) and *Weggehen um anzukommen* (*Depart to Arrive*) (1981), Frank Ripploh's *Taxi zum Klo* (1980), Wieland Speck's *Westler* (1985), Heiner Carow's *Coming Out* (1989), Peter Kern's *Gossenkind* (*Street Kid*) (1991), Marcel Geisler's *Die blaue Stunde* (*The Blue Hour*) (1992), and Percy Adlon's *Salmonberries* (1991). Although certain social commentaries are fascinating for their treatment of homophobia, I have also regretfully excluded them—*Anders als du und ich* (*Different from You and Me*) (1957) by Veit Harlan and *Jagdszenen aus Niederbayern* (*Hunting Scenes from Lower Bavaria*) (1969) by Peter Fleischmann. The documentary format of, say, Jochen Hick's *Via Appia* (1990), *Menmaniacs* (1995), and *Sex/Life in L.A.* (1998) or the collectively produced film on gays and lesbians who survived the Third Reich, *Verzaubert* (*Enchanted*) (1992) is also underrepresented, given the particular orientation of this study. Another film that documents a gay milieu is Peter Kern's *Knutschen Kuscheln Jubilieren* (*Kiss Cuddle Celebrate*) (1998) on a group of aging men who nightly frequent a Düsseldorf bar. Like *Verzaubert*, this cinematic essay records the continuity of gay life from Nazi persecution to the present.

15

Perhaps the most difficult cut was made with regard to Lothar Lambert, whose films on gay men and transvestites include *Paso Doble* (1983), *Drama in Blond* (1984), *In Hassliebe Lola* (*In Love-Hate Lola*) (1994), and *Und Gott erschuf das Make-Up* (*And God Created Make-Up*) (1998). Born in 1944 (and thus of the same generation as Rosa von Praunheim, Fassbinder, and Schroeter), Lambert has directed over twenty films, serving as his own producer, cameraman, scriptwriter, and editor. Already in 1982 the Goethe Institute in New York dedicated a retrospective to his films, and Dagmar Beiersdorf assesses him as "*the* underground filmmaker of Germany" in her documentary on their collaboration, *Kuck mal, wer da filmt!* (*Look who's filming!*) (1997). Lambert's loyal cast of unpaid actors and actresses portrays histrionic sexualities of various types in a slice-of-life Berlin milieu, this very discrepancy giving his films their outrageous, fringe quality.[13] Frequently his actors bring their own stories to the screen and with them an authenticity and human warmth. Among this team of actors is Dagmar Beiersdorf, who has made a number of films, including *Die Wolfsbraut* (*The Wolf-Bride*) (1984) on the thorny attraction between two women of different race and class. Here Lambert plays a transvestite street prostitute, as he also does in its sequel *Eine Tunte zum Dessert* (*A Queen for Dessert*) (1992) and in Beiersdorf's earlier film *Dirty Daughters* (1982). Lambert is his own most convincing and campy actor, from his *Now or Never* (1979) to his most recent film *Und Gott erschuf das Make-Up*, putting on wigs and dresses and unabashedly displaying a plump womanly figure. As with the other films mentioned in the previous paragraph, my decision not to devote a chapter to Lambert and Beiersdorf should in no way be interpreted as an attempt to diminish their important role in establishing the indisputably strong gay and lesbian presence in German cinema.

In its focus on specific directors and, within their oeuvres, on specific works, this book is decidedly not a survey of gays and lesbians in German cinema. Nor is it a German film history that focuses on the cinematic representation of social and cultural attitudes toward homosexuality. To my mind, there are serious shortcomings in these conventional constructions of film history due to certain widespread, largely unquestioned preconceptions about the progressive nature of gay and lesbian representation in cinema, the sexuality of the directors, and the prevalence of the coming-out narrative. A historical approach that would presume to be comprehensive (while in fact being sketchy) would assume facile answers to difficult questions. For instance, bracketing for the moment the categories of bisexual and transgender, does gay and lesbian cinema require that gays or lesbians be depicted in it, and by what criteria does one identify or prove a character's sexuality? Must it restrict itself to so-called positive or accurate images of gays and lesbians?[14] Is there a gay aesthetic that such films develop or adhere to? Does such a cinema require that its director be gay, not to mention its actors, producer, and so on? And if a director does not self-identify as gay, does that inhibit one from deriving queer visual pleasure from his or her work?

For although one's desires infuse a text and perhaps only then render it erotic, a danger resides in this linking of a director's sexual orientation with his or her cultural production. An excellent example to the contrary would be Werner Schroeter's sultry female-female glances in *Der Tod der Maria Malibran* (*The Death of Maria Malibran*) (1971), *Willow Springs* (1972/73), and *Flocons d'or* (1975/76), brilliant performances of unadulterated longing. In other words, because a director is gay does not mean his films have to deal openly with his sexuality: it is not a question of whether an author is "out" in his works. The general pernicious expectation, however, as Douglas Crimp bitingly observes in an essay on Fassbinder, is that homosexuality "cannot merely be there: if there, it has to be in the foreground. No matter what the film's official pretext, the subject is 'coming out'" (70). If the anticipated openness is not evident, the resulting assumption is that the author is in hiding, from himself as well as from the world, allowing the viewer to feel superior in his or her ability to see through to the "truth" of another's intimate self. As Crimp notes: "Anything short of this candor must presumably be subterfuge, an elaborate ruse of writing masking the inability simply to *come out with it*. The complex strategies of the text [are] reduced thus to reticence and mystification" (70).

Regarding a director's sexual orientation as an essence that his or her film makes visible thus blinds one to intricate—sometimes insidious—representational maneuvers: as Edward R. O'Neill notes, if the homosexual identity is seen as a visible essence rather than as a socially constructed category, then how it can operate as a fantasy screen for homophobic projections will be ignored, even by a gay cinema: "Previous gay cinema critics assumed that the meaning of homosexuality was something self-evident, needing only to be made visible and protected against misrepresentation. What such critics failed to see was that the signifier 'homosexuality' covers an enigma and even functions as such" (15). It is in fact this sensibility for queerness in its disruptive function as enigma—not the accurate, authentic portrayal of gay and lesbian lives—that guides the Queer German Cinema.

Just as one needs to question one's assumptions regarding what constitutes homosexuality in cinema, so too the idiosyncratic desires and visions that are brought to the screen in the films about to be studied cannot be taken to represent a uniformly *German* gay or lesbian identity, whatever that would be. In other words, there is nothing innately or timelessly German about the sexualities these films explore. Instead they offer an array of queer cultural practices and, in so doing, either retrospectively or quite consciously advance a critique of the modernist, monolithic narrative of the "gay and lesbian community,"[15] whether it be seen as German or international. By focusing on the singularity of different filmmakers I hope to problematize what a single trajectoried idea of a gay and lesbian "history" or "movement" would be. In other words, I want to begin to theorize what we mean by these terms.[16]

It would be especially misleading if I were to write a teleological story that claimed that German gay and lesbian cinema is more and more out: if worldwide gay cinema begins with *Anders als die Andern*, with its star cast of Conrad Veidt, Anita Berber, and Reinhold Schünzel, as well as the major homosexual rights activist of the period, Magnus Hirschfeld, then this trajectory must be seen in reverse as a decline! The Nazi period and the ensuing fearful climate of the late 1940s and 1950s,[17] in any case, mark a break in the linear narrative. Suddenly then and unforeseeably, in 1971 with *Nicht der Homosexuelle ist pervers*, Rosa von Praunheim traces the stations in the life of an openly gay character. Shortly thereafter, Fassbinder casts himself as a gay man in *Faustrecht der Freiheit* (*Fox and His Friends*) (1974) and unapologetically documents his sexual life in *Deutschland im Herbst* (*Germany in Autumn*) (1977/78). With these films a post-closet milieu springs into being full-fledged; it is this openness that characterizes the Queer German Cinema to follow.

In other words, the predominantly American version of the coming-out story—where an individual comes to terms with his or her homosexuality (often concurrently with his or her coming of age) and steps out of the closet —is largely foreign to the openly queer German cinema.[18] Exceptions would be such mainstream television comedies as Alexander Scherer and Angelina Maccarone's *Kommt Mausi raus?* (*Is Mausi Coming Out?*) (1994) or Heiner Carow's *Coming Out*, whose special situation is that it protests social repression in the German Democratic Republic. To a large extent, this national difference between Germany and America is due to the specificity of the American situation (which, to be sure, has found echoes internationally), namely, that there the civil rights and women's liberation movements created a paradigm for the fight for parity. With no enshrined Bill of Rights to appeal to, identity or assimilationist politics have never been as strong in Germany and consequently neither has the emancipatory narrative of "coming out," differences which make one wary of propagating a myth of the modern homosexual based on a generalized (read imperialistic) notion of its homogenized American version. Sociocultural constellations specific to Germany, by contrast, have guided its representation of sexualities, for instance, the prevalent and popular (that is, not exclusively medical) discourse on sexual intermediacy in the initial decades of the twentieth century or the abolition of the antisodomy Paragraph 175 in 1969. In sum, then, the personal narrative of an individual's "coming out," the collective narrative of a progressively more "out" gay cinema, and the autobiographical narrative of the director's "coming out" in his films are generic, widespread preconceptions about gay and lesbian cinema that do not necessarily apply to the Queer German Cinema.

Emboldened by the films it discusses, this book attempts a defamiliariza- tion. Motivating it overall is the conviction that German cinematic history needs to be defamiliarized by acknowledging its long queer tradition. By say- ing that this legacy cannot be reduced to a list of gay, lesbian, or bisexual di- rectors or characters, I do not intend to erase gay or lesbian specificity. On the contrary, the contemporary rubric "queer" allows one to recuperate land- mark films that unfortunately have not been regarded as gay or lesbian, such as Ottinger's *Dorian Gray* or Schroeter's *Der Tod der Maria Malibran*, and thus have not been seen as grounding a major cinematic tradition. Likewise, be- cause homosexual identities from the first few decades of this century cannot be presumed to overlap with contemporary self-nomination, Weimar cinema, too, can be read unconventionally with regard to sexuality and gender. The focus on "queer" explains why films not explicitly dealing with homosexual- ity—the cross-dressing Weimar comedies—are included for extensive analy- sis. Another shortcoming in the annals of German cinematic history is that the considerable scholarship on Nazi cinema, despite Zarah Leander's huge subcultural fandom, barely addresses how and why she has been read queerly.

This project of defamiliarization and revision of master narratives then carries over to the New German Cinema, which, with the constellation Fass- binder-Praunheim-Schroeter, needs to be recognized as indebted to gay un- derground filmmaking. To the extent that von Praunheim has been isolated and categorized as a gay director, even Germany's representative gay direc- tor, he has been treated as an (even tiresome!) anomaly and his links to his contemporaries have not been explored. This exclusion has rendered New German Cinema surprisingly unqueer—as if it were left unmarked by a gay presence, apart from the occasional Fassbinder film, such as *Faustrecht der Freiheit* and *Querelle* (1982).[19] Yet queer sensibilities lie at the core of this cin- ema—its social transgression, its outsider inventiveness and independence, its predilection for bizarre, hyperbolic characters (particularly its transgen- dered ones), its stress on the discontinuities between desire and gender roles, as well as its camp recycling of images both high culture and mass culture. Similarly, overviews of women in German cinema tend to mention lesbian- ism parenthetically as a theme rather than acknowledge how disturbingly queer the same-sex attractions are that govern Margarethe von Trotta's, Percy Adlon's, and Ulrike Ottinger's work.[20] Conceivably at the root of such omissions is the tendency to read German cinema as sociopolitical commen- tary—a sort of realist paradigm—which would not be conducive to examin- ing either what falls outside a social heteronormativity or what is technically and stylistically innovative. One of the most grievous exclusions has thus been the near absence of investigations into experimental cinema. And scholarship has been totally silent on the work by the lesbian animators discussed in the final chapter.[21] This present book hopes to rectify such neglect by rewriting German cinema queerly. The following chapters, then, are devoted to exploring, as exemplified in specific films, the rich, sensuous detail—the uncompromising, defiantly visible desires—of this queer tradition.

Gender Inverts and Cross-Dressers

Reading for a Queer Weimar Cinema

"Tension. Irregular breathing. Guarded eyes. Suspense. . . . Glistening and shining. Suspense. Suspended desires. Dissolving of knots. No breathing. . . . Phallic lustre of the eyes competes with the beams from the stage lights. Vice!" In such staccato style L. W. Rochowanski describes the spectator's reaction to a dance performance with the lurid title "Dances of Vice, Horror, and Ecstasy" (quoted in Fischer, 73). It starred its choreographer Sebastian Droste and his wife Anita Berber, the naked dancer who took Berlin by storm in the first years of the 1920s. Berber, known to frequent lesbian bars and cafés, was also notorious for having started the monocle and tuxedo craze that spread from lesbians to the heterosexual crowd (one lesbian bar in 1930 even advertised a monocle night where every girl would receive one free). Even more queerly, Berber married one of the most ostentatiously gay men of the period, the equally androgynous-looking Droste, the man whom Magnus Hirschfeld in his 1930 book *Geschlechtskunde* crowned the quintessential inverted artist. Onstage or off, Berber's and Droste's permanently white powdered faces against their darkly painted eyes mimicked cinematic style. Indeed, the excitement Rochowanski describes is one likewise imparted by expressionist cinema, which in eighty years has not lost its optical allure. It is not surprising that Rosa von Praunheim, who also copied a Caligari-look in *Horror Vacui* (1984), harked back again to expressionistic angles, makeup, and Berber's bisexuality in his *Anita: Tänze des Lasters* (*Anita: Dances of Vice*) (1988), making explicit the queer cinematic lineage from Weimar to the present.

As in Berber's dance, it is the body in silent cinema that must be allegorically read; through heightened facial features and hyperbolic gestures, the body betrays its passion and sensuality, with more than a hint of sexual deviance. Exaggeration shows it always already engaged in performance. Clothing, too, in its manifest exteriority, begs to be read as theatrical sign, hence the fascination of silent cinema with concealment and revelation, not infrequently involving cross-dressing. Even before Anita Berber's popularization of the tuxedo, Ossi Oswalda in *Ich möchte kein Mann sein* (*I Don't Want to Be a Man*) (1919) and Asta Nielsen in *Hamlet* (1920) draw other women's gazes appreciatively upon them in their graceful male disguise. Without the pitch of the voice to betray its speaker, but with the delightful deceptiveness of drag, gender in the cross-dressing silent signals the wistful imagining of alternative desires. The gender markers that attire provides do not so much underscore male and female binaries as they threaten to confound them, especially when they appeal to the gaze of both sexes.

A variety of cross-dressing comedies will be discussed here: Ernst Lubitsch and Hans Kräly's *Ich möchte kein Mann sein* (*I Don't Want to Be a Man*) (1919), Paul Czinner's *Der Geiger von Florenz* (*Impetuous Youth*) (1925–26), Richard Eichberg's *Der Fürst von Pappenheim* (*The Masked Mannequin*) (1927), and Reinhold Schünzel's *Viktor und Viktoria* (1933). These illustrate well this gender confusion, but they also unsettle the homo/heterosexual distinction, for with the wardrobe comes the closet and its related concern with appearances and camouflage. At a time when the mannish look was fashionably lesbian and young hustlers, similarly androgynous, wore makeup in the streets, these films provocatively raise the questions: Can transvestism be read as a disguise for homosexuality, a closet whose door is left slightly ajar? What would permit one to read inappropriate dress for queerness, despite a heterosexual dénouement? In what ways does the baroque exaggeration of body and dress intimate sexual as well as gender incongruity? How would the spectator of the time—above all, the gay audience—have decoded the cross-dresser? And is there a particular erotics of looking, as well as a pleasurable oscillation in spectatorial identification, that the cinematic cross-dresser invites? In other words, how do the ambiguous signals that the cross-dresser emits arouse the viewer's fantasies and encourage us to reassess cinematic theories of audience interpellation (from Laura Mulvey to Teresa de Lauretis)? To begin, I ground this allegorical reading of a queer Weimar cinema in the discourse of homosexuality prevalent at the time, which was similarly preoccupied with how to decipher and define gender inversion.

Theories of Gender Inversion

22

The vocabulary used to describe homosexuality during the first third of this century borrows largely from the sociomedical discourse developed before 1900, and bears more similarity to definitions of that period than to those current in our own.[1] The term "homosexuality" was first coined in 1869 by

Karoly Maria Kertbeny-Benkert. Only subsequently was the category of heterosexuality invented, a supplementarity challenging the assumption that heterosexuality has been an unchanging, timeless norm with homosexuality as its deviant. Undeniably, homosexuality was pathologized by many of its early theorists; however, the variety of medical and legal terms used to describe same-sex attraction, among which "homosexuality" was only one, at least avoided the antithetical categorizing that pits straight against gay, a mode of thinking that Eve Sedgwick has criticized for generating a host of binary oppositions into which we believe we can epistemologically fit ourselves and, generically, others. In the following paragraphs I would like to propose that the variegated categories formulated in the late nineteenth and early twentieth centuries to circumscribe the homosexual, although in themselves still testifying to a positivistic, at times pathologizing mentality, nonetheless permitted a variegated cultural representation of sexuality that not infrequently blurred the difference between what we today consider gay and straight, as well as masculine and feminine.

A preemptive strike against a dualistic view of sexuality was already made in 1858 in Johann Ludwig Caspar's (1796–1864) notion of the "psychic hybrid" ("geistige Zwitterbildung") or in Karl Heinrich Ulrichs's (1825–95) use of the category "gender invert" to explain same-sex desire. The latter posited the feminine soul in a male body (the "Urning") or, reciprocally, the masculine soul in a female body (the "Urningin," later "Urninde")—a mixture capable of infinite variation, deconstructing exclusionary binaries. Magnus Hirschfeld (1868–1935) preferred and popularized the term "the third sex," influenced as he was by Ulrichs's notion of psychological even physiological gender inversion as well as homosexuality as a natural, biological phenomenon. Insuring Ulrichs's continued significance into the twentieth century, Hirschfeld's organization, the Scientific-Humanitarian Committee, saw to the republishing in 1898 of Ulrichs's twelve-volume *Forschungen über das Rätsel der mannmännlichen Liebe* (*Investigations into the Riddle of Male-Male Love*) (originally published 1864–79). Examining the significance of Ulrichs's destabilization and relativizing of gender binaries via an ever-expanding third term, Klaus Müller perceptively writes:

> As Ulrichs differentiates them, "masculinity/femininity" develop
> into complex and hence unstable gender attributes. In the third sex
> the possibilities for variation and combinations are played out. In
> developing the "gradation of the sexes" Ulrichs proposed a variety of
> differences that were intended to define the Urning but ultimately
> sublated, though unintentionally, the essentialization of the masculine
> and feminine. . . . With "temporary Uranizing" and the "virilization

23

of the Urning," masculinity/femininity are described as temporary phenomena. (86–87)

Not only did Ulrichs upset a normative gender polarity, his writings can be seen as a corrective to today's leading polarity—the labeling of homosexuality as antagonist to its hetero-counterpart. As Müller points out, through the decoupling of sex and gender, "the Urning embodied an essentially more complex personality than the perverse homosexual" (89), on which the subsequent generation was to focus. Richard Krafft-Ebing was one of the late nineteenth-century German physicians who regarded "contrary sexual feeling" to be a perversion; others include Kertbeny-Benkert, Gustav Jäger, Carl Friedrich Westphal, and Albert Moll. Yet in his *Psychopathia sexualis* (1886), Krafft-Ebing, like Ulrichs, devised various categories whose boundaries were permeable. Regarding the divide between homo- and heterosexuality, his four main categories were psychosexual hermaphroditism, homosexuality (the only category focusing on sexual activity), effeminatio, and androgyny.

In debates stretching into the 1920s there was continued resistance, following Ulrichs's and Krafft-Ebing's lead, to the notion that homosexuality could be defined exclusively or even primarily in terms of sexual practices— a discursive distinction from contemporary thought that becomes important once one searches for cultural representation of the homosexual, especially in cinema, where censorship would have prohibited the representation of sexual intimacy in any case. In his book *Berlins drittes Geschlecht* (*Berlin's Third Sex*), for instance, Hirschfeld claims to prefer his coinage to "homosexuality" because of the genital acts imputed to the latter term, remarking that many homosexual men do not realize or know their "true nature" or are "abstinent by reason of personal predilection [Charakterveranlagung]" (24). The group "Gemeinschaft der Eigenen" surrounding Adolf Brand, editor of the journal *Der Eigene: Ein Blatt für männliche Kultur* (*One's Own: A Paper for Male Culture*) (appearing intermittently from 1896 to 1932), likewise advocated a mythic ideal of strong, asexual friendships ("Freundesliebe") between men. Yet Brand and his following also strongly objected to the implications of effeminacy that adhered to Hirschfeld's notion of the third sex (paradoxically, this criticism did not stop Brand from featuring the androgynous ephebe in the photographs that dotted *Der Eigene*).[2] Hirschfeld, then, in an attempt to sidestep the increasing controversy he faced before the more and more popular virile ideal of self-identified gay men, began to deploy the phrase "sexual intermediacy" ("sexuelle Zwischenstufe"), yet without abandoning his advocacy of the gender inversion theory. This later characterization in fact goes further in resisting a binary, pathologizing conceptualization of sexuality in that it suggests that sexual differences cover a natural spectrum.

Although it would be improbable that the sexual activities and identities of gay men and women of this period were patterned exclusively on Hirschfeld's writings, his influence (especially when compared to that of his sexologist predecessors) is undeniable. His leadership extended from 1899, the year his *Jahrbuch für sexuelle Zwischenstufen* was first issued, to 1930, when he left Germany for a world lecture tour which turned into permanent exile. As Jim Steakley and Manfred Herzer conclude in their epilogue to a reprint of *Von Einst bis Jetzt* (*From Then 'til Now*) (1922), Hirschfeld's history of the homosexual movement provided "an identity-grounding impetus in the birth of a self-aware gay minority in the Weimar Republic" (213). On the other hand, in assessing the historical popularity or veracity of such notions as gender intermediacy, the possibility must not be discounted that medical discourse did not so much create the homosexual as invert as take its inspiration from the gay underground of the time. Richard Dyer has surmised that "the third sex idea may well have been developed as a means of accounting for a predominant gay subcultural style rather than one imposed by science on gay people" ("Less and More," 21).

Any glance into the gay and lesbian journals of the period, such as *Blätter für Menschenrecht* (*Magazine for Human Justice*), *Die Freundin* (*The Girlfriend*), or *Garçonne*, demonstrates the widespread acceptance of a Hirschfeldian in-betweenism, above all in the personal confession, which filled the sections regularly devoted to transvestism.[3] As two contributors emphatically wrote in *Die Freundin*: "There is no total man. This is no total woman. There are only bisexual variations" (1929) and "Nowhere in nature, neither in the plant or animal world, nor in mankind, are there strictly set-apart types. Everywhere we find transitional forms" (1920). Defining the various "Übergangsformen," which included gradations from "monogamy" to "polygamy" as well as degrees of sexual activity, was a task undertaken by many who published in these journals; clearly it was a subject that interested the readers of these magazines. For instance, in an essay from *Blätter für Menschenrecht* (1921) entitled "Four Types of the Same-Sex Person: An Essay in the Elucidation of Bewildering Concepts," a Dr. F. O. Hartog lists four categories—"The Uranian," "The Invert," "The Homoerot," and "The Homosexual"—in descending order, the first being "inventive, artistically, literarily, poetically, politically productive or socially active, creative," while the last, though most often monogamous (!), is said to live only for sexual satisfaction. Hirschfeld's notion of sexual indeterminacy catalyzed an epoch-long project that indulged in imagining various sexual and gender gradations; in fact, one term preferred to "homosexuality" and displaying this fascination for variation was "transmutism." This congruency between Hirschfeld's notion of the third sex and its more popular variations cannot be stressed enough given the tendency that

25

began with Brand to disparage the transvestite and effeminate gay male, a trend that has fed into subsequent attempts to dislodge the discourse on homosexuality from early sexologist tracts, a dual process that ultimately hinders one today from recognizing earlier modalities of sexual self-definition.

Freud too gave currency to the theories of gender inversion or inbetweenism at the beginning of the twentieth century. For Freud (as well as, incidentally, for Wilhelm Fließ and Otto Weininger) the homosexual was an invert, having both a male and female psyche. But not only was sexual identity dual for Freud, sexual object choice was as well—moreover, he reasoned why the two were related. In the *Three Essays on the Theory of Sexuality*, first published in 1905, he writes: "It is clear that in Greece, where the most masculine men were numbered among the inverts, what excited a man's love was not the *masculine* character of a boy, but his physical resemblance to a woman as well as his feminine mental qualities—his shyness, his modesty and his need for instruction and assistance" (7:144). Freud continues: "the sexual object is not someone of the same sex but someone who combines the characters of both sexes." In 1915 he added the crucial conclusion: "Thus the sexual object is a kind of reflection of the subject's own bisexual nature" (7:144). In this later version, same-sex object choice not only characterizes inversion but questions the existence of purportedly exclusive heterosexuality, which, Freud writes, was "also a problem that needs elucidating and is not a self-evident fact," for "all human beings are capable of making a homosexual object-choice and have in fact made one in their unconscious" (145–46). Thus, according to Freud, not only is sexual identity, or varying degrees of masculinity and femininity, unfixed in all human subjects; object choice is equally precarious and fluid.

In the volume accompanying the exposition *Goodbye to Berlin? 100 Jahre Schwulenbewegung*, Andreas Sternweiler offers the intriguing observation: "Next to Magnus Hirschfeld, Sigmund Freud exercised considerable influence in describing homosexuality as a phenomenon of puberty and thus as a developmental stage of the heterosexual male" (110). Sternweiler's remark goes against the accepted notion that psychoanalysis (the inheritor of nineteenth-century sexology) and the popular expression of sexuality move along mutually exclusive paths; in actuality, Sternweiler suggests, through the widespread reception of Freud and Hirschfeld, psychoanalytic acknowledgment of pubescent homosexuality served to legitimize its artistic depiction and hence its visible cultural expression. In fact, the homosexual of medical discourse becomes high fashion in the 1920s, as the visibility of Sebastian Droste and Anita Berber illustrates. Describing the summer of 1923 in Berlin, for instance, Stefan Zweig writes: "Along the Kurfürstendamm made-up boys with artificial waistlines walked up and down—and not only professionals were there; every high school student wanted to earn some extra cash. Even Ancient Rome was not familiar with such orgies as at the Berlin transvestite balls, where hundreds of men in women's clothes and women in men's clothes danced under the beneficent gaze of the police" (333). In the early 1920s transvestite bars and revues, such as Eldorado, the Mikado, Bülow-Kasino, Kleist-Kasino, and Voo Doo, mushroomed and appealed to a wide audience, and by the late 1920s photographs of Eldorado's transvestites could be seen in the main cultural journal of the period, *Der Querschnitt* (*The Cross-Cut*). So popular were the lesbian bars, even among a heterosexual clientele, that one lesbian publication, *Die Freundin*, warned its readers about the dangers of exposure when the owners of an establishment too openly advertised its lesbian chic. At the lesbian Club Violetta's transvestite evenings, numerous thin boyish figures were reportedly seen, while the garçonne look was in vogue among urban lesbians and straight women alike. Named after the novel *La Garçonne* by Victor Margueritte (translated into German in 1924), it featured the short-skirted suit that deemphasized waist and bust and the Bubi-style haircut.[4] Given the popularity of a look that read "third sex," it is by no means improbable that cross-dressing films of the period could be read in light of this cultural subtext, with the understanding that not only gay or lesbian audiences would have recognized the allusion. The erotic impression that the androgynous cross-dresser exudes must therefore be recognized as stylishly, hence purposefully, gay or lesbian. Moreover, if, as Sternweiler claims, "the look of drag queens and gays [das Tunte und das Schwule] possessed at that time avant-garde quality" (*Goodbye*, 123), one needs to reconsider the beautified, effeminized males of Weimar art cinema as one would a Sebastian Droste—creating and enhancing a contemporary gay aesthetic, where, as Stephan Zweig among others documents, an androgynous look with its heavy cinematic eye shadow was prized.[5]

The Third Sex in Cinema: 'Anders als die Andern,' 'Das Cabinet des Dr. Caligari,' 'Ich möchte kein Mann sein,' and 'Der Geiger von Florenz'

German cinema can boast of producing as early as 1919 a more openly gay film than would appear for decades to follow. It was in that year that Richard Oswald directed *Anders als die Andern* (*Different From the Rest*), an educational film that valiantly defended homosexual rights and pleaded for sympathy for men who, unable to alter their natures, were blackmailed. Among its star cast,

Figures 1 and 2.   Anders als die Andern (1919), Conrad Veidt (right) and Reinhold Schünzel (left). Courtesy of the Fotoarchiv, Stiftung Deutsche Kinemathek, Berlin.

which included Conrad Veidt and Anita Berber, was Magnus Hirschfeld himself, lecturing on homosexuality. He was also co-scriptwriter. The villain was played by Reinhold Schünzel, who was later to write and direct *Viktor und Viktoria* and to script *Wochenend im Paradies* (*Weekend in Paradise*) (1952), which Billy Wilder remade as one of the most famous transvestite comedies, *Some Like It Hot* (1959). In *Anders als die Andern*, Veidt starred as the musician Paul Körner, whose brilliant career is terminated once he courageously brings his blackmailer to court, thereby exposing his own homosexuality. The ensuing societal rejection leads him to commit suicide. Paul's character, as Richard Dyer points out, fits that of the gender invert—artistic, sensitive, elegantly dressed, with eyes hollowed by kohl.[6] Indeed, the role created for Veidt a gay fandom: his subsequent appearances both onscreen and off were regularly announced and reviewed in the gay press (see *Goodbye to Berlin?*, 126); and Christopher Isherwood has recorded that Veidt was an idolized presence at one Berlin Christmas costume ball for men (cited in Jacobsen, 21).

Acknowledging the variety of gay images that *Anders als die Andern* circulated, Thomas Waugh appreciatively observes: "Amid its Expressionist gloom, *Anders* projects moments of innocent schoolboy play and devotion, and chaste gay mentorship and coupledom (bowlers and overcoats for a

stroll, arm-in-arm, through the Tiergarten)—not to mention precious inside glimpses of camp extravagance in Berlin nightlife" (380). It was these dance scenes, as James Steakley points out in his fascinating reconstruction of the film's production and reception, that provoked the strongest condemnation among the public: returning to the issue of how the third sex is represented in the film, Steakley queries,

> Is it begging the question to propose that both villain and victim may be seen as sexual intermediates, whose contrary temperaments serve precisely to confound unitary notions of "the" homosexual? . . . Yet

> sexual intermediacy is portrayed most vividly not by these two charac-
> ters but by the film's dance scenes depicting anonymous members of
> the third sex. It will be recalled that it was not the image of either
> Körner or Bollek but the first of these scenes which precipitated a riot
> in one Berlin cinema in 1919. ("Film und Zensur," 32–33)[7]

As Steakley painstakingly documents, the film's sold-out screenings quickly
provoked a major scandal throughout the country and led to heightened film
censorship. Given this reception as well as the destruction of Hirschfeld's library by the Nazis, the only print to survive comes from the Gosfilmofond
in Moscow, with Ukrainian intertitles, heavily edited and shortened. It would
be decades before homosexuality could again be invoked on the screen as directly as in *Anders als die Andern*.[8]

The presence of the gender invert, however, could still be detected among
the most luminous creations of the Weimar screen, as well as in lesser-known
works by its most famous directors. Moreover, the most idolized actors and
actresses of the period were to become gay and lesbian icons for years to
come, Greta Garbo and Marlene Dietrich being the most famous. A few
Weimar films are renowned for their discrete portrayal of same-sex desire—
C. Th. Dreyer's *Michael* (1924), G. W. Pabst's *Pandora's Box* (1928), and Leontine Sagan's *Mädchen in Uniform* (1931). Because Pabst's and Sagan's work has
been discussed extensively elsewhere, I will refrain from doing so here except
to emphasize in the course of my argument how incontrovertibly gay *Michael*
or *Mädchen in Uniform* would have appeared to savvy audiences at the time.[9]
The Weimar gay cinema canon, however, invites expansion beyond these
classics, especially if such concepts as gender inversion and intermediacy are
brought into play. Richard Dyer and Ellis Hanson have already analyzed
Friedrich Murnau's *Nosferatu* as encoding male-male attraction. Dyer colorfully writes: "although Orlok is the sexual predator, it is Thomas, the sex object, whose genitals are on display in his trousers that are loose everywhere
but at the crotch. When Orlok goes down on Thomas as he sleeps, he is not
just making do with male 'blood'" ("Less and More," 23). It may be added
that, neither dead nor alive, the count also exemplifies a "geistige Zwitterbildung," as does the androgynous Cesare in the *Das Cabinet des Dr. Caligari*,
which appeared in the same year as *Anders als die Andern* and starred in both
lead roles the haunting Conrad Veidt.[10]

Cesare seems to belong to a third category that holds other binaries in suspension: as Richard Murphy observes, he is "simultaneously passive and active, innocent and evil, and peculiarly androgynous" (50). Murphy further
writes that "Cesare is simply an exhibited object and that, while he remains a

mere semantic vacuum, he is made to signify only as a consequence of the gaze of the other" (51). But if Cesare is "reanimated or recreated only as the *object* of the spectator's gaze" (original italics, 51), it is because an uncanny quality to this character draws attention to it. What cannot be seen or determined is the allegory of his androgyny: arousing an indefinable anxiety and curiosity yet also desire, he is a figure on which to project spectatorial ambivalence about homosexuality. Not surprisingly, he is also intradiegetically the object of scopophilic fascination. There is something oddly unstable about Cesare that the cinematic audience cannot precisely see, as it gawks before Dr. Caligari's sideshow. The somnambulist's unblinking eyes, painted heavily with kohl, mirror back the viewer's own blind stare. Desperate, the viewer then looks for signs of homoeroticism in the film: Cesare murders Alan in bed with a knife but drops Jane in exhaustion;[11] Francis is voyeuristically preoccupied with Cesare and uses him as a vehicle to "kill" his love for Alan so that he can redirect his attentions toward the socially proper female mate; Caligari necrophilically embraces the dead Cesare; and so forth. But in this film it is less an issue of being able to glean homosexuality as it is one of spectatorial hesitation about Cesare's identity, about the anxiety of not being able to see and comprehend homosexuality. Thus the film teasingly plays upon the thematics of revelation, in other words, of theatrically uncovering what needs to be kept hidden inside the cabinet or closet. In so doing it resembles the staging of courtroom and, subsequently, public exposure in *Anders als die Andern*.

The representation of sexual excess, the thematics of hiding and disclosure, the indeterminacy of identity, the scopophilic fascination with the third sex, the projection of spectatorial desire—a queer reading of *Das Cabinet des Dr. Caligari* announces a set of issues that can profitably be examined in other films of the period. The popular genre of the cross-dressing film is a case in point, as the films *Ich möchte kein Mann sein*, starring Ossi Oswalda, *Der Geiger von Florenz* with Elisabeth Bergner, *Der Fürst von Pappenheim* with Curt Bois and Mona Maris, and *Viktor und Viktoria* with Renate Müller illustrate.[12]

Clearly there is a long stage tradition stemming from the nineteenth century of the female-to-male (f2m) trouser role; Marjorie Garber in fact terms it "the transvestite norm" (*Vested Interests*, 39). French ballet of the nineteenth century was largely female, the male roles taken over by "danseuses en travesti" (see Garafola). Sarah Bernhardt was a renowned Hamlet, as was Asta Nielsen in a 1920 screen version, where she plays an unrecognized female Hamlet who secretly falls in love with Horatio. This depiction of a closeted love should make one look more intently at cross-dressing roles for signs of same-sex longing. Nielsen's hauntingly androgynous Hamlet clothed in black tights and staring out of darkened, cavernous eyes pairs her strangely

Figure 3. *Hamlet* (1920), Asta Nielsen. Courtesy of the Fotoarchiv, Stiftung Deutsche Kinemathek, Berlin.

with Veidt's Cesare; like him she bears witness to an unspeakable, repressed desire. Her Hamlet embodies a fundamental ambivalence not only with regard to her revenge but to sexuality as well. She evokes the bisexual hysteric, cloaking her desire through the histrionics of her mad gestures, mockingly masquerading heterosexual love for Ophelia, yet all the while refusing to divulge her threefold secret—her sexual identity, her plot for revenge, and love for Horatio. One wonders whether she could in fact privately welcome acting—for all intents and purposes being—the boy, for she never abandons the part, even in death. Here silent cinema brilliantly plays on its own muteness and demonstrates the problem of interpreting desire and sexuality, which once doubly silenced and masked grows in its suggestiveness, despite Nielsen's erasure of voluptuousness through her accomplished androgyny.

Nielsen was not alone among Weimar's most famous actresses in assuming more than once cross-dressing roles. The waiflike Elisabeth Bergner too in theater and film played the disguised f2m, as did other, in some instances later, lesbian idols—Louise Brooks (*Pandora's Box*), Marlene Dietrich (*Morocco*), Greta Garbo (*Queen Christina*), Hertha Thiele (*Mädchen in Uniform*), Marianne Hoppe (*Schwarzer Jäger Johanna* [*Black Hunter Johanna*]), and Dolly Haas (*Der Page von Dalmasse Hotel* [*The Page from the Dalmasse Hotel*], *Liebeskommando* [*Love Commando*], *Girls Will Be Boys*).[13] These women complement the beautiful, effeminized male stars of the period, Valentino and Veidt, both gay icons of the period.[14] Bergner was in fact paired with Veidt in *Der Geiger von Florenz* as well as in *Nju*. To extend the links further: one writer of the period even fantasized a connection between the Nosferatu and Bergner, satirizing the philistine reaction to her appeal: "Fathers warn their sons, mothers warn their daughters of seduction by this vampire, this Lilith. To everyone she appears as their darling" (Eloesser, 85). I hope to show how indeed "jedem sie wie sein Liebchen vor[kommt]," how Bergner, playing the gender invert, could arouse gay, lesbian, and straight desires and thus confuse the boundaries between them.

Traditionally, cross-dressing has been a means for a woman to assume male prerogatives where they would otherwise be closed to her. Thus f2m transvestism can be perceived as a challenge to male order, which is why the garçonne look of the 1920s lesbian carried the additional threat of woman's emancipation. Both *Ich möchte kein Mann sein* and *Der Geiger von Florenz* begin their narratives with the young woman revolting against the injunctions of her father or his representative. But the "gender trouble" of these films does not reside solely in their depiction of independent, strong-willed women and their rejection of patriarchal authority. Both films deeply unsettle sexual as well as gender divisions in a way inconceivable for even independent gay cinema as well as mainstream straight cinema today.

When Ossi's uncle leaves on an extended trip in *Ich möchte kein Mann sein* and appoints an autocratic guardian, Ossi decides to take revenge for the restriction of her freedoms by having a man's tuxedo tailored for her. The intertitle reads: "Ossi emancipates herself." In her new garb, she mimics male swagger, revealing it to be mere posturing. If Joan Rivière has discussed fem-

33

Figure 4. *Ich möchte kein Mann sein* (1919), Ossi Oswalda (left center). Courtesy of the Fotoarchiv, Stiftung Deutsche Kinemathek, Berlin.

ininity as a masquerade, then Ossi here shows masculinity to be one as well. She mockingly enters the Lacanian symbolic order. Donning a monocle (as Marjorie Garber points out, a sign of the detachable penis [154]), Ossi now controls and manipulates the gaze.[15] She deliberately plays on the ambiguity of being both hypervisible and yet camouflaged in drag. The destabilization of the correspondence between exteriority and interiority, the maintenance of which bourgeois epistemology polices, is in fact what defines camp. Ossi makes the society around her seem laughable for its inability to see through her obvious disguise. Thus even before the film progresses to its intimations of homosexuality, Ossi performs her impersonation with campy, stylized flair, preparing the way for a more flaming transgression that could not have gone undetected by the spectator primed for the implications of transvestite irony. (Magnus Hirschfeld, incidentally, also coined the term "transvestite" in 1911.)

Having thus fashioned a new garb and gait for herself, Ossi saunters out to practice her role by appreciatively eyeing the women on the street. Although no one in the film seems to notice her high heels and exposed feminine ankle, the camera certainly does, as if to clue the spectator in to the fact

Figure 5. *Ich möchte kein Mann sein* (1919). Courtesy of the Fotoarchiv, Stiftung Deutsche Kinemathek, Berlin.

that gender roles never quite fit. Ossi further draws attention to her unstable, third-sex position when at a ball she powders her nose before a crowd of be-mused women. At this event she also attracts the notice of her guardian, Dr. Kersten, and proceeds to cunningly act out her revenge. Once she espies him talking to another woman, she lures him away, with the result that the woman takes off with yet another man. The icebreaker is thus a homosocial one: the inconstancy of women. Homosociality then veers into the erotic as the two seal their warm "Bruderschaft" not only with glasses of champagne but also a full kiss on the lips. Moreover, they sit before a bouquet of lilacs, a gay-coded flower at the time.[16]

In the course of the evening, the pair drink so excessively that they grope at each other as they leave. In helping Dr. Kersten into his coat, Ossi puts it on wrong, as if in commentary on her own inverted costume. They are now both "inverts." Once together in a fiacre, the doctor falls upon his new young friend with another passionate kiss that is reciprocated. Incidentally, he displayed no previous sexual interest in Ossi as a woman. Because their inebriation totally overwhelms them, the coachman must deliver them to their respective quarters; he mixes up their addresses. The cut to Kersten's keen embarrassment on awakening in Ossi's bed (wearing her feminine, frilly nightcap) and the guilt with which he sneaks out of her home suggest what the editing process omits: that the men could have done more than sleep in each other's quarters. This episode could serve as an early example from cinematic discourse of how the morning-after scene in a strange bed metonymically signifies sex the night before. In fact, when Kersten's butler comforts the crying Ossi, he shows no sign of surprise, as if it were not at all unusual to find a young man in his master's bed. After she regains her composure and, realizing the situation, runs back to her own room, Ossi finally doffs her wig, just at the point when Kersten reenters, witnessing the unmasking. The exuberant final "recognition" scene shows them jumping on the bed kissing.

Der Geiger von Florenz also ends in heterosexual pairing but similarly takes a queer route to it. After running away from the boarding school where her father has put her after her jealous, discourteous behavior toward her stepmother, Renée exchanges clothing with a peasant boy so that she can steal undetected across the border to Italy. The pronunciation of her name is, incidentally, itself gender ambiguous. Once in Italy, she draws a crowd of admirers as she masterfully performs on the violin of a local fiddler. A car drives up with an artist (Walter Rilla) and his sister in it: the artist, immediately captivated by Renée's beauty, whisks her away to serve as his model. They arrive in Florenz, a town that provided earlier centuries with the word "florenzen," slang for sodomy. It is hardly coincidental that the homosexuality of the artist in this film harks back to the figure of creative talent in *Anders als die Andern* and *Michael*, as well as to the aesthetic cultivation of things Mediterranean in the latter.[17]

Once back at his villa, the artist appears naked in the shower, washing up after the dusty ride. Then, wrapped in a bathrobe, he invites the boy to a bath and a rubdown. He seems to have quickly fallen in love with his new model, much to the sister's jealousy, and declares he would marry him if he were only a woman. Both *Der Geiger von Florenz* and *Ich möchte kein Mann sein* can be said to offer variations on the traditional pickup scene between a young male prostitute and his john. The novel *Der Puppenjunge* (*The Hustler*) (1926) by John Henry Mackay describes many such scenes as the story follows a delicate, refined-looking teenage hustler from bars and lounges to the streets. Often the young protagonist Gunther, like Ossi, becomes so inebriated he doesn't know how he arrived in the bed in which he awakens the next morning. The novel also portrays an episode, not dissimilar to *Der Geiger von Florenz*, where an aesthete count takes Gunther in, only to admire him night after night naked on a bearskin throw. The situation of an older man setting

Figure 6. *Der Geiger von Florenz* (1925–26), Elisabeth Bergner. Courtesy of the Fotoarchiv, Stiftung Deutsche Kinemathek, Berlin.

up house with a young lover or protégé is likewise the theme of Dreyer's *Michael*. If the couples in *Ich möchte kein Mann sein* and *Der Geiger von Florenz* live presumably happily ever after, it is because homosexuality is denied in the final shots. In contrast to such a happy end, in *Michael* the artist is betrayed by his young companion for a woman, though again in order to thwart the possibility of real same-sex attraction. Homosexuality remains

37

platonic, idealistic, and, as very clearly in *Der Geiger von Florenz*, artistically inspirational.[18]

Conceivably in order to disguise the threat of overt male homosexuality in *Der Geiger von Florenz*, infatuations spring up elsewhere in the plot, beginning with Renée's intense jealousy of her stepmother, which relegates her to a voyeuristic, masochistic role in the family realignment. Another false lead is the triangle mirroring this one, involving Renée, the artist, and his sister. The sister quickly notices the discrepancy between this peasant boy and his fine table manners and soon thinks she recognizes the disguise. She goes into Renée's bedroom and, in the film's most erotic scene, puts her hand on her breast, ostensibly to confirm her sex but also as if to seduce her, for she then looks at Renée knowingly, pets her, and kisses her fully on the mouth: the two women now share a secret. Was the sister's initial jealousy aroused because she feared losing her brother, introducing the possibility of incest, or because the heart of this handsome girl was being won by another?[19] Such complications necessitate a precipitous yet safe dénouement: the father, played by Conrad Veidt, recognizes in a newspaper the portrait the artist has made of his daughter and hastens to Florence to find her. There he agrees to give her hand in marriage to the artist, thus resolving the strange budding triangles and the potentially incestuous family romances in the plot. As in *Ich möchte kein Mann sein*, the female lead never changes back into a dress and thus in the final scene embraces her lover as a boy. As such a detail indicates, despite the apparent innocence and unselfconsciousness of these comedies, the characters exude the sense that they know more about their queer desires than they are willing to admit openly. To quote Judith Butler: "Sexuality always exceeds any given performance, presentation, or narrative. . . . Part of what constitutes sexuality is precisely that which does not appear and that which, to some degree, can never appear" ("Imitation and Gender Insubordination," 25).

It must be emphasized that these cross-dressing films deviate from the genre in that the initial amorous attraction, sustained until the final scenes, is homosexual, not heterosexual. We can read these films as depicting a woman playing a gay man, of showing the desirability of being a gay man. They could be titled: *Ich möchte kein Hetero sein* (*I Don't Want to Be a Hetero*). This reading for homoeroticism, however, does not exclude a straight enjoyment of these films as transvestite comedies. Nor does it underestimate the competing forces to deny same-sex erotic exchange. But neither can the revelation of the disguise and the conventional heterosexual pairing explain away the pederastic advances. The closure is unconvincing.[20] At best the striking figure of the cross-dresser deflects attention away from the homoerotic leanings of the main male role. Similarly, the established tradition of

38

the "Hosenrolle" conceals its homoerotic valence and its allusion to the sexual invert, whereby dress now stands in for body. At the very least these films seem to say that single-gendered identity and single-vectored desire are restrictive and inhibiting. For this reason, one cannot definitively categorize the characters in these two films as straight, gay, or lesbian—nor, for that matter, under the rubrics invert, or the third sex, for they move too agilely among such groupings. But it can be argued that the ternary concept of a third sex functions as does the current term "queer" to allow for a nonbinary, nonantithetical way of thinking sexuality. It is significant that in *Der Geiger von Florenz* the artist is frustrated at not being able to capture Renée's animated modeling—in fact, he can't get her to freeze in the pose he wants—indicating her unconstrained, unrepresentable sexuality, more suitable for the moving image, the cinema, than for the portrait. Her androgyny, moreover, does not suggest sexual indifference; rather than effacing sexual differences, she heightens them.

So far the male impersonator has been read as signaling the gender invert. But can the man who initiates the advances also be seen as passing—but as straight? Is he coded in any way as homosexual? This question is difficult to address because the dynamics of the closet are deflected onto the hidden identity of the cross-dresser; as in *Mädchen in Uniform* where Manuela, acting the part of Don Carlos, comes out and declares her love for Fräulein Bernburg, so too here the gender invert, the boy object, visibly encodes the homosexual. Writing about the 1920s, Moe Meyer observes:

> Among the invert population itself, the association of homosexuality with transvestism was . . . marked. Effeminate and cross-dressing men defined themselves as homosexual. Their partners, if not exhibiting such outward behavior, were classified as heterosexual by both the gay and nongay publics regardless of their participating in same-gender sexual activity. George Chauncey, in his analysis of courtroom and other public documents of the era, concluded that it was not sexual activity that labeled a man homosexual but his choice and use of particular signifying gestures of social gender role enactment. ("Unveiling the Word," 77)

By today's standards, Dr. Kersten and the artist are the most easily recognizable gay characters, but at the time, regardless of their actions, they did not look the part. They thus do not pose to mainstream audiences the threat of homosexuality that one expects to have arisen, which is not to deny that gay audiences would have been attuned to the homoeroticism of these films. The male lead could have appealed, in particular, as an identificatory model for

39

men-loving men who did not want to appear effeminate and yet who, in the vein of Adolf Brand, worshipped handsome youths. Nor is it solely the gay viewer who would read these men thus. In fact, *Ich möchte kein Mann sein* warns the viewer away from reading Dr. Kersten as straight: Ossi's homely governess flatters herself in thinking the guardian has designs on her; in other words, she misreads his sexual orientation, a position of ignorance with which the viewer would hesitate to identify.[21]

Indeed, it may be the straight-appearing male protagonist who nonetheless engages in covert same-sex affairs who could be seen as the key to allowing male homosexuality on the screen in whatever form in a post-*Anders* censorious climate. Another case in point would be the 1928 *Geschlecht in Fesseln* (*Sex in Chains*), a film primarily about prison reform that could not have expected a sympathetic ear for its cause and simultaneously have told the story of a character who was perceived as homosexual. *Geschlecht in Fesseln* narrates the tragedy that befalls a young couple when the husband, Franz Sommer (played by the director, Wilhelm Dieterle), accidentally kills a man molesting his wife. The sexual deprivation of prison life (one man commits suicide when not allowed to see his girlfriend, Franz hallucinates his wife's presence, and the inmates fashion clay girlie dolls) eventually leads Franz to return the affections of one new prisoner, Alfred, played by the openly gay actor Hans Heinrich von Twardowsky. In a charged nighttime scene, the two lie in adjoining beds as the camera pans back and forth between their faces, each time passing over Alfred's body. The following intertitles punctuate the camera movement:

Franz	"What are you thinking about, Alfred?"
Alfred	"Put your hand on your heart and swear that you won't laugh at me."
Franz	"I'd never laugh at you."
Alfred	"Why don't you say anything? Do you despise me?"

In response, Franz takes Alfred's hand as he stretches it out to him. In the scenes that follow, it is clear from the glances between the two that their intimate relationship continues beyond that one night. When both are eventually let out of prison, Alfred (the first to regain freedom) immediately comes to visit Franz at home, bringing him flowers. Although one of Alfred's gay friends suggests blackmailing Franz, Alfred, in a reversal of the plot of *Anders als die Andern*, displays genuine affection. When the wife, however, catches on to the situation (indicated by her burying her face in her hands), Alfred is forced to withdraw. He apologizes: "Dear lady, if I have ruined your happiness, forgive me," and leaves the flowers behind on the balustrade. The meaning of Franz's cryptic words, "only to you can I no longer return," must now be clear to his spouse: his prison experiences have also altered his sexual desires. Franz and his wife (who also committed adultery during their separation) then jointly commit suicide by turning on the gas in their apartment, their final place of incarceration.

As in so many of these silent films, the looks between the characters (especially the concluding threesome) as well as their gestures betray their sexual relations and desires. Likewise serving as visual codes, the opening and closing of doors and (prison) gates suggest the closet and its misery. Although *Geschlecht in Fesseln* did suffer the censor's cut,[22] that it could have even attempted to portray empathetically the dilemma in which Franz found himself, including understanding for his sexual needs, could only have occurred if he himself were not perceived as gay. Franz, a tall, lumbering, wide-shouldered fellow with broad, dull facial features, is contrasted with the more delicate though still not pansyesque Alfred. In addition, Franz's final reunion with his wife, though in death, further deemphasizes his homo- or bisexuality. Two conclusions may be drawn from this representational ambivalence: first, only once homosexuality is attenuated could such a film, whose main purpose was not to advocate homosexuality but to criticize harsh sentencing and penal conditions, expect to garner a receptive audience. Second, Franz's character offers considerable insight into how noninvert male homosexuality was (or was not) perceived at the time and thus offers a clue as to how to read for homosexuality in other examples of Weimar cinema.

From the Semiology to the Hermeneutics of the Transvestite Film: 'Der Fürst von Pappenheim' and 'Viktor und Viktoria'

I shall return to the unobtrusively gay male role shortly with regard to *Viktor und Viktoria* (1933). In this film, however, as in *Der Fürst von Pappenheim* (1927), transvestism generally becomes more theatrical, indeed associated with the stage, more burlesque, less deceptively natural, and less gender-ambiguous. This shift can be seen as the consequence of the genre becoming more intricate in its farcical plot as time progresses. If one continues tracing the transvestite comedy of errors further, say until *Capriccio* (1938) with its dizzying narrative, one begins to wonder how its secondary characters could possibly be duped by the protagonist's disguise; here Lilian Harvey's delicate figure and shoulder-length blond hair are unmistakably feminine and unandrogynous, especially when compared with Asta Nielsen's roles in *Hamlet* and *Das Liebes ABC* (*The ABCs of Love*) (1916). What occurs, however, in *Der Fürst von Pappenheim* and *Viktor und Viktoria* is that with the narrative twists

41

and turns, in the play between stage and dressing room revelations, what matters most is how the cross-dresser is diegetically seen and interpreted by other characters. The visual spectacle is also crucial at the level of the extra-diegetic spectator: the immediate scenario before one's eyes forces one to suspend awareness of the narrative trajectory (that so-and-so is actually a man or a woman) and to indulge in the fantasy of same-sex amorous possibilities. This dwelling on the image, the captivation by the fantasy, is enhanced by the stage setting, which frames the transvestite pose and thematizes the act of looking. Not unexpectedly, such theatrical gazing and falling in love recurs in more recent queer films: in Monika Treut's *Virgin Machine*, for instance, Dorothee ogles the masturbating male impersonator on stage, and in Ulrike Ottinger's *Dorian Gray im Spiegel der Boulevardpresse* the opera sets the scene for Dorian's falling in love with Andamana. In Ottinger, as in Werner Schroeter too, narrative is halted and moves in fits and starts because of this captivation by the painterly, theatrical, or operatic image. As we shall repeatedly see, these are suspended moments of an allegorical layering of meaning—where one is aware of diametrically opposed yet concurrent readings of gender and sexual attraction.

The opening intertitle of *Der Fürst von Pappenheim* is "Lilac Time in Lovonia." As in *Ich möchte kein Mann sein*, where the odd couple Ossi and Dr. Kersten kiss over a bouquet of lilacs, so here too the gay flower of the period is invoked to alert the astute spectator to an unobtrusive subtext. Significantly, these were not the only two cross-dressing films to draw upon the lilac at a prominent moment. *Das Liebes ABC* likewise begins with lilacs, in this case surrounding Asta Nielsen in a cameo shot. In this film Nielsen teaches her passive, weak-willed fiancé how to be a man by taking on the role herself and dressing in a tuxedo. At the opera she starts eyeing the women in the next loge and invites them over, whereupon they sit in her lap, much to her fiancé's disgust, who now looks the part of the jealous gay lover. In yet another hairdo and suit (much is erotically made of her donning each piece of apparel), she has her fiancé introduce her as a school friend to her father. Her final costume is as a chef with white cap and apron. In each outfit Nielsen is strikingly handsome, her mannered, tailored gestures suggestively queer. The repeated voyeuristic scenes of men looking at her through keyholes thematize the insatiability of the gaze when confronted by this fantastical creature. The film then closes with this gender-experimental couple going off on their honeymoon. Although Nielsen's character was ultimately the one to be duped by further slapstick antics (a male servant impersonates the fiancé's lover, arousing the jealousy of the bride-to-be), she still carries a bouquet of lilacs in the final shot. In *Viktor und Viktoria* lilacs also appear at a pivotal moment—when the male protagonist asks his pal Viktor whether he should buy lilacs or roses for his beloved. By choosing roses, Robert signals that the game of deceptions is about to end, and that he will now treat his companion not as a (gay) man but as a woman.

After its auspicious beginning, *Der Fürst von Pappenheim* shows Princess Antoinette (nicknamed Toni, played by Mona Maris), like Ossi and Renée, trying to escape familial constraints, in this case plans to marry her off to someone against her wishes. She flees on the next train, where she runs into Egon Fürst (Curt Bois), manager of the couturier house of Pappenheim, with his entourage of models. Although Fürst professes his love for these women and they all have fond affection for him, no one takes this little fellow seriously. He is particularly betrayed by former model Diddi, who sits in an adjoining compartment with her latest conquest, a paunchy, rich, and bewhiskered Count Ottokar. As Fürst secretly plays footsie with Diddi, he mistakenly rubs up against the count, beginning a series of encounters where Fürst tries to escape from his clutches, either amorous or vengeful, depending on the slapstick situation. Other not totally uneroticized bodily contact occurs between Fürst and the count on the train: Fürst sucks on the count's finger once it is angrily shaken at him, and he faints delicately across the count's wide chest in simulated fear. Other clues later in the film suggest the count's susceptibility to transgendered flirtations.

Upon her arrival in Berlin, Toni decides to take up Fürst's offer and become one of the girls at Pappenheim's. Little does she realize, however, that her uncle knows Madame Pappenheim. He soon decides to visit the couturier to enlist her aid in finding his runaway niece. As the count, too, comes searching for his delinquent Diddi, the stage is set for a comedy of disguise and mistaken identity, held in the world of designer fashion, an ideal setting for behind-the-curtain quick changes and runway masquerade. The famous double cross-dressing sequence occurs when Toni and Fürst switch costumes, Toni to avoid recognition by her uncle and Fürst to fool the count who thinks his rival dead. Since Fürst is the master of ceremonies at the Frankfurt fashion show, Toni handsomely dons his tuxedo, looking the mannish lesbian, while he appears on the runway in her glittering evening dress with low-cut back, peacock fan, and lavish headdress. Swaying his hips, rolling his large eyes, and enjoying every minute of the masquerade, Fürst looks the perfect drag queen. Indeed, his is no cheap female imitation; the performance is not only convincing but scintillating for the precision with which Curt Bois recaptures the exaggerated feminine gestures and movement from the silent era. The mock title of "Duke of (the House of) Pappenheim," now seems apt—like Rosa von Praunheim or Charlotte von Mahlsdorf, he possesses the

43

Figure 7. *Der Fürst von Pappenheim* (1927), Curt Bois and Mona Maris.
Courtesy of the Fotoarchiv, Stiftung Deutsche Kinemathek, Berlin.

44

fake nobility of the "Tunte." It goes without saying that, in addition, the "von" democratically ridicules the class pretensions of the prince (the uncle) and the count.

Predictably, both the count and the uncle sitting in the audience fall in love with Fürst, although they were initially oblivious to Toni. In his flirtatiousness, Fürst even manages to trip off the runway, for the second time, into the count's arms. The queer pairings constantly shift as Toni's beau now appears backstage: looking like a pretty boy, Toni sniffs the roses given her. The uncle happens to pass by as the two men kiss, whereupon he displays not disgust but pleasant amusement: "I may be old-fashioned, but when I kiss I prefer a pair of female lips." In all these scenes what matters is who sees what; in other words, Toni is not a man kissing another man until she is diegetically perceived as such; Fürst is not a pansy until other men fall in love with him. The queerness of this film dwells on the level of representation or exhibition, which, of course, is what fashion modeling itself signifies. In the sequence of dressing room mishaps that ensue (all evocative of the closet's revenge), "misinterpretations" (in quotation marks because who can question what desire actually seeks) arise from the semblance, enactment, or spectacle presented and its reception. The cue to the audience is that it too must fall for the visually erotic pageant and perceive the actual mise-en-scène—for instance, two "men" kissing—in order to recognize the seductive power of representation. Figuring out who is who in disguise is far too simple an interpretive task; the enjoyment of allegorical reading in this film resides in abandonment to the surface, to the image on display. Very astutely, the film seems to suggest with every character (even with Toni and her suitor) that one only falls in love with a disguise: masquerade and desire are intimately linked.

The film ends where it began, back at the castle. The key to the unraveling of identities is itself a representation—a portrait of Toni, hidden, appropriately for the other images of screens, doors, and partitions in this film, behind a curtain. When Fürst happens upon the portrait, he realizes Toni's true identity. A series of pairings complete the dénouement: Toni is matched with her suitor, who proves after all to be the intended fiancé, Diddi with the old uncle, and the count with Toni's aunt Helen, in whom he recognizes his first love. Helen, towering over the count, is unmistakably played by a man, a clear indication that the other gender inversions of the film must be read not just as slapstick but for their queer sensibilities. Fürst, as the truly odd man out, poignantly whispers at the end, "I think I better fade away." The fact that he was disguised as Toni is never revealed to the count or prince, for no unmasking is required: it is part of Fürst's character to slip into different gender roles. His smooth, hairless skin on delicate legs, arms, and back make him physically appear urningesque, while his astonishing mimicry of the feminine screen gestures of the day seems second nature to him. This third-sex, outsider status is never questioned in the film, for instance, by any of the women being attracted to him. How Fürst would identify himself sexually (he chases women) is immaterial before the spectacle of his personage and its reception.

It must not be forgotten, however, that the presentation of the third sex as spectacle has its historical roots in the pathologizing, medical discourse of the day, a connection that becomes distinctly ominous by the next decade in Germany. Hirschfeld popularized the look of the homosexual through his voluminous depictions of the everyday life of the third sex. Through his collecting and sifting he ended up prescribing and fixating homosexual identity, the detection of which could become a parlor game, which conceivably was part of the popular entertainment in going to see a film like *Der Fürst von Pappenheim*. Whereas the androgyny of Nielsen and Bergner, though still decodable as third sex, remained thoroughly ambiguous, with Curt Bois the transvestite queen is all too recognizable. He thereby becomes the object not only of laughter but derision and hatred as well: the Nazis selected the cross-dressing sequence in *Der Fürst von Pappenheim* to illustrate unnatural, decadent, Jewish sexuality in Fritz Hippler's 1940 propaganda film, *Der ewige Jude* (*The Eternal Jew*). A physiognomic reading of the third sex is quickly deployed not only to burlesque purposes but to more sinister ones as well.

More than any other film we have discussed in this self-reflexive genre of the transvestite comedy, *Viktor und Viktoria* operates on the level of the purposefully ambiguous image—how it is staged and received. In fact, *Viktor und Viktoria* moves away from an iconology or semiology of the third sex to the more uncertain realm of hermeneutics, where it is less a matter of recognizing a sign than of interpreting it. Whereas in *Ich möchte kein Mann sein*, *Der Geiger von Florenz*, and *Der Fürst von Pappenheim*, the deception was always at the cost of the onlookers, here dissimulation is practiced by both major parties, turning the act of reading gender and sexuality into a much more complicated affair. With such complexities, the likelihood of queer desires being able to sneak onto the screen increase.

The basic story already presents a double inversion: as is well known from the Blake Edwards 1982 remake, *Victor/Victoria*, with Julie Andrews (there was also an earlier 1935 English rendition called *First a Girl* and a 1957 German version), the female protagonist plays a man playing a woman. In Schünzel's 1933 film, Renate Müller stars in the lead role of Susanne. Her confidant and coach is Viktor Hempel (Hermann Thimig), a m2f performing transvestite whose stage name is Viktoria. When the flu ruins his voice, Viktor sends his newly befriended Susanne on stage in his stead, this surreptitious replacement giving rise to the dual gender reversals she undergoes. The most intriguing character, however, is the debonair male lead who falls in love with this handsome m2f performer, who continues to play a man offstage. In the Edwards version, James Marchand (James Mason) struggles with his homophobia and potential homosexuality. In the much more sophisticated Schünzel version, however, Robert (Adolf Wohlbrück) coolly accepts his bisexuality: he is just as interested in the Renate Müller character when he thinks s/he's a boy as when he knows s/he's a woman. As Wolfgang Theis provocatively writes: "No gay director has dared so ruthlessly to dismantle the age-old wall [die ehernen Grenzen . . . verwischen] between homo- and heterosexuality as Schünzel in *Viktor und Viktoria*" (23). As in the earlier transvestite comedies discussed, heterosexuality wins out in the end. This time the woman finally changes back into a dress, a move that underscores the heterosexual resolution and deflects attention away from the gay subtext. Nonetheless, Wohlbrück's performance is superb, from the glances Robert gives the boy "Viktor" to his sovereign command of his sexual knowledge (after finding out that "Viktor" is a girl, he does not let on). Recently, the gay museum in Berlin devoted an exhibition to Wohlbrück, offering mild evidence that he himself was gay. Perhaps there is not just one secret his character so masterfully keeps hidden in this film!

The entire mise-en-scène of *Viktor und Viktoria* refers back to the self-conscious performance of gender—both onstage and off—even to the point where in the dance revue dogs are dressed up as men and women. Compared to the Blake Edwards version, the Schünzel original moves very quickly, within the first few minutes, into the realm of transvestism. When Viktor Hempel first meets Susanne Lohr, he shows her his acting portfolio, which includes a photo of him as a female Spanish dancer. In the next scene, Susanne is already dressed as a boy, about to take over the role of her sick friend. In the dressing room we see men clothing themselves as "men"—putting on a mustache or a fake tuxedo—thereby pointing to the arbitrariness of male gender markers. Indeed, although on stage both "Viktors" are female impersonators, throughout the film emphasis is placed on faking the male part. Not only does "Viktor" have to act macho around Robert, who delights in coercing him do male chummy things, such as light up a pipe, drink excessively, and go to the barber shop, but "Viktor" accuses Hempel of not being a man when he is challenged to a duel. Repeatedly we see "Viktor" dressing as a man backstage (much less as the female singer), often with a double mirror in the frame, as if to stress the importance of the image to be seen. Given that the plot is so ostensibly concerned with staging virility, the most "manly" character, Robert, can afford to be the unobtrusive vehicle of gay desires.

As in the preceding silent films (*Viktor und Viktoria* is a musical), gestures and glances as well as costume serve as the semiotic details by which to read queerness into the film. For instance, when "Viktor" comes to the Savoy restaurant with noticeable eye shadow on and a carnation (Oscar Wilde's flower) in his lapel, a series of cuts to women turning their heads to look at him is succeeded by a parallel cut to Robert doing the same. The first time they are

47

Figure 8.   *Viktor und Viktoria* (1933), Adolf Wohlbrück (far left) and Renate
Müller (third from left). Courtesy of the Fotoarchiv, Stiftung Deutsche
Kinemathek, Berlin.

shot together in the frame, Robert approaches him, offers him a light, and
invites him to the bar for a whiskey. At this point Robert still does not know
the boy is a woman, but he is intrigued. During this first encounter, the camera pulls back, making their gestures more suggestive and ambiguous, in fact,
giving Robert's approach the look of a classic pickup scene. Lady Ellinor correctly reads the homosexuality of the situation, saying to "Viktor": "London's
most famous connoisseur of women has fallen head over heels in love with
you." Interestingly, Robert hardly protests being seen as gay. Just as Robert
behaves as if "Viktor" were a man, even when he knows better, so too the
viewer can pretend as much, appreciating their interaction as daringly ho-

moerotic. Whether the pairing is between Viktor Hempel and his surrogate (whereby the two "men" walk arm in arm) or between "Viktor" and Robert, the camera homosocially shoots them together in the frame as a couple. In another suggestive scene, this time after Robert knows "Viktor's" true identity, he comes into the backstage dressing room and seems nonchalantly to come on to "Viktor," holding his arm longer than necessary and lighting his cigarette with his own. "Viktor" here explains his femininity, in reference to third-sex theories, as innate ("angeboren"), a line that is extremely significant for how "Viktor" acts and how he considers himself seen by others. In other words, he not only represents the third sex in this glamorous theater crowd, he self-identifies as such.

In the scenes that follow, Robert constantly gazes at "Viktor," his eyes seeming to dwell on the looks of this invert, as if he enjoyed seeing the ephebe or the gender ambiguity.[23] He is not alone; Lady Ellinor also enjoys the sight of the feminine boy. She and Robert together applauded the gender-deceptive stage act, which they conceivably keep in the back of their minds as they continue to watch "Viktor."[24] Although Robert discovers the deception early on in the plot (his only reaction being a slightly raised eyebrow), he has no desire to disclose publicly "Viktor's" identity. He waits for her to change costume, almost as if he had an appreciation for the vicissitudes of the closet. What, though, is Robert looking at? Renate Müller, though not a Lilian Harvey,[25] is still not as androgynous as Asta Nielsen, Elisabeth Bergner, or Dolly Haas. Her figure is fuller, with more noticeable breasts. After all, she is supposed to be a man able to play a woman (and in that sense resembles much more Hirschfeld's descriptions and photos of feminine-looking men and actual transvestites, although today we notice the incongruity of her role). The consequence of this difference, however, is that Adolf Wohlbrück becomes, much more than the f2m, the center of attention as the eye-catching figure, the handsome male, and hence more the focus of an ambiguous sexuality. By contrast, Viktor Hempel, who performs gender inversion in earnest, plays the role of comic foil, with his character thus being, paradoxically, more transparent.[26]

Much of the story line in *Viktor und Viktoria* revolves around the discrepancy between epistemology and perception. The straight audience that goes slumming at the transvestite revue (very popular in the Weimar period) temporarily suspends its knowledge about the gender of the performers in order to relish the act, for the best drag performances are the ones where one is duped. Robert and his friends certainly are deceived, leading them to jest about attractiveness being a "matter of taste." Later Robert suspends his knowledge about Susanne and treats her as if she were a man. Love, of course, always entails behaving against one's better knowledge. The extradiegetic spectator, too, is involved in this discrepancy between knowing and seeing: he or she is encouraged to suspend disbelief in order to enjoy the proffered homoeroticism. Hermeneutically speaking, such maneuvers are complex: instead of accepting that the transvestite sign is duplicitous (although dressed as a man, Susanne is not a man), the spectator contemplates that maybe the sign is *not* misleading after all and that it might be read literally (Robert *is* attracted to the boyish image). More precisely, the spectator recognizes the performative dimension to signification: the sign must be taken as that which it pretends to be; subsequently one's gender must be understood as that which one performs (if "Viktor" looks and acts the boy, we must consider that on some level of signification he is one; or more prosaically, when "Viktoria" plays the woman, the role is so exaggerated, we know that gender is performed). Alone the shifting names and pronouns, which themselves function as masks, testify to this uncertainty: who is Viktor or Viktoria anyway in this film? As soon as one abandons oneself to the signifier, performance, or spectacle, despite one's knowledge that it may be deceptive (for what signifiers are not?), the possibilities for a queer enjoyment arise. This que(e)r hermeneutics of reading against the grain lets one be captivated by the pleasurably ambiguous sign; it also allows one to search for alternative meanings. These cross-dressing films in their allegorical indeterminacy play upon the fantasies of the viewer.

Transgender Fantasies

Just as the sexual orientation of the characters resists definitive labeling, so too does a psychologizing approach to their actions promise little insight. For instance, however tempting it might be to do so, it is moot to speculate what pleasure the woman derives from being loved as a man, without abandoning her basic nature as woman. Similarly, although Asta Nielsen's Hamlet evokes the ambivalent gender affiliations and histrionics of the hysteric, it would be reductive to analyze the film as a case study in hysteria. Such varying and even conflicted gender and sexual positionings *are* important, however, for the pleasure of the spectator. As the examples mentioned in the last section indicate, audience reception and the spectator's pleasure—both intra- and extra-diegetically—are key to reading these films queerly. It is thus here, in discussing the dynamics of this enjoyment, that a psychoanalytic approach can prove helpful. In the remainder of this chapter, I draw on a 1968 essay by Jean LaPlanche and J.-B. Pontalis entitled "Fantasy and the Origins of Sexuality."

LaPlanche and Pontalis write that there is no single position of identity in fantasy. Rather, the subject "cannot be assigned any fixed place in it. . . . As a result, the subject, although always present in the fantasy, may be so in a desubjectivized form, that is to say, in the very syntax of the sequence in question." "In fantasy the subject does not pursue the object or its sign: he appears caught up himself in the sequence of images" (17). With its broken succession of images, the cinematic screen is temporally and visually structured like a mental fantasy.[27] The spectator, although not bodily represented on screen, is present in a "desubjectivized form," sutured into "the very syntax of the sequence." Especially the tableauesque, stagelike style of early cinema matches the fantasy scenario, where the subject, not unlike the camera, is a passive, largely immobile beholder. Yet despite this passivity, the viewing subject, according to LaPlanche and Pontalis, belongs to and is constituted through each successive position of identification.

Like in a fantasy, the cross-dresser stages the subject in various guises. Like in a fantasy, gender identity is here concealed and distributed through different images of the self. It is fragmented and dispersed. Moreover the duplicity of the impersonated image, like that of celluloid itself, is a captivating illusion, a fantasy construction that is dreamlike and fleeting. In other words, the cinematic apparatus itself, this dream machine, can be seen to create fluctuating gender identities and desires. One could object that silent cinema necessitated an excessive sentimentality and exaggerated yet codified display of physical contact that should not automatically be interpreted as gay. Yet precisely because it is silent, early cinema demands an allegorical reading, one that accounts for the hyperbolic, ever-mutable performance staged for fantasy, and one where gestural exaggeration hints at sexual excess.

Although LaPlanche and Pontalis omit gender from their discussion, theories of cinematic spectatorship have focused almost exclusively on this issue, at times on the transgendered dimension to specularity. In response to the debate precipitated by her groundbreaking 1975 article on the conventional encoding of the agent of the "look" as male and the object of his gaze as female, Laura Mulvey has spoken of the "masculinization" of the moviegoer's position regardless of his or her sex. As she states, "trans-sex identification [becomes] a *habit*" (33) for the female viewer, insofar as she decides to identify with the active male hero. Mary Ann Doane, in an equally important piece, has written that in watching movies women can "manufacture a distance from the image" via masquerade in order "to generate a problematic within which the image is manipulable, producible, and readable by the woman" (54).[28] Consideration of LaPlanche and Pontalis implies that the gaze might not be exclusively male after all. It may necessitate a gender switch for the female viewer but, at least with regard to these Weimar films, it is inherently queer: f2m or m2f impersonations could be seen as preparing the ground for the cross-gender masquerade that the viewing subject engages in as it successively identifies with the "sequence of images" unrolling before its eyes. In other words, the ease with which these cross-dressers pass facilitates spectatorial identification across gender lines. Theatricality unites viewer and performer.[29] Likewise the way in which Kersten, the Florentine artist, or Robert "pass" as straight lures the male viewer into a position of homosexual desire. Thus, these crossings become entangled in sexual choice and work to conceal the homosexual desires of the spectator, unless, of course, he or she wants to recognize them. In sum, if we are examining desires that society has repressed and closeted, then it is paramount to look to fantasy and its psychological workings in order to imagine how those desires could be addressed.

It is conceivable that gay men of the period enjoyed seeing on screen the representation of two men kissing and becoming engaged. The entire staging of a concealment, in other words, of the closet, might also have struck a chord with them. And even though they might not have identified with the gender invert, actors such as Wohlbrück offered models both for identification and for erotic viewing. Likewise, the approving glances Ossi gets from women on the street could appeal to the lesbian viewer. Renée even gets her breast stroked by another woman who gazes longingly at her. The cross-dresser's handsome garçonne look alone is eye-catching and arousing, as "Viktor's" appearance at the Savoy suggests, when both Lady Hildebrand and Robert admire her from afar; erotic delight dwells at the edge or borderline; it fetishizes the clothes. Despite the problematic deception behind such eroticized moments and their eventual betrayal by the narrative closure, nonetheless it is imperative to look for ways in which gays, lesbians, and bisexuals could have negotiated pleasure in the realm of heterosexist popular culture.[30]

And find delight they did, if this one poem by "Ethel" from the lesbian journal *Garçonne* (4 [1930]: 5) is any indication:[31]

An Elisabeth Bergner

Wie Wassertropfen klar und bunt
Spiegelnd im Sonnenschein.
Wie huschender Schatten im Blättergrund,
Wie golden funkelnder Wein.
Wie silberhelles Meeresrauschen,
Gleich eines Rehes scheuem Lauschen.
Wie die Mimose empfindsam und fein

Und wie der Bergquell so licht und rein—
So wie ein Lächeln unter Tränen,
Wie ein Verstecken, wie ein Sehnen
Wie Geigentöne süß und leis':
    Das ist die Bergnerweis.

For Elisabeth Bergner

Like water drops that in the sun
Mirror bright and clear.
Like quickened shadows in forest depths,
Like sparkling, golden wine.
Like silver lighting the ocean waves,
as the shy, attentive doe.
Like a primrose sensitive and fine
And the mountain spring so pure,
Just like a smile that shines through tears,
As if to hide and if to yearn
Like violin tones so soft and sweet:
    That is the Bergner strain.

To take more well-known examples, Garbo's and Dietrich's cross-dressing roles have legendarily fascinated lesbians.[32] Dietrich, in fact, consciously switched gender roles to appeal to various fantasies:

> You could say that my act is divided between the woman's part and the man's part. The woman's part is for men and the man's part is for women. It gives tremendous variety to the act and changes the tempo. I have to give them the Marlene they expect in the first part, but I prefer the white tie and tails myself. . . . There are just certain songs that a woman can't sing as a woman, so by dressing in tails I can sing songs written for men. (quoted in Spoto, 268–69)

Dietrich's phrasing "songs written for men" is ambiguous. Does she sing, dressed in a tux, the butch part to femmes (or to unstated same-sex desire in all her female viewers), or does "for men" mean she is singing to her loyal gay male following? Duplicity and excess of meaning are here erotically charged. Queer, too, is this scrambling of signs.

In a widely anthologized essay published before her work on lesbian cinema and entitled "Rethinking Women's Cinema: Aesthetics and Feminist Theory," Teresa de Lauretis argues that feminist film criticism cannot restrict itself to advocating positive, realistic images of women on the screen

53

nor to uncovering the ideological codes embedded in Hollywood's representation of women. What is missing from both approaches is how a female spectator would look at a film differently: in defining a feminine cinematic aesthetic it is necessary to analyze how a film addresses its spectator as a woman. De Lauretis's insight can profitably be applied to these Weimar cross-dressing films: given internal and external censorship, especially after the debacle of *Anders als die Andern*, it would be unrealistic to search for positive, overt images of gays on the Weimar screen; nor would this cinema lend itself to a critique of ideological biases against homosexuals. In addition, it would not suffice to identify either of the director, main actors, or screenwriter as gay, although such detail enhances the likelihood of intentionally queer moments in any given film. The fact that Friedrich Murnau, for example, was gay may be a starting point for viewing *Nosferatu* queerly but such an approach clearly has its limitations and has not been largely pursued, for instance, by Dyer or Hanson. In contrast, by drawing on former definitions of homosexuality, more open novelistic portrayals of same-sex relations, psychoanalytically related theories of spectatorship, as well as the occasional recorded expression of fandom, we can speculate on how these films could have spoken to the gay moviegoer.

Yet the question remains: is the homoeroticism in these cross-dressing films directed to gay audiences alone? In a more recent essay entitled "On the Subject on Fantasy," de Lauretis has warned against an indiscriminate application of LaPlanche and Pontalis's article "to buttress the optimistically silly notion of an unbounded mobility of identities for the spectator-subject; that is to say, the film's spectator would be able to assume and shift between an undefined 'multiplicity' of identificatory positions, would be able to pick and choose any or all of the subject-positions inscribed in the film regardless of gender or sexual difference, to say nothing of other kinds of difference" (75). Clearly, *Ich möchte kein Mann sein, Der Geiger von Florenz, Der Fürst von Pappenheim*, and *Viktor und Viktoria* cannot be seen as representative of all cinema; but it has been argued here that in enacting a cross-gendered fantasy, they provide a means of access for spectators to cross-gendered maneuvers. Moreover, rather than erase sexual and gender differences, through their sexual transgressiveness they heighten for the viewer awareness of these differences. In fact, elsewhere de Lauretis describes an identification by spectators that could well explain the appeal these cross-dressing films exert on any viewer frustrated with inflexible gender roles. She writes: "What I do identify with is [not the object but the setting of my desire,] the space of excess and contradiction that the role, the lack of fit, the disjuncture, the *difference* between characters and roles make apparent" ("Film and the Visible," 252).

Insofar as the audience of these films knows about this disjuncture—in other words, insofar as the audience is privy to the cross-dresser's true identity—that audience is addressed by the film. Yet, as discussed, the pleasure of these films resides not only in this ironic awareness but also in the suspension at will of this knowledge and the induction into the same-sex fantasy scenario. Despite de Lauretis's warnings, it can be argued that the proliferation of represented desires in these films triggers the workings of fantasy for all viewers. Fantasy yearns always and only for itself: we desire to desire, to fantasize, with the result that all amorous gazes are somehow voluptuous, regardless of who is looking at whom. As spectators, we erotically cathect with the longing, wide-eyed gaze, especially in this hyperbolic belladonna-addicted silent cinema. In a similar conclusion, Janet Bergstrom, through analyzing Murnau's feminized male characters, broaches the possibility of a contemplative visual pleasure that is erotic notwithstanding its passive sexual aim: "Assigning fictional characters fixed sexual identities that correspond to gender is often unhelpful in understanding the movement of desire in particular films. Perhaps there is another avenue available within a psychoanalytic framework which leads toward a non-reductive description of sexual orientation and pleasure, less dependent on gender-defined objects, or simply less object-oriented" (200). She proposes that the spectator could be "encouraged to relax rigid demarcations of gender identification and sexual orientation" (202). The present analysis of other homoerotic Weimar films suggests that the cultivation of this particular mode of looking is not exclusive to Murnau. The cross-dresser halts the gaze, encourages it to dwell on his/her fascinating apparition. This out-of-time suspension creates a space for a pleasurable erotics that Bergstrom points out is nonnarrative.

In this space even the straight viewer can indulge in the homoerotic cinematic fantasy, especially because the heterosexual outcome in these films can allow him or her to do so surreptitiously. Or, as Freud would note, he or she would do so unconsciously anyway. These films facilitate acceptance and neutralize anxieties about homosexuality by depicting it as nonthreatening and unnamed.[33] Moreover, this same-sex fantasy scenario conceivably works for a range of viewers because desirability is represented as emancipatory, irrespective of gender barriers; one is desired as either a woman or a man. In fact, these films suggest that it is the clothing or a particular look that we are attracted to and not the physical sex of its wearer.

Conducive as well to interpellation by spectators beyond the battle lines of gay versus straight is the attractive outlaw status of the lead character in his or her resistance to identity norms. If Ossi does not want to be a man, neither does she want to be a woman, thus rejecting any gender categoriza-

55

tion. With the possible exception of *Viktor und Viktoria*, where Susanne is under compulsion to act manly offstage and ridiculously feminine onstage, these films offer the prospect of escaping from gender and sexual prohibitions.[34] They relax, however temporarily, the dominant order of discourse and, as in the writings of Ulrichs and Hirschfeld, align the subject differently along the gender spectrum, going so far as to undo sexual orientation as a category. Transforming gender, these films intimate that the self can be improvised and processually constituted through self-stylization. They appeal to the transgressive desires to push against strait-jacketing roles. In sum, they offer a wardrobe of selves.

two

"Now I Have a Different Desire"

Transgender Specularity in Zarah Leander and R. W. Fassbinder

Zarah Leander

She died on June 23, 1981, the most beloved German chanteuse ever, the greatest screen idol of the Third Reich, the scintillating star of such melodramas as *Zu neuen Ufern* (*To New Shores*) (1937), *La Habanera* (1937), *Es war eine rauschende Ballnacht* (*An Intoxicating Night at the Ball*) (1939), and *Die große Liebe* (*The Great Love*) (1941/42): her name was Zarah Leander. In the Berlin newspaper *Die Tageszeitung* an anonymous contributor penned in a eulogy: "This evening, on the evening of your death in a Swedish hospital bed, the rain about which you sang in your songs will bring to tears guests at a thousand satin upholstered, dimly lit gay brothels" (July 3, 1981).[1] Reminiscing about the diva, Rosa von Praunheim wrote in *Der Spiegel*: "When in her films Zarah sang with tears in her eyes, vulnerable yet mastering her misfortune, and thundering out against it 'Kann denn Liebe Sünde sein?' [Can Love Be a Sin?] you just had to lie down and identify with her" ("Die Baßamsel," 159). And Paul Seiler, who has authored four books on Leander and starred in Christian Blackwood's film *Mein Leben für Zarah Leander* (*My Life for Zarah Leander*) (1984), similarly confessed: "She played . . . a woman struck down by fate, who has to face a crazy lot of adversities and humiliations, but conquers everything just the same. I identified with that, perhaps unconsciously" (*Zarah Leander: Ein Kultbuch*, 9).

How did it come about that the most famous actress of the Ufa studios, who sang on the radio concert requests for the troops and on whose long-suffering love wives back home were encouraged to model themselves,[2] was at the time and continues to be the most important gay icon Germany has ever known? What motivated her gay fans—in the reception exemplified by Seiler and von Praunheim—to so completely identify with her? Do the lines of such identification run differently for these gay admirers than for her female audience? Are there moments when they overlap? Wherein lies the pleasure of seeing oneself in someone else across gender lines? And what is so powerful in this mirroring that it also takes the form of multiple Zarah-impersonators who still entertain today on cabaret stages and in the transvestite revues that are popular—in another bizarre twist—among an older, heterosexual crowd in Germany?[3] An important feature of German cinematic history is this queer reception of Leander. This model or structure of transgender specularity—a cross-gender mirror identification with the screen image—also infuses the work of Rainer Werner Fassbinder, who counted among his favorites *Zu neuen Ufern* and *La Habanera*, the films Leander made with Detlef Sierck.

Although Zarah Leander probably needs little introduction to Germans, a thumbnail sketch of her career is appropriate for the non-German reader. She was born in 1907 in Karlstad, Sweden, and upon seeing *Peer Gynt* at the age of twelve she vowed to become an actress. In 1931 she caught the eye of the famous theater director Max Reinhardt, which led to her first mention in the German press. In what Paul Seiler dubs the most important year of her career, 1936, she traveled to Vienna to play something of a Garbo-parody in the musical *Axel an der Himmelstür* (*Axel at the Gate of Heaven*) by Max Hansen. As Vienna fell at her feet, Berlin also came calling, with the vice-president of the Reich's Film Board offering her the largest salary that an Ufa star was ever to receive, half of it, as she then negotiated, payable in Swedish crowns. Between 1937 and 1943 she starred in ten Ufa films. Eric Rentschler summarizes her success thus: "She was the Nazi film industry's biggest star, an enormous box-office attraction whose face appeared everywhere, whose records sold millions and were heard constantly in public and on the radio" (*Ministry of Illusion*, 136). In these films she invariably played the same generic role, a woman unjustly cast out of society, true to her loves, and prepared, even determined to suffer for them. With her fiery red hair, light Swedish accent, and lavish costuming, she exuded a touch of exoticism, a femme fatale at odds with the Nazi melodrama that tried to domesticate the woman. Most shocking, of course, was her voice: when Zarah Leander opened her mouth a rich, sultry, mellifluous, and extraordinarily deep voice escaped that left Marlene Dietrich sounding like a scratched record. With song lines like "Kann denn Liebe Sünde sein?", "Jede Nacht ein neues Glück" ("Every Night New Luck"), and "Mein Leben für die Liebe" ("My Life for Love") she garnered the adoration of a gay following even during the Third Reich. In her autobiography, *Es war so wunderbar! Mein Leben*, she writes: "Many people wondered about my friendships with homosexual men. I kept these friendships alive even during the war and was once called in by the Head of Ufa about this" (140). One of these friendships was with the text writer of her songs, Bruno Balz, who composed for her "Kann denn Liebe Sünde sein?" "Der Wind hat mir ein Lied erzählt" ("The Wind Has Told Me a Song"), "Davon geht die Welt nicht unter" ("The World Won't Go Under"), and "Jede Nacht ein neues Glück." Denounced for his homosexuality in 1941, Balz spent three weeks imprisoned by the Gestapo until it was made clear that he was needed for the next Leander film. Patterning the way for her subsequent gay reception, Bruno Balz let Leander be his own voice and ventriloquize his longings.

With her Ufa contract running out, and with no desire to renew it (her Grunewald villa had been firebombed in March 1943), Zarah Leander left Germany that spring to return to her family and home in Lönö, Sweden. Despite her involvement with the Nazi film industry (Paul Seiler repeatedly has maintained that she was naive and unpolitical), her fans welcomed her back to Germany as early as 1948. Already in 1947 she had given a concert tour in Switzerland, for she was by all accounts eager to stand before an audience once again. In addition, starting in 1950 with *Gabriela* until 1966 with *Das gewisse Etwas der Frauen* (*Something Special about Women*), Leander starred in seven films. Her singing career lasted even longer: although she kept announcing that her current tour would mark her swan song, Leander repeatedly appeared on stage until 1978.

By this time, even with the prodigious help of wigs, jewelry, and makeup, Leander could scarcely disguise that she was aging. Yet her by now primarily gay audiences could easily forgive her, especially since she herself began to look like a transvestite. Indeed, toward the end of her performing career she was frequently singing at transvestite balls (*Tuntenbälle*), such as the Ball der Freunde (The Friends' Ball) at the gay Club 70. Rosa von Praunheim campily yet affectionately writes: "Without gays she would have been nothing in old age, and when Zarah sang 'Oi joi joi anderrs rrum' [Oi yoi yoi, the otherr way arround] or called out, 'He junger Mann, ich brauch 'nen Ständer' [Hey young man, I need a stand], then the queens went wild, and a Berlin newspaper wrote spitefully: 'Her concerts are usually on Mondays, because that's the day the hairdressers have off'" ("Die Baßamsel" 158). Although Rosa von Praunheim plays up the bawdiness of such a scenario, it must not be forgotten that in the fifties and sixties, before the antisodomy laws of Paragraph 175 were lifted, Leander's concerts were one of the few places where gay men could meet openly. Yet the extent to which gay life was closeted during this period also cannot be underestimated; admiration for Leander was at that time hardly a public banner for gay pride, and it was only post–Paragraph 175 that her audience became more openly gay and less bourgeois. Among the countless newspaper reviews Paul Seiler reproduces in *Ein Mythos lebt:*

Figure 9.   Zarah Leander
(1960). Courtesy of the Paul-
Seiler Archiv.

Zarah Leander, for instance, only one page is devoted to discreet pieces on
Leander's gay following, and these were solely from 1970 on.

The scholarship on Zarah Leander falls into two basic categories. Focusing on her Ufa films, one set of researchers analyzes the function of the female star in the Third Reich, often concentrating on her films made with
Detlef Sierck.[4] Paul Seiler's impressive output represents the other side of
Leander research, biographical, hagiographic, and satisfyingly full of photos,
including many from her postwar public appearances and films. His work
arises from and in part addresses itself to a gay fandom, although it only incidentally mentions this gay reception as a sidelight to Leander's life. It also
distances itself from the phenomenon of the Zarah-impersonators. Seiler
harbors ambiguous feelings about the host of imitators, many of whom perform intentionally bad parodies. In addition, although admitting that the aging Zarah was an imitation of her former self, he rejects as insensitive the notion that she herself looked like a transvestite.

A study of the extensive gay reception of Zarah Leander needs to be undertaken in its own right. I can only begin to unravel it here by focusing on the issue of audience identification.[5] Specularity, another word for this screen identification, has particularly fascinated Leander scholars of the first type mentioned, but they have investigated it solely in terms of a female, heterosexual spectatorship. Eric Rentschler, for instance, argues that, insofar as women during the Third Reich imagined themselves in the various roles that Zarah Leander played, they were allowed "a source of vicarious pleasure, the pleasure of female audiences whose wish for a heightened existence will never be answered except in their dreams" (*Ministry of Illusion*, 145). This very deferral of desire literally occurs on-screen, Rentschler observes, at the conclusion of *La Habanera*: "Sierck's film leaves Astrée [Zarah Leander] caught between an unbearable foreign condition and a return to a world she once renounced as oppressive. She embodies an impossible desire, a desire that becomes possible only in terms of fantasy representations and never-ceasing postponement, a desire that exists only so that it can never be satisfied" (*Ministry of Illusion*, 145). Because these desires can find no fulfillment, they are contained: "Zarah Leander's performances fueled Nazi culture precisely because they appeared to offer alternative points of identification. Her disruptive outbursts and extreme longings served integrative functions. . . . Films like *La Habanera* demonstrated that excess, irony, and distantiation could reaffirm rather than destabilize the status quo" (*Ministry of Illusion*, 143). Antje Ascheid, too, suggests that part of the excitement that Leander generated was precisely her complex combination of alternating roles—diva, independent woman, martyr, lover, and mother—and that negotiating these discrepancies is pleasurable for the viewer. Lutz Koepnick similarly concludes: "The decisive question as to the cultural status of Leander's star image is therefore not whether her spectacular self-presentation within her films was able to empower female spectators . . . to autonomous identities and distinct modes of identification, but whether and to what extent German fascism succeeded in forging ideologically ambivalent strategies of empowerment back into the mould of their political projects" ("En-gendering Mass Culture," 173). These essays serve as a corrective to an earlier scholarship that, mindful of Sirk's ironic stylization of Hollywood melodrama in the 1950s, sees a similar resistance to Nazi ideology in his creation of the headstrong and eroticized roles played by Leander (even when she is the devoted mother or suffering lover).[6]

It is interesting to note how the terms of debate regarding specularity shift dramatically once the audience becomes a subcultural one. To begin, because the reception is after 1945, the issue of Nazi mass manipulation falls by the

61

wayside, although the function of illusion and audience projection remains, albeit now self-consciously recognized, cultivated, and even indulged in as illusion. Although writing on her reception during the Third Reich, Ascheid could have been characterizing the postwar gay reception: "Her generic persona was significantly dependent on audiences' fantasies of fame and the performance of glamour" (57). To rephrase Rentschler, it is precisely because of the closet of the 1950s and 1960s, where the gay "wish for a heightened existence will never be answered" that one identifies with Leander as the projection for these dreams. Seiler thus characterizes the fan: "The imaginary relationship protects [him] from the real deceptions of everyday life. . . . His stars channel unfulfilled dreams and longings" (*Zarah Diva*, 7). In phrasing that barely disguises the gay spectator, he then writes: Leander "offered protection for outsiders, who with her help could dream of a safe alternative world despite the threatening environment" (*Zarah Diva*, 8).

Also crucial for the second wave of the Leander reception is that the object of study (not just the audience) changes, for the aging chanteuse refashions the picture of the Ufa star. Both the younger and older Zarah resonate when Paul Seiler writes: "We [and it is understood who is meant by this plural] were addicted to Zarah, to her pathos-filled style, her larger-than-life emotional outbursts, her Valkyrie-appearances, her dark, almost masculine voice. For many she was both father and mother, she was also a surrogate drug for vicariously lived feelings" (*Zarah Leander: Ein Kultbuch*, 8). The sincerity of this fascination does not exclude a tinge of camp, as is evident when Zarah's own hyperbole is echoed in Seiler's prose. Zarah herself, as von Praunheim writes, "made fun of the kitsch of her earlier years" ("Die Baßamsel," 159). The possibility of an over-the-top appreciation of Leander (as also seen in the obituaries cited earlier) then reconnects, in terms of Sirk scholarship, the earlier and later stages in this director's career: Fassbinder's camp appreciation of the Hollywood Sirk in his article "Imitation of Life: On the Films of Douglas Sirk," for instance, although I cannot prove it, might have been inspired by the camp status Sierck's leading actress had garnered by the early 1970s, the time Fassbinder discovered the Hollywood melodramas.

Although cross-gender identification might strike many as bizarre (for it is indeed queer), there are diverse points of affinity with Leander that would appeal to a broad spectrum of gay viewers. Rentschler's assessment is correct in many ways: "If Leander's star image was dynamic, it was also flexible" (*Ministry of Illusion*, 139). Correspondingly, one cannot speak of a uniform gay reception of Leander, and by no means is it exclusively focused on her impersonators. Moreover, as photographs from Seiler's archive testify, she also had, though to a much lesser extent, a lesbian following.

Leander's particular transgender appeal resided, of course, in her voice. Described as baritone, even bass, it entered an unnatural, inadmissible range that could signal an erotic dissonance or queerness. Elizabeth Wood's characterization of what she calls the "Sapphonic Voice"—the voice that signifies lesbian difference and desire—can equally apply to Leander's: "Its flexible negotiation and integration of an exceptional range of registers crosses boundaries among different voice types and their representations to challenge polarities of both gender and sexuality as these are socially—and vocally—constructed" (28).[7] Testimonies regarding Leander's queer voice are numerous. The German filmmaker Helma Sanders-Brahms, for instance, in an essay entitled "Zarah," repeatedly refers to the actress's "hermaphroditic voice, half man, half woman" (57), which "seemed to have more body than her actual heavy body" (58). In his most recent book, subtitled *Ich bin eine Stimme* (*I Am a Voice*), Paul Seiler has collected colorful sources from 1931 to the present that extol the actress's voice, although he also perceptively notes that in the immediate postwar years rejection of her vocal gender ambiguity arose from the fearful need to stress one's own "normalcy" (135). Seiler gathers together references not only to the masculine timbre of her voice but also to its sexuality. He cites Günther Rühle, for instance, from the *FAZ*: "One encounters here the strangest erotic phenomenon: the grand beloved, he-she [Mannweib], and supermother [Übermutter]" (139). A reviewer, presumably male, from 1948 writes: "one easily succumbs to the strange charm of the masculine voice" (142). Another from 1949 speaks of "the somewhat perverted appeal of hearing a woman sing erotic songs in the baritone range" (143). In 1960 a Viennese newspaper mentioned her "vocal-cord sex" (148). And Renate Helker retrospectively writes in 1995: "The voice is the place where the desire of the body articulates itself" (155). This phantasmatic voice indeed recreates, by transgendering, the body that speaks it. It is then no wonder that Leander's own transgendered apparition would inspire other dreams and fantasies of transforming the body, particularly to have it imitate her model, only in reverse, now male-to-female. Indeed, the two Zarah-impersonators that I have heard perform live, Christina and Tim Fischer, are so remarkable because their haunting and haunted voices possess the phantasmatic capacity of evoking Zarah's presence: in this gender-bending reincarnation, a woman's masculine voice thrillingly issues from a man's body (in Christina's case, dressed as a woman).

63

What is left unstated in the above quotations, though, is how the listener identifies with the voice. Just as Bruno Balz could transfer his desires to the songs he wrote for Leander, so too could Leander ventriloquize for others. Listening to her voice in one's head, it became one's own. Especially with eyes closed one could easily imagine Leander as a man singing about same-sex love. The lyrics, too, were conducive to specular identification for gays: to attend a Leander concert was a liberating, energizing event, especially when she would belt out songs that affirmed and validated one's sexuality, such as "Kann denn Liebe Sünde sein?", "Einen wie Dich könnt' ich lieben" ("I Could Love Someone Like You"), or "Heut' abend lad' ich mir die Liebe ein" ("Tonight I'll Invite Love Over"). Seiler writes, again skirting explicit mention of sexual orientation but making it understood: "when she intoned in her songs against a hostile environment, then it also was an emancipatory outlet for her audience" (*Zarah Diva*, 8). Seiler's own evasive allusion to who constituted this audience patterns itself on the indirectness of Balz's lyrics—both call for a gay allegorical reading.

Leander's appearance also had masculine qualities despite the extremely feminized roles she played (she never assumed the trouser role, as did Dietrich and Garbo). As indicated, she was very large, broad-shouldered, and flat-chested. Detlef Sierck had recourse to various staging tricks—directing the male lead to stand on boxes, dressing Leander in decorative hats, sparkling jewelry, and advantageously cut gowns—in order to distract from her heavy figure (see Läufer, 55). In her autobiography, Leander herself admits that the cameraman "Franz Weihmayer often performed magic [zauberte], for in reality I was never as beautiful as in his film shots" (137). Thus even before her later career as a chanteuse, Leander was already in disguise in the 1930s, her body made to pretend that it was different from its reality. Yet despite her corporeal oddity, she was indisputably gorgeous: the diva queens could thus both empathize with the regret of inhabiting the wrong body yet also launch themselves into this dream of being courted by such men as Viktor Staal (*Zu neuen Ufern* and *Die große Liebe*).

The plots of her films (and I will concentrate on the Sierck dramas) could also resonate with her gay followers. In *Zu neuen Ufern* she plays a British variety singer, Gloria Vane, who protects her no-good lover, Sir Albert Finsbury (Willy Birgel), from calumny by pleading guilty to the forgery he committed, for which she is sent to prison in the Australian colonies. Although his company is stationed nearby, Major Finsbury refuses to compromise his ascendant career by helping Gloria and betrays her devotion by planning to marry the daughter of Sydney's colonial governor. The female prisoners, meanwhile, can only shorten their sentence by marrying one of the settlers. Thus Gloria is humiliated not merely by hard labor but by standing in a lineup of women paraded before their would-be husbands. Even after Henry, a handsome, strapping landowner (Viktor Staal), chooses her, she runs away to find the sleazy Major, to whom she is still true. Only when Finsbury removes himself from the picture (by committing suicide, portrayed as a cowardly act), does she reluctantly agree to wed Henry. In *La Habanera*, too, she makes the wrong match and ends up the Swedish wife to the cruel, jealous Puerto Rican Don Pedro (Ferdinand Marian). She longs for the snows of her homeland and can only leave her virtual prison on the island once her husband dies of a fever, freeing her to travel back to Sweden with the chivalrous and attractive Dr. Nagel (Karl Martell).

In both films the affiliations she enters into are the wrong ones; the conventional marriage partner is not the one she would naturally choose, so that her desires are perpetually directed elsewhere.[8] In this sense, her roles and desires can be said to be queer ones, bucking the social norm. In addition to emulating her courage in the face of such adversity, her gay public, as Seiler and von Praunheim intimate, also could empathize with this representation of ostracism, loneliness, and melancholy. Leander could suffer for one and prepare the way. Stylized, her distress seemed beautiful and transcendent and allowed for an identification that a realistic mode never would have permitted. Moreover, her refusal to unburden her heart and her determination to remain stoically silent mirror the tremulous life of the closet. In *Gabriele* this silence estranges her from her daughter, in *Damals* (*At That Time*) (1942) it lands her in jail, and in *Ave Maria* (1953) it leads to self-imposed exile. In all three cases, the closeted Leander assumes a new name and identity to escape detection.

Because her sorrows and hardships need to be hidden from society, the Zarah Leander character can only express herself obliquely or allegorically, that is, through the body. Her darkly hued voice, where, as Helker writes, the body articulates itself, thus sings in a whisper, falters, haltingly tries to breathe, as she struggles to stage this prohibition. Like the songs, the close-ups on Leander's face suspend the narrative flow. Her eyes, too, bespeak her sadness. Even her luxurious dress in *La Habanera* as well as her bodily weight seem to want to protect her and hide the vulnerability of her unloved body. When recourse to action is denied the suffering woman, it is her body that becomes melodramatically expressive. If Leander's characters are not permitted to verbalize their grief to others, at least they can express it somatically and thereby preserve depths of feeling and fend off depression. This histrionic display through costume, voice, downcast features, and gesture then compensates for the deprivation and loss. In addition, by so venting rather than closeting her overwrought feelings, Leander ventriloquizes for her similarly mute fans. The viewer longs to identify with this freighted pure display, to be transported by Leander's own melodramatic overstatement. Here allegory, the melodramatic genre, and fan psychology all operate according to a logic of semiotic substitution.[9] The fascination with Leander's visage comes from this inability to read its allegorical enigma: in closeups or in star photos the fan can gaze at her face forever, precisely because the expression speaks otherwise and remains unfathomable. In the static tableau that mesmerizes the gaze her sorrow is unreadable because it is itself made the spectacle.

Such displacement and masking link Leander to the structure of transvestism. Marjorie Garber writes: "Psychoanalytically, transvestism is a mechanism that functions *by displacement* and *through fantasy* to enact a scenario of desire" (366). One can thus see Leander's somatic expression as a kind of dressing differently, an indirect discursive code that requires special reading, even a cult interpretation, which of course her gay fans gave her. At the same time she generates a structure of displacement and substitution that eventually leads to her own appearance and voice being copied by her transvestite impersonators.[10]

Yet this is not to say that Leander functions as the origin of simulations. She operates so successfully as a figure on whom to project fantasy (facilitating thereby imitation across gender lines) because she has always signified a substitute onto whom desires could be transferred. From the start of her career to its close, Leander stood in for another. To begin, she was invited to Ufa to become Germany's Garbo and Dietrich. Koepnick extrapolates: "Leander's star persona was characterized, and jeopardized, by ostensible signatures of simulation: whereas film stars commonly derive their charisma from a peculiar jargon of individual authenticity, from presumed continuities between on- and off-screen persona, Leander entered the German film industry as a substitute, a mere copy measured against what she was supposed to replace. Hence the extravagant press campaign that accompanied her move to Nazi Germany: an attempt to naturalize her stardom, don her in an aura of exceptionality, and make audiences forget about the fact that her stardom designated nothing other than the presence of an absence" ("En-gendering Mass Culture," 164). This process of simulation then continued into her later career, though now she imitated herself. Seiler writes: "At the end Zarah seemed to me to be a disguise [Verkleidung] of herself" (*Ein Kultbuch*, 15). Rosa von Praunheim unabashedly writes: "Zarah made an ass out of Zarah, made fun of the kitsch of her earlier years" ("Die Baßamsel," 159). She gave the impression of a transvestite, he says, with her strong body, large hands and feet, and flat chest, which is to say she imitated her imitators. Likewise Sanders-Brahms points out that "gays loved Zarah, because she already almost wasn't a woman, and she was close to the queens through the exertion it took still to be [feminine]" (60). Zarah ironically topped all these comments by asserting that she could impersonate herself better than any other impersonator.

But even when one turns to the Zarah of the Nazi cinema one notes how she parades or imitates femininity, presenting it as a masquerade. In writing about *Die große Liebe* (directed by Rolf Hansen), where Leander plays a singer, Hanna Holberg, Irene Dölling observes that onstage Hanna is the representative image of the desired, eroticized woman:

> In stage costume that presents her body as desirable, with blond wig and heavy makeup, she is at first a "moving image," a mask (and not "herself"). She is the embodiment [Zurschaustellung] of "femininity" as masquerade, which is made clear in the subsequent dressing room scene, when in removing her makeup and changing her clothes her "true" face and her "actual" character appear. With this difference between image and person it is then possible to see the reconstruction of her "femininity" in the rest of the story. (19)

In a very similar scenario at the start of *Zu neuen Ufern*, Gloria Vane also performs on stage: Koepnick writes that

> Sirk's diegesis is at pains to provide the viewer with a clear sense for the artificiality and constructedness of the singer's frivolous stage persona. The camera follows and reframes her movements on stage from ever-changing points of view and focal lengths. Frequent cuts and abrupt shifts between the myriad of perspectives draw the film viewer's attention to the fact that what we see is not the recording of an artistic expression, but a truly violent process of dismemberment— male desire mapped onto and exploiting the surface of Vane's body.

By contrast, in a parallel scene later in the film, "Gloria now rebuffs any attempt to transform her body and stage presence into a pleasurable commodity" ("Sirk and the Culture Industry," 101–2) and is booed off the stage for not complying with her male audience's demand for light entertainment, instead singing the sad song, "Ich steh' im Regen."

Since the pathos of the offstage character is equally a Sierckean construction, what occurs here is the *simulation* of the revelation of a "true" self. What matters then is the *representation* or *performance* of the closet with its contradictory dynamics of preservation and role-playing. Dölling and Koepnick suggest that Hanna and Gloria act out or stage the dis-identification with their role as spectacle: they expose identification with the theatrical persona as a dis-possession. One sees this distantiation again in *Damals*, *Gabriela*, and *Ave Maria*, where the heroine—to her own detriment—assumes a false name in order to protect her daughter. These characters signify the desire for a natural sign—to finally be what and where one appears to be. Insofar as the

67

postwar West German society did not provide in its heterosexual matrix equality and respect for homosexuals, such a desire understandably found strong resonance among Leander's gay fans. Their identification with her thus contains or repeats her characters' move of dis-possession—a complex and paradoxical doubling back of the moment of withdrawal in the act of identification with the role. The cross-gender specularity additionally rein-scribes and underscores the gap between nature and role, self and other, for it too betokens the desire to be where one cannot. Camp, in fact, arises from the representation of this separation. Identification with Zarah thus means that one indulges in occupying a panoply of incongruent positionalities. In other words, transgender specularity is conceivably so enticing a process be-cause it entails imaginatively balancing several contradictory moments in the phantasmatic grafting of another's image onto one's own self-perception and self-presentation. The rich overlapping, the multifaceted fantasy, is in itself pleasurable, a matter for elation.

This palimpsest-like mapping becomes even more intricate in the imagi-nary world of spectacle to which the aging Leander devotes herself. Here she more forthrightly takes the female as spectacle and plays with it, her own self-construction displaying an element of gay pride. In other words, she takes the body that society generally wants to closet—here the older woman—and puts it on display as visually captivating and even more vampish than on the stage of *Zu neuen Ufern*. She deliberately draws attention to her weight and glittery apparel, which become the fetish through which the loss (of her youthful looks) is perceived and yet also restored. Not only is her voice gender-ambiguous but her status as a former movie queen whose past image res-onates in the present image parallels the bifocal vision of the transvestitic spectacle, whose visual allure resides in such hovering between alternatives. Most importantly, Leander now organizes the stage event and places herself before an unorthodox gaze, a subversively different yet still admiring male gaze, one that instead of objectifying her undertakes the gender-transgressive act of identifying with her. She subverts the gaze, moreover, through the overwhelming, disarming power of her voice, which became even deeper with age. Such a powerful realignment of the spectacle, of course, is what Le-ander's fans came to venerate in her.

In writing, as scholars apart from Seiler do, on Leander's pre-1945 screen persona, Knut Hickethier notes: "The impression of the artificial, of broken pathos, the ambivalence between devotion and distance distinguish Leander's performance from the near-banal theatricality [Schauspielerei] of many [of her] contemporaries. One would also want to call this posture 'postmodern,' were it more pronounced" (cited in Lenssen, 2). I would like to suggest in conclusion that this "impression of the artificial," that distance from her role that Dölling and Koepnick also note, actually disappears in Leander's later incarnations. In her career as diseuse before gay audiences what occurs is precisely the opposite. It is now truly postmodern: the distinction between artificial performance and authentic expression collapses and becomes immaterial, for it is the theatrical and unabashedly synthetic Zarah who asserts her legitimacy. She proudly sang, "So bin ich und so bleibe ich" ("So I am and so I'll stay"), in a pre-1990s version of "We're here, we're queer." The starlet who could not give up her stage career until she was forced to by ill health at the ripe age of 71, three years before her death, thrived on performance and refused to hide her enjoyment of interacting with her fans. As Johannes von Moltke writes about the nature of the diva phenomenon, what counts is the "staging of the whole person," "the sublation of the riddle of the private in the extrovertedness of the diva" ("Die Diva," 220). Her gay admirers cheered her on in her defiance of the closet, where critics of her garish extrovertedness wanted to push her. As Paul Seiler writes: "The audience received especially well the impression that she lacked perfection; it loved the loose tone of her interviews, in which she liked to ironize herself and tried to destroy the myth of the unapproachable screen goddess of her youth" (*Ein Kultbuch*, 109). The distance between screen idol and public further collapses in the phenomenon of Leander simulations (especially if the impersonation is seen as reciprocal). Spectacle thus equally occurs in the arena of the audience. In these various ways, then, Zarah Leander succeeded in reintegrating spectacle with the space of her audience, who was as true to her as she was to it. Hers is an excellent example of where the site of reception becomes the site of production. Indeed, in the second half of this chapter I want to examine the cinematic production of Rainer Werner Fassbinder for its intricate reception of Leander—how he treats the issue that she raises of transgender specularity.

Rainer Werner Fassbinder

It is curious that although Fassbinder's biographer/friend/actor Harry Baer lists *Zu neuen Ufern* and *La Habanera* among the director's favorite films (195), Fassbinder himself only discusses the Hollywood Sirk in his essay, "Imitation of Life: On the Films of Douglas Sirk" (1971), and barely mentions Sirk's previous career in Nazi Germany. The omission is even more glaring given that one of the characters in his play *Der Müll, die Stadt und der Tod* (*The City, Garbage and Death*) (1975), the unrepentant ex-Nazi Müller, is a Zarah Leander impersonator, as if to signify therewith Müller's continued fascination with National Socialism. Why would Fassbinder link a post-1945 reincarnation of Leander with the Third Reich while eliding the same link with regard to the post-1945 director?[11] Although it would be fascinating to speculate why Fassbinder did not include discussion of Sierck's Ufa films, or to examine if via *Lili Marleen*, which deals with the Nazi production and commodification of spectacle, Fassbinder answers the question of melodrama's investment and hence Sierck's involvement in the Third Reich, these are not problems the rest of this chapter will address. They lead down paths different from the issue of queer gender performance that Leander introduces and that I want to pursue in Fassbinder. Instead I want to propose that just as Detlef Sierck haunts as an absent figure the Douglas Sirk essay, in a number of films Fassbinder made in the late 1970s and early 1980s Zarah Leander is the unstated model—a ghost—behind the main characters. Just as *Angst essen Seele auf (Ali—Fear Eats the Soul)* (1974) is a remake of *All that Heaven Allows* (1956), so too Zarah Leander reappears in various guises in *In einem Jahr mit dreizehn Monden (In a Year of 13 Moons)* (1978), *Lili Marleen* (1980), *Die Sehnsucht der Veronika Voss (Veronika Voss)* (1982) and *Querelle* (1982). When characters in these films echo Zarah Leander they also raise the issues that circulate around her figure—female mimicry, homosexuality, and camp. Their very mirroring of Leander, moreover, underscores how identity is constituted through specularity. Zarah Leander is thus key to articulating how femininity is masqueraded in Fassbinder and whether, in terms of camp, it matters if this performance is undertaken by women or men. She thereby opens the door to the intersexed fantasies in Fassbinder and the longings that such gender transgression signifies.

Just as the investigation of specularity in Leander begins with the simulation and hence commodification of femininity—both in her own screen roles and among her female audience—so too echoes of Leander are to be recognized foremost in Fassbinder's female characters. It is here that one can begin to track her spectral appearances. Two of his films tell the story of Nazi stars, but as if splitting Zarah Leander into two characters—one a popular diva (*Lili Marleen*) and the other an actress (*Veronika Voss*). The two periods in Leander's career likewise underscore this split: *Lili Marleen* takes place during the Third Reich, while *Veronika Voss* tells the fate of a now aging Nazi screen idol in the early 1950s. To be sure, the real-life models for both leading roles are not Leander directly. Sybille Schmitz, a favorite actress of Goebbels who later was blacklisted by him, committed suicide in 1955: she provided the model for Veronika Voss.[12] *Lili Marleen* is based on the life of the singer Lale Anderson, whose love song by that title was famous throughout war-torn Europe. As Thomas Elsaesser summarizes, her "song, originally called 'Der Wachposten' written by Hans Leip, with music by Norbert Schulze, [was] the hit of 1943, when it was played every night by Radio Belgrade, the Germany Army broadcast station in occupied Serbia. Adopted also by other Wehrmacht radio stations, and even heard on Allied and Russian radio, it became a kind of signature tune for the men in the trenches all over Europe. The song was briefly banned by propaganda minister Goebbels for being defeatist, but this ban was lifted again in the face of massive protests" (150).[13] This borrowing from the lives of Andersen and Schmitz, however, in no way excludes the possibility of Leander likewise resonating in these films and thereby underscoring, as Fassbinder sees it, the commodifiable interchangeability of the Nazi image of the star. To see Veronika Voss and Willie (the woman who sings the song "Lili Marleen") not only as copies of Schmitz and Andersen respectively but also of Leander is to emphasize their common function as representations or simulations of femininity. In other words, it is not so much that Zarah Leander is referenced directly in *Veronika Voss* and *Lili Marleen* (one can see the latter also as a remake of other Nazi melodramas, such as *Wunschkonzert* [*Request Concert*] and *Schlußakkord* [*Final Chord*] but that Leander has helped create the constellation of images associated with the Nazi diva that Fassbinder not only draws upon but also deconstructs as cliché.[14]

Let me begin with the performance of femininity in *Lili Marleen*. In an interview about his plans for the film, Fassbinder comments: "In its self-portrayal the Third Reich did have a lot to do with spectacle . . . its impact has a great deal to do with the aesthetics of staging" (*Anarchy*, 66). *Lili Marleen* demonstrates in particular how the woman as image is coopted for the fascist spectacle. Not only is Willie's voice commodified as a technologically reproducible object for consumption over the airwaves but her body, too, is placed on stage to entertain a mass audience. Hanna Schygulla plays the part with her signature lethargy and passivity, evidenced particularly when Willie is dragged back to the spotlight after having tried to commit suicide, her face bloated and pale, and her movements zombielike. She is revived so that the Germans can refute the claims of the international press linking her disappearance to the existence of concentration camps. Having lost her will to live, she is now merely a vehicle for the Nazis to manipulate. Elsaesser writes on this scenario: "The facts of her attempted suicide and of the concentration camps, different realities and incommensurate in themselves, are subsumed under her star image as pure sign, available for manipulation and transfer from one discourse (show biz performance) to another (genocide and politics)" (159).

Even more than the pawn of the Nazi propaganda machine, she is the victim of the momentum her own song gathers, as it is appropriated by a reception that not even the government can control. As the song becomes too popular, its excessive repetition becomes lame, and stultifies. Even the film spectator senses this exhaustion, hearing the song over and over (Willie performs it seven times in the course of the film). Its refrain "wie einst" ("as before") underscores its repetition. The crippling quality of this empty iteration is literalized when one sees soldiers awaiting its soothing broadcast night after night in the trenches, just as they also await their deaths. Fassbinder cuts back and forth from shots of bombs exploding and limbs flying to the crescendo of applause for the singer. The song thereby suggests a fatal distraction from reality as well as a secretly desired, orgiastic death, both elements that testify to what Bathrick calls "the horror of the culture industry in the service of mass destruction" (50).[15] Even more distracting were, of course, Zarah Leander's songs, whose titles such as "Davon geht die Welt nicht unter" ("It's Not the End of the World") and "Ich weiß, es wird einmal ein Wunder geschehen" ("I Know that Someday a Miracle Will Occur") seem retrospectively sinister in their deceptive optimism. Insofar as these songs too form the undercurrent to *Lili Marleen*, they contribute to what Bathrick terms "the film's hidden and not so hidden referentiality" and its "systems of inscription" (39).

Fassbinder further metacritically comments on the technological reproduction of the female voice in a scene where Willie's love, Robert Mendelsson (Giancarlo Giannini), is incarcerated and a nonstop recording of "Lili Marleen" is piped into his cell. Like a record constantly skipping, the same snippet is looped ad nauseam. The truncated song reminds Robert of Willie's absence but it also signifies that as a commodifiable product, her voice is already disincarnated when sent over the airwaves. It awakens the desire to put a face to the voice, which means that the song functions as an empty signifier onto which fantasies and desires can be projected. By dragging the half-dead Willie onto the concert stage, the Nazi machinery can be seen at work, creating the illusion of an actual woman at the source of the song, yet using her as a puppet through whom desires can be channeled. One of these fictions is that Willie is Lili Marleen, for so she autographs her photos, thereby erasing any identity separate from the star image. The song itself demonstrates how easily these identities slip, disconnecting the singer from what she sings about: the lyrics belong to a first-person male voice who addresses an absent woman, speaking of how he will wait under the lantern, as Lili Marleen once did. Through this distancing, Lili Marleen becomes an absence signifying a longing, who is not even the subjectivity who expresses this longing. By virtue of this disembodiment, soldiers can identify with the first-person male in his melancholic waiting, yet they can also fantasize about both the woman singing the song and the mysterious Lili Marleen. The song was conceivably so popular because the channels of fantasy it prompts are so nomadic and unspecifiable.

In *Veronika Voss* Fassbinder also comments on the vacant position signified by the Nazi star image. The film moreover demonstrates how ingrained and addictive the performance of femininity can become. Veronika Voss (Rosel Zech) is a character who feels she has to keep up a facade of urbane elegance in order to meet the expectations she imagines others having of her. She wants to be recognized as the familiar image she once was from the Ufa screen and dresses and coifs herself so as to garner that recognition. If others forget, she reminds them of her former glamour so that she can picture to herself the woman they see, thereby bolstering her self-image. Veronika thus creates mirrors around her that shield her from the truth—that she is actually a drug addict. In other words, she is an example of the continuum between Nazi and postwar Germany that Fassbinder depicts elsewhere, most clearly in *Die Ehe der Maria Braun* (*The Marriage of Maria Braun*) (1979): Veronika Voss tries to make a comeback in movies by appealing to her earlier star status, for she wants to be seen still in the 1950s as living on the Ufa screen. Those that appreciatively recognize her, like the proprietor of the jewelry shop, are also nostalgic for the Nazi regime, signaling that the draw of this recent past occurs via its image repertoire.

In another scene Veronika Voss likewise illustrates her masquerading of femininity: in a flashback to her married life in the 1940s, her husband (Armin Mueller-Stahl) asks why they cannot be just who they are. By replying that "when an actress plays a woman who wants to please a man, she tries to be all the women in the world," Veronika reveals how she performs the woman she expects or imagines the other desiring and how this image is that of a generic femininity. His response—"I drink to tune out, and you drink to build yourself up, to make yourself big, beautiful, seductive, unique"—reveals how her specularity is another, related addiction. It is interesting that her suicide occurs when she is locked away from others, when there is no more gaze to confirm her existence—when her narcissistic self-viewing loses its prop.

Especially when she sings a husky farewell torch song to her friends, Veronika Voss's Leander/Dietrich imitation borders on camp, which always highlights that modicum of difference between screen idol and its imitations, a difference Veronika tries to bridge but cannot. She thereby lacks the clear self-awareness of the impossibility of mimicry that accompanies camp. The parallel, however, raises questions: If Willie and Veronika Voss imitate fem-

73

ininity, what is to distinguish them from the male-to-female transvestite who likewise does so, especially if their model for femininity is Zarah Leander, who herself has been seen through the transvestite lens? If Fassbinder's hero-ines Maria Braun, Willie, Lola, and Veronika all display an element of taw-driness—in other words, if he underscores their less-than-perfect glamour—to what extent are they similarly transvestitic?

Johannes von Moltke sees the theatricality of feminine role-playing (espe-cially with Hanna Schygulla) in Fassbinder's films as camp: "In the case of Schygulla, this embodiment is marked, like the parodies of the drag per-former, by excess: she is not simply a woman of the fifties, but one who is con-stantly playing at playing a woman of the fifties [in *The Marriage of Maria Braun*]" ("Camping in the Art Closet," 98–99). I would qualify, however, that these female characters, although they manipulatively wield their femininity, do not treat it as camp, as the aging Leander does, for camp is not only the ex-cessive imitation of femininity but the awareness of the *failure* of the imitation: this difference—the queer reinscription of masculinity—is then what consti-tutes camp. Hence only insofar as Veronika Voss or Maria Braun can be seen as nonfeminine in their imitation of femininity—that is, only insofar as they can be read as transvestitic—are they also camp.[16] Rosa von Praunheim's alle-gorization of Fassbinder's female characters follows this tack: "His women fig-ures were, like with Tennessee Williams, always a part of his transvestitic soul" ("Schwul, pervers, kontrovers"). Campy, too, was Fassbinder's rechristening of the males in his entourage: he himself was "Mary," Kurt Raab was "Emma," Dietor Schidor was "Kitty," and Peter Kern was "Paula." This gender rever-sibility leads us to ask in which of Fassbinder's films does the male-to-female imitation or a gender-bending male femininity come most prominently to the fore? In other words, how can the paradigm of gender masquerade and in-congruity that Leander introduces be nuanced to cover a spectrum from one Fassbinder work to the next? And are echoes of Leander present in these works, keys to interpreting their gender transitivity?

It is almost commonplace to read the lesbian characters in *Die bitteren Tränen der Petra von Kant* (*The Bitter Tears of Petra von Kant*) (1972) as drag-ging as gay men. Kurt Raab, for instance, writes in his biography of Fass-binder: "This play could have just as well been performed by six men, it was actually a man's piece, it was a play about a part of his life, his history with Günther Kaufmann" (162). In addition to *Faustrecht der Freiheit* (*Fox and His Friends*) (1975), the only film with an almost entirely gay cast of characters is Fassbinder's last, *Querelle* (1982). Fassbinder counted Jean Genet's novel, on which the film is based, among his favorites and had always wanted to film it (as did Werner Schroeter). *Querelle* incants an ode to gay sex and the phallus;

even in the stage design by Rolf Zehetbauer the rampart turrets resemble erect cocks. In one of the few appreciative reviews of the film, Ed Sikov observes in words that still hold true today: "Rarely, if ever, has an openly gay director of Fassbinder's stature had the opportunity to film the work of a major gay author whose works deal with gay people" (40). However, if Fassbinder's female divas are not far from gender travesty in their exaggerated performance of femininity and the characters of *Die bitteren Tränen der Petra von Kant* can be imagined as gay men, is it possible that in *Querelle* too Fassbinder hints at this structure of male-female reversibility? It would be interesting to ask whether and how Fassbinder violates the macho world of prisons, bars, ship decks, and workers' barracks by implanting on the male body indices of femininity, thereby resignifying masculinity and deconstructing the gender divide via homosexuality, though without recourse to stereotypical notions of the homosexual as pansy or fairy.

Querelle lends itself particularly to this allegorical reading of gender signifying otherwise or queerly when one considers that Fassbinder himself was at pains to point out the oblique representation at work in Genet's novel, which he tried to match with his "surrealist landscape" (*Anarchy of the Imagination*, 169). In the "Preliminary Remarks" on the film, Fassbinder wrote that "as far as discrepancy between objective plot and subjective fantasy is concerned, Jean Genet's *Querelle de Brest* may be the most radical novel in world literature." Genet's world operates according to "singular laws" and obeys "an astonishing mythology." Putting this universe on film meant for Fassbinder that "every gesture means something else; in each case it is something essentially more, something greater, generally something sacred" (*Anarchy of the Imagination*, 169). As we shall see, gender and sexuality indeed operate according to their "singular laws" in this film, radically breaking with conventional mores to structure a new "mythology."

Only one major character in *Querelle* is a woman, Lysiane (Jeanne Moreau); however, announcing the trans-sexed momentum in the film, at one point she too is encoded as gay male. Mario, the police officer (Burkhard Driest), says about the sex between Robert and Lysiane: "But when they make love, it's like with gays" (140).[17] Robert (Hanno Pöschl) is brother to Querelle (Brad Davis), and their love for each other represents the strongest homosexual bond in the film, though it is unconsummated. Lysiane, because she goes to bed with both of them, functions as the substitute or go-between for their homosexuality. In other words, because the threat of incest prohibits a sexual love between the brothers, it can only find expression via the intermediary Lysiane. This triangle would classically exemplify what Eve Sedgwick outlines in *Between Men*[18]—the traffic in women in order to deflect away from homosexuality—were it not that in *Querelle* homosexuality is hardly repressed. It is indeed so pervasive that Lysiane, too, signifies as gay, paradoxically *because* she substitutes for gay relations. Through her Fassbinder thus queers in an extremely provocative way the only heterosexual relations in the film. Lysiane, of course, embodies another Zarah Leander figure in Fassbinder's repertoire, though now Leander as the worn, aging diva. As a chanteuse at her husband's bar (singing "Each man kills the thing he loves"), Lysiane performs in a deep voice that encodes her as a male-to-female transvestite. Paradoxically, it is the exaggeration of femininity, here also signified by the black boa and black sequined dress, that make Lysiane, like Zarah Leander, look like a drag queen. Reflecting on her role in *Querelle*, Jeanne Moreau tellingly reveals: "I am quite familiar with the phenomenon of a dual personality. I am conscious of my own masculine traits and I also recognize feminine traits in men" (99).

As Moreau intimates, Lysiane is only one example in *Querelle* of transgendering, one-half of the chiastic switching of sexual roles. This symmetry distinguishes the film's highly structural arrangement. Through theatrical stage settings, garish yellow lighting, allegorical allusions to the passion of Christ, and the poetic interweaving of narration and intertitles, Fassbinder creates a mood of artificiality. *Querelle*'s "obliteration of verisimilitude" (Sikov, 41) also arises from its formal alignment of characters who often mirror each other, as seen most clearly in that one actor plays the roles of Robert and Gil. Because of this matching, Gil Turko acts in Querelle's eyes as a sexual stand-in for Robert (as does Lysiane). Even Nono (Günther Kaufmann), the black gay bartender married to Lysiane who anally penetrates Querelle, can in the twisted doublings of the film be seen as a replacement for Robert, the one Querelle really loves but cannot approach because he is both brother and, ostensibly, heterosexual. Thus Lysiane accuses Querelle in a statement that is otherwise incomprehensible: "If you really slept with Nono, you did it only because you love your brother immortally" (170). Underscoring these doublings is the text flashed onto the screen: "For the first time Querelle kissed a man on the mouth. It seemed as if his face hit against a mirror, that threw back his own image" (43). Given this insular gay world of doppelgänger and same-sex partners, what then appears intriguing are the cracks in the mirror that insert gender discrepancies and thus multiply the perverse angles to the sexual configurations Fassbinder explores via Genet. Or to deploy the metaphor of the mirror differently: just as the mirror presents the image backwards, so too does the male visage reflect its opposite, femininity.

In her capacity as reader of tarot cards, Lysiane is an interpreter of the other characters. One can turn to her as a kind of clairvoyant outsider to find

Figure 10. *Querelle* (1982), Jeanne Moreau. Courtesy of the Fotoarchiv, Stiftung Deutsche Kinemathek, Berlin.

how to allegorize the male homosexuality Fassbinder depicts. She presents the love between the brothers as a kind of specularity; she says to Robert, "your statue-double [Doppelstatue] mirrors itself in both its halves . . . you live in your brother, in his eyes" (138). In this symbiosis there is no place for a third term for the woman: "the two of you regard only yourselves! I don't even exist. . . . There is no place for me between you two" (138–39). The reason Lysiane can be excluded from this economy of the same is because, in their very mirroring of each other, the men begin to perceive in each other a femininity, a sort of distortion or trick of the mirror that points to an element of bisexual desire in homosexuality, which indeed lends it its impetus. Lysiane says to Querelle: "You two love each other. You love each other, with your beauty" (140). Likewise, the narrative voice-over intones about the brothers: "Surrounding them—and only for them—there existed a world from which the image of the woman is banned. The absence of the woman forces the two men to draw femininity somewhat out of themselves. They discovered the woman" (117). In other words, the excluded term of femininity deconstructively turns out to determine the economy of male homosexuality, which is not as enclosed upon itself as first appears.

Several other examples illustrate this transgendered gay fantasy, which oc-

77

curs primarily at moments when the gaze becomes reflective and languorous. To be sure, homophobia (and misogyny) surface in the film linked to a derogatory feminization of gay men: Theo taunts Gil by calling him "a little girl" and his pal Roger his "girlfriend" (77). Homophobic and closeting, too, is Gil's pretense that he is hot for Roger's look-alike sister while being attracted to Roger's own delicate features. Yet he soon drops the pose to openly exclaim, "You are really as pretty as a girl" (134). In *Querelle* femininity is discerned in the entire range of male characters, from the comely Roger to the macho stud Nono and leather daddy Mario, thus turning Theo's homophobic catcalls inside-out and affirming an almost sublime male femininity. In their knife fight, for instance, the brothers call each other "arousingly beautiful" (109); Querelle finds Mario, too, beautiful (71); while Lysiane comments about Nono that "sometimes he exudes a kind of femininity, by some delicate movement or another" (101). Lieutenant Seblon (Franco Nero), the most introverted and self-reflective of the gay characters, notices that his passion for Querelle makes "the woman in [him] all the more sensitive, tender, definite and therefore sadder" (111). In eroticizing his own body, he imagines it compositely, having breasts: "My hands formed two female breasts over my chest, as if they were propped up there" (130). Finally, Querelle, whose very name suggests a queer "elle," is cast with the pretty face of Brad Davis, who plays his part subdued and always soft-spoken, the opposite of what one would expect from a murderous outlaw. Sikov writes: "A passive sexual object, the antithesis of masculinity under patriarchy, Querelle is also the object of visual examination: by Seblon, by the brothel's madam, Lysianne [sic], by Querelle's brother, Robert, by another murderer, Gil Turko, and, ultimately, by the audience" (41).

This feminization across the characters is thus linked to their being made a spectacle. In part it also is tied to a passive anal eroticism and sexual submission, but not exclusively, as evidenced by Querelle's switchability and the fact that the "tops" Mario and Nono are also feminized.[19] Even the double-sexed Seblon, who Querelle derogatorily calls a *Tunte* ("queen"), maintains his authority as officer over the sailors and conquers ("besiegt," 167) Querelle in the end. The feminization is not encoded as an emasculation or mark of inequality; rather, it instates a kind of parity between men, a willingness to give and receive love.[20] Hence Lysiane refers to "male passivity" as the "desire to give and to receive" (113). In other words, although still moving within a binary gender structure, Fassbinder uses it to unlock the male/female, active/passive essentialist grid and simultaneously to deconstruct the exhibitionist macho gay world of sweaty, muscular bodies, fracturing it into various, ever-shifting prisms of desire that are open to bisexual inflections.[21]

One could argue that the radicality and lawlessness of *Querelle* lies not so much in its bringing of anal sex to the art film or in its glorification of sexually motivated violence, but in this unconventional gender subversion that homosexuality invites. This anomaly and transgressiveness are additionally indexed via unnatural sets and lighting and formulaic doppelgänger-constellations, as if only in such an antimimetic, allegorical mode could Fassbinder unleash such queer fantasies. Indeed, the artificial setting and acting seem to betoken a fantasy scenario and, true to this, the film's eroticism lies not only in the visual display of stripped torsos but also in the thoughts and perceptions of its characters. Sex occurs on a phantasmatic stage, where the erotic gaze is freed from its empirical moorings and indulges in fanciful pleasures of seeing unconventional marks of gender difference mapped onto the bodies of others. Thus Gil voices the queer similarities between Roger and his sister that turn him on. Seblon's closeted diary fantasies about Querelle contain the film's most erotic passages and enter a realm of sublime masochism where the Lieutenant pictures himself being "shattered" ("niedergeschmettert," 162). The narrator encourages us, too, to see Querelle as a figment of our own imagination: "By and by we recognized how Querelle had already become our flesh, larger in us, how he developed in our soul and devoured the best in us" (81). This fantasy world moves into the mythological as Querelle envisions himself in a Pièta tableau vivant—as the dead Christ lying in the arms of the transgendered Seblon. And the very process described earlier of Querelle's loving his brother (and hence, through this double, himself) via other characters—Lysiane, Nono, Gil—leads equally back to the phantasmatic, imaginary world of sexuality, to its structure of refracted, prismatic specularity, or to what the narrator calls "that sublime heaven where all the doubles [Ebenbilder] are wed to one another" (174).

Usually identification acts as a stabilizing mechanism which consolidates, even rigidifies, the ego. Veronika Voss performs femininity in order to reify and confirm her identity as someone desirable. In *Querelle*, however, identification with the woman is a risky, destabilizing move that splinters and deterritorializes the self, carrying one into unknown, unpredictable realms of desire. This libidinal situation is both volatile and richly layered, as attraction lies in seeing alterity (femininity) inscribed onto a male body. Fassbinder thus breaches social codifications by envisaging new, compositely gendered identities and desires. Although a feminist reading of *Querelle* might object either to the phallocentrism of the film or to its misappropriation and colonization of what is perceived to be "feminine," it must also be recognized that to manipulate femininity unveils it as a construct and that to rearrange identity and desire across genders means a breaking down of misogynist defense mechanisms. The film by Fassbinder which goes furthest in exploring the labile, intersexed psyche is, of course, *In einem Jahr mit 13 Monden* (*In a Year of 13 Moons*). Whereas in *Querelle* the transgendering is imagined, in *In einem Jahr mit 13 Monden* it becomes enacted.

In einem Jahr mit 13 Monden resembles *Veronika Voss* in that both films demonstrate how the masquerade of gender cannot be sustained. Yet even though *Veronika Voss* and *Lili Marleen* display how femininity is a construct and spectacle, they do not plumb the depths of despair about the impossibility of assuming an identity via gender the way *In einem Jahr mit 13 Monden* does, a film that shows the social and emotional consequences of going so far in the imitation of femininity as to physically change one's sex. Moreover, the jouissance of the trans-sexed body in *Querelle* is now absent; in his earlier film Fassbinder mercilessly lays bare how gender transgression is reviled by society and how the individual suffers from this rejection. And yet, as we shall see, *In einem Jahr mit 13 Monden* does lead to *Querelle* in the way it articulates a longing for a space in which contradictory desires can be expressed.

The film begins by visually and acoustically disorienting the viewer, as if throwing the spectator in the gender-destabilized realm that the protagonist inhabits. As the titles roll, we can make out in the dawn a man picking up a hustler in the park. The lighting, extreme close-up, editing, and frame resist giving a clear picture of what is occurring: it appears that money is exchanged, a shirt is removed, and a mouth kisses skin. Then gender confusion arises as we see hands groping under a woman's lace panties for the penis. The hustler starts to struggle with his john and yells out to his pals: "he says he's not a guy, he's a woman" (5).[22] The others join him in stripping and beating up the person whom we subsequently find out is the male-to-female transsexual Elvira Weishaupt (Volker Spengler). Ending this sequence, Elvira's clothes are thrown into the river; her undressing is neither a revelation nor an explanation, only an exposure of nakedness and vulnerability. Because her assertion of being a woman does not clarify the situation, the difference is underscored between who one says or represents oneself to be and who one is, between enunciated and enunciator. If it is impossible to determine one's identity, then no assertion or encoding can act as a substitute. Consequently, *In einem Jahr mit 13 Monden* suggests that the performance of gender codes is a futile gesture in defining identity, that it cannot be undertaken playfully or experimentally, and that the attempt at conformity meets with ridicule and isolates one further from others.

In the course of the film bits and pieces of Elvira's past are narrated, in part by her, in part by others, while additional stories are recounted that allegorize her own (such as Soul Frieda's dream of the cemetery or Zora's fairy tale of the brother snail and sister mushroom).²³ It is as if this illegible, gender-nonconformist body needed to be narrated in order to be inscribed with meaning. Elvira's life must be mirrored in other social outcasts—the prostitute Zora, the recluse Soul Frieda, the vendor with kidney cancer, the suicidal man, and the deaf voyeur—so as to be signified. However, these attempts at ex-centric representation fail to justify Elvira's life to herself, so that in the end she chooses suicide. In a nutshell her story is the following: Several years prior to the film's opening shot, Erwin Weishaupt traveled to Casablanca to undergo a sex change. The impetus was an off-hand remark made by the person Erwin loved, Anton Saitz (Gottfried John), who said, in response to Erwin's declaration of love, "that would be nice if he was a girl" (42). In other words, the operation was undertaken not at the bequest of Saitz but in order to please him, and conform to the image Erwin felt was expected of him. The act radicalizes and stands for Erwin/Elvira's disassociation from his/her own self and a self-mutilating, imaginary, submissive dependence on another. Prior to meeting Saitz, Erwin had married Irene, the daughter of his employer, and had a child with her, contacts that he still upholds and indeed wants to tighten (they never divorced). At the time the film begins Elvira has been living with Christoph, whom she had long supported as a prostitute but who now rejects her continued devotion. Elvira narrates these two segments from her life—before and after the operation—while she takes her friend Zora on a tour through a slaughterhouse, where one can hear the cries of the dying animals punctuating her tale. In another sequence we also learn of Erwin's devastating childhood as an orphan, told by the Catholic sister who helped raise him. The dénouement unwinds as Elvira returns successively to the individuals who were important to her—Sister Gudrun, Saitz, Irene, even the reporter Hauer to whom Elvira had told her story and on whom she calls when abandoned by the others. Yet they are all unwilling to resume their former bonds with her and thereby to tie the past to who Elvira is in the present. Unable to achieve narrative continuity, she returns to her apartment to at least give her life an end.

As indicated, her sex change can be seen as an attempt to reflect back the image she anticipates others wanting from her: she literalizes Saitz's callous retort. Here the inescapable Lacanian command—that we desire the desire of the Other—leads Elvira down a spiral to ultimate degradation. Repeatedly Elvira tries to reflect social codes and norms, to match this demand that she imagines is made of her, yet every attempt to recode her body makes it more incomprehensible and monstrous in the eyes of others. The initial scene is a case of how she cannot make the masquerade work: even in the subculture, norms oppress and straitjacket. Elvira tries to get a job in her old line of work as a butcher—again by wearing men's clothes—but here too she fails to pass. The seeds for such a desperate mimicry lie in her childhood. Sister Gudrun says that little Erwin "was forced to learn how to lie" once he "discovered that the more he said to each [sister] what she wanted to hear, the better it went for him" (25). Then in order to protect himself he started provoking rejection in order to anticipate its coming, with the result that the sisters began to fear him. The rift between what others perceive and how Elvira perceives herself is most painfully illustrated when her partner Christoph comes home. He tells Elvira what he sees, "a fat, sickening, useless blob of flesh" (8) with a face "so bloated and ugly it's disgusting like it was some kind of degenerative disease" (7). Yet when he holds Elvira's face up to the mirror for her to see it for herself, all she sees is her loving him instead. This nadir thus converts into the utopic as Elvira moves for a moment beyond identifying with the gaze others cast upon her, in other words, beyond specularity. Traveling along this trajectory, she sporadically comes to use her transgendered inbetweenism not in a mimicry of others' desire but precisely in order to express, bodily, "a different desire" (47).

Her path is full of obstacles, especially because sexuality in Fassbinder's universe is, like gender, relentlessly conformist. This demystification directly pertains to sexual choice: although Elvira loved Saitz, she did not identify with being gay. Thus, after the operation, sex with men is something she has to get used to: "it took a few years and I really had to try very hard. I really had to make an effort, but I did it. Even though it was hard, I learned how men smell, so it doesn't smell like an odor that makes me sick anymore" (22). Just as she moves between wearing women's and men's clothes, so too does she not fit into a gay-straight dichotomy, proving it to be unnatural and arbitrary. Her attempts at performing any one of these binaries only points to her dissociation from them; because they are borrowed, gender markers cannot author the self. Yet in order to gain acceptance Elvira has constantly to try to resignify herself within the hegemonic order, and she carries the melancholy of failing to do so. She painfully internalizes the guilt of rejection, saying to Sister Gudrun, "I've ruined my life," to which the nun replies, "No one ruins his life by himself. The world which people have made for themselves does that" (24). The man who hangs himself in Saitz's deserted office building likewise draws a distinction between an inhospitable world and the suffering individual: "The suicide desires life, but is just dissatisfied with the conditions under which it has come to him" (33). The very imbrication of the individual and society, however, means that the former never acquires an independent, distinct identity, which Elvira has experience enough to realize. She thus cannot be said to be on a search to find herself or to acquire a sexual identity.[24] As

Elsaesser rightly says, the film is "about an inverse quest: the dissolution of self, the un-making of identity" (210). It is therewith an indictment of the oppressive constructs of identity and the self, especially as these are categorized through sex and gender.[25] Silverman likewise concludes:

> The film critiques our existing system of sexual differentiation for its inability to accommodate a figure who can be assimilated neither to masculinity nor to femininity, while at the same time maximizing the intransigence of these categories in such a way as to undermine utterly any gesture on its protagonist's part toward the recovery of a phallic identification. (*Male Subjectivity*, 216)

As opposed to this failed attempt to consolidate the ego via the process of identification and assimilation, Kaja Silverman has cogently argued that Elvira's anatomical loss dramatizes a masochistic yet ecstatic divestiture of self. This masochistic bliss is intensified through an externalized identification, which Silverman calls heteropathic or ex-centric, as with the dying cows in the slaughterhouse. Transported outside himself, Erwin "resonates to a pain which is no longer his 'own'" (*Male Subjectivity*, 262).[26] Yet there is another path Elvira follows, which is the opposite of self-debasement. However much she stutters, Elvira does come into her own language at the end.

Interestingly, Elvira shows the most composure when she has to muster strength to visit Saitz in his office after years of separation. In the one role that she plays successfully—perhaps because it provides the distance of hyper-artifice—Elvira dresses as Zarah Leander, wearing the same widow's outfit as Astrée does as she leaves Puerto Rico on a ship to her native Sweden, in *La Habanera*. Both women don a black tight-bodiced dress with black gloves and a wide-brimmed black hat with a veil. Elvira likewise comports herself with Leander's erect pose and dark, soft-spoken voice. At the close of *La Habanera* Astrée's final words are that she has no regrets about her life in Puerto Rico, and one senses that going back to Sweden with Dr. Nagel will also not bring her full happiness; Leander's characters perpetually pine for "new shores." Astrée's refusal to regret is, I believe, key to understanding Elvira's own last words.

The importance of finding a vocabulary of one's own is mentioned twice in the film. First, Elvira cites the famous lines from Goethe's *Tasso*: "And if, as a man, I am silenced in my agony, give me a god to speak of how I suffer" (14). Elvira places the words in Christoph's mouth, while she herself voices what she in vain waits to hear coming from others, "I will not desert you in such need" (14). The second reference to the necessity of signifying oneself authentically (that is, not via a narcissistic specular identification with the im-

Figure 11.   *La Habanera* (1937), Zarah Leander. Courtesy of the
Paul-Seiler Archiv.

age expected of one) occurs when the camera takes a close-up of a note
tacked up in Soul Frieda's apartment: "What I fear most is if one day I'm able
to put my feelings into words, because when I do . . . " (22).

While Elvira goes back to her apartment to commit suicide, the reporter
Hauer plays the taped interview with Elvira. Rendered as a voice-over as her
friends and family appear too late to prevent the suicide, Elvira's words are so
poignant because they become a memento from beyond the grave. Com-

Figure 12. *In einem Jahr mit 13 Monden* (1978), Volker Spengler as Elvira. Courtesy of the Fotoarchiv, Stiftung Deutsche Kinemathek, Berlin.

pelling too is how Elvira struggles to articulate her desires. As pure voice, symbolically speaking she is released from the scopic prejudices that her transgendered body provokes;[27] hence this disembodied voice is granted a special authority. As her words make clear, her authenticity and integrity reside not in a gender or sexual affiliation she could call her own but in her articulation of a need, whose very nature is that it cannot be defined, and can elicit then no response. Elvira sees her life as a process and not as specified by a fixed identity: "What is being happy? Of course, I'm not happy. There is no such thing as happiness. We search, and it's the process that's exciting, not the result, happiness" (47). She acknowledges in a telling but short phrase: "Now I have a different desire" (47). Like Astrée, Elvira comes to realize that she had not been a passive victim of others but had made choices that were based on her sexual desire, curiosity, and hope. And like Leander's characters she exists in her longing for love. Among the last words she utters on the tape are: "Life is, or was, still some kind of hope. Somehow it meant comfort, or, like I said before, desire, or maybe I was just curious to experience these things" (50). Hence, like Astrée, Elvira affirms her past and the vagaries of her desires: "Maybe I'd like to. . . . I don't know, maybe I'd like it with Anton. Or maybe I'd like it with Irene. Or maybe . . . " (47). Her probing and receptivity are signified by the very pauses that are pregnant with possibilities.

Thus rather than viewing Elvira's inbetweenism as a torture, one sees her turn it around to be an exploration of different, rich channels of desire. Moreover, rather than concluding that Elvira's identity can only be negatively expressed—as neither male nor female, neither gay nor straight[28]—one comes to recognize that she bisexually loved Irene, Anton, and Christoph and that she undertook the sex change not to comply with Saitz's wish but to satisfy her curiosity "to experience these things."[29] Hers is the attempt to move beyond projecting the image others demand of her to experience freely the contradictions of being interchangeably male, female, bisexual, and transgender. Her exercise remains, though, "still some kind of hope," for *In einem Jahr mit 13 Monden* ultimately portrays social and sexual conformity as an inescapable prison. Fassbinder does not romanticize transgender but presents it as a transgression lived every day.

In conclusion, I should like to reconsider the various positions on the representation of gay sexuality in Fassbinder—but in terms of a transgender reading. Like Rosa von Praunheim's work, *Querelle* and *In einem Jahr mit 13 Monden* are remarkable for how their characters are open and out about their sexualities. Their queer desires are neither inhibited nor repressed; they are also not psychologized, as if Fassbinder, like von Praunheim, refused to ruminate about the psychological roots of homosexuality and thereby apologize for the behavior of gays.[30] Ed Sikov further observes: "Unlike Frank Ripploh's *Taxi zum Klo*, with its documentary tour of Berlin with true-to-life gay people, or even Fassbinder's own *Fox and His Friends*, *Querelle* audaciously presumes that the world it represents is not a subset of a larger world. . . . It simply takes [homosexuality] as a given, and it is this affront that our cultural arbiters cannot tolerate" (42). Although he does not refer to this article, Al LaValley would be sympathetic to Sikov's positive appraisal of *Querelle*, for LaValley challenges the director's critics, such as Rosa von Praunheim and Richard Dyer, who wished to have seen more evidence in Fassbinder's oeuvre of the 1970s Gay Liberation Movement and its cry for social change toward and among gays.[31] LaValley energetically counters: "That [these films] pay no attention to the tenets of Gay Liberation yet somehow come out of them, seems to me a mark of their power and continuing excitement. They face issues that few films from the gay community have looked at, and they link these issues to the various major emotional, psychological, historical, and social issues that Fassbinder explores in his other films. They touch on issues of class in the gay world, exploitation, varied life styles, emotional breakups, s-and-m, gender confusion, the role of looks, body types, race, the role of women vis-à-vis gay men, even the size of a gay man's cock—all issues that have been given little treatment in gay film" (137).

LaValley also briefly mentions that Fassbinder seeks "to show that the gay male can embody both male and female roles, much as Genet dissected them" (137). I have argued that this dual embodiment gives insight into male homosexuality while it complicates any attempt to categorize this sexuality as unambiguously male-centered: *Querelle* and *In einem Jahr mit 13 Monden* cannot unproblematically be called "gay" films, for gay male desire is not always same-sex. Fassbinder presents the subject as a highly contradictory, libidinally nomadic force field, the sum or alternation of unruly desires. In this sense, then, sexuality in these films is outlaw and transgressive: it rearranges the codifying, mutually exclusive binaries of the symbolic social system, including not only male/female and active/passive but also mono/bisexuality. Through such an unconventional queering of gay male sexuality Fassbinder opens doors to opulent, labyrinthine fantasies, and indeed addresses though this angle "issues that few films from the gay community have looked at" (LaValley, 137). In addition, his work looks ahead to such transgender films of the late nineties as von Praunheim's *Vor Transsexuellen wird gewarnt* (*Transsexual Menace*) (1996), Scheirl's *Dandy Dust* (1998), and Treut's *Gendernauts* (1998).

The various referencings of Leander in Fassbinder's works, moreover, emphasize how he presents sexuality and gender as layered, citational, and hence allegorical. By indirectly imitating Leander, various characters show how specularity cleaves the image, never identically replicating it. Whereas *Lili Marleen* and *Veronika Voss* rehearse this imitation in terms of femininity as spectacle (and reveal its reactionary, fascist foundation), *Querelle* and *In einem Jahr mit 13 Monden* radicalize this splitting to figure forth a subversive specular desire—the ultimate desire not only to be the other but to be the other sex. However brief they may be, the allusions to Leander in *Querelle* and *In einem Jahr mit 13 Monden* offer an entry point for unraveling a fascinatingly complex gender transitivity.[32]

Chapter

The Pink Peril

Rosa von Praunheim

Given that the notoriety of Rainer Werner Fassbinder's bisexuality has lent worldwide renown to the queers in *Die bitteren Tränen der Petra von Kant*, *Faustrecht der Freiheit*, *In einem Jahr mit 13 Monden*, and *Querelle*, one might almost forget that another German director was making radical films about gays even before Fassbinder. Although his enemies may be loathe to admit it, Rosa von Praunheim is unquestionably the most important figure in the Queer German Cinema as well as the most energetic spokesman for the gay movement in Germany in the last quarter century. Born in 1942 in Riga, Latvia, as Holger Mischwitzky, he chose the name Rosa von Praunheim to remind people of the pink triangle ("Rosa Winkel") that homosexuals had to wear in Nazi concentration camps. He is the senior of Fassbinder, Wenders, and Schroeter by three years, and, since Fassbinder's death in 1982, is Germany's most prolific filmmaker, with forty films up to *Neurosia* (1995) and still counting. From this mock autobiography back to his first film, the similarly self-preoccupied *Von Rosa von Praunheim* (1967), his output has been steady, with new works always in production, the latest being a high-budget feature, *The Einstein of Sex: The Life and Work of Dr. Magnus Hirschfeld* and *The History of Homosexuality from Stonehenge to Stonewall and Beyond*.

Like Ulrike Ottinger, he initiated his artistic career as a student of painting (1961–67). In the late sixties he began experimenting in film (also in creative writing with his unpublished novel *Tagebuch in Rosa* [*Diary in Pink*]), at which time he befriended Werner Schroeter, working together with him on *Grotesk-Burlesk-Pittoresk* (*Grotesque-Burlesque-Picturesque*) (1968), *Schwestern der Revolution* (*Sisters of the Revolution*) (1969), and *Samuel Beckett* (1969). They also each produced a *Macbeth* (1970 and 1971) starring Magdalena Montezuma.[1] Von Praunheim's collaboration with Elfi Mikesch similarly began in the late 1960s with their photo-novel *Oh Muvie* (1969). It was to continue with her taking over his camera work in *Leidenschaften* (*Passions*) (1971–72), *Horror Vacui* (1984), *Ein Virus kennt keine Moral* (*A Virus Knows No Morals*)

(1985), *Anita: Tänze des Lasters* (*Anita: Dances of Vice*) (1988) and *Feuer unterm Arsch* (*Fire Under the Ass*) (the third part of the AIDS trilogy, 1990). Rosa von Praunheim's filmic breakthrough came in 1970 with *Die Bettwurst* (*The Bolster*), a hilarious parody of bourgeois marriage, starring his aging aunt Luzi Kryn who was paired with a squirrely fellow named Dietmar Kracht, who overnight became the darling of the artistic underground scene in Berlin. But his most renowned work, *Nicht der Homosexuelle ist pervers, sondern die Situation, in der er lebt* (*It's Not the Homosexual Who Is Perverse, But the Situation in Which He Lives*) (1971) truly launched von Praunheim's career, as well as the gay movement in Germany, through the public debates that accompanied its screenings. Distribution of the film brought him to a post-Stonewall United States, where he contributed to the gay liberation and later AIDS activist movements in a number of significant documentaries, including *Armee der Liebenden oder Aufstand der Perversen* (*Army of Lovers or Revolt of the Perverts*) (1972–76), *Positiv* (*Positive*) (1990), and *Schweigen = Tod* (*Silence = Death*) (1990). Attuned to the seriousness of AIDS at an early date, Praunheim had already produced the feature-length part-musical, part-morality play *Ein Virus kennt keine Moral* in 1985.[2] His most recent feature-length documentaries continue in this thought-provoking tradition: *Vor Transsexuellen wird gewarnt* (*Transsexual Menace*) (1996) presents transgender activism in the States, while *Schwuler Mut* (*Gay Courage*) (1997) reviews, as its subtitle indicates, "100 Years of the Gay Movement in Germany and Beyond." The latter film developed from the exposition held in Berlin in 1997 on the same topic, for which von Praunheim curated several events. He is currently helping to organize a large exhibition to be held in Berlin in 2001 on gays and lesbians in the Third World.

The success of many of Rosa von Praunheim's films, beginning with *Die Bettwurst*, is due in large part to his ability to let his actors and actresses demonstrate the vitality and uniqueness of their personalities on screen. If Werner Schroeter had his Magdalena Montezuma, Ulrike Ottinger her Tabea Blumenschein and Delphine Seyrig, and Monika Treut her Susie Sexpert, Annie Sprinkle, and Eva Norvind, then Rosa von Praunheim has taken this cultivation of the star personality even further with the vibrant "women" around whom he has constructed a number of his films. These actresses include the singers Evelyn Künneke in *Ich bin ein Antistar* (*I am an Anti-Star*) (1976) and Tally Brown in *Tally Brown, New York* (1978) as well as Lotti Huber in *Horror Vacui, Unsere Leichen leben noch* (*Our Corpses Are Still Alive*) (1981), *Anita: Tänze des Lasters* and *Affengeil: Eine Reise durch Lottis Leben* (*Life Is a Cucumber*) (1990), and the male-to-female transvestite Charlotte von Mahlsdorf in *Ich bin meine eigene Frau* (*I Am My Own Woman*) (1992). *Stadt der verlorenen Seelen* (*City of*

Lost Souls) (1982/83) stars an entire cast of transvestites, transsexuals, and trapeze artists. In fact, the broad spectrum of "queers"—the loud, extreme, not mainstream personalities—that he brings to the screen prevent him from being classified solely as a "gay" director. His activist documentaries likewise borrow their strength from the fascinating individuals he captures on celluloid. Accompanying *Armee der Liebenden*, for instance, is a book by the same title that devotes its chapters to key movers and controversial figures in Gay Liberation before, during, and after the Stonewall riots, including Christopher Isherwood, Jim Kepner, Bruce Voeller, Tom Reeves, and Fred Halsted, persons interviewed in the film. Similarly, in *Positiv* he gives ample camera time to Larry Kramer, the founder of the Gay Mens' Health Crisis and subsequently Act Up, as well as to the singer and founder of People With Aids Coalition, Michael Callen. *Schweigen = Tod* derives its power from the performance artists, painters, and writers David Wojnarowicz, Emilio Cubiero, Keith Haring, and Allen Ginsberg, among others. Regarding his entire work, von Praunheim has said that it is almost all documentary: "Even the feature films are with real people, strong personalities that I build in documentary fashion into my films" (*Rosa von Praunheim*, 73).

Given the extent to which from its inception Rosa von Praunheim's oeuvre has relied not so much on the strong hand of its author as on collaboration with colorful personalities, it is not surprising that Rosa von Praunheim more than any other director of his era has been involved in the mentoring of younger generations of filmmakers, including Frank Ripploh and Michael Stock in Germany and Phillip Roth in the United States, in whose *I Was a Jewish Sexworker* (1997) he appears. Furthermore, *Zero Patience* (1995) by the Canadian John Greyson is indebted to *Ein Virus kennt keine Moral*. By candidly addressing gay issues in his oeuvre, von Praunheim has performed a groundbreaking task in widely opening closet doors for gay cinema. The daring, sassy quality to Monika Treut's work, including its humor and irony, for instance, is unthinkable without him. In *Verführung: Die grausame Frau* (*Seduction: The Cruel Woman*) (1985) and *Die Jungfrauenmaschine* (*Virgin Machine*) (1988) one can see Treut building (on) this queer cinematic tradition, with Elfi Mikesch, her cinematographer and informal film instructor, serving as the personal link back to Rosa von Praunheim. Given this springboard, Treut's works from the eighties show her running an edge ahead of the New Queer Cinema directors of the 1990s, such as Bruce la Bruce (*No Skin Off My Ass* [1990], *Super 8½* [1994], *Hustler White* [1996]) and Gregg Araki (*The Living End* [1992], *Totally F***ed Up* [1993], *The Doom Generation* [1995], and *Nowhere* [1997]). What connects Rosa von Praunheim to this recent cinema is a predilection for histrionic performance, the heightened stylization of self, and hyperbolic, over-the-top expression. Indisputably, other gay German filmmakers such as Lambert, Schroeter, and Ottinger share these tendencies, but although these older directors presage the younger generation, only von Praunheim is regularly counted within the group because of the stridently "out" content of his work. Another way of reconfiguring this history of New Queer Cinema would be to claim Rosa von Praunheim as the bridge between it and its largely unrecognized predecessor, the New German Cinema.[3]

Rosa von Praunheim not only has been at the vanguard of the international movement of queer cinema but has also served as Germany's most prominent gay political activist. This figurehead status is extremely controversial, not least because it is perceived that he sets himself up as the spokesman for the German gay community, a position many in Germany resent. The gay press, for instance, has called him a gay Führer and Gummi-Rosa (Rubber Rosa, for his loud plaidoyer for safe sex).[4] In addition, he has aroused the anger of both gays and straights for outing several famous show business personalities and politicians on German television. Clear evidence of Rosa von Praunheim's penchant for unabashed self-display can be found in his recent autobiography/diary, *50 Jahre pervers* (*50 Years of Perversity*), where his sexual prowess and promiscuity are amply paraded, as well as the frank admission that he was intensely jealous of the successes of Fassbinder and Schroeter; he even admits his relief at Fassbinder's death (281). It is not easy to detect irony in these pages; in fact one marvels at its absence. Ironic distance regarding his own foibles, however, does guide the filmic rendition of this half-century of perversion. Although *Neurosia* may still strike viewers as self-indulgent, it deploys several techniques of self-effacement and self-parody missing from the written autobiography;[5] indeed, its conceit is that Rosa von Praunheim is presumed shot dead by one of his many enemies, while a reporter, played by the transvestite Désirée Nick, digs up dirt on his life for her hit TV show. She interviews relatives, former friends, and colleagues, most of whom have little good to say about him. Paradoxically the film becomes more a vehicle for these other characters than for its director, a strategy of withdrawal that explains many of von Praunheim's tactics both cinematically as well as politically.

Another telling example of this audacity and talent for provocation, paradoxically combined with a tendency to pull back and observe the fallout, is the controversy surrounding the appearance of his AIDS trilogy in Germany in 1990. The set is comprised of the two documentaries on AIDS activism in New York, *Positiv* (79 min.) and *Schweigen = Tod* (55 min.), and a less affirmative one on the scene in Berlin, *Feuer unterm Arsch* (50 min.), a juxtaposition that proved incendiary. As *Armee der Liebenden* already testifies, Rosa von

Praunheim was heavily influenced by the gay movement in the United States. Although we see and hear him posing questions to his interviewees in this film, for the most part he retires as documentarian to celebrate the accomplishments and leadership of others. This admiration for strength in the face of adversity is even more evident in *Positiv* and *Schweigen = Tod*. It is no wonder then that Rosa von Praunheim would take the strident Larry Kramer and passionate David Wojnarowicz as models for his own AIDS activism in Germany.[6] Unfortunately, this adulation and emulation was read as foreign and unwelcome once imported to Germany: in the July issue of the gay magazine *Magnus*, whose lead story was the controversy surrounding the première of the AIDS trilogy, one journalist reminded Rosa, addressed derogatively as "she," that the Act Up successes in New York were limited after all (34), while another sarcastically wrote that learning from America was learning to triumph (25).

What produced this bilious response was a polemical article on AIDS that Rosa von Praunheim had published in *Der Spiegel* in May 1990—exactly when the trilogy was about to be screened in its entirety and travel through Germany.[7] With the intent of inciting dissent, von Praunheim had stated that PWAs carried responsibility for their own infection and hence their own death in having remained passive toward the virus. Moreover, he attacked gay health organizations in Berlin for harboring heavily subsidized AIDS professionals and bureaucrats. If such recklessness were not enough, he also criticized gays from the former East Germany for their nonchalant attitude toward the disease. To the general public it appeared that the gay movement was internally divided; to gays it was transparent that Rosa had no right to put himself up as their spokesman. Some called for a boycott of the trilogy; others suggested punishing him by robbing him of his artistic, mock-aristocratic name. Recalling this period in his autobiography, the filmmaker wondered what demon had possessed him to write such incendiary material (373). In the interview in *Magnus* that fateful summer, however, he did admit to having said what was incorrect in order to provoke, the intent being to save lives (26).

This odd pattern of polemics followed by retraction, though not recantation, whereby Rosa von Praunheim acts successively as agent provocateur and observant documentarian, can be seen as early as 1971 in the reception of *Nicht der Homosexuelle ist pervers*. As with the AIDS trilogy, the director requested that public discussion always follow the film's screenings. And he repeatedly stated that the film itself was less important than the reactions it elicited. The film premièred only two years after Paragraph 175 of the penal code criminalizing homosexuality had been lifted. Time was obviously ripe for a collective coming out that would parallel the revolution in the American community after the Stonewall riots in 1969, but the film too must be credited for initiating change and debate. In the chapter that follows I want to examine this seminal work closely—not only for its complex interweaving of discourses that not surprisingly led to a heated discussion and the instigation of the gay rights movement in Germany but also for its status within von Praunheim's oeuvre. In fact, much of the controversy over this film can be clarified by tensions latent in subsequent works by this director. Similarities include a mock seriousness or polemic, the toying with the biographical story and its pretensions to revelation, an affinity for eccentric characters whose normalcy or representative status is nonetheless ironically claimed, the intersplicing of competing narratives, the deconstruction of pornography, stratified layers of role-playing, the acting out of socially constructed gender and sexual identities, a camp attitude toward social strictures and norms, as well as a proclivity for the *Stationsdrama*, a theater piece composed of sequential, allegorical stations. It is from such a comparative perspective that I then want to examine von Praunheim's 1991 film on Charlotte von Mahlsdorf, *Ich bin meine eigene Frau*. A later chapter on "Lesbians Abroad" will look at another of his documentaries, *Überleben in New York* (*Survival in New York*) (1989), a film that von Praunheim called his most successful (*50 Jahre*, 356), on three German women living in New York City.

'Nicht der Homosexuelle ist pervers, sondern die Situation, in der er lebt'

The *Schwulenfilm* (*Faggot Film*) as Rosa von Praunheim provocatively calls this work, is frequently lauded as the first gay activist film worldwide, although from the start it provoked anger on the part of its gay audiences both in Germany and North America.[8] On its release in 1971 in Berlin the first German gay organization was founded. Its appearance on German television on January 31, 1972, unleashed a more widespread debate. It was originally to be screened on the national network, the ARD, but the ARD pulled out at the last moment, giving contradictory reasons for its decision and leaving only the local Cologne WDR station to air it. On the one hand, network officials feared that the film would confirm and strengthen prejudices against homosexuals. On the other hand, they claimed, much less altruistically, the need as a public institution to serve the majority in their programming. A year later *Nicht der Homosexuelle* did show on the ARD channel although still not in conservative, Catholic Bavaria. On this occasion (January 15, 1973), a discussion about the film was also broadcast, as well as the address of a gay organization in Münster, where later the first gay rights demonstration was held. In addition, as Charlotte von Mahlsdorf writes in her autobiography (158), East German gays had watched the broadcast and wanted likewise to form groups of solidarity. The general press condemned the film for its perversity, while its leftist branch criticized the film for its classless, apolitical nature. Gays felt attacked by the castigating voice-over and reacted defensively against the negative stereotypes.[9] Not to be discounted in this reception history is that with the initial televisation Holger Mischwitzky came out to his parents.

Given that the *Schwulenfilm* launched the gay movement in Germany, it is amazing that Rosa von Praunheim made it without knowledge of the Stonewall riots. Nor is Stonewall mentioned in the German press that records the film's reception. It was not until von Praunheim traveled for the first time to the States with the film that he was exposed to gay liberation. The reception of the *Schwulenfilm* in the United States was no less controversial and prolonged than in Germany. In 1972 the film screened at the Museum of Modern Art, followed by a heated discussion that formed the basis for a half-hour documentary, which showed the audience receiving the film as anti-gay. It was argued that the film failed on two major accounts: it did not bring to light public aggression against gays and it did not assertively promote homosexuality. Only later in 1977, at the two-week-long sold-out screenings at New York's Film Forum, was the work accepted as insider critique. Amazingly, further films were made of the debates at other venues in the United States, which led to a body of films that could be screened with the original, allowing the audience to compare its reactions to that of others. By the conclusion of the decade, however, the tide was turning definitively against the self-accusatory portrayal of gays. As Dietrich Kuhlbrodt summarizes in his 1983 book on Rosa von Praunheim: "at the end of the seventies the public wanted a confirmation of the successes of the gay movement, and Praunheim's film from 1970 did not offer a gay love story but reminded one of problems that still had not been solved" (*Rosa von Praunheim*, 126). Today, almost thirty years after Stonewall, one clearly does not expect that gay cinema needs exclusively to depict love stories nor to be unselfcritical; nonetheless, it is inconceivable that contemporary gay cinema, even its high camp mode, would portray the plethora of negative gay stereotypes that *Nicht der Homosexuelle* does. It is furthermore hard to imagine that the final rallying cry "Out of the toilets and into the streets," chanted as it is by a commune of men lounging around naked, could ever have served as an efficacious call to solidarity, although this scene does have documentary value

94

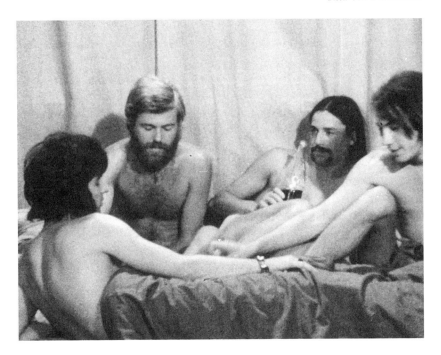

Figure 13. *Nicht der Homosexuelle ist pervers, sondern die Situation, in der er lebt* (1971). Courtesy of Rosa von Praunheim.

in illustrating how difficult it must have been to begin organizing group politics.[10] But it is precisely the entire history of this reception, not one particular moment in it, that demonstrates how disparate, even self-contradictory, the voices are that Rosa von Praunheim pits against each other both intratextually and extratextually.

The film traces the story of Daniel (Bernd Feuerhelm), a young man from the provinces, coming to the big city and moving from one gay subculture to the next. His adventures begin on the streets of Berlin, where he meets Clemens (Berryt Bohlen), who invites him home for coffee. Soon Daniel is living with Clemens and believes he has found in him the love of his life. The two try to imitate a bourgeois marriage and its lifestyle. But after four months of this tedium, Daniel is cruised by a rich older man (the fashion designer, Ernst Kuchling) who entices him to move into his villa, where he encounters a group of older gays, pretentious in their appreciation of fine art and classical music, who fawn over him. In his progressive disenchantment, Daniel realizes that his rich friend is only using him as a plaything. He leaves to work in a gay café and learns to dress fashionably, at which point the film

95

parades ostentatious late-sixties outfits. This preoccupation with body and looks continues at the swimming pool where Daniel spends his free time. At this hangout men stand around to be admired by other men, and the camera lingers over their muscular torsos. Two years later Daniel is no longer content with meeting men in elegant cafés, boutiques, and beaches but seeks out pickups at the bars for quick sex. He moves on to the darkly lit parks where the leather daddies congregate, the "tense choreography of men who silently moved about without ever exchanging a word." He finally descends to the public toilets where hustlers hang out as well as frustrated, closeted types and aging gays who are no longer attractive; the latter only end up being beaten by punks. Daniel's penultimate stop is a transvestite bar, the single sequence where some actors seem at ease and to be enjoying themselves. There he meets Paul, who takes him back to his commune (*Wohngemeinschaft*) where a group of men, lying around naked, openly criticize their superficial, closeted lifestyles, sexual hangups, fashion, and conformity. Calling for gay emancipation, they advocate social engagement and collective organization against discrimination. Their nakedness contrasts with the film's earlier focus on trendy, even outlandish dress.

Throughout the film the acting is wooden, with the men usually standing around isolated from yet posing for each other (not that they actually look at each other). Daniel himself is a slight, nondescript man with a shiny, expressionless face evocative of a wax figure or marionette. Initially, Rosa von Praunheim considered casting the singular Dietmar Kracht from *Die Bettwurst* as Daniel but decided against this choice in order to show not camp perversity but lack of personality in the lead role. Despite Daniel's varied adventures—sexual and otherwise—he remains impassive, until he appears transformed in the crowded transvestite bar dancing where, like the other patrons, he momentarily looks normal in an interactive, slice-of-life setting. The camera suddenly has an appreciation for unique physiognomies; the characters sing and applaud. The difference reminds us of who Daniel might actually be and hence underscores his earlier incarnations as fabrication. Moreover, the distance with which Feuerhelm plays his character prevents the spectator not only from wanting to identify or empathize with him but from taking the stations of his life as credible. As von Praunheim explained in his book *Sex und Karriere*: "I didn't want a story with which people could identify but images that were exemplary in their alienation" (15).

The entire film is a compilation of voice-overs, beginning with the dubbed conversation between Clemens and Daniel and ending with the gay men in the commune; their lips move but clearly not in synch with their words. Paradoxically, the only apparent synchronization is in the bar where a transvestite sings (or lipsynchs). The only exception to the constant voice-over flow occurs during the night episode in the park where the camera cruises in silence the bodies of men in leather and chains. The predominant voice-over (scripted with the gay sociologist Martin Dannecker) is a castigating commentary on the behavior of "faggots," together with "fags," a word used ninety times in the film.[11] As the director has pointed out (*Rosa von Praunheim*, 54), the part is read in the provocatively nagging high pitch of a queen (*Tunte*). Other and often conflicting voice-overs include the inner voice of Clemens, Daniel's letters to his parents, two queens dissing the fashion of an older fag followed by a punk crying "gas them, castrate them," as well as a steamy literary narrative that casts Daniel's adventures as a racy soft-porn novel. This narration begins as Clemens and Daniel kiss undressed in bed: "Clemens desires Daniel and his boyish body whose firmness for Clemens is so pleasingly different from the soft contours of a woman. As far back as he can remember, Clemens has been strongly attracted by men. He adores Daniel's shy, boyish behavior and his naive wonder. As a result of his strict upbringing, Daniel has to struggle against strong feelings of sin and guilt . . . " Betraying the triteness and artificiality of this pulp genre, however, is the totally dispassionate lovemaking.

Collectively, the effect of these voice-overs is an assault of information, their disparity necessitating a varied reception. Of the soundtrack, von Praunheim observes: "it is very important, this destabilization, this over-exertion of the spectator, in opposition to these long takes . . . the spectator or critic can interpret uncommonly a lot into the film" (*Rosa von Praunheim*, 54). Together, the voice-overs serve various functions: to begin, marking a rupture from the visual image, they call attention to the fact that cinema is a technical construction that mechanically weds sound to image and hence cannot be taken as mimetically reproducing reality. This split emphasizes that the fictional biography of Daniel can make no pretense of accurately depicting a gay lifestyle; it accents as well the work's status as art film as opposed to documentary, were such a juxtaposition not in itself simplistic. Although the voice thus remains cut off from the body (especially in the silent, dimly lit "leather freak" scene), it complements the static acting, insofar as both signify a disembodiment and elicit a persistent spectatorial disidentification. In other words, Daniel, like the gay men serving as props around him, cannot be read as possessing subjecthood or individuality. On the one hand, this lack could be said to illustrate the censorious commentary that condemns faggot shallowness. Yet, insofar as the actors embody stereotypes, the spectator is suspicious of their validity, just as he or she remains skeptical of the appropriateness of the voice-over lecture. Indeed, because this one scathing tract is juxtaposed

97

with other narratives, its authority is challenged. The competing discourses beg to be aligned with and against each other, whereby their separate attempts to define the homosexual implode: the very conflict between discourses deconstructs the homosexual as legible category.

Nonetheless audiences reacted negatively to the entire film, based on this virulent editorial that is fascist in its attempts to secure the borders of homosexuality and unrelenting in its anti-gay rhetoric (it only ceases with the transvestite bar and commune scenes). Provocative as well is the fact that documentary conventions discourage the deployment of an authoritative voice-over that one resists. To illustrate with a couple of excerpts: "The less fags are capable of human relations among themselves the more they need a substitute. The desire for happiness and fulfillment is exploited by industry and diverted away from people to products. Furniture, television, and a new car are for straights what the latest fashion is to the fag" (in the café scene). "Fags find it hard to keep a lover; full of vanity and guilty conscience they look into each other's eyes searching for true love; they dream of an ideal lover who doesn't exist" (the night scene in front of the bars). This discourse is additionally difficult to adjudicate precisely because it is free-floating: there is no face to attach to it to help decipher who would deliver it and with what motive. It oscillates between a semi-psychologizing tone and, with its critique of gay consumerist and bourgeois mentality, a Marxist posture. Especially after the intervening decades of gay pride, this tirade, despite its consciousness of class differences, seems excruciatingly politically incorrect, although at the time it was received by some as acceptable in-crowd critique. Others saw it as the projection of a pre-Stonewall voice of self-incrimination. Although this discourse shares certain concerns with early gay-liberation tracts—consciousness-raising critiques of how gays mimic the role-playing of straight societal institutions, how they engage in such reprehensible practices as cruising, or how they retreat into a make-believe world—unlike these manifestos, it fails to offer creative solutions.[12]

Nicht der Homosexuelle bears comparison with the reception of Matt Crowley's *The Boys in the Band*, a successful play before Stonewall but panned once produced as a film in 1970 by William Friedkin. Although the casting remained the same, the self-loathing and self-pitying drunken characters were no longer appropriate, believable, or authentic models for a liberated gay consciousness. But whereas *Boys in the Band* was daring in its time for its uncompromising readiness to depict the strains in the lives of gay men, Rosa von Praunheim ultimately relativizes the accusatory voice-over and delegitimizes it. This exterior commentary demonstrates that it is the symbolic, dominant order, that is, the situation in which one lives, that produces the category "homosexual." In Foucauldian fashion, it is this persistent discourse from the outside that creates a matrix into which the subject must be fitted, into which he performs himself. Yet at the same time the subject is forced to comply, he is also cruelly chastized for his conformity. The voice-over reproves: "In order to be accepted into the company of fags, a young homosexual is forced to give up his own personal interests for allegedly more homosexual interests and ideals." No "I" precedes or can even follow from this imitative process: hence Feuerhelm acts out a puppetlike, affectless character. Yet the denaturalization of his performance ultimately subverts the norm to which his character is supposed to adhere. This critical remove from the spectacle being enacted paradoxically robs the self-important, condemning voice-over of its authority, for the homosexual never identifies with the role apportioned to him. The commentary thus falls short of its aim and fails to elucidate; it is doubly disembodied. As the title indicates, it is this deficiency that makes the discourse on the homosexual—not Daniel himself—perverse.

In yet another way the attempt of the voice-over to accuse the homosexual of base conformity fails. Through the accumulation of alienating techniques beginning with the split between image and sound, the film leaves a disturbing, pervasively "queer" feeling. Moe Meyer has offered a definition of queer "based on an alternative model of the constitution of subjectivity and of social identity. The emergence of the queer label as an oppositional critique of gay and lesbian middle-class assimilationism is, perhaps, its strongest and most valid aspect. In the sense that the queer label emerges as a class critique, then what is opposed are bourgeois models of identity" ("Introduction," 2). Although the Marxist stance of the voice-over condemns the faggot for his "middle-class assimilationism," the way in which the faggot exceeds and thereby erodes normality is continually present in the film. Such moments include but are not limited to the over-the-top dress and gestures of Kuchling in the role of Daniel's patron, the sheen of leather and metal in the park scene, and the transvestite parading as a yodeling grandmother in the penultimate episode. Although the voice-over insists on the faggot's desire for conformity, what the visuals emphasize—paradoxically all the more so because the faggot doesn't speak—is his queerness. Even the opening and closing credits, where a single rose is sketched against a pink backdrop, signal Rosa's camp pride.

If, on the level of enunciation, it is claimed that faggots are only concerned with their appearance both to society at large and to themselves, the sets, lighting, camera movement, and editing—in addition to the acting—invert this claim by showing that the mechanisms by which we see and represent life actually fabricate this superficiality; they do not reproduce it. Robert van

99

Ackeren's camera remains cool and distant, resisting the Hollywoodesque shot-countershot. It either stands statically in front of the bars, tearooms, and cafés, refusing to enter; or it slowly pans, cruising the men. The deliberate sequence of tableaux, the mechanical posing of the actors as if for a photograph, and the sudden cuts to a new scene make one aware of the film as fabrication. The cinematography thereby joins the soundtrack and acting to present the self as exterior or carapace, intimating that discourses about homosexuality will always be condemned to falsity. The allegoresis of the homosexual, the running pseudo-psychologizing annotation, is only a mock disclosure of the "truth" of sexuality. Rosa von Praunheim thereby sets the audience of this film into a mise-en-abyme of interpretation. Just as the voice-over misses the mark, so too are all discussions about the film condemned to inappropriateness—a move that paradoxically generates the ongoing discussion that the film's reception history demonstrates. Ultimately, the film makes its spectator uncomfortable with any right to "interpret" homosexuality.

By thereby undermining the ostensible attempt to establish a taxonomy of homosexuality—of its exterior signs of dress, hairstyle, gesture, bodily physique—Rosa von Praunheim undermines the very workings of representation and belief in visibility. Richard Dyer has argued in his article "Seen to Be Believed": "The prevalent fact of gay typification is determined by the importance of a social category whose members would be invisible did they and the culture not provide lifestyle signs with which to make recognition possible" (*The Matter of Images*, 25). Although Dyer acknowledges that typecasting of a gay character "has the disadvantage that it tends to reduce everything about that character to his/her sexuality," he also reasons that "it never allows the text to closet her or him, and it thus allows gay sub-cultural perspectives to be always present in a scene. For gay readers and audiences, in particular, this allows a place in the text from which to view the proceedings" (24–25). Keeping these distinctions in mind, it appears that Rosa von Praunheim's film can be read both as a refusal to closet gays and as a litany of various gay types—but not ones that a gay audience would want to recognize, let alone identify with. Although the film does not claim that invisibility is the only alternative, it does question the appropriateness of classifications. Although presented as something known and circumscribed, the stereotype functions in von Praunheim as a mask for something hidden.

100

The film thus brilliantly plays with the construct of the closet. Although it appears with this first openly gay film (amazingly, the only other contender is *Anders als die Andern* from 1919) that its director sets ajar the closet door, he refuses to show what is actually inside. The gesture of revelation is solely that: Daniel projects merely the surface or sheen of an identity and deflects our probing gaze. Von Praunheim thus ironically points to the opened closet as an empty frame, which like the cinematic apparatus itself is expected to put on show "the homosexual." Cinema as closet holds the promise of revelation, but actually distorts our vision. It forces us to reflect on what is hidden as well as to confront our own voyeuristic desires. The shots demonstrate this point when repeatedly, despite the scenes of nudity, the penis is hidden: at the beginning and at the end when Daniel is lying down naked, his penis is carefully shielded, as if von Praunheim wanted to thwart our pornographic desires, to deemphasize focus on this member, and to protest against how the gay body is often represented.

Yet paradoxically, as in camp, Rosa von Praunheim also turns the closet into a stage for spectacle. In fact, he pushes spectacle to its limit via the external voicing of an intense self-abnegation. He provocatively and incessantly deploys the term "faggot," which even more than the current usage of "queer" carries a derogatory edge. Through the voice-over, the faggot is degraded and exposed. But if shame is something one feels when a hidden part of oneself is revealed, shame is not enacted in the film. Daniel is never aware of the gaze upon him nor of the implications of the voice-over. Shaming, unlike in Fassbinder, never hits its target. The closet connotes the abject, despised body (which German directors from Fassbinder and Schroeter to Ottinger are remarkable for exorcising by putting it on display). What is especially fascinating about *Nicht der Homosexuelle* is its ability to engage this abjection without repeating it; in other words, von Praunheim manages to deflect mortification.[13] Especially in the transvestite bar scene—the only time the camera goes inside a public establishment—strange physiognomies and dress are proudly put on display. Criticizing Fassbinder for making "bourgeois films" rather than "minority films," von Praunheim says that in his own work it was always important "to show the physical defects or defectiveness in people, thus outsiders who are seen by society as inferior or faulty, and to show that they live with self-assurance and strength" (*Rosa von Praunheim*, 60).

How, though, is the conclusion to be interpreted in light of the sequences that precede it? How could this section have prompted gay rights organizing throughout East and West Germany? Again, in this scene a rift opens between the visuals and the soundtrack, signaling a continuing irony: if synchronization signifies a speaking from and with the body, then this scene would indicate the impossibility of speaking authentically. Other details make this finale hard to envisage as politically efficacious: The men seem preposterous as they lounge around, sharing a bottle of Coke and mouthing claims as sententious and strident as the previous voice-over. Daniel, looking as waxen and passive as ever, reclines femme-like with a blanket draped

101

over him. Moreover, Praunheim appears to parody the communal setting as he later did in *Horror Vacui*, the story of a sect brainwashed by Madame C (Lotti Huber) to believe in "optimal optimism." Most significantly, the cry to boycott parks, tearooms, and even bars seems absurd by today's standards of gay pride, where all varieties of sexual expression are not only accepted but flaunted.

Nonetheless, that these oddities were disregarded proves how radical its message must have been to the generation first watching it. As opposed to the predominant, admonishing voice-over heard earlier in the film (which by the close has petered out, exhausted), here criticism issues from a plurality of voices. It no longer comes from the outside but is self-motivated. To be sure, it echoes a number of problems previously uttered—the whorehouse atmosphere of the bars, the antipathy between queens and butches, the false ideals of eternal love and marriage—but what is new is the constructive call for erotic freedom and political organization. The names of anti-gay workplaces are to be publicized; blacks and women are to unite as oppressed minorities; gays now advocate joint action and fighting back. Important, too, is the developmental trajectory Daniel follows: he ends up in a consciousness-raising group rather than indulging in private shame, as the voice-over would have predicted.

The significance of *Nicht der Homosexuelle* lies in the debates it provoked but also in its place within Rosa von Praunheim's oeuvre. If one compares this film to the one that immediately preceded it, *Die Bettwurst*, the extent to which social role adaptation is ironically exaggerated becomes more apparent. The moments of frivolous camp gesture and dress in the *Schwulenfilm* can be more readily enjoyed as hilarious and subversive; even the stern voice-over seems over the top. In *Die Bettwurst* it is heterosexuality that is ironically performed. Von Praunheim's middle-aged aunt Luzi and the young, queer Dietmar Kracht become an unlikely couple that go into ecstasy about the most mundane aspects of their bourgeois lifestyle. Singing Zarah Leander's "Ich weiß, es wird einmal ein Wunder geschehen," Dietmar prances around the apartment vacuuming and goes into sexual convulsions while enjoying a shower. Luzi adores performing for the camera, constantly turning to it with a sparkle in her eye while she primps and preens. Announcing a trend that several of the director's later works will follow, the characters perform their own unbelievable lives: Dietmar was literally a member of a criminal gang, a detail that is integrated into the story. Luzi plays herself and films in her own apartment. Initially one might assume, given Rosa von Praunheim's penchant for autobiographical disclosure as well as for this rehearsal of the life narratives of his actors and actresses, that he ascribes to an expressive model of the self, in other words, believes that through display some interior truth about the self is revealed. Yet quite the opposite proves to be the case: theatricality is here not in the service of a self-finding. *Nicht der Homosexuelle*, too, emphatically mocks the biographical narrative as well as parodying the time-honored German genre of the *Bildungsroman*.

This pseudo-biographical mode—whereby a retracing of the conventional stations in a person's life is contrasted with a bizarre self-performance —continues through *Ich bin meine eigene Frau* and *Affengeil* to *Neurosia*, a film that resembles *Nicht der Homosexuelle* not only in these elements but additionally in its faux self-castigation. What these films from the early 1970s also share with von Praunheim's later gay rights documentaries, in particular his work on New York artists protesting AIDS, *Schweigen = Tod*, is a hyperbolic, stylized theatricality. Even after he was informed by the pathos of AIDS activism, von Praunheim never abandoned a distanced, Brechtian approach to gay issues. Perhaps most significantly, what continues from *Nicht der Homosexuelle* to today is his refusal to rehearse the coming-out narrative of life before and after the closet. This difference shows to what extent von Praunheim is a step ahead of most gay and lesbian American filmmakers leading up to the New Queer Cinema. American prime-time television, which outed its first leading gay character in May 1997 with *Ellen* (starring Ellen Degeneres), follows this earlier pattern of narrating a character's discovery or coming to terms with his or her sexuality. Daniel, by contrast, does not dwell on establishing that he is gay. He certainly never defends but does accept his sexual orientation. Another powerful instance in Rosa von Praunheim's works of this matter-of-fact attitude to sexual and gender nonconformity is *Ich bin meine eigene Frau*, the life story of the male-to-female transvestite Charlotte von Mahlsdorf.

'Ich bin meine eigene Frau'

Like the *Schwulenfilm*, *Ich bin meine eigene Frau* takes a chronological, biographical story line—this time of an actual person, the Berlin celebrity and lifelong cross-dresser Charlotte von Mahlsdorf—only to disrupt and complicate the narrative. Just as the 1971 film interjected various voices to accompany Daniel's chronicle, so here Charlotte comments on her own life as various actors reenact scenes from it. Often her doubles disrupt the cinematic illusion by discussing with her how events actually transpired. In other words, just as the voice-overs interpret and narrativize the homosexual, so too do these actors as well as Charlotte herself interpret and retell her past. By self-reflexively calling attention to the reconstruction of her story and thereby to the film as fabrication and manipulation, Rosa von Praunheim encourages the viewer to assess the dichotomy between naturalness and artifice, credibility and unbelievability, authenticity and theatricality in the person of this transvestite. Thus how the film represents, not just what it represents, becomes relevant to the issue of the representation of gender.

Throughout the film, Charlotte, who wears no makeup, little jewelry, and clothes no more fashionable than those of a homely grandmother, comments repeatedly on her inborn attraction to women's apparel and feminine way of being. Because she straightforwardly asserts her proclivities, she forestalls either any accusation of gender dysphoria or the temptation to treat her cross-dressing as camp. Given the blatant discrepancy with her biological sex, however, these comments raise a number of questions: In describing herself as a *weibliches Wesen*, a "feminine creature," does Charlotte essentialize femininity or unhinge it from the sole domain of women? Does she construct gender or appropriate and internalize it? Does her garb as dowdy old woman bespeak domesticity or sexual liberation? Is her cross-dressing innate or acquired, artless or studied? Does her dress constitute or express who she is? Given that Charlotte does not ironically distance herself from the mask, on what level can we invoke Judith Butler's notion of gender performance, not to mention high camp, in discussing this film? And are there differences between how Charlotte explains her life and how von Praunheim chooses to represent it, hence in how these questions might be answered?

Rosa von Praunheim's film follows many of the incidents Charlotte recounts in her autobiography by the same title (published in 1992), staging them as vignettes interspliced with Charlotte's own narration, either to the camera or in voice-over. The film begins with a youth (Jens Taschner) taking the S-Bahn to the Mahlsdorf suburb of Berlin, where he greets an older woman descending the steps of a villa. This is Charlotte, and the mansion is the Gründerzeit Museum, where she "lives like a woman from the turn of the century." After a few shots from the interior of this museum, the narration begins with the youth lovingly dusting and polishing furniture at the home of Charlotte's great uncle, where she was born as Lothar Berfelde in 1928. The next vignettes show the youth at an antique shop and anxiously witnessing the destruction of a Jewish home in 1942. Charlotte encourages the boy: "Yes, you played it exactly as it happened." Other early scenes include his trying on the gowns of Aunt Luise (herself a member of the "third sex," who gives her nephew Magnus Hirschfeld's *Die Transvestiten* to read), a tender romp with a farmhand in the hay, and ominous scenes that intimate the bullying, violent nature of his father. Indeed, in order to protect his mother, the

Figure 14. *Ich bin meine eigene Frau* (1992), Ichgola Androgyn, Jens Taschner, and Charlotte von Mahlsdorf. Courtesy of Rosa von Praunheim.

young Lothar was compelled to bludgeon his father to death, a crime for which he was psychiatrically evaluated and imprisoned. The Allied invasion sets the boy free, and we see how he makes his way home through the deserted, bombarded streets of Berlin.

In 1946 Charlotte moves into the destroyed Friedrichsfelde castle to try to restore it, at which point the next actor, Ichgola Androgyn (a favorite actor of Michael Brynntrup), steps in to inquire how she lived after the war—as man or woman. Subsequent scenes with Ichgola Androgyn include her being seduced by the elderly equestrian officer Herbert von Zitzenau (for whose household she served as a domestic and with whom she sustained an erotic friendship lasting several years), a scene in Elli's beer bar where the proprietor welcomes gays and lesbians, and the tearoom pickup and subsequent s/m role-playing with Jochen, her lover for 27 years. In the later episodes, which reenact her persecution by GDR officials (dismissal from the Märkisches Museum, the threat to tax and impound the belongings of her Gründerzeit Museum, an attempt to lure her into informing on other gays, and interrogation by a perplexed border guard), Charlotte plays herself, a calm, composed individual with disarmingly frank yet polite responses. In the final scenes we see her sharing meals with her lesbian housemates; visiting the grave of her mother, who died in 1991; reminiscing about her acting and consulting at the DEFA studios in Babelsberg; attending the première of Heiner Carow's *Coming Out* (which was on the night the Wall fell, November 9, 1989); and remembering the vicious Neonazi attack on the first joint East-West gay and lesbian gathering. The film ends with her curtsying to applause on her receiving the *Bundesverdienstkreuz*, the Cross of the Order of Merit, in 1992.[14]

Of necessity the cinematic version omits much of the fascinating detail Charlotte recounts in her book. Yet as recompense we amply get to see "Lottchen" herself, her friends, and the interior of her museum. The film repeatedly draws attention to how it must metonymically represent events from her life, thus its awareness of documentary limits. The destruction of the Jewish household is rendered only insofar as a few belongings are dashed onto the street at night as the antique dealer and his apprentice wend their way home. The murder of the father is visually anticipated as he undresses before bed, with a cut to Lothar sneaking down the hall to a kitchen cupboard. The bombing of Berlin is represented with sirens and exploding shells on the soundtrack, while the youth runs down a deserted street. The skins' attack is likewise only represented through their foreboding approach to Mahlsdorf. This avoidance of violence and melodrama matches well Charlotte's own stoic calmness (her lips are usually drawn in a taut line, emphasizing her determined jaw), as well as the composed pacing of her autobiography. Both Charlotte and her director let the gravity of the situation suggest itself without embellishment, a restraint not appreciated in the press, which regrets that "even the most remarkable, shocking key scenes of her life in the role-playing episodes hardly emit atmosphere or 'move' the spectator" (*Magnus* 4.11 [1992]: 79).

The breaking of the melodramatic illusion is also foregrounded by the introduction of the two actors playing Charlotte before they assume their roles. As noted, the film begins with Jens Taschner riding the train to Mahlsdorf, establishing the real-life frame into which the reenactment is set. The vignettes are interrupted by Lottchen's encouragement to her actors and their questioning of her motivations. This Brechtian alienation technique is especially startling when the character playing the father drops his brutal facade to talk with Charlotte about her parents, again effectively dispelling suspense. On another occasion it is not the narrative that is suspended but the frame, as a bell rings calling Ichgola Androgyn away from Charlotte to enter his role-playing with Herbert von Zitzenau. This fanciful alteration between frame and story, fiction and reality, Charlotte and her incarnations (including herself in the later recreations) functions to rob the documentary of its generic seriousness, even pretentiousness. Ironically commenting on the documentary format of the interview, the film likewise fabricates a series of interviews or interrogations with so-called authorities—with the Nazi psychiatrist, East German border police, and Stasi spies.

Similar to its subversion of documentary conventions is the film's thwarting of the spectator's purient, voyeuristic desires. In the two early scenes at Aunt Luise's home, for instance, Lothar is caught off guard by his aunt looking on, first when trying on her clothes and then when undressed with the farm boy. Yet the aunt foils her role as our scopophilic stand-in insofar as she immediately voices her respect for Lothar's privacy. To the same effect, the self-consciously staged scenes of sexual role-playing with Herbert and Jochen tease with a pornographic subject matter that fails to ratify pornography's claim to "real, live" sex or satisfy what Linda Williams calls "the frenzy of the visible." Herbert takes photographs of "Charlotte," revealing her male genitalia under a woman's dress, but her penis remains limp. The black-and-white photos inserted into the diegesis, moreover, are not as one might expect, Charlotte's originals; they were taken of Ichgola Androgyn with Rosa von Praunheim's camera. These photos are thus copies of the actor copying Charlotte, thereby holding the pornographic investment in actuality at double remove. The spanking scene with Jochen is likewise tame and untittilating, with Charlotte herself matter-of-factly bending over fully clothed to show Ichgola Androgyn what position to take. Charlotte's subsequent admission that she and Jochen stayed together 27 years further domesticizes and renders harmless the s/m games. Despite the campy, mechanical acting, Rosa von Praunheim mutes the spectacle and insists on the anti-sensationalist character of this cross-dresser. In these reenacted scenes he toys with the promise of erotica while withholding its delivery, a double strategy foreign to the autobiography, whose most suggestive photo is an old workbench with a couple of bamboo canes and straps lying on it.

Besides deflating pornographic expectations, these scenes also erode what a documentary on a "queer" is generally purported to uncover, namely, the "truth" of a person, which Foucault has underscored is taken to reside in his or her sexuality. The elaborate casting, editing, soundtrack, and narrative raise in fact the uneasy suspicion that perhaps too much control is being exercised in this film, in the sense not that a fakeness or artifice overwhelms Charlotte's story but, quite the opposite, that this constructed complexity is designed to hide her from too close scrutiny. Charlotte's unusual and admirable life raises more questions than the film (or the autobiography, for that matter) is prepared to answer. Indeed, if for much of her adult life Char-

lotte von Mahlsdorf has been a public persona—giving museum tours, organizing the East German gay movement, playing parts in the East German
film industry—then it is not inconceivable that she masquerades here again
for the camera.

We are not allowed to forget that *Ich bin meine eigene Frau* is not cinéma
vérité, and that what we see revealed is selective. If Rosa von Praunheim as
filmmaker re-produces Charlotte's life (even though her own voice narrates
and hence gives approval to the representation), the director through the
antimimetic framing devices points to the derivative nature of his work. By
borrowing or lifting from this other person's tale, he acknowledges that he
cannot represent the original. In fact, most of von Praunheim's work plays
ingeniously with this discrepancy between biography and fictional performance, between authenticity and fabrication. *Die Bettwurst* stages the most improbable marriage, thereby mocking the heterosexual institution; separately,
however, Luzi Kryn and Dietmar Kracht act out their own personalities and
histories. *Die Stadt der verlorenen Seelen* is little more than a vehicle for a
group of transvestites to parade themselves through dance and song within a
loosely concocted narrative about the employees at a "Burger Queen" restaurant. At its première the film was not even watched by the audience but
accompanied a party where the celebrating actors again could star as themselves. *Anita: Tänze des Lasters* juxtaposes the contemporary story of an elderly woman, played by Lotti Huber, who imagines being the famous 1920s
nightclub artist Anita Berber with expressionistic scenes from Berber's decadent bisexual life, here enacted by Ina Blum (who also played Dorothee in
Treut's *Die Jungfrauenmaschine*). And whereas *Ich bin meine eigene Frau* recasts
scenes from Charlotte's biography with actors, *Neurosia* fictionalizes Rosa
von Praunheim's death in order to interview real people who knew him.

Given the highly self-reflexive, constructed nature of *Ich bin meine eigene
Frau*, then, the question arises of how this intricacy pertains to the issues of
gender performance in the person of Charlotte. To what degree is she likewise self-conscious and to what extent is she active in constructing her gender? Moreover, how do the theatrical reenactments work in counterpoint to
Charlotte's own transvestism? In what respects does Charlotte stage herself
and, if her acting is subversive, then what is she parodying?

On several occasions, Charlotte emphatically announces her femininity.
For instance, she explains to Ichgola Androgyn that she is a "feminine being
in a masculine body"; with Jochen she could be "a real woman." Her deci-
sions are wisely governed by "feminine reserve" and around older men she
feels "protected the way women do." All these statements are presented assertively and unironically, suggesting that her feminine tendencies are neither

an anomaly nor a performance. It would be incorrect, however, to conclude that Charlotte assumes there is an essential, unchanging, ahistorical quality called "femininity." First, by declaring "I am my own woman" she stresses the unique, individual way in which she is a woman. Second, by appropriating the feminine, she unhinges it from being something essentially attributable to women. Third, by averring that she is an exact replica of her mother and that her mother lives on in her daughter, Charlotte takes as her model not all women but specifically her mother. By also identifying with her great-uncle, she further prevents one from categorizing by gender what was formative in her personal development. It should also be noted that unlike the popular conception of the drag queen, the image of femininity to which she adheres is not flamboyant or exaggerated but restrained and even domestic, and her domesticity is not a role to which she is resigned or condemned but one she openly chooses. She additionally specifies and historicizes what she understands by femininity by identifying with a type of woman at the turn of the century; and in her sexual role-playing with Herbert von Zitzenau she acts out and thereby parodies class differences in tandem with gendered ones.[15] In other words, she confirms Judith Butler's statement that "there is no one femininity with which to identify, which is to say that femininity might itself offer an array of identificatory sites" (*Bodies That Matter*, 239).

The ease with which Charlotte sits in her own femininity prevents one from pathologizing or psychoanalyzing her case, a significant distinction considering the medical discourse that arose around the transvestite precisely during the period to which Charlotte is otherwise drawn. Given that the voice-off Nazi doctor questioning the youth after the murder of Berfelde senior is mocked (the child does not even know what "sexual intercourse" means), any other attempt to interrogate Charlotte's life psychologically risks being equally off-track. Despite the fact that the Oedipal fantasy of patricide comes true, both film and book dwell neither on any subconscious motivation for the killing nor on any possible effects on Lothar's later development. The only indirect, yet unelaborated connection the film makes between the violent filial bond and Charlotte's later life is that the child receives from the father a bare-bottom spanking for playing with dolls. The film leaves unexplored whether the child takes a subversive delight in the punishment or whether the later s/m games are a working through of this childhood trauma. Despite the biographical narrative, *Ich bin meine eigene Frau* thus resists launching into a confession, especially not one confided to the spectator as psychoanalyst. Just as Charlotte conserves and preserves the past at her museum, so too she protects her own privacy. Hence there are no photos of her earlier life inserted into the film as one would expect from a biographical documentary. Conse-

109

quently, the spectator is left to challenge why he or she would presume Charlotte to be responsible for telling everything.

With such considerations it is clear that Charlotte's investment in drag is
neither naive nor unreflecting, despite the absence of apparent psychological
motivation, the lack of camp, as well as her essentialist claim to femininity.
Her gender performance is artfully unselfconscious. For the most part, the
film displaces theatrical, deliberately stilted masquerade onto the other actors. Yet it must also be noted that Charlotte does drag as well in the films she
starred in, in her previous sexual role-playing, and when she dons a wig to attend parties. The division between veracity and masquerade blurs even more
once mapped onto the stereotypical documentary claim to tell the "truth"
about the past, to reveal how things "really" were, for here bygone reality unveils itself precisely as masquerade. Nor is the by-now-deconstructed opposition between authenticity and performance, truth and costume applied to a
separation between straight and gay, as indicated when the father pulls on his
Nazi uniform with its tall leather boots: the film suggests that there are much
less innocent ways for people to dress than in women's clothing.

In the wake of Judith Butler's writings on gender performance, it is frequently assumed that drag is automatically subversive of gender limitations,
a site for critical agency insofar as it "disputes heterosexuality's claim on naturalness and originality" (*Bodies That Matter*, 125). Butler herself, though, has
cautioned: "What has been understood as the performativity of gender—far
from the exercise of an unconstrained voluntarism—will prove to be impossible apart from notions of such political constraints registered physically"
(94). She questions, moreover, "whether parodying the dominant norms is
enough to displace them; indeed, whether the denaturalization of gender
cannot be the very vehicle for a reconsolidation of hegemonic norms" (125).
The question arises whether Charlotte von Mahlsdorf's cross-dressing, because it is unironic, serves effectively to parody reiterated, reified gender
norms. In other words, does she sufficiently denaturalize what one assumes
to be a man or a woman?

Given the historical contexts in which Charlotte has lived unconventionally as a transvestite and as an unconventional transvestite, it seems that these
questions are limited in their ability to address her wider political activity, if
the aim in posing them in the first place is to examine individual agency and
potential political contestation in drag. Following in the steps of the autobiography, the film *Ich bin meine eigene Frau* repeatedly shows how successive
regimes—National Socialism, the German Democratic Republic, and, most
recently through the Treuhand reappropriation of East German property,
the Federal Republic of Germany—have destroyed or threatened to rob

Charlotte von Mahlsdorf as well as other citizens (such as the Jews during the Third Reich) of their homes and belongings. Here Charlotte's steadfastness and determination, coupled with flexibility and ingenuity in improvisation, are exemplary; rather than have the East German government confiscate the museum and its holdings, she royally gives them away to the visitors. Her political subversiveness is much more detailed in the autobiography, where, for instance, she recounts the East German sell-off of antiques for Western currency and how she competently strove to prevent it, whereby her actions indict both Communist and capitalist greed.

She has endeavored to rescue the past in her curatorial capacity, and also with regard to documenting and transmitting the history of the third sex as well as gay life in the GDR. Her unique story and the lives with which she has intersected serve to highlight the many differences within both the gay and transvestite communities in Berlin. Moreover, the degree to which Charlotte can make the claim to being "her own" person in a society that levels individuality in favor of collectivity can be considered an insurrection. Thus Charlotte's gender disruption (which I do not want to diminish) needs to be seen as part of a larger resistance to social conventions and oppressions, a courageous insubordination through queer social visibility in the forms of gay activism, sexual nonconformity, personal allegiances in the face of harassment, and commitment to historical preservation. These engagements go significantly beyond a deconstruction of the "illusion of an abiding gendered self" (Butler, "Performing Acts," 270), where much American queer theorizing on drag has remained focused.

The very best of Rosa von Praunheim's work is engaged precisely in this queer visibility, where the gendered and sexually unconventional subject is placed center stage, such that his/her presence becomes an affront to the bourgeois status quo and an encouragement to all queers. When von Praunheim can capture the political edge to this histrionics his work excels; without it his movies run the danger of seeping into self-indulgence and silliness, as in *Stadt der verlorenen Seelen* or even *Neurosia*. Two of his most complex works, *Nicht der Homosexuelle* and *Ich bin meine eigene Frau*, problematize the very advocacy of visibility, though, by demonstrating that visibility also serves as a disguise; the scintillating masquerade hides more than it puts on show. Charlotte's seemingly trite, cliched statements about femininity and its gentility screen the complexity of her constructed femininity and coyly divert attention from her nonconformist sexual role-playing. And in their theatricality and constant interruption the reenactments from her life testify to the illusion of biographical confession. In *Nicht der Homosexuelle* the discourse

111

that outs and shames the homosexual, that makes him painfully visible, paradoxically makes him all the more unreadable. The wooden acting and cool, withdrawn camerawork likewise conceal rather than display the homosexual. The spectator, moreover, resists the stereotyping. Perplexing its audience, the film generated an entire national gay movement that tried to define the homosexual and the situation in which he lives.

This dialectic between an ornate visibility and subtle concealment lies, of course, at the crux of allegory. To repeat: by isolating the image, allegory gives the impression of clarity and precision despite its semantic obscurity. Through its visual sharpness it pretends to open, direct statement. In actuality, though, it calls attention to oblique signification and threatens illegibility. Allegory's theatricality both cloaks and unveils. Rosa von Praunheim's films may not share in the allegorical, baroque optic surfeit of Ulrike Ottinger nor in the esoteric, operatic allusions of Werner Schroeter. He does not restage the medieval passion play, as does Ottinger in *Freak Orlando*, Schroeter in *Der Rosenkönig*, or Michael Stock in *Prinz in Hölleland*. But he does explore the realm of ornate, bizarre desires and selects the physiognomically strangest and most striking actors for his roles. Most important, he allegorically hollows out the biographical narrative—as in *Neurosia* actually hiding himself from view in a cellar and substituting for his presence excerpts from his films and diaries as well as snippets of mock interviews with friends and relatives. Yet again, as in *Nicht der Homosexuelle*, Rosa von Praunheim demonstrates the futility of one's presuming to read the homosexual: he and his characters remain just too queer.

four

"The Passionate Evidence" of Werner Schroeter's *Maria Malibran* and *Der Rosenkönig*

Despite his prolific output and scintillating vision, Werner Schroeter's films were poorly distributed upon their release, only rarely rebroadcast on German television, and subsequently never reached video circulation in the States. They are unjustly among the least known in the New German Cinema. Only in France have his films been consistently reviewed and lauded, one his most ardent fans having been Michel Foucault. This uniquely francophone recognition extends to the present: at the 1996 première in Lausanne of his latest work, *Poussières d'amour / Abfallprodukte der Liebe*, Schroeter was awarded the prestigious *pardo d'honneur* for his entire oeuvre, which at the time was comprised of thirty films and forty-two theater and opera performances. But if Schroeter's cinema, occupying, as Ulrike Sieglohr puts it, "a transitional space between avant-garde and art cinema, neither quite narrative, nor quite abstract" ("Excess Yearning," 197), has not attracted a wide public, nonetheless has been intensely admired by other German filmmakers. It has aroused both adoration and jealousy from such auteurs as Rainer Werner Fassbinder, Wim Wenders, and Rosa von Praunheim. Over the years Schroeter collaborated with a number of directors of this generation (he was born, like Fassbinder and Wenders, in 1945): Fassbinder's *Beware of a Holy Whore* (1971), for instance, opens with Schroeter nonchalantly narrating a silly anecdote. While they traded off actresses in their experimental films, Schroeter and von Praunheim worked and travelled together in the late sixties and early seventies. In addition, like von Praunheim and Monika Treut, he frequently relied on Elfi Mikesch as camerawoman. The gay world of German cinema is a close but prolific and diversified one.

Given such intersections it is ironic that the issue of gay politics publicly divided these filmmakers in the late seventies. In a notorious article that appeared in *Filmkritik* in 1979 entitled "With Fond Greetings to Champagne-Schroeter," Rosa von Praunheim attacked his devoted friend for not openly acknowledging his homosexuality and refusing to take an activist stance in the gay movement. Werner Schroeter had declined to sign a coming-out declaration for the magazine *Stern*, according to von Praunheim, "with the smug reply that *Stern* wasn't serious enough for him. He much preferred the tidbits of gossip in the same periodical" (quoted in Rentschler, *West German Filmmakers*, 194). Continuing his sarcasm, von Praunheim took his fellow filmmaker to task for his cliches about gay pederasts, aging prostitutes, crazed mothers, and the courageous poor in his recently released *Neapolitanische Geschwister* (*Kingdom of Naples*). Apparently, while posturing as sympathetic to the lower classes, Schroeter would finish "his shooting with champagne and caviar" (193).

In the ensuing debacle over these accusations, Fassbinder jumped to Schroeter's defense in an eloquent homage, which in turn was the occasion for devastating, sardonic comments on other filmmakers. About Schroeter himself, Fassbinder wrote that he would "in years to come assume a place in film history similar to one I would describe in literature as somewhere between Novalis, Lautréamont, and Louis Ferdinand Céline. . . . [He] has been graced with a much clearer and more comprehensive gaze onto this globe that we call earth than anyone else who produces art, no matter what kind. And just a little bit, it seems to me, this fortunate and privileged soul has access to strange and marvelous secrets of the universe" (196–97). The praise continued in a listing of directors who, according to Fassbinder, borrowed from Schroeter, including Daniel Schmid, Ulrike Ottinger, and, above all, Hans-Jürgen Syberberg. The latter Fassbinder declared a pilferer, a "trafficker in matters of plagiarism" and "a quite resourceful Schroeter-imitator" (198). As to Rosa von Praunheim, "he actually thinks he alone has the right, a monopoly of sorts, to use the medium film to reflect his own or whoever else's homosexuality" (199).

The soap-opera scandal unleashed by von Praunheim's typically provocative accusations thus not only pulled a number of leading German filmmakers into a debate but outed the problem in the New German Cinema of its frequently hushed gay voice. Although Fassbinder refused to pick up the gauntlet and address cinematic gay representation, von Praunheim did raise pressing questions about cinematic closeting and gay cliches. For Schroeter's silence is symptomatic of larger issues: it poses the question of the New German Cinema's engagement in and commitment to gay representation and therefore of how to read (for) homosexuality in its films. The same queries apply specifically to Schroeter's oeuvre: Can he be labeled a gay director, independent of his sexual orientation, and what would that categorization mean or entail? Does his refusal to come out publicly have a bearing on homosexuality in his films? Does Rosa von Praunheim have the right to read a blatantly negative portrayal of a homosexual (as "fat and disgusting," trying "to fondle a little boy") as "a demonstration of [Schroeter's] homosexual self-hatred" (193)? Since such a cliched representation is alone reprehensible, what is gained and what is at stake when a director's life (or others' perception of it) is confused with his art? On a different note, what is the result of comparing Schroeter to Rosa von Praunheim, who directly confronted gay issues and the tensions between the self-representation and the societal image of gays in 1971 in *Nicht der Homosexuelle ist pervers*? Can Schroeter then be said to be unconcerned with any sort of recognizable, that is, out gay dimension to his work? Do we see here an aestheticism divorced from gay identity politics? Or is von Praunheim untrue to Schroeter in focusing on this one gay character? Ultimately, how can one take his attack as a challenge to read same-sex desires in Schroeter differently?

Schroeter's own statements linking homosexuality, beauty, identity, and ideology are illuminating for how he undermines the commonplace separation of sexual politics from aesthetic ideals. In his discussion with Foucault, for instance, Schroeter asserts "I've said it since my childhood: for me, it's an advantage to be gay because it's beautiful" (quoted in Courant, 43). And in an interview with Daniel Schmid he candidly associates being gay with yet another quality that again has little to do with a core sexual identity, or even with sexual activity or predilection: "For me homosexuality is absolutely not a psychological fact, but rather a social reaction against a materialist environment" (*Werner Schroeter*, 60). For Schroeter, sexual normalcy is an anathema to the artist struggling in all other respects against the social system. Homosexuality is less an innate predisposition than a conscious rejection of heterosexuality. Sexual preference itself thus becomes a political and aesthetic statement, and moreover is an issue that, pace Rosa von Praunheim, Schroeter is not shy to address in the public, printed forum.

Schroeter's reflections on the tie between homosexuality and art, however, offer few keys to unlocking the workings of same-sex desires in his films. For instance, the erotic gazes between women (as in *Der Tod der Maria Malibran* or *Willow Springs*) or the use of transvestites (such as Candy Darling in *Der Tod der Maria Malibran*) hardly serve the sole or primary purpose of affronting the bourgeois status quo. Equally restrictive would be von Praunheim's exclusive focus on what he perceives to be gay stereotypes. Nor would Schroeter's own sexuality serve to explain the predominantly sapphic relations in his work. More fundamental, it seems to me, is how Schroeter breaks apart a conception of normative identity through an ecstatic passion that ruptures and deterritorializes the individual: the question then to be raised is why this passion is frequently encoded as queer.

Schroeter's cinema abounds in histrionic affects and fragmented signs of an intense yet unnamable passion that, because it dares not speak its name, already whispers queerness. From his earliest work in 8mm on Maria Callas (1968) to *Abfallprodukte der Liebe* Schroeter has been fascinated by opera's ability to give voice to illicit passions.[1] With its campy acting, exaggerated miming, and lipsynching to a constantly changing soundtrack, as well as with extended poses and long shot durations, Schroeter's production appears manneristically Romantic. Throughout his years of filmmaking, Schroeter has maintained a fascination with exoticism and emotional exaltation—from his roots in experimental, low-budget, underground filmmaking (including *Neurasia* [1969], *Eika Katappa* [1969], *Der Bomberpilot* [1970], and *Salome* [1970]) to more pronouncedly narrative films (*Neapolitanische Geschwister* [1978], *Palermo oder Wolfsburg* [1979], *Der Rosenkönig* [*The King of the Roses*] [1986], and *Malina* [1991]).[2] In this cinema the possibility of a coherent, communicable selfhood—the linchpin of bourgeois ideology—dissolves, with ecstasy taking its place as an antithetical state into which one falls. The mesmerized same-sex gazes of Schroeter's characters, held in suspension by his immobile camera, alongside postsynchronized soundtracks pieced together from pop kitsch as well as Callas's unfettered pathos, bear witness to and instigate a queer transport that disarticulates individuality. The excess and nonconformity of a passion addressed to a member of one's own sex bespeaks a revolutionary intransigence that unhinges social and cinematic norms. Schroeter, moreover, expresses these same-sex desires "deviantly," that is, through silent, allegorical articulation.

The Schroeterian gesture, through its exaggeration bordering on camp, sets up an implicit dichotomy with what the gesture can deflect away from or hide—namely, an interiority. Thus how an interiority would be infused or informed by sexuality (and consequently how homosexuality could come to be seen as a distinguishing mark of one's identity) carries little interest for Schroeter. As opposed to the prevalent ideal of portraying a personage or character with psychological depth on the screen, Schroeter's actors move in a fantasmatic world of operatic gesture, manneristic excess, and the allegorical display of affect. Indeed, the dichotomy between a transparent interiority and an enigmatic surface characterizes the difference in signifying potential between symbol and allegory. Developing this dualism further, Foucault compliments Schroeter on his ability "[to abandon] entirely the psychological film" and to present instead the visual signifiers of "bodies, faces, lips, eyes." What comes into play is "a sort of passionate evidence" that, unlike Bergman's films, for instance, does not try to excavate what is happening between characters. As Foucault puts it, "you've lost your way in life, in your writing, in your filmmaking, precisely when you want to interrogate the nature of the identity of something. Then you've missed the mark [c'est loupé], because you enter into classifications." The task of the artist is not to name but to lend "a coloration, form, and intensity" (quoted in Courant, 44). Although Foucault is talking about creativity in general and not about sexual identity in particular, nonetheless his observations could be deployed in an understanding of what homosexuality in Schroeter's films is not ("the nature of [one's] identity" or a "classification") and where it possibly could be gleaned instead (in the "passionate evidence" of "faces, lips, eyes").

Although Schroeter's films resist an investigation of the psychological motivation of his characters, they do invite the sensitivities of psychoanalysis, as a conceptually different kind of study that attends to the level of the symptom. The symptom, like allegory, operates on the plane of the hermetic signifier; it is a kind of clue or index that the economic transactions or circuitry of the psyche are at work. Yet it resists an archeological probing of the unconscious, which remains hidden, unknowable, or, as the word itself suggests, inaccessible to consciousness. As Slavoj Žižek defines the symptom, it is "a particular, 'pathological,' signifying formation, a binding of enjoyment, an inert stain resisting communication and interpretation, a stain which cannot be included in the circuit of discourse, of social bond network, but is at the same time a positive condition of it" (*Sublime Object*, 75). It is not surprising that Schroeter refers to authors such as Novalis and Lautréamont (as Fassbinder does writing on him), who also were obsessed with the oneiric stage and its hieroglyphic, circuitous signification. In Schroeter's cinema, as Foucault intimates, it is not the interior of the heart or mind that is brought to light, in the sense that the identity, past, ambitions, or drives of an individual are revealed. Rather, the exterior emerges as impenetrable yet scintillating surface or enigmatic visual gesture (his characters rarely utter a word or, when they do, frequently chant the same phrase, turning it into a quotation). Schroeter's is a cinema of pure, external signs or symptoms without an etiology.[3]

It is not surprising, given his fascination with pageantry, that this filmmaker increasingly worked as a director of theater and opera, from Kleist's *Kätchen von Heilbronn* and Lessing's *Emilia Galotti* to Wagner's *Lohengrin*. Spectacle, as representation of an exterior, appeals to Schroeter for all its optical splendor, artificiality, stylization, and ultimately banality. The purpose of the rest of this chapter will be to examine how this theatrical, fantasmatic, hallucinatory universe with its stylized, allegorical "passionate evidence" of "lips and eyes" is linked to the envisaging and revisioning of queer desires. I shall look primarily at a work that Schroeter took to be his best, *Der Tod der Maria Malibran* (1971), the first in a trilogy of films on the love, suffering, and death of women, including *Willow Springs* (1972–73) and *Flocons d'or / Goldflocken* (1975–76) (which will also be drawn into discussion). The chapter then concludes with a study of *Der Rosenkönig* (1986), Schroeter's most explicit film to date on male-male desire. Whereas *Der Rosenkönig* can serve as an example of Schroeter's more narrative films after 1978, *Der Tod der Maria Malibran* exemplifies his earlier discontinuous, epiphanic style of filmmaking.

'Der Tod der Maria Malibran'

Born in 1808 in Paris, Maria Malibran was one of the nineteenth century's greatest mezzo-sopranos. She studied under her father, the tenor Manuel Garcia, who trained her mercilessly. In her book, *Opera, or the Undoing of Women*, Catherine Clément recounts how in Malibran's story biography and role, art and life, intertwine. At the age of fifteen Maria Malibran sang Desdemona opposite the Otello of her father in Rossini's rendition, afraid that, should she not meet his vocal demands, he truly would strangle her in the final scene (29). Schroeter takes such mythicization to produce a film that tells less about the life of Malibran than about devotion, subjugation, and the ecstasy of the voice. Indeed, Maria Malibran, whose range commanded three octaves, provided the ultimate Romantic narrative of art and death. Clément writes that "she died young, at twenty-eight. She had a riding accident and was wounded in the head. That very evening she played in Bellini's *La Somnambule*. For one last time she was sublime, wearing makeup and a wig that hid her bruises, in a role where the torpor of her injuries strengthened the strange, hallucinated aspect of the young girl who sings in her sleep. Then she lost her voice, and finally her sight. Six months later, still singing, in spite of everything, she died" (30). According to Schroeter, the final, fatal song was from Rossini's *Semiramide* (1823), which the soundtrack to *Der Tod der Maria Malibran* replays in a version with Maria Callas. In their introduction to *En Travesti: Women, Gender, Subversion, Opera*, editors Corinne Blackmer and Patricia Juliana Smith select *Semiramide* as their classic example of the female-to-male cross-dressing genre that provides Romantic intrigue between two women and hence a luxurious mingling of female voices. Queen Semiramide of Babylon falls in love, unbeknownst to her, with her own son, Arsace, a role composed for the mezzo-soprano. In the final act she is slain by Arsace while trying to protect him. Schroeter, as will be seen, extends this deadly, passionate longing for one's own sex to make it the ruling conceit of his film.

Other tales about Maria Malibran suggest that a queer sexuality was not restricted to her stage characters. In *The Queen's Throat*, Wayne Koestenbaum quotes the diva as saying: "I never feel the slightest desire [for men]. . . . I feel such disgust!" She asks her husband for a separation with the explanation: "I think a theatrical life demands a great deal of calm and the life of a virgin which is what suits me perfectly *I am very happy as I am now*" (100). Koestenbaum also recounts that "audiences speculated that Maria Malibran was not anatomically a woman, but an androgyne or hermaphrodite—an aberrant physique to match her voice's magic power" (104). She would often sing male parts and is known for her Otello as well as Desdemona. Morever she inspired queer desires, with her most illustrious admirer being Georges Sand, who, Terry Castle writes, "first assumed her sleek top-hatted costume . . . precisely in order to procure cheap standing-room tickets (available only to men) at the Théâtre des Italiens where Malibran was performing" (26). In her history of how famous divas inspired homoerotic emotion, Castle notes that Sand wrote her husband in 1831 after abandoning him: "I saw Madame Malibran in *Otello*. She made me weep, shudder, and suffer as though I had been watching a scene from real life. This woman is the foremost genius of Europe, as lovely as a Raphael madonna, simple, energetic, naive, she's the foremost singer and foremost tragedian. I'm mad about her." In addition, Malibran inspired the writer's short story, *La Prima Donna*, as well as, Castle suggests, her love affair with the actress Marie Dorval, "who bore a striking resemblance to the Spanish singer. . . . There is more than a little hint that she wished to recreate in the flesh the idealized passion for Malibran."

Schroeter's *Der Tod der Maria Malibran* concerns itself with such acting out of idealized passion. With its predominantly black backdrop and painted sets, the film presents a dark stage on which the artificiality of the opera, the fictional creations of the imagination, and same-sex ardor are paraded. It is broken into three sections: the first sequence shows isolated shots of rhapsodic, strangely agonizing women in love; the middle section tells a harrowing tale of a winter journey; while the concluding part elliptically enacts the passionate death of Maria Malibran.

"THE EYES"

To the music of Brahms's *Alto Rhapsody* (a setting of Goethe's Sturm-und-Drang poem "Harzreise im Winter"), *Der Tod der Maria Malibran* begins with a closeup of a woman's face from whose right eye is drawn away a sharp instrument.[4] As blood streams down her face, the woman holds one hand over the left eye. Then her other hand gently covers the bleeding eye, as if to protect the wounded organ. Together with the enucleation the hands compound the impairment of vision. Brahms's rich, chromatic harmonies and the sonorous, opulent alto voice underscore the discrepancy between sound and im-

119

age, hearing and seeing, hence further point to the theme of blindness. Later in the film, in the middle section entitled "Federico Garcia: The Father of Maria Malibran," the story behind the blinding is revealed. An androgynous young woman, cross-dressed in a type of Robin Hood outfit with pants and feathered cap (Christine Kaufmann), wanders over wintry mountains to Eisenstadt. Just as in "Harzreise im Winter," where the wanderer is swallowed up by an inimical nature and the pathway loses itself in the bushes, here too the snow, forest, and loneliness threaten the young woman. On her way, she meets a mysterious top-hatted man named Hugo (Magdelena Montezuma, who otherwise primarily plays Malibran). Once the two seem hopelessly lost in the woods, Hugo demands in exchange for a piece of bread the woman's eye. The knife then gouges both the loaf and the orb; however, true to the fairytale setting and costuming, at the end of this sequence the woman jumps for joy at miraculously having her eyesight restored.

This severed relation between cause and effect, motivation and consequence, is characteristic of the metonymic disjuncture that pervades the rest of the film with its enigmatic, scattered tableaux. The image of the blood-stained cheek and injured eye at the start of the film raises questions that are thus barely answered by this later episode: What is the reason for the blinding? Is it a sacrifice or punishment, and what for? Or does it function as a symptom, "an inert stain resisting communication and interpretation"? What will the spectator or the characters see or not see as the film progresses? Does the blinding lead to an inner revelation? Does it signify a different, cinematic vision? The subsequent series of shots—variations and recombinations of the same scenario of one woman gazing at another woman or two women gazing at each other—underscore the primacy of the optical theme in the rest of the film, yet in so doing reconfirm the urgency of these questions.

First an intertitle announces that the problematics of the gaze have everything to do with a blind passion. Schroeter reprints Heinrich Heine's "Der Asra" from the collection *Romanzero*, a poem that tells of a pale slave dying of love: "Und mein Stamm sind jene Asra, / Welche sterben, wenn sie lieben" ("And my tribe are the Asra, who die once they love"). The Romantic theme of *Liebestod* is taken up as well in *Der Rosenkönig*, again in fairytale and epithet-like fashion at the beginning, as a voice-over states, "when two children kiss without being able to speak, one of them must die." In *Der Rosenkönig* the two "children," one of them the son of the Magdalena Montezuma character, are young men who fall in love. Thus in the context of Schroeter's films, Heine's deadly love intimates one forbidden not by class or racial differences but by the norms of heterosexuality. This ill-fated homoerotic attraction evokes the opening line from the poem "Tristan" by one of Heine's contemporaries, August von Platen (though ironically, given that Heine publicly taunted von Platen for his homosexuality): "Wer die Schönheit angeschaut mit Augen, / Ist dem Tode schon anheimgegeben" ("Whoever looks upon beauty is already given over to death"). In *Der Tod der Maria Malibran*, censored same-sex love expresses itself paradoxically by the very absence of its utterance: lips move but do not form words. Unable to rely on its naming, this gesticular love speaks through the eyes, which, as von Platen's poem suggests, are themselves the messengers of death. As Corrigan describes *Der Tod der Maria Malibran*, its "facial poses textually crystallize the expressive look itself as a deathly pale brilliance, a kind of death mask, born on the edge of darkness" ("On the Edge of History," 15).

Against a black backdrop and the continuing entreaty of Brahms's plaintive lines, "O who will heal the pains?" ("Ach wer heilet die Schmerzen?"), Magdalena Montezuma, in Biedermeier dress, lifts her eyes to gaze at another woman wearing a low-cut gown, who in her weight and harsh, made-up features signals the transvestite (Manuela Riva). As Magdalena Montezuma raises lips to this face, the other woman opens her mouth as if to lipsynch but without any attempt at matching the soundtrack. (Later her voice indeed proves to be male.) Not only is the ear confused but, because of the drag deception, the eye as well. The next take is a close-up of two faces in profile, proximate but not looking directly at each other: the one is the transvestite, while the other looks androgynous. The third is a medium shot of two women with long hair, eyes downcast in melancholy. One of them turns, touching her own face as if trying to contain her rapture at the sight of the other. The subsequent takes are recombinations of these paired women, displayed either in adoration of each other or kissing.[5] Do these women desire each other or inflame an unspecified longing by mirroring their ardor in each other?

The presence of the transvestite clearly signals queerness and complicates the designation of this passion as exclusively lesbian. Indecision about gender and sexual affiliations is in fact the objective here: if Manuela Riva betrays her male sex, another transvestite passes impeccably—Andy Warhol's Candy Darling, who later sings the songs "Ramona" and "Saint Louis Woman." This male-to-female drag casts the female actors (Magdalena Montezuma, Christine Kaufmann, Ingrid Caven, Annette Tirier) as engaged in a similar feminine masquerade with their makeup, gowns, and exaggerated Romantic affects.[6] Here the operatic and Biedermeier dress—tokens of artistic sensibility and bourgeois culture—mesh with a touch of camp, though not in the sense that burlesque or parody take over. Rather than maintaining a self-conscious distance from the roles they play, Schroeter's best actresses, Magdalena Montezuma and Carla Aulaulu,[7] are known, like the divas Maria Mal-

Figure 15. *Der Tod der Maria Malibran* (1971), with Christine Kaufmann, Magdalena Montezuma, and Candy Darling. Courtesy of the Fotoarchiv, Stiftung Deutsche Kinemathek, Berlin.

ibran and Maria Callas, for throwing themselves into the roles they assume, as if their transport came in merging with their histrionic presentation. Schroeter's "camp" is here performed in avant-garde high seriousness—verging, however, because of the long, often motionless shots, on the edge of trivialization and lethargy.[8] Schroeter himself said of the mutual relativization of camp and art: "I don't make any differences between kitsch and culture. . . . For me kitsch is camp. There are no gaps between kitsch and art. It is stupid to look for traditional values in art and culture, you only need to look for the living spirit" (quoted in *Werner Schroeter*, 14).

Announced at the start, this enthralled female-female gaze continues through the film, its queerness emphasized further when Magdalena Montezuma dresses in male attire as Hugo and stares down at the androgynous Christine Kaufmann.[9] Yet what are these eyes trying to say? By no means is this gaze always met, for more often than not the other woman seems impassive, self-absorbed in melancholic withdrawal, or the eyes peer off into space, past or through the other's visage. In takes showing a single woman, the wide-eyed looking seems to betoken foresakenness, a pure seeing, and an absolute, objectless yearning. With no countershot or with misdirected eyeline matches, the spectator is not informed of what these women could be surveying. Hence the cinematic stasis reminds one of what is absent from the frame and consequently of one's own blindness and longing to see. These women could be observing nothing, as the black backdrop evokes, or their vacuous gaze could signal an intent listening to the soundtrack, in which case hearing paradoxically also signals a kind of blindness. But because there is no clue that the music is actually apprehended by the characters, this surmise remains speculative. On all accounts, whether it be from the perspective of the internal or external viewer, vision is—to cite "Harzreise im Winter"— clouded (*umwölkt*). The actresses' eyes are held open as if, not being able to see, they wanted melancholically to devour everything around them. Hence in the middle of the Hugo episode to see, to keep one's eyes, means to give up nourishment, the loaf of bread the stranger conditionally offers. This connection between the open, exposed eye and the equally soft cavity of the mouth is suggested further by the link between the first and last images of the film: the blood trickling from the eye at the start is matched by the blood that flows from the mouth as Magdalena Montezuma / Maria Malibran expires at the end (an image Schroeter later recalls in *Flocons d'or*).

Eyes thus articulate a demand that cannot be met and mark the site of vulnerability and an inner wound. They signal as well the theme of misguided passion with which they are linked throughout the film. In one episode, for instance, Magdalena Montezuma silently mouths words to a voice-over that

123

retells a passing encounter with a sailor on the street. The woman notices the inviting, knowing look he throws her way and wonders what he sees in her. Had she probed deeper into what it was, she muses, it would have been like looking into the harsh, blinding sun. Significantly, the two do not stop and the vectors of desire never meet. Nor is the demand met in a following sequence, shot from a distance at the Munich Olympiaberg, where Magdalena Montezuma stumbles after a man named Alfred (recalling *La Traviata*) who refuses to turn around to her insistent cry, "Wait for me. Please don't leave me. Don't you remember me?" In this reverse tale of Orpheus and Eurydice, the other's gaze is withheld and yet at the same time the woman is the object of shame for all other eyes at the park and for the camera voyeuristically tracking from above.

SAPPHIC DESIRES

Thus although this film dramatizes what the Heine and Goethe poems announce—unrequited passion—at the same time it also depicts women gazing enraptured at each other. Are these two moments contradictory or somehow related? Inasmuch as the same-sex gazing transpires against a black background, a theater curtain, or in nature where human presence is otherwise invisible, it occurs in an imaginary, even oneiric realm, the only space in which a closeted homoeroticism could unfold. Both the solitary gaze and the lesbian gaze betoken an impossible desire, fulfilled only in the imagination and sublimated in the artwork. The enchantment of these women suggests that they are responding to the beauty of each other, the music, or both. Here lesbian desire, held at a distance by the stationary, frontal camera and signified by the feverish yet ultimately chaste gaze and kiss, takes on the qualities of the disinterested artwork. In writing on Goethe's "Harzreise im Winter," David Wellbery observes that its poet "attain[s] to a desire that is unbounded by attachment to corporeality, a sublimated love that proves to be . . . the resource of poetic achievement" (373). The circumstances surrounding Brahms's composition are also telling for their intimations of a closeted passion: Brahms had fallen in love with Clara Schumann's twenty-four-year-old daughter Julie but kept his feelings to himself. Shortly after hearing news of her engagement to a Count Marmorito he presented Clara with the *Alto Rhapsody*, which she named in her diary "his wedding song." It is no wonder that Schroeter selected this music to open his film on aestheticized sorrow, an impossible queer desire, its sublimation in the worship of beauty, and the artist's (Malibran's) sacrifice of life for art.

Yet another dimension to this female gaze problematizes a reading of it as indicative of unalloyed, active desire for another woman. It is unclear whether the women are the source of each other's desire or if they see in each other the reflection, now doubled and intensified, of their own private longing. In other words, it is ambiguous whether the women are desired or desiring, whether they identify with the other woman or take her as the object of erotic interest. This ambivalence between identification and desire lies at the heart of theories on lesbian spectatorship.[10] Does identifying with a female body on the screen entail or exclude desiring it? Does admiration of another woman, including her eroticism, encode the spectator as queer? And does an empathetic or appreciative identification necessarily mean that it is narcissistic, ratifying the female ego? In other words, is homosexuality being defined as narcissistic object choice? These questions resonate in Lewis and Rolley's statement on the lesbian gaze: "the identification is not just with the women in the picture ('I want to look like that') but with their state of being looked at ('I want to be the object of the desiring gaze') by a *female* viewer" (182).

Certainly, when Schroeter frames the women facing each other, he alludes to the diptych, the Rorschach test, or the looking glass.[11] The repetition of the dual visages from one shot to the next likewise implies mirroring. This still captivation before the image evokes the myth of Narcissus, frozen in admiration of his own reflection. His ideal object remains untouchable and distanced, for to reach out to it would disturb and dissolve the placid waters that contain it. Schroeter could be accused of encoding the lesbian as narcissistic, but it seems rather that here identification and emulation enhance lesbian desire. The closeness between Schroeter's women imparts a palpable element of sexuality; shot tightly together in the frame, they testify to a certain eroticism of proximity. Moreover, the gaze can be so voracious that its active quality, its lesbianism, cannot be denied nor dismissed as a regressive, narcissistic, and hence passive pleasure. If same-sex visual fascination is at work in Schroeter's films, it is a pleasure he proposes should be taken.

In addition, and more important, the mirroring establishes a pattern that queers the spectator's relationship to the screen. Rather than reinforcing optical distance, the stasis of the image functions as a mirror to the spectator, transforming the viewed object into an intimately known one. Corrigan brilliantly writes à propos *Willow Springs* that its images "attract and hold the spectator by means of an hypnotic fascination put in place by the exhibition of an excess. Instead of distancing or alienating the viewer, the film thus absorbs the viewer directly into the exhibition itself" ("Operatic Voice," 52).[12] As when one glances into a mirror and all else disappears except for one's gaze, so too in *Der Tod der Maria Malibran* the background dissolves and one stands mesmerized by the gaze. Because the longing remains undefined, the spectator can interpolate him- or herself with ease into the position of desiring subject and identify with the fervent gaze. The film thereby appeals to the pure desire to desire. It actualizes Schroeter's vision of art as a "cataclysm of unlived longings" (quoted in *Werner Schroeter*, 59).

Wim Wenders ingeniously noted how Schroeter responds to this desire to watch to one's full. Schroeter's cinema, he writes, indulges the scopic drive that possesses one when one sees, for instance, Marilyn Monroe, Elvis Presley, or Mick Jagger perform. "Werner Schroeter's films are the way one wants movies with Marilyn Monroe to be, actually the way one wants everything to be, especially at the movies" (14), he notes. I would take Wenders's remark two steps further: first, as this insatiable, entranced viewing is itself represented on the screen, it conditions the spectator's own viewing and enables the passion Wenders describes. Second, insofar as it establishes itself as a female-to-female relation, it encodes the viewer as lesbian, regardless of his or her own sexual predilections. Schroeter thus turns the cinematic apparatus with its capacity for celluloid mirroring, screen projection, and scopic jouissance into an instrument for rendering desires queer.

'OBJET A'

To investigate spectatorship in terms of the cinematic apparatus is to invoke such film Lacanians as Baudry, Oudart, Metz, Mulvey, and Silverman, yet Lacan's own characterization of the gaze as an example of the *objet petit a* begs for specific consideration. According to Lacan in the *Four Fundamental Concepts of Psycho-Analysis*, the *objet a* is posited by desire to replace an irredeemably lost relation to the unattainable Other. Imagined as a remnant from this Other, it possesses an emotive richness that is allegorical in the sense that its referent belongs to a submerged past; as compensation, its artifice, also like that of allegory, is elaborate. The *objet a* reassures and comforts by filling in the gaps, by papering over the void in the subject, thereby becoming invested with the function of surplus. Slavoj Žižek clarifies:

> *Objet a* is simultaneously the pure lack, the void around which the desire turns and which, as such, causes the desire, *and* the imaginary element which conceals this void, renders it invisible by filling it out. The point, of course, is that there is no lack without the element filling it out: *the filler sustains what it dissimulates*. (*Metastases*, 178)

126　　In Lacan's words, "the *objet a* in the field of the visible is the gaze" (105). The subject longs to have the gaze rest on him, as once did the maternal gaze, whose current absence can be denied by the presence of its substitutes. The subject can jubilantly declare that, no, he has not lost the mother but regained her in this other form. Schroeter's camera is transfixed on this beatific, enraptured gaze which appears everywhere. It is fascinated by it and responsive to it, registering the slightest flutter of the eyelash. The face, whose eyes and lips are enhanced through the contrast of makeup and lighting, is often shot in close-up, as if the child at the mother's breast were looking into her eyes. This gaze cum *objet a* thereby becomes the chimerical object of fantasy; this "passionate evidence" permits one to read all and intuit everything into it, as if in repudiation of the wounded, castrated eye at the beginning of the film. In addition, as Žižek points out, because it both conceals and marks the void, the *objet a* gives rise to the contradictory emotions of elation and melancholy, rapture and tedium that Schroeter's camp and ceremony elicit.

The strength or phallicity of the gaze is not only evident in this beatific mode but metamorphoses as well under Magdalena Montezuma's superb acting into a fearsome, imperious one. In certain scenes she stands with a devastating, impassive stare over another woman, who either looks back entreatingly or grovels and gropes on the floor. This chastizing maternal gaze is enacted as the paternal one in the central section on Malibran's father, where Magdalena Montezuma's sovereign gaze is paired with the young woman's blinding, as if to suggest that the subject cannot see when faced with the Other's gaze. Lacan writes: "I see only from one point, but in my existence I am looked at from all sides" (72). He reminds me that I never look from a safe, objective distance, for another gaze will always catch me unawares. "In the scopic field, the gaze is outside, I am looked at, that is to say, I am a picture. . . . What determines me, at the most profound level, in the visible, is the gaze that is outside" (106).[13] It is no wonder that the Christine Kaufmann character is blinded before this annihilating gaze and that her eyesight is restored once Hugo disappears.

The imperious gaze of Magdalena Montezuma is even more evident in the two films that completed Schroeter's trilogy. *Willow Springs* was shot in the Mojave Desert after Schroeter had traveled to Los Angeles with the intent of making a film about Marilyn Monroe. It is ostensibly about three women (Magdalena Montezuma, Christine Kaufmann, and Ila von Hasperg) who inhabit a deserted, run-down house and about their sadomasochistic, jealous relations. The domineering and priestesslike Magdalena rules over the beautiful Christine and the initially servile but then rebellious Ila, who takes up with a teenage boy named Michael who appears one day at their doorstep (initially Rosa von Praunheim was to play the male role). After spying on Michael and Ida having sex, Magdalena dreams or foresees the two leaving and her shooting them in retribution. In this bizarre wild Western, filled with mirrors and reflected images, the dream indeed becomes reality. As the mu-

127

sic swells in the final moments after Michael and Ida's collapse, Magdalena walks out alone triumphantly into the desert, her hands held high.

Reducing the others to insignificant objects, Magdalena looks on repeatedly throughout the film, even when her unstable, wandering eyes seem inwardly focused. Sometimes she looks like an uncanny, ghostly double, whose omnipotent gaze presides over all events. In one instance, the camera pulls back from Christine to reveal a dirty window (or is it a mirror?) framing Magdalena's approach from the desert. At first the glass image looks like a reflection and we think Christine also stands outdoors. At the last moment we see that Magdalena comes to the window from the outside to peer down at Christine inside, who thus proves to be the one entrapped in an enclosure. Magdalena's imperiousness plays on various registers. It seems to signify the fantasy of an omnipotent female gaze, exhilarating for its reversal of the traditional objectivization of the woman. To the extent that she evokes the phallic mother, her gaze embodies the *objet a* that arouses not just anxiety but also a strange, familiar pleasure. It also expresses the voracious determination to enjoy everything, especially the other women: her viewing thus embodies the cinephile's secret desire to see all, the reason for which she enters the theater. But insofar as Magdalena's apparition, in the scene just described, also dupes the spectator, one is reminded of how she represents the Other-cum-cinematic apparatus which one cannot tame to one's own desires. In fact, this film conditions the viewer to anticipate anxiously, for every shot, a countershot revealing her presence looking on. Again, her vision signifies the blindness of all others concerned.

Schroeter's subsequent film in the trilogy, *Flocons d'or*, is comprised of four parts with a frame. In the third part, entitled "Coeur brisé,"[14] "the beautiful madwoman" (Andréa Ferréol) wearing spiked pumps, gartered stockings, and a low-cut negligée goes out onto the streets of Avignon stalked by "the American assassin" (Magdalena Montezuma) wrapped in a leather coat. According to Schroeter, the latter is "on the lookout for living sacrifices for her hungry soul" (quoted in *Werner Schroeter*, 173). The two women finally meet up in a bar where they dance together while a third woman, "the murderous soul" (Bulle Ogier), looks on; the trio form an erotically charged group whose alliance is never clarified. In the subsequent section "Réalité?—Vérité," Magdalena Montezuma again plays a shadow (in an outlandish dark blue gown and feathers), this time to the ever-feminine Udo Kier in the role of a supposed child murderer. Additionally, in the first two sections she appears like an angel of death (or is it vampire?) to embrace and kiss the body of the deceased. In "Cuba en 1949," for instance, blood flows from her mouth to besmirch in necrophilic fellatio the unzipped crotch of the dead heroin addict.

In all these episodes, as omnipresent witness Madgelena Montezuma stands in for the invisible camera; yet at the same time she embodies the camera's effects—its undead, shadowy images.

"THE LIPS"

Along with the gaze, Lacan designates the voice as another prime example of the *objet a*, the remnant from the (maternal) body, fetishistically imbued with significance.[15] The voice, arising out of the dark cavities of the body, departing from its source, evokes a wholeness but points to a kind of acoustic amputation. The ambivalence between a resonating plenitude and the abjected part characterizes Schroeter's treatment of the voice, which is either worshipped in its operatic glory or denigrated through pop sleaze. The acoustic image, working in tandem with the visual one, also signals this oscillation, for repeatedly in Schroeter the presence of one evokes the absence of the other. On the one hand, the transport produced by the voice suggests that one has no need of vision, that one can close one's eyes in order to improve one's hearing, which in fact the stasis of the Schroeterian image seems to want to encourage. On the other hand, the nondiegetic use of music raises the question of where it originates and its relation to the image. Does it accompany the thoughts of the person on screen? Is it what they hear or what they imagine hearing? In other words, is it in their head, issuing from off-screen, or neither? Because the voice that exudes from the lipsynching mouth is obviously not the original, displacement and visual disorientation occurs. The voice itself is optically encoded through the full, painted lips. As with the heavy eye shadow, lipstick fetishizes the body part; it both draws attention to and yet covers the empty mouth, this emblem of desire. Moreover, the painted eyes and lips, turning the face into a mask, distract and dominate the viewer, thereby functioning as the Lacanian stain that optically deceives.

Despite the enveloping richness of the operatic voice that opens and closes Schroeter's films, the vocal organ is repeatedly deprecated. On the level of the image, blood trickles from the mouth, for Malibran's divine song brings death; earlier a knife is held to the throat.[16] On the level of the soundtrack, the voice is frequently broken off (especially in *Willow Springs*, where the diegetic music comes from a record player on site, so that one hears the scratching of the needle against plastic). Together with the switching from one recording to the next, extended silences remind one of the temporality and mutability of the voice and one's listening. In addition, the recordings can be old and poor; entirely instrumental or cheesy pop tunes displace the diva's song. Such interruptions sully the pure voice, making unattainable the sublimity longed for.[17] Schroeter's cinema thereby conjures, in

Wayne Koestenbaum's words, "the abjection and sadness that lie buried in listening" (147).[18]

It is extremely paradoxical that the very richness of the music, punctuated by recitations from *Hamlet* and Heine, points to the presence of silence, visualized in the open mouth of the actress. Schroeter's films, while serving as precursors to MTV, thereby also harken back to the silent era. Even the subtitles recall early cinema's intertitles. The extensive use of music emphasizes, moreover, as in silent films, the need to read the bodily gesture as supplementary discourse.[19]

Thus signaling its own incomprehensibility, the voice—like the foreign languages Schroeter repeatedly introduces in dialogue, citation, and song—functions as symptom and gesture,[20] pointing to its sheer opacity and materiality. Repeated or rehearsed for its own sake, the voice epitomizes theatricality. Although issuing from the corporeal interior, its texturedness represents a kind of surface or exteriority. Or, put another way, the soul for Schroeter is constituted through its artifice and exposure. This display of (vocal or visual) gesture is thus a process of disembodiment—which also occurs when voices are mapped onto another source through deliberately out-of-synch lipsynching, when the character of Maria Malibran is played by several actresses, or when one sex eccentrically acts out the role of the other in transvestism. Moreover, in its distance from its origin, the voice on the soundtrack signals its status as copy, a fact emphasized through the mimicry of lipsynching. The citation of Heine, Shakespeare, and Poe also points to a gesticular iteration, as does the incantation of the same phrase over and over (for instance, "Ich sehne mich so nach dir").

Yet perhaps in order to battle alienation and death, which the copy pervasively evokes, Schroeter's cinema also bears witness to an insistent desire and the desperate hope that one's longing can be fulfilled in an ecstatic, authentic present. There are reasons for arguing that this desire is not just bold but queer. Both the internal and external listeners share in the desire that the voice performs: it is a second self that can utter what one cannot. Thus, although they rarely speak (but only declaim), Schroeter's characters with their open lips seem transvestitically to embody a being-in-voice. Insofar as it marks displacement from the body, the voice signifies not only a kind of transvestism but a closeting as well—a separation of the visible from the invisible. And ironically, perhaps via its imperfection, the voice embodies a dissonance that, like the gaze, can bespeak an odd, unnatural desire; it eroticizes idiosyncrasy.[21]

This sexual dissonance can be tied not only back to the original Maria Malibran, with whom this section started, but to the actual voices in Schroeter's films. In a fascinating essay entitled "Sapphonics," Elizabeth Wood writes:

> I call this voice Sapphonic for its resonance in sonic space as lesbian difference and desire. Its sound is characteristically powerful and problematic, defiant and defective. Its flexible negotiation and integration of an exceptional range of registers crosses boundaries among different voice types and their representations to challenge polarities of both gender and sexuality as these are socially—and vocally—constructed. (28)

In a footnote Wood observes that Pauline Viardot and her sister Maria Malibran possessed the huge range of the Sapphonic voice, as did Nellie Melba and Emma Calvé, who had been trained in vocal methods originating with Viardot and Malibran's father Manuel Garcia and their brother Manuel Garcia (57). The darkly hued alto and mezzo voices for which Schroeter has an affinity seem to embody this Sapphonics, which Wood calls "*both* butch and femme, *both* male and female" (32). The film, of course, begins with the *Alto Rhapsody* but additionally contains, among other songs, Marlene Dietrich's androgynous "Mundharmonika"; Candy Darling's transvestitic "St. Louis Woman" and "Ramona"; Catarina Valente's husky "Spiel noch einmal für mich"; and Callas's "O mio babbino caro" from Puccini's *Gianni Schicchi*. Just as Schroeter transforms the viewer into a lesbian one, so too he constructs "a lesbian listener for whom the singer serves as a messenger, her voice as vessel, of desire" (28). Wood continues: "The Sapphonic voice is a destabilizing agent of fantasy and desire. The woman with this voice, this capacity to embody and traverse a range of sonic possibilities and overflow sonic boundaries, may vocalize inadmissible sexualities and a thrilling readiness to go beyond so-called natural limits, an erotics of risk and defiance, a desire for desire itself" (32–33).[22] Wood could have been describing the ardor and force behind Schroeter's operatic cinema.

'Der Rosenkönig'

Der Rosenkönig takes up the themes of love and death announced in the trilogy of *Der Tod der Maria Malibran*, *Willow Springs*, and *Flocons d'or* and links them most prominently in the image of red roses that are increasingly portrayed dripping blood. The conventional symbol of the rose thus becomes macabre and mawkish, with its traditional valence further reversed through association with a male instead of a female character and with homosexual

131

Figure 16. *Der Rosenkönig* (1986), Mostéfa Djadjam and Antonio Orlando. Courtesy of the Fotoarchiv, Stiftung Deutsche Kinemathek, Berlin.

rather than heterosexual love.[23] Perhaps alluding to the same-sex attraction in Richard Strauss's *Der Rosenkavalier*, the "Rose King" seduces another man. In addition, for Schroeter connoisseurs, the red rose, held high by two embraced hands, recalls the same image from the segment in *Eika Katappa* where two young Neapolitan men fall in love, only to have the one tragically die.

Like the films produced after the trilogy, *Der Rosenkönig* has a more realistic setting and clearly delineated plot, while still relying on long, photographic takes that suspend the narrative. The story concerns a mother (Magdalena Montezuma) and her grown son Albert (Mostéfa Djadjam) who together run a rose farm in the desert of Portugal. The son has horticultural aspirations, attempting to propagate an ideal rose; his hothouse serves as a metaphor for the realm where exotic, forbidden desires grow. One night he discovers a youth (Antonio Orlando) stealing from a local church and locks him up in their barn, where he binds him to a chair and feeds him. Albert develops a sadistic, erotic relation to his captive, who in his very passivity seduces. Even when the youth has the opportunity to escape he returns to the barn, despite the mother's attempt to bribe him to leave. She is repeatedly shown wandering through her house and a ruined chapel on her property, obsessed by her increasing estrangement from a son she holds dear, looking as if she has a premonition of some catastrophe. In an image that suggests a kind of penitence as well as the externalization of (black) blood, she smears tar over her face, highlighting thereby her eyes, which stare out as luminous globes from the jet mass. Indeed, she is often shot as a kind of voyeur, listening to her son's comings and goings. In the end, her anxieties prove true, for Albert slays the "Rose King" in a passion (both in the Christian sense and the secular one), and inserts roses into the bodily lacerations. This multivalent symbol of the roses richly condenses intimations of death, beauty, and a gay love.

Conceivably the three most important events in Schroeter's life were the deaths of the women who meant the most to him: his mother; shortly thereafter, Maria Callas; and two and a half weeks after the shooting of *Der Rosenkönig* Magdalena Montezuma, on July 15, 1984, from intestinal cancer. On the death of his mother Schroeter said that he experienced the most immense self-alienation, although he also confesses that he subsequently was more productive than in previous years (*Werner Schroeter*, 69). His thoughts on Callas's passing also revolve around the proximity of death and art. In the eulogy published in 1977 in *Der Spiegel* he commented on the diva's ability to immobilize time through the very force of her expression. In face of the fact that death is "the only objective fact of our existence," Callas's art demonstrated the "desire to halt time" and "to ignore the finitude of human desires" (quoted in Courant, 10). In an interview with Daniel Schmid he similarly comments on how in opera, in the moment, the transience of life is forgotten (*Werner Schroeter*, 67). At the close of the interview he speaks of how he lives each day to its full, so that death loses its terror, that is, the thought that with its arrival one might have missed something (*Werner Schroeter*, 83). Indeed, in discussion with Foucault he states, à la Rimbaud, "Chaque jour je suis un autre [Every day I am an other]" (quoted in Courant, 46). Thus death seems to produce for Schroeter a productive relationship to life and art as affirmations of the ever-changing present moment. As a diva in *Eika Katappa* declaims upon dying: "Life is very precious, even right now." The anticipation of an end thus paradoxically allows Schroeter to redefine time and temporality. This realization can be achieved, as he intimated with regard to Callas, especially through surrender and excess.

Der Rosenkönig illustrates in various ways this proximity of death to the present and death to art. Given the connection between beauty and the rose, the insertion of rosebuds into the lacerated body suggests that art grows from such a wounding. The body of the captive youth is itself presented to the camera as a lifeless but exquisite statue for the eye to dwell on; in one pose he is tied to a pole like Saint Sebastian and in another he is draped across Albert's arms as in a statue of the Pièta. Indeed, the extraordinary beauty of the camerawork by longtime collaborator Elfi Mikesch[24] is itself inseparable from the notions of mutability and death. Images such as the dangling roses, the pounding seashore, or water trickling at a fountain are shot so exquisitely that one almost forgets their hint of triteness. Set in opposite pairs (desert/roses, fire/water, light/dark, blues/reds), their optical splendor is so intense that they take on an almost tactile quality. Yet despite their immediate brilliance, these still images, brought about by the lingering of the camera, paradoxically testify to an awareness of death. They mark a desire either to halt the passage of time or to show how the camera can slow its progress.

The ravages of time are portrayed with even more overt allegorical clarity in the scenes at the ruined chapel, with its cobwebs, decaying statues, and shattered glass panes. The mother repeatedly wanders through this space, as if trying to establish a relationship to the past. Her diary, yellowed photographs, letters, and other objects metonymically assembled on her table likewise seem to evoke a past that holds memories for her that are not imparted to the viewer. Yet while the settings seem heavy with allusions to the past, the film also affirms the living present and equates it with vision, as in the phrases "but we live from what is" and "whoever lives will see." In other words, this film epitomizes cinema itself in its ability to make its viewer reflect on what time and actuality are. For cinema is a temporal art that can capture the present yet at the same time remind one that its arrested images are spent, reduced to shadows on celluloid. As such, cinema itself is inherently allegorical, arising from the past, displaying the temporality of its signs, and yet veiling its origin by the deceptive immediacy of its images. Like the musical recording that Schroeter relies on so heavily, cinema is an ephemeral art that nevertheless has stabilized and captured a past moment. In Schroeter's version, cinema is manic in its visual intensity and excess but depressive in its ultimate awareness of the fleeting moment.

Given that Magdalena Montezuma was already dying of cancer during the shooting of *Der Rosenkönig*, one wonders how anticipation of the loss of his closest companion might have affected Schroeter in the conception of the film itself with its themes of death and temporality. Compared to her earlier roles, Magdalena Montezuma here looks notably thinner, even gaunt, with her already large eyes and wide cheekbones even more prominent. Her movement is restricted, as if she were in pain. These penultimate, fleeting traces of an individual, whom Gary Indiana called "the greatest European actress since Anna Magnani" (48), render her performance unutterably precious, like that of Cyril Collard in *Les Nuits Sauvages*. We cling to every shot of her, not wanting to believe that these images belong to the past. One can imagine Schroeter editing the film, always coming back to the close-up of her face and hands, as if to recapture her presence. Given the dolorous circumstances surrounding the making of *Der Rosenkönig*, it is therefore odd that death in the film is displaced onto a male character, although it is the female character whose suffering is rendered most visibly. Magdalena Montezuma is often depicted alone or in close-up, as if she were no longer of interest to her indifferent son but solely to the camera. In her loneliness she seems to have more intimacy with the relics in the chapel and objects in her house, like the piano keys and photograph she besmirches with her tar-stained hands. In one scene she embraces a little boy, clasping him to her, as if wanting to recapture her relationship to her son. She is both the *mater dolorosa* and *mater de la rosa*, who renders her abjection visible by dirtying her face in tar and sand.

As noted earlier, the close-ups of the female visage play upon the fantasy of closeness to the mother. It is thus curious that the fantasy of giving and bestowing maternal care is transferred onto the relationship between the two men. It was already noted how Albert poses as the Madonna in a Pièta-like tableau, paralleling the role Magdalena Montezuma plays as a live statue of Maria who appears before the feverish youth. Albert also acts out the mother when he feeds his prisoner, undresses him, washes him, and asks if he has been hurt, thereby resignifying the motherly part as latently sadistic. When stealing offerings at the church, the youth speaks to the religious statues, saying that he needs the money not for himself but for his dying mother. Clearly, Albert robs the mother of her son in order to become her himself.[25] In the meantime, the mother / Magdalena Montezuma remains dying.

What this entire scenario disturbingly suggests is that the forgetting or repudiation of the female allows for the gay male relation and its representation. What I propose to examine is first how gay sexuality is represented, then in more detail how the mother-figure intersects with the couple formation, and finally how this triangulation involves a kind of queer transsubstantiation of desire.

Although *Eika Katappa* and *Neapolitanische Geschwister* deal secondarily with intimate relations between men, *Der Rosenkönig* is Schroeter's only film that foregrounds male homosexuality. Whereas the lesbian dimension to *Der Tod der Maria Malibran*, *Willow Springs*, and *Flocons d'or* resides primarily in the ecstatic gaze and kiss, in *Der Rosenkönig* it is the naked body that is put on display. Albert undresses the youth to wash him, his hand lingering in close-up over the youth's torso and then genitals. The only other marker that their desire has become carnal is a cut to their calves and feet entwined. In other words, although more explicit in its physicality than these earlier films, *Der Rosenkönig* still holds at an aesthetic remove its erotic object. Along with the

135

examples of Christian iconography (the sheep, the stable, the [crown of] thorns, the pierced body, and sacrificial death), the staging of this love, especially in the long shots that portray the barn as a cathedral, recalls a ritual performed on an altar.[26] This tendency to distanced display is of course reversed in the necrophilic finale with its extreme close-ups of the bleeding (hence feminized?) body, as if to suggest that gay intimate experience can only occur through violation and death.

Like the work of Jean Genet and Fassbinder's *Querelle, Der Rosenkönig* is daring in its portrayal of a brutal, sadistic dimension to homoeroticism—its willingness to admit a link between physical attraction and mutilation, between aggression and beauty. It also seems to suggest that the violence arises in the aftermath of a closeting: the captive is locked away, occasionally the object of little boys peering in through the cracks in the barn. His relation with Albert carries an air of secrecy and the illicit. Only in the end, after he is slain, is the youth's body taken by Albert into the open, into the rose garden. The opening prediction, repeated in the course of the film—"when two children love each other without being able to speak, one of them must die"—intimates not only that the two men speak different languages but also that they are not able to speak their love, or not permitted to do so.

Yet arguably more provocative than the portrayal of a destructive, repressed gay sexuality is the relation of the Magdalena Montezuma character to this sexuality. Schroeter contrasts an anxious maternal love with its false, hence deadly substitute, suggesting that the repudiation of the former leads to the latter. The gay relation is impossible from the start because it is paradoxically both mediated and prohibited by the mother. In the erotic triangle, the mother's spurned attentions carry sexual overtones, especially when she leans over in her bedroom to listen across the wall to what her son is doing in his bed. The scene visually evokes Genet's *Un chant d'amour* where the camera likewise pans through a wall to another prison cell and depicts the sexual tensions between the two incarcerated men.[27] In Schroeter's film the traveling camera marks the mother's inability to see what it does, to peer to the other side. As in *Der Tod der Maria Malibran*, Magdalena Montezuma's wide-eyed looking betokens an emptiness she longs to fill. To further complicate triangulation, Albert, as a grown man, seems to play the role in the household of the husband, whose departure is alluded to. The Magdalena Montezuma character is thus doubly abandoned. This rejection, however, occurs not just on the level of narrative. It is interesting that Magdalena Montezuma played in life a similarly suffering, maternal role to Werner Schroeter. She accompanied him everywhere, cooked for him, served as his secretary, and even slept celibately with him. If he had a male lover, she would simply turn aside in the bed. Rosa von Praunheim writes that "She dedicated her life to him and sacrificed everything for him" (*50 Jahre pervers*, 172).

With such similarities between art and biography, the questions arise: In *Der Rosenkönig* did Schroeter finally create for Magdalena Montezuma a role that approximated her actual relationship to him? Is the film a tribute to the fervor of her passion and forgiveness? Does it reflect Schroeter's contrite recognition of her love or yet again its denial? Furthermore, if she is the one who is literally dying and Schroeter had lost his own mother a few years before, why would he displace the act of bereavement onto a mother mourning the loss of her son? Regardless of how these questions are answered, if they can be, they point to the emotive intensity residing at the core of this film, an intensity that allegorically expresses itself through rich pictorial allusions (Georges de la Tour, Caravaggio), musical citations (Puccini, Johann Strauss), theatrical gesture, and religious ritual.

What this allegorical signification permits, and what the triangular erotic constellation likewise implies, is that one's desire can be represented through that of another. The borrowing from another body recalls a vampiric transsubstantiation: the roses, the color of blood, begin to drip blood. This metamorphosis or transfer also occurs queerly across gender divisions. Just as the character played by Magdalena Montezuma expresses the emotions of a jealous love, in a sense closeted love, so too the female voice bears the expression of gay male desire. In the gender reversals of *Der Rosenkönig*, Albert's sublimated passion is communicated as through ventriloquism, via the female operatic voice singing the aria "Vissi d'arte" from Puccini's *Tosca*, "I have lived for art and love." His passion is also signified indirectly via Magdalena Montezuma's tortured facial expression and ultimately via the desecration of the youth's life and beauty. My point is not to reduce the tale to a psychological explanation of Albert's behavior. It is not so much that the character of Albert feels the need to repress or closet his attraction to the youth, as well as to remain impassive toward his mother, resulting in the final eruption of violence, but that Schroeter recognizes that all desire works surreptitiously and bizarrely. With Schroeter we find a cinema of phantasmatic, displaced, and distanced desires.

What thus becomes important in reading this director's eloquence is not the psychology of repression (which is certainly not, as Rosa von Praunheim would read it, as applied to the person of Werner Schroeter) but the enigmatic, scintillating articulation or surfacing of the symptoms of desire. Through gesture, voice, and even another's suffering, passion is literalized. Unlocalizable in one subject, it is queerly transmutable from one gender to the next. The issue of who is the agent or object of desire is subordinate to the very articulation of desire. This semiotic "deviance," then, is what renders Schroeter's cinematic language allegorical.

As Fassbinder knew, Werner Schroeter's mark on the New German Cinema was striking and indelible; the legacy of his influence can be detected far beyond the directors Fassbinder listed in 1979. The visual repertoire of the Queer German Cinema, as we shall see in the following chapters, borrows extensively from Schroeter. This is a cinema that focuses on the allegorical remnant, on the fragment where desire metonymically lodges. Insofar as it points to the larger whole that it can only intimate, the fragment signifies its own longing. Schroeter is captivated by the partial, hence fetishistic, indirect, and fragile circuitry of queer desires, whose presence is rendered in the "passionate evidence" of the bodily fragment, in the "eyes and lips," and collected together in a pastiche of discontinuous, inevitably interrupted tableaux. In Ulrike Ottinger, Michael Brynntrup, Ursula Pürrer, and Hans Scheirl one finds a similar allegorical autonomization of images, the fetishistic, baroque excesses of gesture and clothing, and a preference for ironic, camp flamboyance that cannot clearly be decoded and that masks the inexpressibility of desire. In addition, one consistently encounters the performance of cross-gender desires, as well as a histrionic acting out of same-sex desires, which are, first and foremost, audacious in their demands.

five

Allegory, Androgyny, Anamorphosis

Ulrike Ottinger's *Dorian Gray*

More than any other filmmaker discussed in this book, Ulrike Ottinger displays a strong, sustained affinity for allegory. Its ritual nature already comes to the fore in *Berlinfieber* (*Berlin Fever*) (1973), a filmed "happening" by Wolf Vostell, where cars ceremoniously drive over dinner plates heaped with salt. Ottinger's interest in accumulated fragments continues all the way to another recording of events in Berlin, *Countdown* (1990), where on ten successive days she took her camera to randomly shoot different waterways in the city. As these early and late examples testify, Ottinger presents sequences of enigmatic, discrete images that despite their signifying opacity nonetheless possess the visual allure and pictorial clarity that characterize allegory. She has the unique capacity to endow even the documentary genre, as in these two films, with an allegorical sensibility. The very discontinuity in their flow of images could be explained as a remnant of allegorical epic. Allegory, in Quintilian's sense of it as an extended metaphor, frequently relies on the longer narrative form, as in the psychomachia or related stories of the quest, pilgrimage, or voyage (such as *The Fairie Queene*, *Pilgrim's Progress*, *Gulliver's Travels*, and *Moby Dick*). Once the allegorical meaning propelling the narrative is removed, and with it a clear telos (such as salvation), the disparate stations gain independent weight and create a paratactic, episodic structure, as, to give a twentieth-century example, in Kafka's *Amerika*. With an educational background in painting, Ottinger experiments with the static tableau and the radiant, isolated image, which go hand in hand with her often disjointed narrative to endow her work with an "allegorical effect."

One of the most obvious features of Ottinger's films is that they document a travel or quest where the "goal" remains shrouded in obscurity, while the stations along the way stand out vividly. In *Madame X—Eine absolute Herrscherin* (*Madame X—An Absolute Ruler*) (1977), for instance, seven women from around the world, including the American housewife Betty Brillo, the European artist Josephine de Collage (played by the filmmaker Yvonne Rainer),

139

and the native Noa-Noa from Tai-Pi, come to join the beautiful but cruel pirate Madame X on her ship *Orlando*, with her promise of danger, love, and adventure. The lengthy first section of the film is devoted to depicting sequentially the individual journeys of Madame X's followers as they arrive from around the globe to meet her, after which various episodes from their joint exploits are rendered. In another example of the quest, *Bildnis einer Trinkerin* (*Ticket of No Return*) (1979), an anonymous, silent alcoholic flies to Berlin for an extended tour of its watering holes. Writing on "the protagonist's purposefully purposeless quest," Miriam Hansen notes that the various Berlin locations "do not add up to a social topography . . . but represent allegorical stations in the protagonist's experiment of lived-out fantasy" (202). As she appears in one locale after the other in her extravagant costumes, the drinker is accompanied by a bag lady and spied upon by a chorus of three purportedly upright women in houndstooth suits—Exact Statistics, Social Question, and Common Sense—who embody the didacticism and sententiousness of the allegorical strain. The drinker's connection to a mythologized womanhood is pronounced by the initial voice-over: she is "a woman of exquisite beauty, of Classical dignity and harmonious Raphaelesque proportions, a woman, created like no other to be Medea, Madonna, Beatrice, Iphigenia, Aspasia." In another feature-length film by Ottinger, *Freak Orlando* (1981), the allegorical dimension is announced in the subtitle itself, *Kleines Welttheater in 5 Episoden* (*Small World-Theater in 5 Episodes*); here the discontinuous plot sequels through the various incarnations and persecutions of Orlando/Orlanda. Ottinger's short *Superbia—Der Stolz* (*Superbia—Pride*) (1986) likewise borrows the metaphor of the allegorical medieval or baroque stage in illustrating one of the seven deadly sins. Included in an omnibus film entitled *Seven Women, Seven Sins* (other directors include Helke Sander, Chantal Akerman, Bette Gordon, and Valie Export), *Superbia* selects as its central image the very structure of sequential listing or parade that informs the collective project. In a triumphal procession that evokes the dance of death, allegorical figures march by in outlandish dress and arrogant poses. Finally, *Johanna d'Arc of Mongolia* (1989) takes up the travel motif announced in *Madame X* to present a group of Western women riding the Orient Express, their unanticipated destination being a matriarchal society in Mongolia.

In all these films the sequence of episodes refuses to culminate in any one scene of anagnorisis or peripeteia, as if the series could continue indefinitely and randomly. What precise transformation the female adventurers in *Madame X* or the protagonist in *Bildnis einer Trinkerin* undergo along their journey is left open to interpretation. Notwithstanding, metamorphosis—whether it be signaled through change in costume, gesture, or even sex (as in *Freak Or-*

lando)—runs as a constant theme throughout Ottinger. In other words, that transformation occurs in these episodic narratives cannot be denied; what its actual nature is, however, remains mysterious. This allegorical obscurity additionally derives from Ottinger's magnificent, glossy costuming that halts the eye, making it dwell, as does allegory, on decoration and ornament, in other words, on the enigmatic surface. Thus the striking garments and accessories of Ottinger's characters (even her frequent use of midgets or obese women) further interrupt the broken narratives and present the spectator with tableau-esque, even statuesque, materiality.

A study of the allegorical function in Ottinger's cinema would be a mammoth undertaking, and frustrating, given that her esoteric images and ateleological narratives resist an exegesis that would pinpoint meaning. Perhaps the magnitude of the problem explains why no scholar has attempted this project, even in preliminary article form. As an antidote I hope that focus on one particular film, *Dorian Gray im Spiegel der Boulevardpresse* (*Dorian Gray in the Mirror of the Yellow Press*) (1984), might help one begin to understand the allegorical workings in her oeuvre. Particularly, I want to argue how the urgent call for reading that allegory prompts, given its signifying structure that relentlessly separates images from their potential meaning, are key to the riddle of sexuality and gender in her work. Frequently the bizarre, visually captivating quality to Ottinger's work lies not only in the ostentatious costuming but, related to this, in her penchant for transvestite, androgynous characters and the disturbing eroticism they evoke. As if taking the lead from her immediately preceding film, *Freak Orlando*, Ottinger uses the trope of gender-switching to make it her major conceit in *Dorian Gray*: the primary male role is played by a 1960s androgynous-looking model, Veruschka von Lehndorff, who at times even seems to sport a five-o'clock shadow.[1] Yet unlike the Weimar cross-dressing films analyzed earlier, here the disguise is never revealed, not even directly mentioned in the film itself. This silence relates to allegory's own enigmatic discourse as well as to the overt thematization of the binaries secrecy/disclosure, private/public, and innocence/initiation that run throughout the film.

I thus propose a study of queer genders and desires in Ottinger via issues raised by allegorical structure and signification. My approach consequently veers from that of most scholars, who have concentrated on visual pleasure and other registers of women's desire, including female-female desire, primarily in *Madame X*, *Bildnis einer Trinkerin*, and *Johanna d'Arc of Mongolia*.[2] Yet feminist, even lesbian issues do not always overlap with queer ones; indeed, they often conflict. For instance, Ottinger is not reluctant to cast same-sex relationships between women as possessing an unsettling erotic dimension that

141

is premised precisely not on a preoedipal symbiosis or mutual appreciation between women.[3] Instead the lesbian dimension can grow from sexual differ-ence and deviance, as evidenced in the transgendered attraction of *Freak Or-lando* or the dominant/submissive role-playing with its s/m iconography in *Madame X.* Yet apart from Mary Russo's chapter on *Freak Orlando* in her book *The Female Grotesque: Risk, Excess, Modernity,* no study tackles the aberrancy or queerness at the heart of Ottinger's work, an uncanniness that allegory through its evasive signification markedly underscores.

Another thesis which I should like to explore is Judith Mayne's on the in-direct lesbian eroticism in *Bildnis einer Trinkerin.* She situates the "lesbian sig-natures" in this film as speaking "the marginality of lesbianism" and "another register of desire altogether" (154). What fascinates me in particular is how Ottinger elaborates "that marginality into a visual and narrative momentum of its own" (149), in terms of this present investigation, how queer desires and looks inform an aesthetic of startling apartness and enigmatic significa-tion. Perhaps because of its puzzling transgendered protagonist, a feature it shares with *Freak Orlando, Dorian Gray* has not been the focus of readings from the perspective of female eroticism and hence comparatively little has been written on it and not from a particularly queer perspective.[4] But given that *Dorian Gray,* like *Freak Orlando,* alludes in its very title to the canon of gay and lesbian literature, it promises to be a prime candidate for investiga-tion in terms of its queer sensibilities, especially regarding such issues as the epistemology of the closet, transgendered performance, and visual fascina-tion with the strange spectacle.

The Allegorical Effect

In the central section of *Dorian Gray,* Frau Dr. Mabuse (Delphine Seyrig)[5] takes her prodigy Dorian through a "horror program of the city by night." She promises to show and explain to him the world, as they step down a manhole and pass through dank, dark underground corridors. Dr. Mabuse plays Virgil to Dorian's Dante in this descent through hell, a perverse rendi-tion of Alice's fall down a rabbit hole into Wonderland, or, as the title sug-gests, her Adventures through the Looking Glass. Dr. Mabuse is the calcu-lating mastermind behind the popular press; she is the elegant, deceptively charming, behind-the-scenes tycoon running tabloid publishing around the world. Like her namesake, the quick-change artist from Fritz Lang's films *Dr. Mabuse, The Gambler* (1922), *The Testament of Dr. Mabuse* (1932), and *The 1,000 Eyes of Dr. Mabuse* (1960), she is a sinister manipulator of images. At the start of the film Dr. Mabuse announces to the male media moguls gathered around her (with such names as Mr. Charles Chronicle, Mr. Standard Telegraph, and Mario Scandalo) that they will no longer "live off other people's stories . . . smoothing complex matters, reinterpreting them for our own purposes, trivializing, scandalizing the simplicity left over." Instead they will create their own celebrities and scandals, which she proposes to do by fashioning over the vain young Dorian Gray, making him into a pawn in a worldwide scandal to be publicized as a serialized novel (*Feuilleton-Roman*) in the yellow press. For "Operation Mirror" she plans to match this independently wealthy man with a beautiful actress and track the ups and downs of their affair, which she in fact orchestrates. Thus, as Dr. Mabuse and Dorian later descend together into the sewer world of wayward delights, she makes sure photographers are on hand to capture him indulging in excesses, photos that will appear in the next day's newspapers.

This underground trip, which begins with the drinking of strange elixirs and ends with Dorian in an opium den, exemplifies Ottinger's allegorical tendencies. The voyage begins with a dinner of sumptuously prepared platters that float by Dr. Mabuse and her guest. The chain of buoyant exotic dishes mirrors the serial structure that the entire nocturnal adventure will follow. Fortune cookies contain cryptic messages—"Tears in the Third Eye," "The Black Egg is questioned," "The Seven Sisters control the Twelve"—while Dr. Mabuse's exegesis of them—"That means the Seven Roosters"—is equally incomprehensible. Ottinger turns the riddle into yet another one, making this entire sequence an allegory about allegorical obscurity.

At the first performance in the underground sideshow five characters are playing with dice, and when Dorian joins in they laugh uproariously at the result of his throw; again, the scene of reading is puzzling. Dorian and Dr. Mabuse then walk past two leather-clad women embracing. They move on to a satiric scene depicting a masochistic retired civil servant lying Maratlike in a bathtub who pleads to be insulted; a man then comes to urinate in his tub. At the next stop in this bizarre tour two sailors kiss and then enact a ritualistic knife fight that ends in a mutual stabbing. Throughout Dorian and Dr. Mabuse stand at the corners of the frame, not unlike the patrons of medieval religious paintings who are depicted looking up in adoration at biblical scenes. The two visitors next see, in succession, three children chanting in a circle; a lady Viennese doctor performing weird experiments on naked, prone bodies; and a pantomime of a woman knifing a doll. Finally, Dorian joins a group of men gawking at a dollar strip joint before which bare-breasted overweight women (or are they transvestites?) parade up and down. As the group rushes to dance with the women, Dorian ends up partnered with another

man. Next, while Dr. Mabuse pays a Chinese man to prepare opium for Dorian, the latter watches Siamese twins as they dance and sing. He then settles
into a large cement pipe to smoke the narcotic, as if to suggest he is entering
the world offered him by the smaller pipe.

Others around Dorian in this oddest of opium dens try either to remember or to forget. Voices call upon him to remember, yet although the following images evoke ones previously seen in the film (the skinned boar's head a
child pulls on a string is linked to the pig tethered to Dorian in the opera),
how these images reconfigure or organize his past is unclear. Roswitha
Mueller has suggested that the film's recurring imagery (such as the twin and
trio configurations) creates yet belies an effect of narrative coherence; it supports a "contradiction between linear traditional narration and modernist autonomy of the fragment and repetition for its own sake" (186).

The consecutive images, corridors, and pipes all suggest both rites of passage and the travel narrative. Just as in Dr. Mabuse's inferno Dorian drifts
from one station to the next, so too in his dream he wanders through a sea of
stones. Yet despite the trope of the journey, Dorian's peregrinations are as
aimless as the absence of narrative in the most discontinuous of print media,
the newspaper. One could cast this very dichotomy—one that Mueller defines as occurring between the illusion of narrative continuity and its dissolving into fragments—in terms of allegory. The central section of the film resembles the type of allegory that Joel Fineman sees as "primarily horizontal,
such as a picaresque or quest narrative, where figurative structure is only ca-
sually and allusively appended to the circuit of adventures through time"
(31). Yet although the various stations mark like a clock Dorian's passage
through the hours of the night, a sense of temporal progression is missing.
The numerous scenes are seemingly interchangeable, and their list could
conceivably be contracted or prolonged.

"Horizontal" allegory, then, is less quest than anti-quest. If Dr. Mabuse is
initiating Dorian through the viewing of elaborate rituals, what he is being
initiated into is not revealed. The "horizontal" allegory presupposes a trajectory, yet without a goal, even an intermediate one, to measure progression,
the disparate scenes remain disconnected, isolated, and singular.[6] Separated,
each gallery that Dorian views paradoxically gains in both pictorial vividness
and semantic obscurity. Paul de Man articulates the discrepancy as follows:
"The difficulty of allegory is . . . that this emphatic clarity of representation
does not stand in the service of something that can be represented" ("Pascal's
Allegory," 1). The accumulation of visually intriguing images is both stimu-
lating and yet oddly melancholic, precisely because they are depleted of all
but formal significance. To the same effect, Fineman writes: "if allegorical

themes are in a sense emptied of their content by the structure that governs them, if the particular signifiers of allegory become vehicles of a larger structural story that they carry but in which they play no part, they are at the same time ostentatiously foregrounded by the very structurality that becomes immanent in them" (33).

This hollowed out "horizontal" structure opens room for the counterpoint of another form of movement, that of descent. Instead of developing linearly, the plot takes the spectator down into an abyss or vortex of non-meaning. The underground space offers no sense of direction and appears instead like a maze. This episodic narrative turns as well into a compendium of static tableaux. Ottinger's films seem like sequential collages radically juxtaposing images so as to highlight the gaps between them. Moreover, the camera, as it accompanies Dorian on his voyage, remains withdrawn from each gallery. The spectator's desire to peer more intently at this mix of a freak and peep show is thwarted. Thus despite the voyeuristic scenario staged—of performances of often lewd actions before the intradiegetic spectators—the situation is one of allegorical illegibility and distance. Only the illusion of visibility and sensuousness is created: sense itself is absent.

Dorian and His Doubles

Yet perhaps even more uncanny than the bizarre scenes on Dr. Mabuse's horror tour is Dorian's reaction or rather visible lack thereof. Dorian is an impassive viewer who does not try to interpret the strange scenes before him. He maintains a polite, unchanging expression that betrays only his dullwittedness. This lassitude turns Dorian the spectator into a spectacle; he himself becomes a victim of allegorical petrifaction. Rainer Nägele perceptively writes:

> In allegorical theater, in theatrical allegory, fullness takes on the brutal materiality of stuffed skin, shell, and puppet. No transfigured interiority expresses itself. . . . The scene of show . . . is constituted by pure acts of looking and nothing else. Through this structure theater is intimately linked to allegory. In contrast to the classic-Romantic symbol, allegory does not hide the split between signifier and signified. It stages it. (27)

145

Emphasizing their deadened, allegorical function, the actors in the sideshow resemble marionettes in a puppet theater. As is the case with the fighting sailors or the obese marching prostitutes, their movements are awkward, wooden, and consciously staged. They repel rather than invite audience involvement, identification, or interpretation. Like these actors he views, Dorian is on display for the tabloid spies and photographers. Dr. Mabuse herself is always eyeing him, and clearly in his androgyny he is a fixation for our scopophilia as well. Because he is uncannily lifeless, like an ornament or marionette, Dorian attracts the gaze. Indeed, he is literally Dr. Mabuse's puppet. Correspondingly, as if to signal his awareness that the gaze is upon him, he emits a stiff air of being uncomfortable in whatever situation he finds himself. Cast as a puppet come to life, he raises the question of whether he is alive or dead. This query becomes, as we shall see, actual at the end of the film when, during his apparent funeral, Dorian seems to have come back to life and speeds by in his red sports car, running over and killing his mourners, including Dr. Mabuse. In ultimate revenge for having been used as a pawn, he then appears at the close to have taken over her role as queen of the publishing industry. But not only does Dorian command the uncanny power of the lifeless (or the immortal?), he also is ambiguously neither male nor female.

The split between the actor (a woman) and role (a man) is not dissimilar to the one between signifier and signified in allegory. In both cases—the theatrical and the linguistic—a homogeneity, transparency, or interchangeability between the binary terms is missing. The major question this film raises is thus inherently an allegorical one—how to read the opaque signs of Dorian's gender. For instance, does his effeminate appearance, coupled with the allusion to Oscar Wilde's fictional creation, signify that he represents a gay man? Does the fact that Dorian is played by a woman mean that his love interest in Andamana (Tabea Blumenschein) is lesbian? And is there a connection to the scenes in the sideshow that imply queer sexuality? In other words, does Dorian in this "Operation Mirror" see himself represented in the two leather-clad dykes, the two sailors homoerotically stabbing each other, or in the same-sex doubling of the Siamese twins, who seem to reflect his narcissism? And what is the implication of his being swept up to the stage to dance with another man? Such questions regarding the horror tour as allegory—with its clues to Dorian's sexuality—invite further explanation through reference to the frame story surrounding it.

The central, functionally digressive section to *Dorian Gray* is in part fascinating for its juxtaposition with the main story. If the nocturnal tour follows the allegorical plot of descent and exploration, with at least pretensions to the possibility of self-discovery, then the frame tells a very different tale. It is about the creation of an individual without any depth whatsoever, of a mannequin for the yellow press who appears solely as a two-dimensional image on its front pages. Dorian is supposed to be transparent to the masses that read his face on newsprint. Ironically, the real Dorian is only a simulacrum of

Figure 17. *Dorian Gray im Spiegel der Boulevardpresse* (1984), Veruschka von
Lehndorff and Tabea Blumenschein. Courtesy of the Fotoarchiv, Stiftung
Deutsche Kinemathek, Berlin.

his snapshot. Dr. Mabuse has molded him to be the image she orders to be
photographed.[7] Here simulacrum and allegory overlap, for both mark ir-
reparable distance from an "original" referent.

Yet there is a difference: if allegory is traditionally tantalizingly hard to
read, then Dorian is an absolutely uninteresting character to read (apart from
the gender ambiguity, to which I shall return). Dr. Mabuse tells the media
moguls at the start that the person she has selected for her plan is a "beautiful, somewhat dull, inexperienced young man." Even his pastimes are boring:
when she asks him what he does in the evening he confesses he watches TV
with his Chinese servant, who bears the ironic name of Hollywood (Toyo
Tanaka).[8] The supreme irony is that in her ruse Dr. Mabuse pretends that
Dorian hides something secretive and fascinating which only the tabloids can
reveal. The scandal she devises is the following:

Dr. Mabuse introduces herself to Dorian Gray with an invitation to accompany her to the première of an opera. The performance begins with the

master of ceremonies (Toyo Tanaka) announcing the colonialist story as he stands before a stage. As the curtain unfolds and the camera draws back, we see that the proscenium frame has been erected on a deserted beach, on which the opera itself transpires, with the cliffs next to the shore serving as the magnificent box seats from which Dorian and Dr. Mabuse watch the spectacle. Dorian sees himself in the opera: Veruschka von Lehndorff also plays the role of Don Luis de la Cerda, Infante of Spain, who falls in love with the beautiful Andamana, ruler of the isles his men have just conquered. The clash the opera erects between woman and man, nature and culture, native and European, innocence and cunning, heathen and Christian, between the stiff, self-important Don Luis and the statuesque, naked Andamana, is deceptive in its opposition. Clearly, Andamana with her elaborate headdress and bared bosom is as much a product of Western (male) imagination as is Don Luis in his cumbersome, ostentatious Baroque costume, even more flagrantly so. She is certainly the object of Dorian's fantasy. First narcissistically captivated by seeing his own image perform,[9] Dorian then falls in love with his double's sweetheart, who significantly bears the same name on stage as off. Yet in case he does not fully realize his amorous state (since he is so dumb), Dr. Mabuse has to inform him of it, adding that she is jealous. As a creator of media images, she is well aware that desire is triangular and that its support is phantasmatic.

The rest of the film traces Dr. Mabuse's plot; it follows the romance between Dorian and Andamana to its demise in their apparent, consecutive deaths—of course, announced in her newspaper. The first glitch in Dr. Mabuse's plans occurs when a photo appears from among those taken by her spies, showing her paying large sums of money to the Chinese man for Dorian's opium, thereby betraying her behind-the-scenes setup of the whole affair. As a media tycoon, Dr. Mabuse knows full well that the image controls a person, not vice versa, so that the moment she appears in a photo she knows her influence is beginning to wane. She discovers the mistake as her helpers flash on TV monitors scenes of their newspapers being bought up around the world, with Dorian at the top of the headlines. These stills on the TV monitor demonstrate that we never see directly how Dorian is being read by the scandal-hungry masses. A public reception of Dorian would in fact breathe life back into his image, but Ottinger is intent in showing how Dr. Mabuse's hollow world revolves incestuously around itself. Thus what Ottinger here depicts is an unending series of copies—the photo (on TV) of a photo (from a newspaper) reproducing another photo (of Dorian). Dr. Mabuse's three aids are themselves allegorical acronyms for the roles they play, suggesting that they have no identity outside their professional service: Passat = Program for Semi-Automatic Keyword Selection from Texts (Irm Hermann), Golem = Computerized Investigation Method (Magdalena Montezuma), and Susy = Search System (Barbara Valentin).[10] Dr. Mabuse orders these human robots to find the incriminating photographic negative, an ironic term for the "original" copy we never actually see. The negative reappears later only on another photo on the TV monitor (yet solely when enlarged), showing it in Dorian's hands. Once in possession of the image (rather than being it) Dorian begins his revenge on Dr. Mabuse, which, as already noted, ends with him appropriating her role.

These themes of doublings and narcissistic love, of course, link Ottinger's *Dorian Gray* to Wilde's.[11] Dr. Mabuse is simultaneously the artist Basil Hallward, who paints the portrait of Dorian, and Lord Henry Wotton, who plays up to Dorian's egocentrism and creates the reactions he wants to see in him. Like Wilde's protagonist, who falls in love with his own portrait and kisses it, so too Ottinger's hero leans his cheek rapturously against his mirror image. Wilde's character Sibyl Vane, who commits suicide over Dorian, marginally resembles Andamana: both characters are actresses, both function as Dorian's mirror, and Andamana truly literalizes Vane's name in her own vanity, second only to Dorian's. There are other minor resemblances: Wilde's Dorian also goes to an opium den and eventually leads a sordid underground life. He kills Basil with a knife, the instrument Ottinger's equivalent uses in attacking Dr. Mabuse and her "cocks," the media kings who at the end have donned rooster masks. Roswitha Mueller additionally notes: "Harking back to Oscar Wilde's novel, the stabbing of Mabuse can of course also be seen as the annihilation of his own image, both of the media image created by Mabuse and the reflection of his own character in Mabuse" (187). But where the film significantly differs from its literary model is in the inseparability of Dorian and his media image; in the novella, of course, the portrait reveals Dorian's inner, hideous soul, while its original retains the appearance of purity and an unmarred delicacy.

Wilde's play between life and art—such that art literally imitates life (the portrait mirrors Dorian's descent into depravity) and life imitates the timeless beauty of art (Dorian does not age)—takes a different turn in Ottinger's postmodern film. Here life and the simulacrum become indistinguishable, as Dorian betrays no individuality or psychological depth and hence can provide Dr. Mabuse with the two-dimensional photos she needs. Moreover, if there is in Wilde an attic where the uncanny portrait is stored away, then in Ottinger there is no private space of Dorian's that is not revealed to the public. His supposedly secret rendezvous with Andamana, even their lovemaking, are broadcast to the world. Thus the first glimpse we have of him is

149

when Hollywood pulls back the curtain to his bedroom, a gesture of disclosure that is repeated throughout the film. The closet, if one were to look for it, must be found on a completely different level of the text.

The Masquerade

What is closeted and never revealed, of course, is that Dorian is a woman. If Miriam Hansen, in drawing upon the Wildean allusions in *Bildnis einer Trinkerin*, refers to dandyism as "sublimated transvestism" (203), then *Dorian Gray* literalizes transvestism in its protagonist while dispersing the scene of sublimation throughout the text. The entire discourse that this "mock thriller" (Mueller) is based on—Dr. Mabuse's scheme that pits disclosure against secrecy, public against private, knowledge against ignorance, and truth against falsification—can be seen to be generated from the repressed, unspoken secret of Dorian's gender. The greatest scandal is not the one Dr. Mabuse fashions but that a woman plays a man's role, making what is truly illicit about the affair between Dorian and Andamana its potential queerness.

This oddity can be taken in various ways. First the couple could be seen as only aping a Hollywood romance; their heterosexuality is, after all, constructed, faked, and staged by the press. Second, if Dorian is a woman, then his attraction to Andamana would be lesbian. Especially the photos flashed tantalizingly briefly across the screen of the two in bed elicit a sense of an affair even more taboo than what the tabloids purport to unveil. Moreover, what Russo claims of Magdalena Montezuma in *Freak Orlando* could be said of Veruschka von Lehndorff: it "adds an important trajectory in that she plays a woman playing a man *to another woman*" (104).[12] Third, and even more strangely, Dorian's appearance could be decoded as gay. Like his namesake he leads an effeminate, dandyish lifestyle, which explains the considerable lack of erotic tension between him and Andamana. In all these cases, Dorian's enigmatic sexuality invites a queer reading.

Dorian's bivalence demonstrates how Ottinger challenges gender matrices and the stereotypical roles they assign. By having a woman play a man, she emphasizes how Dorian himself acts out male swaggering. In the opera he struts about stuttering "ich, ich, ich" and generally basks in his position as the desired male, his stiffness mimicking and substituting for phallic potency. Ottinger herself writes about this casting decision: "therefore not only the role of Dorian Gray but also the role of the man is played by a woman" (quoted in *Ulrike Ottinger*, 170–71). If Lacan wrote "virile display itself appears as feminine" (*Feminine Sexuality*, 85), then Ottinger seems to bitingly reply: only once a woman acts out virile display does it appear as display. Dr. Mabuse too can be seen in this light of subversive gendering. Her namesake is male and she displays traditionally male traits of dominance and aggressivity, yet she also resembles the controlling femme: her assertiveness toward Dorian is arguably where the most erotic charge in the film is generated. Similarly, Andamana in her pompadour hairstyle and red taffeta gown can be seen as impersonating femininity. As in her lead roles in *Madame X* and *Bildnis einer Trinkerin*, Tabea Blumenschein plays her hyperbolic part with a cool distance that is heightened by her assigned speechlessness. Each in their own way, Veruschka von Lehndorff, Delphine Seyrig, and Tabea Blumenschein present gender as a facade and performance. If Dorian signifies artifice, then he also signifies the gendered self as artificial and prosthetic.

I do not want to suggest, however, that this dialectic between appearance and recognition, role and truth, is something that the spectator is invited to master and could see through, for the film serves as a constant reminder that vision is always marred by méconnaissance. In a chapter from *The Threshold of the Visible World* devoted to *Bildnis einer Trinkerin*, Kaja Silverman writes that Ottinger's film "stresses that there can be no direct access to the 'self,' and that even the subject's relation to the literal mirror involves all kinds of cultural coercions" (58). The alcoholic, according to Silverman, seeks narcissistic gratification through specularization, but her self-image fails to bolster the fantasy she wishes to have of herself. *Dorian Gray* too indicates that the mirror held up to its main protagonist by the yellow press cannot offer him an image he can unambiguously identify with or define himself by. Cultural representation, which the tabloids signify, always distorts the subject's self-perception. Thus Dorian comports himself stiffly, as someone who apprehends himself from outside himself, who feels the gaze of the camera, this inscription of Otherness, upon him. And yet vain Dorian also loves the reified image that others form of him, which is why Dr. Mabuse chooses him as her victim in the first place and why she constantly informs him of who he is and how he is feeling. In an interview, Ottinger noted that Dorian likes to see his mirror image in the newspaper, even when it is distorted or when it reflects something which does not exist or which he does not appear to be (*Ulrike Ottinger*, 169).

But if Dorian never sees himself from our perspective (as vain and dull), that does not mean that by contrast our gaze is all-knowing. The supreme irony of *Dorian Gray* is that by casting Veruschka von Lehndorff as Dorian, we are the ones who are caught off guard. In the dialectic of the gazes, we are reminded of our inability to see when we look at Dorian and in him perceive a man. Thus the optic misrecognition (but with it fascination) is ultimately

151

ours, not his, proving that Ottinger knows even better than Dr. Mabuse that eroticism lies in the play between secrecy and disclosure. As a personal, rather burlesque confession of such blindness yet also captivation: when I first saw the film, I entered the theater with no forewarning as to what it was about. I missed the clue in the initial credits that its title character was played by a woman. Thus I was profoundly disturbed every time his/her image appeared on the screen. I was confused by the appearance of the five-o'clock shadow and anxiously looked for the tell-tale swelling of the breasts, which I didn't find. Instead, I was confronted with the ostentatious marker of sexual difference in the naked breasts of Tabea Blumenschein and the women parading before the dollar strip joint. In writing on this film, Chris Straayer presumed a much less duped viewer: "The viewer knows that Dorian's covered chest is actually female, but this cannot be separated from the narrative/performance and visual experience of him/her as male. The male chest therefore becomes eroticized" (75). But was the chest male? Every time the curtain was drawn open to Dorian's sleeping quarters, I hoped to find revealed some indication of the actor's sex but only saw him dressed. Veruschka von Lehndorff aroused a scopic fascination that was insatiable. I could never look closely enough, and was relieved when the final credits resolved the ambiguity for me, especially because I felt I was rehearsing the classic psychoanalytic scenario of the child's anxiety—does she have it or not?

In Lacanian terms, Dorian's androgyny functions anamorphotically, as a stain that both provokes yet ultimately blocks one's vision.[13] His body and dress are a constant reminder of the viewer's scotoma. His queerness functions as a scintillating surface or screen behind which the viewer cannot see. The diegetic emphasis on how Dorian is constantly being spied upon and photographed, implying that his life is transparent to the public eye, thus makes mockery of the extradiegetic spectator for whom Dorian's androgyny is unreadable. Moreover, the fact that the other characters are ostensibly impervious to his gender indeterminacy hinders secondary identification with these characters and hence a suturing of oneself into the film. Ottinger thereby uses gender-bending visual alienation as a tool against the classical Hollywood cinematic apparatus.[14]

This indecidability of the sex of one's object of vision characterizes, of course, the operations of fetishism. According to Freud in his 1927 essay "Fetishism," the fetishist is latently homosexual: with the fetish in place, covering or dissimulating the genital area, its user can imagine that his object choice is male (that is, uncastrated, for the fetish covers the frightening site of imputed female castration), but, lest the threat of homosexuality be too strong, he can remove the fetish at will to prove to himself that the object choice is a woman after all. The fetish transfixes one's gaze in order to divert it from nakedness revealed. In general, Ottinger's scintillating costuming functions fetishistically to attract and deflect the eye, halting it at the surface. It is libidinally invested for its proximity to the skin. Especially in the roles played by Tabea Blumenschein, who designs and sews her own costumes, the sumptuous dresses, often made of stiff materials such as leather and taffeta or decorated with hard objects such as mirrors and sequins, endow her with a certain phallicity, most notably in the skin-tight, studded leather suit in *Madame X*, where she plays an imposing dominatrix. Having maimed her right hand, to deny its loss Madame X wears an imposing fetish in its place, a gauntlet with a silver knife extending as its tip. Her dress and behavior thus evoke for the fetishist both masculine and feminine attributes. Insofar as this bivalence is mapped onto a female body, which the female viewer could identify with and/or desire, Ottinger appropriates the domain of the fetish, conceived in Freud as exclusively male, for a visual female erotic.[15]

In Dorian's case (he also wears a red leather suit while riding his moped or car), his eccentric body turns him into a fetish. The spectator can indulge in a constantly reversing play of disavowal: "I know very well that Dorian is played by a woman, but all the same . . . " or "I know very well that Dorian is a man, but. . . . " In his position as either male or female, Dorian can serve to disavow any lack. In addition, if one can read into Dorian signs of either masculinity or femininity, what becomes seductive or attractive about the masquerade is the extent to which it signifies sexual difference alternately.[16] One could even venture a definition of queerness as the fetishistic detachment and highlighting of these contradictory signifiers. For that a queer cinema dismantles the system of sexual difference does not mean that sexual markers are absent from it; it does not regressively deny sexual differences so much as underscore them.

The question arises, however, in his or her struggle between epistemology and desire, does the fetishist always see what he or she wants to see? *Dorian Gray* is a highly unusual specimen of the cross-dressing genre. Other examples clearly share with Ottinger's film the fascination of disbelief: how is it, we ask, that the transvestite's performance can be executed so perfectly? But from the Weimar cross-dressing films to such contemporary examples as *Paris Is Burning* (Jennie Livingston, 1990), a documentary about drag balls among poor Black and Puerto Rican gay men in New York, or *Dream Girls* (Kim Longinotto and Jano Williams, 1993), a documentary about the Takarazuka revue, where actresses play all the men's roles, we know, when we watch, what the actual sex of the performer is, despite the seamless passing. Our pleasure is dependent on this superior knowledge; in fact, we see the

153

transvestite both in and out of costume. Chris Straayer labels such switching temporary transvestism as opposed to trans-sex casting, "where sexual disguise is produced profilmically" (43). *Dorian Gray* is one of her few examples of the latter genre: Ottinger refuses to show Veruschka von Lehndorff as a woman, although the entire plot unwinds around the topic of leaking sexual secrets. Ottinger thereby reminds us that one does not always see what one wants to in the masquerade. Gender performance can only be liberating and subversive when the spectator masters the irony and recognizes the deviance from the gender norm. In *Dorian Gray* the gender performance is more disquieting than emancipatory because visible contradictions in Dorian's gender are erased. Had the disguise been unconvincing, the viewer would feel his/her sense of mastery over gender reconfirmed, although paradoxically at the cost of repression: as Straayer writes, "It is a fear of actual cross-sex passing that necessitates the convention of inadequate disguise" (57). Dorian indeed arouses this anxiety. Moreover, this difference between trans-sex casting and temporary transvestism explains why Ottinger's films lack the campiness prevalent in Rosa von Praunheim's or Lothar Lambert's films, where camp performs an open secret and presupposes irony and hence a spectator in the know. The tinge of the improper, fake, or camouflage is missing from Ottinger, where instead the artifice is immaculately constructed and sustainedly performed.

Thus it is not only on the level of the plot that Dorian is a purely exhibited body. For the viewer of the film as well he is *donné à voir*, destined to be scrutinized for his denaturalized physiognomy. Dorian therewith joins a host of other sexually ambiguous freaks or, as I would like to call them, queers in Ottinger's repertoire, where they are intradiegetically the subject of spectatorial fascination as well as ridicule. In *Madame X,*[17] for example, an androgynous shipwrecked Belcampo (Mackay Taylor) is rescued by Madame X's ship, and is the only "male" character tolerated among the all-female crew by virtue of his gender indeterminacy. Because he cannot speak except in gestures, his voice does not betray him. His very name alludes to the attractive play of camp, and indeed he serves as a jester to the nautical court. When he saves a tiny Russian sailor, he homoerotically hugs and fondles him, further emphasizing his queerness and providing a spectacle for Madame X (she represents an imperious, omnipresent gaze much like Magdalena Montezuma in Schroeter's *Willow Springs,* who also polices an all-female community). Another dual-gendered, queer character who is strangely eroticized by virtue of how s/he solicits our look is Orlando/Orlanda (Magdalena Montezuma), the eccentric transformational body in *Freak Orlando.* Over the ages s/he consecutively takes the form of a three-eyed Cyclops, a two-headed body, a man

Figure 18. *Dorian Gray im Spiegel der Boulevardpresse* (1984), Veruschka von Lehndorff as Dorian. Courtesy of the Fotoarchiv, Stiftung Deutsche Kinemathek, Berlin.

who aberrantly has fish scales for hair, and finally a female master of cere-monies in a contest for the most ugly freak. As with Dorian and Belcampo, gender ambiguity makes Orlando the focus of intradiegetic spectatorial cap-tivation, but also of persecution; one episode reenacts, like the opera in *Do-rian Gray*, the Inquisition. Orlando, who repeatedly finds company among the physically deformed, is a social outcast. But s/he also takes performance into his/her own hands when, in conclusion, s/he hosts a burlesque outdoor stage contest entertaining and starring other freaks. Comically, the winner is an ordinary middle-aged businessman for psychopharmaceuticals who inad-vertently walks onto the stage.

Like the freaks who perform at the ending of *Freak Orlando* and like the third enigmatic eye of Orlanda Zyklopa shown in close-up at the beginning, Dorian embodies the Lacanian gaze that looks back and makes us aware of our viewing and inability to comprehend what we see, no matter how much we stare. Thus it is not Dorian as freak who is the object of the gaze, but we who are the blinded subjects. For this reason, I would maintain, Dorian tri-umphs in the end, where the sequence and outcome of events become confusing to the spectator. At first it seems as if Dr. Mabuse elaborately stages Dorian's funeral, complete with dromedaries in the cortege. The sanctimonious burial of a media celebrity recalls the ending of Volker Schlöndorff's *The Lost Honor of Katharina Blum* (1975), where the death of a devious tabloid journalist draws the hypocritical newspaper world together in mourning.[18] But Ottinger parodies Schlöndorff's ending by resurrecting Dorian, who triumphantly speeds by in his red sports car (though we never see his face), running over and killing the guests. The final image then presents Dorian in a suit giving orders, for he has now taken over Dr. Mabuse's position. Just as Dorian's hybrid gender and consequently vague sexuality trump our looking, so here too his bivalent status as neither dead nor alive surprises the viewer: he holds a newspaper announcing his death. The entire concluding section breaks unexpectedly away from narrative predictability and reassurance.

With this ending Dorian as queer has triumphed. By destroying social constructions of himself he has become powerful. Looking straight into the camera with hair slicked back and wearing a pinstriped dark suit, Dorian suddenly seems to have mastered his own image and has moved from an effeminate style to a butch one. For the first time, Veruschka von Lehndorff looks like a Wall Street dyke dressed for success and able to manipulate the symbolic order, represented by the newspaper she is holding, with its headlines, "Dorian Gray Dead." It is another, metamorphized Dorian we see.

This episodic, even incoherent series of events takes us back to our opening discussion of the allegorical narrative and raises the question: to what extent does Dorian's gender pertain to the allegorical effect? As a gender-ambiguous as well as artificial, statuesque, and undead figure, Dorian is another unreadable allegorical object in this film. Like allegory, Dorian proclaims his own artifice. He moreover demonstrates the link between allegory and perversion: they both signal something not quite right and threaten to embody something not fully understood. Like allegory, perversion belongs not to a natural order but to an ornamental one. As the ending underscores, Dorian represents a misleading sign that camps up its status as sign, making the desire for a definite referent (does he signal masculinity or femininity, homosexuality or heterosexuality, defeat or victory?) all the stronger. Furthermore, allegory shares with Ottinger's experiment with the closet an investment in the epistemological order of truth and deceit, secrecy and disclosure, accompanied by the intent of thwarting this order. The film repeatedly illustrates how "truth," especially of one's gender and sexuality, cannot be fully revealed, despite the attempt by the hegemonic regime (here represented by the media) to do so. Instead this "truth" remains cloaked in allegorical enigma.

SIX

Lesbians Abroad

The Queer Nationhood of Monika Treut et al.

In the productive years for German lesbian cinema during the 1980s and 1990s, the crossing of gender boundaries and heterosexual norms frequently came to be associated with a different kind of boundary crossing—that of place. As mentioned in the previous chapter, already in 1977 in Ulrike Ottinger's *Madame X* women come to the piratess from around the world and take to the high seas. Although each woman in Madame X's entourage maintains her camp, exaggerated national identity (Flora Tannenbaum from Germany, Betty Brillo from suburban America, and Noa-Noa from Polynesia), together they colorfully mix and mingle on board. Two years later in *Bildnis einer Trinkerin (Ticket of No Return)* Ottinger again has her lesbian heroine crossing borders and taboos: a luxuriously dressed but silent foreigner flies to Berlin for a self-indulgent drinking spree. On the streets and in the bars of Berlin the alcoholic is a markedly exotic woman. Yet despite her otherness, the nonverbal friendship between the drinker and the bag lady suggests that a female mutual attraction can transcend cultural differences. Later in *Johanna d'Arc of Mongolia* (1989), the Western women slip into the foreign culture and, through bonding with the women there, wear the new culture as their own, without misappropriating or colonizing it. Through their woman-identified closeness, the outsiders both participate in the matriarchal civilization and stand in appreciative awe of it, in Ottinger's investigation of the manifold registers of female desire. Here lesbian desires bridge cultural differences yet are also aroused by them. As Brenda Longfellow writes: "*Johanna d'Arc of Mongolia* repeats this erotic scenario of orientalism, mediating lesbian desire through the desire for a racial and cultural other. . . . Here difference does not provoke anxiety—it is, precisely, the lure and the cause of desire" (135). Similarly, in discussing *Bildnis einer Trinkerin*, Judith Mayne speaks of Ottinger's "eroticizing of the thresholds and boundaries that exist among women" (142). In this chapter I hope to offer several other examples of how national and erotic frontiers are traversed by lesbians.

After Ottinger's groundbreaking films of the 1970s, more examples of the lesbian abroad arise in the 1980s and 1990s. For instance, in her *Novembermond* (*November Moon*) (1985) Alexandra von Grote sets the loyal, self-sacrificing love between a Jewish woman from Berlin and a French native in Nazi-occupied Paris. In her earlier *Weggehen um anzukommen* (*Depart to Arrive*) (1981) the relationship between Regine and Anna breaks up, with the latter leaving for the French countryside to recuperate and rediscover herself. The brief lesbian affair in Ingemo Engström's *Flucht in den Norden* (*Flight to the North*) (1985) occurs in Finland, although it quickly gives way to a torrid heterosexual love affair.[1] After the female homosociality of most of her films, Margarethe von Trotta finally broached lesbianism directly in *Die Rückkehr* (*L'Africana*) (1990), again taking Paris as the prime setting. And in *Salmonberries* (1991) Percy Adlon shows two cultures, that of an East German exile, Roswitha, and a woman of native American heritage, Kotzebue (played by country singer lesbian idol, k d lang), coming together first in icy Alaska and then in Berlin, to which the two travel in search of Roswitha's past. The film simultaneously maps cultural crisscrossing as the encounter between femme and butch.[2] Less known are Stefanie Jordan's short *Crude* (1996) on the leather crowd at the Folsom Street Fair in San Francisco and the recent lesbian video documentaries by Mahide Lein and Dorothea Etzler on the problems of speaking openly about taboo desires in sexually less tolerant societies: made together with Pakaipei Sue Maluwa-Bruce, *Schick mir mal eine Postkarte* (*Send Me a Postcard*) (1997) depicts daily life in Zimbabwe, while *Weisse Nächte in Hell-Blau und Rosa* (*White Nights in Light Blue and Pink*) (1997) documents the lesbian and gay gatherings in today's Russia.

The most renowned of the directors setting her women characters abroad, however, is Monika Treut. It is not surprising that she has a stronger lesbian cult following in America than in Germany, for, apart from her first film *Verführung: Die grausame Frau* (*Seduction: The Cruel Woman*) (1985), all her films were produced in an American context. Two of her best-known features, *Die Jungfrauenmaschine* (*Virgin Machine*) (1988) and *My Father Is Coming* (1991), depict the heroine crossing the Atlantic to set up housekeeping in San Francisco and New York City, respectively. Her collection of documentary shorts *Female Misbehavior* (1992) is devoted to four strong personalities from America. Although it takes place in Treut's home town of Hamburg, another short, *Taboo Parlor*, marks Treut's first brush with Hollywood producers. It was included in the omnibus film *Erotique* (1994), itself an international endeavor with contributions from female directors from the United States, Germany, Hong Kong, and (originally) Brazil. Likewise cosmopolitan in spirit is Treut's video *Didn't Do It for Love* (1997) on the dominatrix Eva Norvind, who currently lives in New York but comes from Norway, has lived around the world, and is fluent is several languages. Much of Treut's fascination with this personage lies in Norvind's adeptness in traversing boundaries—sexual as well as geographic. Finally, Treut's subsequent documentary *Gendernauts* (1998) investigates women from San Francisco who cross the gender divide by experimenting with varying doses of testosterone.

Theoretically speaking, all these films—from Ottinger's to Treut's—serve to investigate how current discourses on sexuality and place intersect. They raise a number of fascinating questions: How can the lesbian thematic reassess problems of social assimilation, territorialization, and appropriation? Conversely, how does the trope of mobility inform issues of gender and sexual affiliations? Are there ways in which sexual difference is recoded as ethnic and racial otherness, and what are the problems that such representation of an alterity present? Moreover, can the juxtaposition of sexual and national identity liberate one from the deterministic assumption that sexuality is cultural inheritance? Are nationality and sexuality inevitable and natural or variable and expropriable? In raising these questions, such films variously discover new ways of expressing how multicentered realities can be. They thus challenge static views of identity alignment.

German cinema is conceivably in a privileged position to attempt such an investigation, when one considers that gay and lesbian identity politics is arguably less highly profiled and activist in Germany than in the States, a difference that makes its cinema more flexible and inventive in the ways it encodes sexual preference. Monika Treut, for example, has surmised that one of the reasons for a greater openness toward homosexuality in Germany and consequently a less politicized gay rights movement is "that after the Third Reich, and with the constitution of the Federal Republic of Germany, people have become very sensitive—have had to be very sensitive—when defining others as outcasts" (Gemünden, Kuzniar, Phillips, 4). Although I recognize how risky it is to speculate about the parallels between the weighty subjects of nationality and sexuality (and I hope to show that these films do so in very sophisticated ways), perhaps it can be said that the lack of a postwar German national identity, or resistance to such an identity, together with this sensitivity to "defining others as outcasts," has made certain directors open to queerness as resistance to restricting affiliations and classifications. The eagerness with which a number of German directors sent their lesbian heroines abroad, I think, indicates a preparedness to address the problem of ostracism (which arises from anxieties about the stability of one's own ego) by advocating flexible, provisory selfhoods. The lesbian residing overseas, in these films, renegotiates her sexual desires and identity in terms of the society around her.

159

Given the wide selection of films that treat the lesbian abroad, I want to focus my inquiry by discussing three films. In the first two films, Rosa von Praunheim's *Überleben in New York* (*Survival in New York*) (1989) and Monika Treut's *My Father Is Coming*, the lesbian immigrant to New York is able to come out to herself and others in her newly adopted home, thanks to its welcoming gay community. This openness to sexual alternatives sets the tone for a broadmindedness toward other cultural differences as well. The German background of the recent newcomer barely sets her apart in this multiethnic and multiracial metropolis; there is hardly any question of her not fitting into certain strata of American society. The third film I shall discuss in detail is a delightful short, *Heldinnen der Liebe* (*Heroines of Love*) (1997) by the young Berlin filmmakers Nathalie Percillier and Lily Besilly (whose work will be treated in more detail in the last chapter). In *Heldinnen der Liebe* lesbian faces lesbian on the "no-man's land" of the deserted war front, where enemy lines meet. Again queer solidarity overrides divisions between countries, as the French and German female soldiers (played by the directors themselves) fall in love.

Rosa von Praunheim's 'Überleben in New York'

Rosa von Praunheim's *Überleben in New York* is a documentary about three German women who, each in their unique way, establish new lives for themselves in the Big Apple. The film is in German, with the occasional English interview translated in voice-over. As these women alternately narrate in bits and pieces the history of their sojourns in New York, the camera roams throughout the city, noting its diversity of race, class, and culture. The editing mitigates and breaches divisions and differences; as von Praunheim cuts from one woman to the next, the spectator senses a fluidity and commonality between them, as if their lives stood for the flux of life in Manhattan.

These women have crossed not only national borders but racial divisions as well. Uli, a nurse and animal rights activist, falls in love with a Guardian Angel and lives for three years with him in Harlem as the only white woman in the neighborhood. She then hooks up with an emotionally disabled white Vietnam vet. Anna, a go-go dancer and psychotherapist who counsels in an African-American Catholic school, marries a black man whom she met dancing and whose stylish flair matches her own striking appearance. Claudia, the third woman, comes to the United States with a German boyfriend, whom she dumps when her lesbian tendencies start to grow. Before the camera she enumerates what New York has helped her realize: the extroverted element in

Figure 19. *Überleben in New York* (1989), Anna, Rosa von Praunheim, Claudia, and Uli. Courtesy of Rosa von Praunheim.

her personality, the freedom to acknowledge who she is, and the total opening of herself. She admits to having been confronted with complete truths about herself. Claudia's Atlantic crossing thus suggests the crossing that her coming out also marks. Yet in a characteristic mode for the Queer German Cinema, which, as I argued in the introduction, is predominantly post-closet, Rosa von Praunheim concentrates on Claudia's current life as a lesbian and not on the stations of her sexual awakening.

To get her green card, Claudia marries an underground theater star who specializes in transvestite parts and who enters the marriage as if it were another stage role. It is her lesbian partner Ryan who locates John for Claudia. If Claudia's "marriage" is theatrical and queer, then the other two women make straightness seem like drag. The hyperbole with which Anna and Uli display femininity suggests a conscious, controlled playing with sexual norms that bespeaks a queer sensibility, despite the fact that ultrafemininity is normally (and is here) associated with heterosexuality.[3] Anna, for instance, performs at the go-go club with cool, amused detachment, using moves calculated to arouse men. Uli wears doll-like garb—dressed either totally in bright red with matching accessories or in shades of pink (perhaps in honor of Rosa)—with two

Figure 20.   *Überleben in New York* (1989), Anna. Courtesy of Rosa von
Praunheim.

large ponytails tied up with conspicuous bows. She carries a Little-Red-
Riding-Hood basket to complete the look. These women present themselves
as playing with gender and experimenting with sexual self-expression. In addition, their willingness to appear before the camera serves as a crucial dimension to their conscious articulation of an eroticized selfhood. In one scene in
particular, Claudia, who is probably in her mid- to late forties, poses as a nude
model in an artist's studio, evidently comfortable not only in front of the artist
but before the camera as well. The fact that the three women have freely
adapted to their new environment and thrive in it underscores how they have
constructed identities for themselves, including their sexual components. By
documenting their lives, Praunheim exuberantly affirms their choices.

Central here is the fact that sexuality, for which Claudia's lesbianism is
paradigmatic, is encoded as a realignment of national and cultural affiliations.
In this shift what is important is not that German and American cultures are
compared: there is no dichotomous weighing of the pros and cons of each
country, for Claudia, Anna, and Uli live in the here-and-now of New York.

National heritage is thus incidental and decidedly not formative. Moreover, Praunheim in no way stereotypes these women as German, as Percy Adlon does with the characters Marianne Sägebrecht plays in *Out of Rosenheim* (*Bagdad Café*) (1988) and *Rosalie Goes Shopping* (1990).[4] What is important instead is the naturalness with which Praunheim's women have adopted a different cultural lifestyle. In the postmodern mélange of this film, they step over prescribed ethnic and gender roles as well as sexual and racial taboos without making a big deal of their nonconformity. Furthermore, the new identities they assume do not appear arbitrary or frivolous, as if they were simply donning clothing or costuming (despite the importance of dress just discussed). Anna, Uli, and Claudia do not give the impression that they are merely tourists playing at being American: their originally fashioned cross-identifications sit comfortably on them. In other words, despite the autonomy they exercise in their sometimes flamboyant lifestyle choices (which links them to Praunheim's other lead roles, Lotti Huber in *Anita: Tänze des Lasters* and Charlotte von Mahlsdorf in *Ich bin meine eigene Frau*) and in order to deter us from jumping to the conclusion that gender performance is synonymous with inauthenticity, all three women give the strong impression of sincerity and conviction.

It thus must be underscored that to attribute their individuality to the move to New York would be a reductive reading of the film that would rob the women of their own agency. Undoubtedly, New York exposes these women to unfamiliar and varied experiences, but Praunheim does not thereby suggest that the new cultural and social environment determines their characters, insofar as the three never express the need or desire to be assimilated. In other words, the new location signals or signifies their individuality more than it is the cause of it. Just as these women energetically experiment with different sexual identities, so too, by not dwelling on their nationality, do they portray national character and its inheritance as arbitrary and the concept of it as inappropriate. There is an ethics of cosmopolitanism at work here that derives from the same spirit as sexual tolerance. In addition, the novelty as well as the odd diversity of America that these German women (together with Praunheim) appreciatively experience—the *queerness* of this new land (to use the word as a trope)—paradoxically makes them fit in as foreigners. Here I deploy the word "queer" guardedly not to reify otherness (in this case, the otherness of America) but, on the contrary, in Eve Sedgwick's definition of the term, to refer to "the open mesh of possibilities, gaps, overlaps, dissonances, and resonances, lapses and excesses of meaning [that can't be made] to signify monolithically" (*Tendencies*, 8).

163

Monika Treut's 'My Father Is Coming'

Before turning to the more complicated narrative plot of *My Father Is Coming*, I want to consider how the biographical narrative of Eva Norvind in Treut's more recent work, *Didn't Do It for Love*, exemplifies the director's fascination with the crossing of national and sexual boundaries, and how she deftly intersects cultural and sexual matrices. The documentary is based on the life of the Norwegian Eva Norvind, who was born in 1944 and moved with her mother to France in 1958 and from there alone to New York in 1960. During the 1960s she starred as a blond bombshell in Mexican B-movies. Treut gives a synopsis of her subsequent life as follows: "She spoke out for abortion and women's rights and was kicked out of Mexico. She went to what was still the Soviet Union and became a professional photographer. In the '80s she was New York's most famous dominatrix, and she still runs a dungeon in midtown. And she said to me, 'Monika, I'm so tired of being a dominatrix. I just came back from India. I'm working every year now with Mother Teresa.' By now, she speaks eight languages fluently: Norwegian, Swedish, Danish, German, French, Spanish, English, and Italian. She's learning Japanese and Arabic, and she's also taking courses in Swahili. She's a cultural chameleon" (Gemünden, Kuzniar, Philips, 11). Treut problematizes Eva's lifelong journeying by closing *Didn't Do It for Love* with the latter's insight: "It's easy to travel around the world, what's difficult is to stay in one place with myself." Eva's transgression of national borders and cultural mores is thus not unreflectively celebrated by the video; Treut recognizes the psychological costs and causes of her subject's malleable character.

The central section of *Didn't Do It for Love* is disturbing, though exhilarating. It is composed of a gorgeously shot black-and-white sadomasochistic interlude between Eva in her leather outfit and the naked, prone young woman on whom Eva plays with a knife and flame. Just as Eva's national identity is complex, so too is her sexuality. She speaks as openly about her intimate affairs with women as with men. And clearly her heterosexual relations, whether staged or not, are queer in their unconventionality, for instance, in the campy clips from her 1960s movies or in her current partnership with a much younger African American, whom she met through the personals. As we shall see with Treut's other female heroines, Eva cannot be classified as hetero, lesbian, or even bisexual. Especially in her exploration of sadomasochism, she is, to rephrase Treut, "a sexual chameleon." Treut takes her fascination with metamorphizing sexualities even further in her newest project on women who experiment with testosterone dosages and who thereby push

Figure 21.   *Didn't Do It for Love* (1998), Eva Norvind (left). Courtesy of Monika Treut.

back gender frontiers and deconstruct the male-female binary. They create a third sex that seems more natural than the first two.

As in *Didn't Do It for Love*, in *My Father Is Coming* Treut explores the criss-crossing of exotica and erotica; here individuals representing the gamut of unconventional sexualities and various ethnicities meet in New York. In brief, this is the story of *My Father Is Coming*: Vicky (Shelley Kästner), who waits tables and tries to land acting jobs, gets a visit from her rather over-weight German father Hans (Alfred Edel). When he first arrives, he behaves like a stereotypical German tourist who comes to colonize and civilize America: he brings sausage in his suitcase and insists one can't find the likes of it in New York; he asks if at least the water is potable. Yet the more obnoxiously he behaves as a foreigner, the more he is reminded by others of the Germans' Nazi past. Vicky, in the meantime, hits a streak of bad luck. While her father lands a spot in a commercial, Vicky auditions in vain to get a part in Annie Sprinkle's new film *Pornutopia*.[5] Then she is torn in her amorous leanings: she finds herself attracted simultaneously to a handsome female-to-male trans-sexual and to her co-worker, a Puerto Rican woman named Lisa, who suf-fered abject poverty in childhood and now loves to eat. When her father dis-

165

covers the two women in bed together, after Vicky has acted as if her gay roommate Ben were her husband, he (the father) disappears. After a kind of New Age sexual experience with Annie, exposure to sex shops, and an encounter with a middle-aged guru who practices skin-piercing, Hans, espying Vicky in a bar, goes in to tell her he accepts her lifestyle. He toasts America and soon leaves for home sporting a baseball cap.

Jo, the transsexual, states that "people should have the choice to become who they are." One's past—whether it be one's nationality (Hans), class (Lisa),[6] or even sex (Jo)—can be altered. Who a person is can never be taken for granted despite all appearances. Treut seems to suggest, moreover, that one becomes who one is through acting. Hans begins his transformation by starring in a commercial, and Vicky appears to fully realize her passion for Lisa in a torch song she performs at a club. In a fine example of the simulacrum, Annie Sprinkle even makes an audition for a porno flick an occasion for imaginatively experiencing sexual ecstasy—or so it seems. Conversely, the real "put-on," the marriage, is seen through as just an act.[7]

In a scene in Vicky's apartment, the camera pans across a poster of Marlene Dietrich in a man's suit: is this immaculate actress gay or straight, German or American? If sexuality isn't something given but something one becomes or acts out, then nationality too is a matter of performance. The opening sequence shows Vicky auditioning for a part as a German tourist in a Chinese restaurant and being coached to behave like a concentration "camp" commandant. The scene exposes American prejudices against Germans, yet it also suggests that national affiliation is a pose or put-on anyway. The film points out that in order to have your nationality recognized, you have to act it out, thereby suggesting that it is not something readily knowable or readable, let alone natural. Thus Lisa, who speaks like a native New Yorker, says no one believes her when she says she is Puerto Rican. Hans's boorishness and heavy German accent make his adherence to his national identity look ridiculous. Then, in adopting American culture, Hans and Vicky make Americanisms—like the baseball cap—seem arbitrary. This is not to say that the film levels ethnic or cultural differences or is fundamentally indifferent to them, but that it plays up their queerness. This film portrays nationality, American as well as German, as a form of drag.

Significantly, neither Vicky nor Hans could pass as Americans, yet they can cross over into the new culture. Rather than flawlessly imitating American speech, dress, or gestures, they retain the marks of cultural difference. Indeed, one could say that Treut has them adopting a nationality that is not their own in order to highlight and resignify these differences ironically. The gap between performance and "original" clearly emphasizes that one is not

Figure 22. Monika Treut. Photo by Elfi Mikesch. Courtesy of Monika Treut.

what one performs, yet not in any negative sense. By the end of the film, Hans no longer takes as natural and self-evident what we as viewers saw as arbitrary—namely, his German prejudices against America. Instead, upon being exposed to the theatricality of porn and skin-piercing artists, Hans himself becomes accepting of and even playful with signifiers of identity. We in turn become accepting of his overweight body, and welcome, as does Annie Sprinkle, his expressions of sexual desire. In other words, the citationality of a nationalistic mode of behavior that makes Hans look ridiculous does not have to be compulsory, as it is for him at the start of the film, but can be voluntary and playful.[8] Rejoicing at playing a part in a commercial and earning big bucks for it, Hans learns to cite and mime American custom with ease.[9] Nor is Hans's mimicry of American custom a question of assimilation—in other words, of his need to recognize himself in the signifiers of another culture and to remain in this country. That this does not occur is not a disappointment to him but rather a liberation from fixed identity categories, the source of judgmental prejudice; hence he accepts his daughter's sexuality, which, significantly, is also not easily pigeonholed.

167

If Hans crosses not only the Atlantic but also (in his *coming* of age) the taboo that older men don't have the right to explore new sexualities (let alone have them depicted on screen), then Vicky too crosses various sexual norms. She is implicitly classed as a femme when Ben asks her if she has ever made it with a dyke, and indeed she plays the femme to Lisa's butch.[10] But she also tries, unsuccessfully, to pass as a married, straight woman (and even faintly comes on to Ben at one point when they are alone together in her bedroom watching gay male porn). Moreover, she welcomes Jo's hot attentions, and only later finds out that Jo is a transsexual. Are we to read Vicky's variegated sexual interests as a mark of indecisiveness or ambivalence, especially when compared to other characters who more actively pursue their sexual desires? Or is she best characterized as a bisexual femme who knows she wants it all? That we do not know the answers to these questions is in itself significant.

Biddy Martin has noted the subversive potential of the femme for deconstructing reifying gender categories:

> The very fact that the femme may pass implies the possibility of denaturalizing heterosexuality by emphasizing the permeabilities of gay/straight boundaries. In a sense, the lesbian femme who can supposedly pass could be said most successfully to displace the opposition between imitation (of straight roles) and lesbian specificity, since she is neither the same nor different, but both. (113)

Vicky's femmeness does demonstrate the permeability of gay and straight boundaries,[11] especially when she feels attracted to Jo, leading us to speculate whether she is fascinated by his manliness, his femininity, or the confusion between the two, and whether her attraction is intensified after she learns of Jo's sex change. Thus, despite her passivity in comparison to other characters, the very mutability of Vicky's desires places her in a central position in the film, around which the others circulate. She may not define herself as lesbian, but what is important is that she experiences lesbian sex and directs her desires to characters who are not straight. Treut thereby eschews adherence to sexual identity categorizations.[12] In an interview, Treut has said,

> I'm not very much in love with the identity concept, because I think it's somewhat restrictive—the idea that people have a single identity. We have so many different parts and we're made up of so many pieces that it's difficult to say "I'm a lesbian" to describe a whole self. . . . This labeling gives . . . a sense of false identity, be it via sexuality or ethnicity or bodily appearance. (Gemünden, Kuzniar, Phillips, 4)

In terms of nationality, Vicky performs a key role: neither German nor American, in Biddy Martin's terms, "neither the same nor different, but both," she deconstructs the opposition. In addition, Treut avoids, as does Praunheim, propagating the prevalent image of America as the land of (in this case erotic) freedom. These directors do not equate sexual liberation with exposure to America or queer sexuality with being American, as it might seem in a facile reading of the travel narrative in these films. Indeed, the butch-looking women in *My Father Is Coming* hail from different countries: Vicky's two neighbors are Hungarian, and, as mentioned, Lisa is Puerto Rican.[13] Moreover, Ben goes after Latino men. In other words, neither von Praunheim nor Treut simplistically map sexual preference onto national differences, an insidious move that would reify gay/straight and native/foreign oppositions. Insofar as their characters *cross* boundaries, Treut and von Praunheim work against a binary mode of perception that creates otherness, whether it be sexual or ethnic exoticism.

This crossing or permeability stands in distinct contrast to earlier German films, such as Werner Herzog's *Stroszek* (1976) or Wim Wenders's *Alice in den Städten* (*Alice in the Cities*) (1974) and *Der Stand der Dinge* (*The State of Things*) (1982), that made the trip to the United States seem like exile. Praunheim's and Treut's work, exhibiting no nostalgia for life back home, is also distinct from the longing for family that infuses Chantal Akerman's *News from Home* (1977), where a constant voice-over reads a French mother's letters to her daughter in New York. Praunheim and Treut are thus closer to the postmodern sensibility of Wenders's *Bis ans Ende der Welt* (*Until the End of the World*) (1991) which makes its travelers seemingly at ease at stopovers around the globe. Yet an important difference sets *Überleben in New York* and *My Father Is Coming* apart from these other films occurring in the United States: the effortless crossing of cultural barriers is simultaneously a very natural crossing or obscuring of heterosexual gender boundaries. Queer sexuality rather than nationality becomes the major (now positive) signifier of difference.

In sum, in their studies in postmodern cross-culturalism both Treut and Praunheim advocate a truly queer nationhood. In the foreign land, one's search for identity leads neither back to one's cultural roots nor to adaptation and assimilation but to an allegiance to queerness, which is to say, to the productive dissonances in the cross-identifications that compose one's personality. The very word "queer" affirms both one's immigrant and sexual status as an outsider and marks them not as stigmas but as performance, and thus as chosen. Praunheim's and Treut's immigrants do not so much discover a monolithic America and try to fit in to its social structure as they construct a community of another culture for themselves. They (and we, the spectators) see this country through their eyes. The determining paradigm for this queerying of national and cultural identity is the receptivity both films demonstrate to a range of sexual expressions and experimentation.

Nathalie Percillier and Lily Besilly's 'Heldinnen der Liebe'

In *Heldinnen der Liebe*, Nathalie Percillier and Lily Besilly also postulate the utopia of a queer nationhood, one that would deconstruct nationalistic differences. And like *My Father Is Coming*, it uses comedy to diffuse the tension between the oppositions it sets up. Winner of the prestigious Teddy Award for best gay and lesbian short at the 1997 Berlinale,[14] *Heldinnen der Liebe* is a ten-minute slapstick comedy that is accompanied by piano, clarinet, accordion, and tuba music, played by the all-female Swiss band "Les Reines Prochaines."[15] Shot in super-8 at 18 frames per second but reproduced at 24 frames per second, the film has a stylishly dated, "jerky" look. Nathalie Percillier plays Jeanne Derc, a French soldier left behind at the front by her fellow troops because they didn't want to wake her. The film cuts to the German Ute Hau, played by Lily Besilly, wandering aimlessly through the woods, having lost her battalion eleven days ago. Whereas Jeanne settles down to a picnic lunch à la française, Ute enjoys a Wurstchen that squeaks every time she bites into it. The two women are also signified by different musical leitmotivs, in Jeanne's case with strains of the "Marseillaise." Once Jeanne discovers a pair of heavy German white briefs, she knows that the enemy is nearby. In the delightfully ridiculous detail of this film, Ute captures Jeanne by lassoing her. The intertitle announces a cut to "weeks later": the women are kissing warmly. They have set up a tent, tend a cabbage patch, and shoot their own game (shooting into the air at a tiny fish that lands in the frying pan). When the weather gets too cold, they decide to pack up camp and, after months of wandering, land at the Brandenburg Gate, where they are photographed by curious tourists. In the throng we also see the cinematographer Stefanie Jordan behind the camera.

On many levels, *Heldinnen der Liebe* is sophisticated for its dialectical presentation of ethnic, gender, and sexual differences. Primarily, it is a send-up of ethnic stereotypes and renders harmless the national differences that lead to enmity. The directors play upon these differences yet override and deflate the hostilities that chauvinism generates. National character becomes a matter of drag, signified by underwear and food. By this camping, and via the cross-cutting that characterizes the first half of the film, *Heldinnen der Liebe* foregrounds ethnicity as the primary trope of difference; however, it is undermined by the other signifier of difference, lesbianism, which takes over in the second half. In this brilliant juxtaposing of nationality and sexuality, patriotism and militarism are staged as a pose or front that is dropped once the women fall in love.

Figure 23. *Heldinnen der Liebe* (1997), Lily Besilly and Nathalie Percillier.
Courtesy of Heldinnenfilm.

The male/female binary is likewise subverted by casting women in traditionally male roles. Jeanne portrays soldierly male behavior as drag as she
pompously marches up and down, shouldering her rifle. The mild, self-ironic
lesbian/feminist statement of the film is that, rather than fighting, women
prefer to sleep in, fall in love, and devote themselves to domestic duties. Yet
Heldinnen der Liebe does not leave lesbians unscathed by its humor; it pokes
fun at the women by stereotypically showing them content to be with each
other over the years, even decades, oblivious to the outside world. Especially
the near-sighted Ute parodies the cliche of the lesbian as plain and homely.

In terms of its representation of space, the film serves as a metacommen-
tary on where lesbians can find safe refuge—in this "no-man's land," this
tiny plot abandoned by men and forgotten by the rest of the world. The issue of territorialization and appropriation, too, is transformed by the lesbian
thematic: instead of conquering the land of the enemy, they set up a home
and garden. The ending likewise alludes to the joining of opposites (not just
German/French but East/West and past/present), when the women suddenly appear as if sent in a time capsule to the post–cold war Brandenburg
Gate. By gleefully reconfiguring such grand themes as politics and history in

171

terms of lesbian love, *Heldinnen der Liebe* lends the term "sexual politics" a new twist. The film moreover suggests that its heroines infuse their sexual politics with personal commitment. The directors themselves stand in front of the camera and thus go public as lesbians. And, insofar as Percillier herself is French, living and working in Berlin, she allegorizes her own narrative in the film, showing how she too has traversed national boundaries.

A National Cinema?

The breaking down of barriers between native and foreign cultures in *Heldinnen der Liebe*, as in *My Father Is Coming* and *Überleben in New York*, leads one to reflect on the terms of a German national cinema. Treut's example is especially telling but not unique. Given that so many of her films have been produced abroad, one may ask to what extent they are German; her films have received more approbation and distribution in the United States than in Germany; mindful of her audience, even the pun in the title *My Father Is Coming* is untranslatable in German. Treut herself has said:

> I feel that people in this country [the U. S.] are more interested in my work and take it more seriously. I aim for an international audience. And the reason I survive in the business is because my films appeal to audiences from different cultures. Apart from the U. S., I have an audience in England, Holland, Australia, Canada, and now also in France. That's why I shoot in English—to have greater access to different markets. (Gemünden, Kuzniar, Phillips, 5)

Rosa von Praunheim, too, has produced several documentaries in the United States and ends his recent film *Schwuler Mut — 100 Jahre Schwulenbewegung* (*Gay Courage — 100 Years of the Gay Movement*), which takes place in Berlin, with a segment in San Francisco as the gay world capital. He and Treut are at the top of an extensive list of German gay and lesbian directors making films abroad. In addition to the lesbian directors named at the beginning of this chapter, several gay male directors deserve mention—Jochen Hick (Rio, *Via Appia* [1990]; U.S.A., *Menmaniacs* [1995] and *Sex/Life in L.A.* [1997]); Jürgen Brüning (Thailand, *Maybe I Can Give You Sex?* [1992]), and Jörg Fockele (New York City, *Spokes* [1996] and *Rules of the Game* [1997]). Wieland Speck begins *Westler* (1985) in California, with two men looking out at the Pacific Ocean, but then turns east to tell the love story between a West Berliner and an East Berliner. Werner Schroeter, too, has traveled around the world making films.

These numerous examples call into question our assumptions about the coherence and uniformity of a national cinema. On the one hand, more often than not, German films and videos today are being made with international casts, production teams, locations, and funding sources. In the queer cinema this globalization occurs simultaneously with a kind of queer cosmopolitanism and consolidation—through the meeting with gays and lesbians in other countries (many of the films listed above are documentaries, including Treut's and Praunheim's) and through screenings at gay and lesbian (film) festivals worldwide. Given this scenario, one needs to ask to what degree it makes sense to speak of a national cinema. On the other hand, in this book I have argued that the Queer German Cinema *is* unique—its story is significant not because of anything German about the sexuality portrayed but because of the cinematic tradition that began strongly in the Weimar era and picked up momentum again in the 1970s, a heritage boasting a long list of illustrious directors. Yet insofar as this important branch of German cinema has not been recognized as exceptional, noteworthy, or consequential in German cinematic historiography, the evidence presented in this book does question how we are conditioned to regard, study, and teach German cinema and its definitional contours. In this way, then, the Queer German Cinema profoundly interrogates the boundaries of this national cinema.

Seven

A Gay Melancholia

Michael Stock's *Prinz in Hölleland*

In large part because of their youth, the directors to be discussed in the final three chapters have yet to see their time and fame come, a situation that this book tries to remedy. In the case of Michael Stock, it is particularly unfortunate that his film *Prinz in Hölleland* (*Prince in Hell*) (1993) has not found distribution and is known only to those who might have caught it at film festivals. It is a narratively complex masterpiece that hauntingly combines the charm of a Romantic fairy tale, the grandeur of a Baroque *Trauerspiel*, and the grimness of the Berlin drug scene. Encouraged by Rosa von Praunheim to make the film, Michael Stock was only twenty-five at the time. *Prinz in Hölleland* is sexually explicit and emotionally intense, and Stock has subsequently encountered difficulty funding his next feature-length script on another taboo topic, father-son incest. This film was to be entitled *Manuel: Die Aussöhnung* (*Manuel: The Settlement*). Despite this setback, Stock is currently planning a collection of short takes on gay and lesbian life in Berlin, while working full time for the TV program *Liebe Sünde* on Pro 7. Not only has he starred in such shorts as Jürgen Brüning's *Er hat'ne Glatze und ist Rassist, Er ist schwul und ein Faschist* (*He Is Bold and He Is a Racist, He Is Gay and He Is a Fascist*) (1994) and Peter Jürgensmeier's *Finale* (1998) and played the German hustler in Todd Verow's *Frisk* (1997), but he also takes the lead role in his own film as the heroin junkie. It is this engagement of his self in the film that lends *Prinz in Hölleland* its vehemence and conviction.

Prinz in Hölleland was filmed in Berlin in September 1992. Not only is it post-wall but, with its matter-of-fact gay sex, post-closet and post–identity politics as well. It mixes the gruesome reality of sex for drugs and death by drugs with an astonishingly innocent make-believe atmosphere. To do so, the film juxtaposes two narrative strands. The one is told by the jester Firlefanz in the guise of a fairytale puppet play about the love between the Prince and the miller's son, who flee together into the woods to escape the wrath of the King, who cannot accept his son's "unnatural" love. Once in the dark forest,

Figure 24. *Prinz in Hölleland* (1993), Stefan Laarmann as the miller's son and Michael Stock as the prince. Courtesy of Michael Stock Filmproduktion.

the Prince succumbs to the conjurer's enticements in the form of a hallucinatory white powder. The miller's son, though, rescues his beloved from the
forest and carries him back to the King, who promptly arranges their marriage. Although performed intradiegetically on a puppet stage, this tale also
continues intermittently as a voice-over that accompanies scenes from the
main plot: it allegorizes the story of Firlefanz's friends, the beautiful but
heroin-addicted Jockel and his sensitive, concerned boyfriend Stefan, a story
that in turn seems to allegorize the split between the former East and West
Germanies. Their circle of friends includes Micha (who enjoys sex with
Jockel), Sabine, and the young Sascha (the son of Sabine and Micha). In a
milieu that is uniquely early 1990s Berlin and has since vanished in urban development, these youths live communally as squatters in abandoned construction trailers in Kreuzberg. They are apparently without jobs or occupa-
tions, although Jockel trades sex in exchange for a hit from his dealer Ingolf.
As they wander through drag bars, demos, and bouts of group sex they appear cast off and adrift from society. In the end Jockel is first brutally beaten
by Neonazis, and then, in the relentless downward spiral of this film, dies
from a dose of heroin laced with strychnine.

   This unsettling disparity between the playfulness of the fairy tale and the
horror of Jockel's life sets the stage for other tensions in this film, or rather,
releases them. The foremost question that arises upon viewing *Prinz in
Hölleland* is why it does not address AIDS—indeed, it blatantly depicts both
needle-sharing and unprotected sex with multiple partners. Although such
practices, as well as the death of young gays, clearly evoke AIDS, the film notably does not name the virus. It is as if the shadow of AIDS is so omnipresent and dark that it cannot be summoned by name, nor need it be, for
a community ravaged by it and cognizant of how to combat it. Given this, it
is curious that Stock was severely criticized in the gay German press for depicting rough, unprotected sex, as if this sex were presented enticingly or
pornographically. Here AIDS consciousness phobically denies the prevalence
of risky sexual behavior, and neglects how the film evokes the specter of
AIDS precisely because it is not discussed among the characters. Moreover,
in addition to showing how a younger generation of gay men are not pro-
tecting themselves, the film strongly intimates that mainlining will kill one
sooner than AIDS anyway. In this respect it is a much more responsible and
realistic film than Danny Boyle's hyped, trendy *Trainspotting* (1996).

   In addition to AIDS, what the film also only indirectly addresses is the past
of its characters: post-wall Berlin is clearly post-Oedipal and post-Freudian as
well. Although we have brief indications that both Sabine and Jockel were
sexually abused when younger, Stock decidedly does not probe the actions of

his characters psychologically but instead focuses on their living in the immediate present. This emphasis endows the film with both its free-spiritedness
and its dejection: this youth obviously has no future. Nor, as just mentioned,
is the split between Jockel and Stefan clearly allegorized as the split between
the former East and West Germanies. Instead the newly "united" Germany is
a "Hölleland," and the protagonists live in the no-man's land at the edge of
Kreuzberg where the two parts join—or where they do not.

It is this hesitation to name—to clearly spell out the meaning behind the
allegories that inform the film—that Firlefanz and his fairy tale thematize.
The tale runs parallel to the other events but at the crucial end diverges, suggesting that its ability to signify and hence clarify the lives of Stefan and
Jockel fails. Its moral warning goes unheeded by Jockel. Firlefanz, after trying to talk to Jockel and as if foreseeing his death, breaks down and tears at
his clothes, bemoaning the emptiness of his words. His attentive observations
and fanciful recasting of Stefan and Jockel's lives are pointless and ineffectual.
Thus, in a scene where Firlefanz reads Tarot cards, he draws in succession the
hanged man, signifying helplessness and rigidity, and his own card, that of
the jester. In another scene, he spouts off to Stefan about all being vanity. But
when Stefan confronts him about what his riddles mean, the jester just shrugs
his shoulders. With his belled cap and pointed shoes, he seems to have come
from a medieval mystery play, but one that announces death without trans-
figuration. Moreover, his dress—the heavy makeup, strings of fake pearls,
skirts, and fishnet hosiery—suggests a queer gender performance, neither
male nor female, child nor adult, real nor fictional. Protesting a rigid division
between the sexes and signifying the utopia of a third gender, Firlefanz is the
most revolutionary, taboo-breaking character. But his performance, although
exuberant, is not, as Judith Butler would have it, emancipatory, but profoundly melancholic in its citation of a make-believe world, the realm of
childhood innocence, imagination, and androgyny, which Firlefanz is power-
less to summon back. This is Romanticism pushed to its limit, to its breaking
point.

Both Firlefanz's costume and his pseudonym make up a mask, whose function, Lacan notes, is "to dominate the identifications through which refusals
of love are resolved" (*Feminine Sexuality*, 85). Like a child but unlike all the
adult characters in the film, Firlefanz does not engage in sex: his mask is a
strategy to counter the refusals of love or rejections that Micha, Stefan, and
Jockel at one time or another experience in the course of the film. In a significant reversal, the recovering Jockel wheels the healthy Firlefanz out of
the hospital, alluding to an earlier intimation that Firlefanz had been institu-
tionalized (in the "nuthouse"). Although he is a voice of reason and sobriety

Figure 25. *Prinz in Hölleland* (1993), Wolfram Haak as Firlefanz. Courtesy of Michael Stock Filmproduktion.

in the film, Firlefanz is ironically the character most pointedly associated with mental instability. Like the other binaries his character represents, the sane/insane dichotomy is inextricably fused: his clearsightedness is simultaneously a paralyzing vision into the futility of hope. It is precisely because he is so close to this despairing reality that he needs a mask to protect him, to deflect the other's gaze, and yet also to represent this surface where inner and outer collide. Because the vulnerable jester cannot distance himself from his mask, he never appears in any other garb. In other words, his costume is not a masquerade that he could abandon at will. In fact, when he is robbed of it he dies: the very last scene shows us the little boy Sascha stealing Firlefanz's crown and boot—the metonymic signs of his magical gifts—as well as his puppet of the Prince (for Jockel too is dead).

Sascha, forced to live in a fairytale world that kindly filters reality, can be said to inherit the jester's madness. The boy is often present as witness and one wonders, in a film that repeatedly shows observation of sexual intercourse by a dispassionate or disgusted third party, what the child thinks when he sees his father having sex with Jockel in a scene that uncannily contrasts idyllic escape with mounting tension. It is fantasy that permits Sascha not only to cope but to register and acknowledge violence: in his imagination the puppet Prince actually suffers sunburn and later bleeds. To return to the end: the boy's anger finally explodes when he scolds Firlefanz for telling a tale that was too real. Suddenly no longer a spectator, he kicks a stool from under the jester's feet, leaving him in agony, dangling, suddenly naked and shaven, from a rope. Firlefanz's dog—as we know from Albrecht Dürer, Melancholia's companion—licks up the involuntary release of the hanged man's excrement. This scandalous ending is one that the filmmaker refused to edit out in order to guarantee a distributor for the film.

At the same time that Stock can be so shockingly direct, he can also be elusive and suggestive. The title *Prinz in Hölleland* itself is marvelously evocative—of the "Totentanz," Milton, a truly Grim(m) fairy tale, and *Alice in Wonderland*. But in its polysemy, the title accomplishes the opposite of a Christian allegory, in which meaning, though arcane, is ultimately fixed and stable. The title *Prinz in Hölleland* gestures back to the time when such allegorical meaning was evident and sacred precisely in order to mark the difference. In contrast to this past time, language and representation, signified via the figure of Firlefanz, now point to self-deception and failure in the face of heroin addiction, Neonazi violence, and the gulf between East and West Germany. This is not to suggest that meaning in this film by virtue of its self-reflexivity is ultimately evasive. The film does reflect on its inability to represent loss, but this self-consciousness is hardly playful postmodernist metatextuality.

179

As discussed in the introduction, according to Benjamin and De Man, allegory underscores the disjuncture between sign and referent, such that its oblique referencing displays an uncertainty and detachment about language's ability to signify. Allegorical discourse is hence fragmentary and scattered. Given this skepticism, it is paradoxical that precisely the separation of sign from referent calls for and enables theatrical representation, in other words, the hyperbolic style that characterizes much allegory: allegory exaggerates as if to make up for its own inarticulateness. Firlefanz's puppet stage and his queer gender performance are examples of such theatrical, flamboyant allegory, but their very exaggeration betrays an underlying ambivalence and depression about their ability to signify.

Prinz in Hölleland deviates from many films discussed so far that deploy allegory to play with the veiling and unveiling of same-sex desires. Stock's work is openly gay, showing no concern for issues of the closet, even to the extent that the sex depicted in it is graphic and unapologetic. It is thus all the more interesting that the allegorical element is extremely strong in this film, betraying its connection to other German cinematic representation of queer desires, or at least to the continuing presence of allegory in this tradition. In the lineage of such theatrical and yet melancholic allegorical discourse in the Queer German Cinema, Stock compares most with Fassbinder (as the casting of Harry Baer in the role of Ingolf arguably signals, as well as the drug-related death of the director). Both Stock and Fassbinder produce not just allegory but what I would like to call "reallegory." Reallegory juxtaposes the indirectness or discontinuity in allegorical signification with a shocking proximity to reality—in particular, the display of the abject body. An example of reallegory would be the realistic final image of *Prinz in Hölleland*: as if Jockel's demise weren't stark enough, suddenly the spectator is confronted with an image that is far too close for comfort—the facticity of the body as superfluous, dead, waste matter. If Firlefanz previously wore a mask to cover and protect his emotions, now the image is reversed and his insides are horrendously displayed.

The character played by Michael Stock also calls for discussion in terms of reallegory. He is undoubtedly a figure whose life is ruled by monetary exchange and hence the Lacanian symbolic order—drug-dealing, as Stefan interprets it, is a sign of the capitalist West, with I. G. Farben holding the patent to heroin. But what exceeds this order is Jockel's bodily need for heroin and for his other dependency, sex. He accepts all forms of penetration and is not merely addicted to drugs but to pure risk. It is via Jockel that the audience is brought face to face with a stark reality, a return of what society represses—namely, the subjugation to immediate bodily gratification. Moreover, the realistic, nonpornographic depiction of sex confronts the gay community with what it cannot afford to ignore and yet what it protested in this film—the darker side of sexuality. Throughout the film Jockel's body is on display, game for impersonal encounters, shivering from withdrawal, or taut in anticipation of the hit. His gaunt face with its kohl-darkened eyes is repeatedly shot in close-up. He is particularly vulnerable to the violence that erupts in German society; his body lives out the country's internal divisions and lack of control, as is intimated when he sits twitching from narcotic dependency in front of a mirror, the camera revealing the dual images. How is it then that this proximate, abject body can be the subject of allegorical distantiation?

Stock's impetus in producing his film was the heroin addiction of a friend. The film indeed has the moralistic strain of the allegorical genre, although it simultaneously is drained of faith in reform. It parodies, in the characters of Stefan and Firlefanz, self-righteous sententiousness. Yet what is revealing about Stock's inspiration for the film is that he casts himself as his friend, subjecting his own body to display on screen as a sexually and otherwise physically abused character, a substitution and humiliation that has Christ-like resonances. Indeed, these echoes begin with the title: just as Christ suffers and dies for mankind's sins and descends into hell, so too Jockel journeys through "Hölleland"—with the difference that death meets him at the end. The horrors the film depicts are designed to serve as a warning to the addict.

But the role of Jockel is far more intricate than a reduction of the story to that of moralistic, cautionary tale would suggest. In taking over the part of the junkie, Stock relinquishes control of the camera to stand before it and becomes subject to his own project, again placed in a passive, submissive state. Moreover, his acting out of death is an identificatory move that serves dual functions—sacrificial substitution and preemptive bereavement. The drug abuse leaves Jockel drained of affect and out of touch with life around him, just as would the loss of a friend. At times the camera zooms in on his motionless and made-up face, as if he were one of Firlefanz's puppets. By playing a deadened, indifferent figure, Stock acts out the symptoms of personal loss or the fear of it. According to Freud in his essay "Trauer und Melancholie" ("Mourning and Melancholia"), mourning ceases with the recathexis or redirection of psychic energy toward the self that was once invested in the other. By standing in for his friend and thereby redirecting the energy to himself, Stock appears to be engaged in the work of a preemptive, anticipatory mourning. But insofar as the self and other here merge (as even the similarity of the names St*ock* and J*ock*el intimate), how can mourning be accomplished? Moreover, what is Stock not saying, and hence covering up, by casting himself as another? Is then melancholia (as an interminable, unspec-

181

ified mourning) here at work instead? The relation between melancholy, allegory, and the film's self-referential discourse on representation lead to such a surmise.

According to Freud, in melancholy the ego becomes poor, taking itself as the object that is lost, as opposed to mourning where the object is lost and acknowledged as such. In melancholy, the shadow of the object falls upon the subject. Because of this confusion, even interchangeability, between self and other, the loss becomes too close and hence unnamable. The inability to acknowledge the other as separate from oneself—in other words, to signify the deprivation—ends in mutism. By miming his friend in performing the role of Jockel, Stock acts out the depressive who destroys himself in order to preserve the other. He takes his body as the tomb or crypt in which to encase and protect the real heroin addict. Progressively becoming more wooden and inflexible, the character Jockel rejects dialog with Stefan and Firlefanz and descends into self-engrossed silence.

Words come from the mouth and in their absence much else is ingested and injected to fill the void. Orality pervades the film—from fellatio and repeated scenes of heavy kissing to, in the descent that is visualized in the stair imagery, the eating of excrement in the final shot. Food itself is related to death, as when the chicken is slaughtered for dinner. Stefan drinks excessively in order to forget. Drugs—sniffed or injected—likewise are taken to fill the inner void but only entail death. Reduced to an animalistic level, Jockel and Micha shoot up rat poison. This film thus portrays the gamut from *Künstler* and *Überlebenskünstler* to *Hungerkünstler*. In a scene where an East German hitchhiker asks Stefan if he and his friends are artists, the latter ironically replies, "*Überlebenskünstler*." But as we have just seen, Jockel and company are not only not artists, insofar as the film self-critiques the efficacy of artistic representation, but they fail to be survival artists as well. The more appropriate name for their wasting away in the Kafkaesque conclusion would be *Hungerkünstler*. Micha hungers, as he says, to develop and find himself; but this arty affectation rings hollow. It sounds more like an excuse for not sharing parenting with Sabine; it leads him to narcotic experimentation with Jockel. The latter, who at one point leaves before dinner saying he's not hungry, longs, like Kafka's character, for some other nourishment, a desire that his addiction to sex and drugs signifies.

In contrast to Jockel, Firlefanz embodies a different depressive response to language. In fine jester tradition, he is appropriately melancholic. To repeat, he represents how ineffectual and insufficient language is either to alter or simply to narrate the course of events. Although he tells the story of the Prince, he, unlike Stefan, is late in coming to realize the severity of Jockel's addiction. Moreover, his fairy tale must conform to convention and hence in its happy end diverges radically from reality. As noted, his inability to name characterizes melancholia: the object of mourning cannot be signified. Hence the allegorical indirectness of this film, most blatant in the absence of any discourse on AIDS. But unlike Jockel's melancholy that ends in fatal silence, Firlefanz tries to paper over the deprivation through an exuberant language that he knows is wanting. He is the manic who parades on stage, claiming to have rescued all loss through his manneristic signification—his dress, his gestures, and his puppet theater. His artifice, esoterism, and style aim to countervail the void. Through his baroque spectacle he pretends to expel and exorcise the demon "H" that controls their lives.

But are Stock's and Firlefanz's roles so different? Stock does not just play the character of Jockel but, like Firlefanz, is himself the director of a performance. On the one hand, insofar as both narrators die in the end, we can see Stock too doubting the efficacy of his own medium. His moralizing tale parallels the shortcomings and fate of Firlefanz's. Thus by staging his own fall into silence, Stock as narrator can be read as admitting the futility of his work, a confession which explains the profound sadness that pervades the film. As with Firlefanz, performance (here of the role of the drug-abused friend) fails to substitute for more effective action. Yet, on the other hand, unlike Firlefanz, Stock does not narrate his story in order to watch it as a nonparticipant from the outside. Instead he risks a frightening closeness to addiction, beating, and death through acting them out. Indeed, it is even incorrect to say that he is merely acting: the sex is neither mimed nor alluded to through editing cuts. If the sex is real, then the mainlining could be as well: how does one tell the difference? And what would the difference signify? Such questions raise the issue of the truth residing in Stock's performance, of the inseparability of fact and fiction. If Firlefanz's play fails to substitute for more effective action and insists on its purely fictive happy end, then Stock's performance differs in its vital proximity to contemporary issues: he openly grieves and protests the loss of gay youth to homophobic violence, heroin, and AIDS.

In *Gender Trouble* and *Bodies That Matter* Judith Butler extensively discusses the melancholy of gender performance in the formation of heterosexuality. According to Butler, the heterosexual disavows same-sex affections and sympathies and, further, refuses to grieve the loss of homosexual love. Counterphobically, the heterosexual hyperbolically performs and identifies with the masculinity or femininity he or she cannot love. "The straight man *becomes* (mimes, cites, appropriates, assumes the status of) the man he 'never' loved and 'never' grieved; the straight woman *becomes* the woman she 'never' loved and 'never' grieved. It is in this sense, then, that what is most apparently performed as gender is the sign and symptom of a pervasive disavowal" (*Bodies That Matter*, 236). By contrast, Michael Stock demonstrates how performance and identification can function therapeutically in the work of mourning, which is not to underestimate his risk-taking. He openly avows his love and acknowledges through his performance the limitless loss of gay men's lives. To apply Butler's words regarding public monuments to AIDS such as the NAMES Project Quilt: in this film, the "publicization and dramatization of death . . . call to be read as life-affirming rejoinders to the dire consequences of a grieving process culturally thwarted and proscribed" (*Bodies That Matter*, 236).

In many ways *Prinz in Hölleland*, itself a work of social protest, very much depicts and thereby indicts its public absence. What strikes one about the Berlin it displays is how far removed it is from belief not only in 1960s street theater but meaningful street activism. As they walk against the flow of antiracist demonstrations in Berlin, Micha and Jockel show how ignored and abandoned *they* are by German society. The film gives no indication of parental or societal concern for the grown children, a disregard that recurs in Micha's relationship to his own son. Indeed, the absence of public responsibility is encoded throughout the film as the absence of paternal accountability.

If the film grieves the loss of gay youth to drugs and AIDS, then it also grieves the loss of the empathetic father. Poor, even evil parental substitutes take his place. One of the film's opening shots is that of Micha sleeping with his son, a confusing image intimating child abuse for the viewer not yet apprised of their relationship. The only older father figures are the drug pusher and the leather daddies, who penetrate Jockel orally and anally in the cellar scene, taking advantage of his sexual readiness. The sole character who behaves like a father is Firlefanz toward Sascha, who kills his benefactor in the end. The notable absence of actual fathers paradoxically points to an Oedipal plot underlying the film, as this ending indeed suggests. Hence the only good father is purely fictional: the Puppet King. Unlike his evil counterpart the sorcerer, the Puppet King has no equivalent in the world outside the fairy tale. Although this father initially casts out his son (interestingly, the accents of Micha [Swiss] and Jockel [Swabian] also designate them as displaced), he also welcomes the Prince back, together with the miller's boy, and announces their wedding.

Considering that Michael Stock's year of birth is 1968, the film could be read as an indictment of the 1968 generation's abandonment of their children and the shortcomings of activist sentiments. The 1990s antiracist demonstrations that Stock documents in *Prinz in Hölleland* target violence against

184

so-called foreigners, but they do not protest Neonazi violence against a less obvious other, namely, homosexuals. Nor can Neonazism be combated by mere sloganeering, like the words on Stefan's T-shirt saying "Gib die Nazis keine Chance." Jockel mocks his friend's well-meaning attempts to fight heroin addiction by posting placards, and Firlefanz's brand of street theater is likewise ineffective: he performs it before junkies oblivious to its message. It is no wonder that this youth apathetically ignores radio broadcasts concerning the blockade of Sarajevo and xenophobic violence in Germany. The lack of connection between East and West is further symbolized in a scene where the aural and visual, too, are severed: on an outing to the Muggelsee, Stefan and a former East German hitchhiker complain about their mutual misunderstandings. While the soundtrack renders their conversation, the camera resolutely follows the exterior of the bus until the hitchhiker jumps (is kicked?) off. The landscape of Berlin symbolizes not the reunification but cultural and social disintegration of Germany.

Yet despite this bleak picture, in a sense Berlin is briefly still a magical forest of colorful life, for the ephemeral existence of its youth makes Stock's city an object of nostalgia, a fairytale setting. This ambivalence about innocence infuses the entire film. Despite its nihilism, *Prinz in Hölleland* conveys a remarkable emotive intensity and resilience through the characters' bids for love and friendship, even when these are sought in casual sex, which is portrayed without condemnation and as natural. To be sure, *Prinz in Hölleland* depicts the falling apart of communication between its characters, yet it is their resulting vulnerability that is so disturbingly poignant. The film bears empathetic witness to the plight of homeless gay youth.

Chapter

Experimental Visions

Brynntrup, Müller, Schillinger, Scheirl, and Pürrer

The Viennese experimental director Ilse Gassinger describes her postproduction manipulation of images as follows:

> Sitting at the intersection of analog reproduction and digital image processing, I work with, among other things, methods of deciphering, displacement, deconstruction, and remontage. Searching for aesthetic principles of order, I always come back to the vitalism of chaos, of the hidden, of rapid thought, and of the imprecise. Methodological procedures that match a condition of oscillation. (Quoted in Schüttelkopf, "Da zeigt sich Wirklichkeit," 105)

Operating out of the technically well-equipped Medienwerkstatt Wien, in 1986 Gassinger fashioned the cleverly stylish and visually sophisticated *Quick Lunch* to Lydia Lunch's acid pop lyrics, "Let's go to the other side." Starting with super-8 material transferred to video, she toyed with the image to produce an exciting peep at girls wiggling their naked legs, their polka-dotted summer skirts waving wildly, their panties revealed—fleeting impressions set in a dynamically pulsating frame of primary colors. Gassinger further writes: "The gaze in *Quick Lunch* is voyeuristic; half-naked women in red dresses. My desire for the body, the female body is voyeuristic. . . . Basically I concentrate on the body, for if I eliminate language and narrative plot, only the body is left. The language that is communicated is basically a body language" (quoted in Schüttelkopf, "Da zeigt sich Wirklichkeit," 106, 108).

Body language fetishistically or voyeuristically caught by the momentary glance is erotic, because as a fragment it wants to be read. It invites, but to what is left open. Gassinger takes this glimpse and enhances it as fragment through the image processing she describes, underscoring the "vitalism of chaos, of the hidden." Her methods of "deciphering, displacement, deconstruction, and remontage" could equally apply to the creative work that has been accomplished in German gay and lesbian experimental filmmaking in

186

the years since her precocious *Quick Lunch* was made. Here the cinematic tradition of allegory with its seductively enigmatic, elliptical signification reaches its culmination. Whether one considers the work of Michael Brynntrup, Matthias Müller, Claudia Schillinger, or Hans A. Scheirl and Ursula Pürrer—the five directors discussed at length in this chapter—one encounters an art that indulges in the visual enjoyment of suspended, unhinged, transient images which resist translation. As Matthias Müller writes, experimental films are "created in emotional border territories, spaces between which cannot, or will not, be named. The interest of the experimental filmmaker is rarely dedicated to those phenomena which have found their definitive expression. Instead, they share an interest in ambiguity, in the unsettled states which cannot be classified. In a place which obtains before language" (5). Although such allegorical indetermination and disconnected signification may frustrate the viewer, they also may serve to arouse. The five directors to be discussed here stymie the acquisitive mastery of the gaze at the same time they give it pleasure.

Fragmentariness alone thus becomes eroticized, the allure of the not shown. This cinema fetishizes the partial object relying on brevity, intensity, and obliqueness. Its disjointedness in turn creates a cult object: if the isolated image emits an air of mystery, then experimentalism turns its very products into auratic incarnations to behold, each film a body of tantalizing, mosaic-like glimpses. The postproduction manipulation of images reminds us that what we see is barred from legibility, for which reason, as Judith Butler points out, it is instead exteriorized and performed.[1] This highlighting of the visual display leads to experimental cinema's predilection for found footage, montage, and the overlapping and disintegrating of images. The very layering and juxtaposition of screen images resembles skin next to skin, and often literalizes this comparison. Polyphony is represented not only optically but also acoustically in complicated, nonsynchronized soundtracks, as in the compositions by Dirk Schaefer and Robert Henke, who have written for several of the filmmakers discussed here.

Insofar as this cinema searches out strategies of incongruity, it is related to camp, which also tries to denaturalize the norm and contradict seeing. Michael Brynntrup, for example, even in his most autobiographical moments, mocks the purported self-revelation and presents his persona as figuratively in drag. Such a cinema will thereby profoundly question norms of identity, whether gay or lesbian or other. Thus "the unsettled states which cannot be classified"—to cite Matthias Müller again—include those of queer sexualities. In excess of conventional coding, queer desires are as nomadic and exploratory as the experimental medium itself. Generally speaking, in both this aesthetic and homoerotic innovation (or in their inseparability), the German contemporary gay and lesbian short differs sharply from its counterpart in English-speaking countries, which tends to be more narratively linear.[2] To be sure, there are plenty of German films (and I shall mention several in the following pages) that offer slice-of-life vignettes and a humorous take on human foibles. By and large, however, the German gay and lesbian short is less accessible to popular viewing, given its unpredictability and fringe flair.

In this chapter I concentrate on five directors who grant particular attention to the iconic, visual status of the production over its narrative thrust and over adherence to real-life settings. Brynntrup, Müller, Schillinger, Scheirl, and Pürrer have each already amassed a body of work, with the first two having garnered numerous awards and the acknowledgment of retrospectives. Scheirl and Pürrer's *Rote Ohren fetzen durch Asche* (*Flaming Ears*) (1992) has received wide American video distribution as well as something of a cult underground status. The field of German experimental cinema is so vast, however, that such a selection necessarily omits discussion of other important texts, a number of which I at least want to mention in the following paragraphs. This richness and diversity paradoxically arise from economic scarcity. The evershorter supply of government grants and subsidies,[3] compounded by the lack of private sponsoring, demands that the contemporary director work on a small scale, usually with a nonprofessional cast, hence novelty and visual dazzle result more from the invention of the imagination than from the benefits of a large purse. Because of ever-dwindling government support, moreover, the experimental artist cannot hope to characterize his or her work as belonging to an *Autorenkino*, or auteurs' cinema, which saw its heyday in the 1970s and early 1980s. Yet the technical innovations and artistic signatures of these current filmmakers bear similar critical scrutiny:[4] it is here that the most ingenious work in German cinema is today to be found.

Who are these filmmakers? Among the gay male directors who merit more attention than space unfortunately allows, Wieland Speck is probably the best known—but more for his feature-length film, *Westler: East of the Wall* (1985), and for his programming as director of the Panorama section at the Berlin film festival, than for his shorts. These fall into the more realistic, narrative side of the spectrum and include *David, Montgomery und Ich* (1980), *Das Geräusch rascher Erlösung* (*The Sound of Sudden Salvation*) (1983), *Bei Uns Zuhause* (*At Our Place*) (1981), *November* (1989), and *Zimmer 303* (*Room 303*) (1991). Notwithstanding their everyday settings, Speck's films have a quality of reverie to them, as can be seen most clearly in *Zimmer 303*, where the friends and family of an AIDS patient have flashbacks to scenes from their life with him. A number of gay shorts fit under the rubric of the realistic vignette. Such is the case with *Finale* (1998) by Peter Jürgensmeier, starring

Michael Stock as a hustler who encounters his john, a police commissioner, in an interrogation cell. *Dreck (Dirt)* (1995) by the brothers Dom and Ben Reding tells the conventional story of a teenager's sexual awakening, and presents scenes from his daily life in Cologne. Yet *Dreck* also explodes with two surrealistic images—one of two men making love covered in mud and, in conclusion, of the glass windows and doors of the protagonist's house being blown out, suggesting the shattering of his humdrum world.

Even shorts that move into the area of the documentary similarly play with the borders to the experimental, artistic realm. Jürgen Brüning, for example, documents how gay men counterphobically react to Neonazi violence against them by adopting the skinhead look. In *Er hat'ne Glatze und ist Rassist, Er ist schwul und ein Faschist (He's Bold and He Is a Racist, He Is Gay and He Is a Fascist)* (1994), Brüning alternates talking-head interviews with such playful scenes as gays in Doc Martens and shaved scalps marching in rank and file, roses flitting by the screen, and penises swirling around to form the swastika. He humorously ends with the quotation from Brecht (1933): "Be careful what kind of skin you pull back, you never know what head will appear." Brüning has also authored the documentary short *Maybe I Can Give You Sex?* (1992) on male homosexuality in Thailand and together with Mark Goldstein *What Is the Relationship between Rosa von Praunheim and the Male Strippers in San Francisco?* (1990), precisely the question that the viewer asks upon seeing the film. Brüning now produces, in addition to gay pornography, films by its New-Queer-Cinema offspring, Bruce la Bruce and Ela Troyano.

Jörg Fockele deserves special mention as a consistently productive, ingenious filmmaker from Hamburg who worked on the collective project *Verzaubert (Enchanted)* (1992), a documentary interviewing gay and lesbian survivors of Third Reich persecution. Fockele now lives in New York, where he produced his two most recent pieces. In *Spokes* (1996) an uptight young man from Liechtenstein meets a black youth on a bike, whose charm finally breaks through the former's iciness. *Rules of the Game* (1998) is a warm, engaging, 48-minute documentary about four articulate kids from New York who talk about being gay and transgender. Fockele allows them to choose a costume, set, and musical theme to present a fantasy about themselves in music video format. Fockele's earlier work is sheer camp. It includes *Angesichts ihrer fatalen Veranlagung scheidet Lilo Wandas freiwillig aus dem Leben (In View of Her Fatal Inclination Lilo Wandas Gives Up the Ghost)* (1994), where Ernie **189** Reinhardt immaculately performs the role of a fur-clad transvestite who first poises her cigarette holder, takes a long drag, and coolly announces her suicidal intention before slipping the pistol between her ruby-red lips. The underground piece *Analstahl (Anal Steel)* (1990) makes the excesses of Jörg

Figure 26.   *Er hat'ne Glatze und ist Rassist, Er ist schwul und ein Faschist* (1994).
Photo by Nan Goldin. Copyright, Jürgen Brüning Filmproduktion.

Buttgereit, Christoph Schlingensief, and John Waters seem tame. Bad too is the homely woman in *Frau und Geschlecht* (*Basic Instincts*) (1993), who enjoys gay porn and sneaks unconscious men into her apartment. Elegant, by contrast, is *Alice und der Aurifaktor* (1995), a fifteen-minute fairy tale on sign language that takes its inspiration from Expressionist cinema. Fockele's films are among the most visually captivating and creative coming from Germany today, as the numerous awards he has received testify.

Stefan Hayn is another important gay male director. He has authored the anarchic, surrealistic work *Fontvella's Box* (1991), as well as *Schwulenfilm* (*Gay Film*) (1989–90), *Tuntenfilm* (*Film of Queens*) (1989–90), *Pissen* (*Piss*) (1989–90), *Klassenkampf in Amerika* (*Class Warfare in America*) (1993), and *What to put . . . ?* (1994). Hans Scheugl's *Prince of Peace* (1993) treats the subjects of religiosity, porn, and public washrooms in Vienna, while Kristian Petersen's *Pilka* (1995) deals with what can be accomplished with shaving cream. Likewise bizarre are the surrealistic worlds of Las Theuerkauff (*'Der Kleine' zeigt:*) "*I can't help Marcel*" (['*The Small One*' *Presents:*] "*I Can't Help Marcel*") (1998) and the short he made with Heiko Kalmbach, *Ein Mann liegt in der Badewanne und bekommt Nasenbluten* (*A Man Lies in the Bathtub and Gets a Nosebleed*) (1995). The feature-length, antinarrative, philosophically and architecturally inspired films by Heinz Emigholz—*Die Basis des Make-Up* (*The Basis of Makeup*) (1985), *Die Wiese der Sachen* (*The Meadow of Things*) (1987), and *Der zynische Körper* (*The Cynical Body*) (1990)—should also be listed for their intimations of male homosexuality, as should the videos by Marcel Odenbach.

The concluding chapter on dyke noir animation will study a number of women filmmakers who overlap with the category of the experimental. Among the lesbian shorts that tell a brief drama in a realistic milieu can be counted Ulrike Zimmermann and Claudia Richarz's *La Triviata* (1983), Elke Götz's *Mein ist Dein ganzes Herz* (*Your Heart is All Mine*) (1992), Claudia Huttenlocher's *Letzte Tropfen* (*Last Drops*) (1997) and the lesbian bar-scene parodies, birgit durbahn's *Mit den besten Wünschen* (*With Best Wishes*) (1982), Katrin Barben's *Bar Jeder Frau* (*The Bad Girl Bar*) (1992; winner of the Ursula Prize at the gay and lesbian film festival in Hamburg), Sylke R. Meyer's *Rituale des Werbens* (*The Rites of Wooing*) (1995), and Nathalie Percillier's *Mein 37. Abenteuer* (*My 37th Adventure*) (1994–95). The bar-scene genre is particularly important for its depiction of a lesbian community, a dimension often underrepresented in lesbian cinema. Its humor primarily resides in the hyperbolization of butch-femme role-playing. In the related comic vein are Hucky Porzner's *Strech as Stress Can Be* [sic] (1995) on the constrictions of women's bathing suits, Kerstin Ahlrichs's *Switch to Where the Flavor Is* (1996) on a dyke's fantasy billboard after the motto "Don't come to maleboring country," and Ewjenia

191

Figure 27.   *Spokes* (1996). Courtesy of Jörg Fockele.

Tsanana's beautifully inventive *In Farbe* (*In Color*) (1996), where the artist paints with her pendulous breasts. Barbara Klingner, who has documented the 1997 Berlin Christopher Street Day Parade in *Karneval der Ratten oder wie quer darf queer sein?* (*Carnival of the Rats, or How "Quer" Can Queer Be?*) (1997), fantasizes butch-femme encounters at public toilets in her short *Klappenansichten* (*Views of the Urinal*) (1996). Bettina Flitner's *Aktenzeichen XX ungelöst* (*Files XX: Unsolved*) (1991) with the subtitle *ZDF Ihr Pogrom* (*ZDF Your Pogrom*) is a hilarious take-off on a popular German television series that reenacts actual crime scenes and invites the audience to call in with leads; here Hella von Sinnen (Germany's only well-known out lesbian comedian) stars in various male and female roles as both TV announcer and deviant character. An early film on cross-gender performance is Marion Kellner's *Make Me Wet* (1984), a videoclip to the music of Unknown Gender.

In a more serious vein is Bettina Flitner's *Mein Feind—Geschichte einer Ausstellung* (*My Enemy—The History of an Exhibition*) (1992), which records the coarse, unsympathetic reactions to a street installation about abused women and their revenge fantasies, whereby the question of what constitutes art and its function is raised. Monika Treut's *Bondage* (1983), Cléo Uebelmann's 53-minute *Mano Destra* (1985) to music by the Vyllies, and Stefanie Jordan's *Crude* (1996) with a soundtrack by Robert Henke treat through stunning black-and-white photography, inventive pacing, and peculiar camera angles the thrills of the leather s/m scene. Barben's *Casting* (1995) likewise experiments with s/m role-playing. Sexually rough and daring are the videos by photographer and live artist Krista Beinstein, *True Love* (1989), *Hafenexzesse* (*Harbor Excesses*) (1990), and *Bad Girls* (1990–91), as well as the filming of one of her performances by Ulrike Zimmerman, *Free Fucking* (1985). Lyric, narratively elliptic, and visually experimental, by contrast, are Zimmermann's *Touristinnen* (*Tourists*) (1986), as well as Ilse Gassinger and Anna Steininger's *Verzehren Verzerrt* (*Devour Distorted*) (1984), birgit durbahn's *Messages from the Cave* (1990), and Suse Bohse's *Time Is All There Is* (1995).[5]

Along with Monika Treut's *Gendernauts* and Hans Scheirl's *Dandy Dust*, Heather Cameron's short *Transit* (1999) contributes to the new foray into f2m transgender. *Transit* begins by using the architectual transformations on Berlin's Potsdamer Platz (where East and West Germany meet) as a metaphor for transitioning from male to female and for crossing the boundaries between the looks of the lesbian butch and those of the gay male. Unlike Treut in *Gendernauts* and Rosa von Praunheim in *Vor Transsexuellen wird gewarnt* (*Transsexual Menace*), Cameron rejects the fetishing of hormone therapy and of San Francisco as the transgender mecca. In this documentary, the trendy demimonde meets instead at Berlin's Café Fatale.

Figure 28. *Weit weit weg* (1995), Bjørn Melhus as Dorothy. Courtesy of Bjørn Melhus.

Of particular note for its queerness is the intellectually stunning work by Bjørn Melhus, where the director himself plays both male and female doppelgängers and where the Lacanian mirror stage meets the Baudrillardian video stage. In *Das Zauberglas* (*The Magic Glass*) (1991) a lifeless TV viewer insipidly converses with his female double who appears in the boobtube— they both repeat phrases over and over without communicating. In *Weit weit weg* (*Far far away*) (1995) Melhus plays Dorothy from *The Wizard of Oz*, dressed in pigtails and a hideous green bow and dress (Julia Neuenhausen is his resourceful stylist in all films). Living in a concrete world of apartment blocks and TV antennae, Dorothy gets her thrills from dial tones and is devoted to her porcelain Toto (whose appearance is acccompanied by ominous chords on the soundtrack). She chats via a luminescent yellow cellular phone with a replicant of herself across the ocean in New York, whereby her phrases "Hello, my name is Dorothy" and "It is wonderful" are echoed back to her. For Dorothy[1] there is no place like her uncanny home for security, especially with its ever-encroaching walls. Dorothy[2], meanwhile, continues to reduplicate and appears on Prime Time News (the Oz of the 90s), where the TV announcers also start saying "My name is Dorothy." Here the indistinction between TV and reality, the living and the undead is complete, and irony (which registers such difference) becomes obsolete. Dorothy[2] affirms to her TV audience: "I'm not going to leave here ever, ever again, because I love you all." In *No Sunshine* (1997) Melhus plays genderless, plastic twin dummies who float around like astronauts and lipsynch to snatches of "luv me . . . luv you" and "yeaaah" and "nooo." In all three films, the mimicry becomes sheer, hollow repetition, matched by Melhus's wonderful ability to put on an idiotic, expressionless smile. He is beyond performing gender identities, even parodically; instead performativity becomes total redundancy, with the result that queerness is no salvation from the uniform world of TV and video. Even drag, which usually emphasizes gender difference, here reinforces the overwhelming sense of sameness and lethargy. In his redefinition of gender fuck as undead replication, then, Melhus goes beyond the parameters of this book and deflates the outlaw gender theatricalization in Praunheim, Schroeter, Ottinger, Treut, Brynntrup (on whose projects he has collaborated), and, if this can be imagined, even the eccentricities of Scheirl and Pürrer.

Michael Brynntrup

1. The copy decomposes the original. The pulse of the machine brings an end to the art of the free hand.
2. The retina turns into a coordinate system, the picture into wallpaper.
3. The art of disjointed, mediated body parts is over. The only possible original now is the living picture without go-between.
4. The original is motion. Identity is denied.

With this manifesto from his 1984 film *Handfest—freiwillige Selbstkontrolle* (*Handfest—Voluntary Self-Control*), Michael Brynntrup (alias Brintrup and Brinntrup) announces the theme that will run throughout his work—the dissolution of the original and individual via replication. In this film, an intertitle—"Self-Portrait with Skull"—announces a series of images of Brynntrup looking like *Seinfeld*'s Kramer, with mouth and eyes wide open; as each blowup draws us closer into his pupil we see a skull form and then disintegrate before our eyes, as if linking mechanical reproduction to death. In *Herzsofort. Setzung* (*Heart. Instant[iation]*) (1994), via rephotography and digital alteration Brynntrup manipulates an already stylized image of himself, transforming it to the rapid patter of a camera clicking, so that we are left with the impression of the total, albeit virtuoso, mutability of the subject-image. Although his face is cut into frames and rearranged like a Cubist puz-

195

zle, Brynntrup is right in denying this to be an "art of disjointed body parts"; instead the picture becomes a living thing via the pulse of the clicking camera and computerized music. The serialization draws us closer and closer into the face, forcing us to study it; yet in the maelstrom, depth reverts into the opposite of sheer surface. Nothing is revealed about the intimate self, although here as elsewhere in his films, Brynntrup puts himself on display. Or, precisely because the human visage can be so malleable and anamorphically changed, our eyes are captivated by its two-dimensional image. It exerts a fascination not unlike the optical illusions of Baroque allegorical still life.

Michael Brynntrup has premièred his work more than ten times at the Berlinale and has shown twice at the Museum of Modern Art, once at the 1987 Cineprobe Film Exhibition and once in a retrospective entitled *Lebende Bilder. still lives* in 1992. This Mephistophelian manipulator of screen images is indisputably one of Germany's most significant filmmakers today. Unfortunately, as with his cohorts in the experimental, underground vein, the venues for his work are still few and far between. German film studies still needs to wake up to the exciting productions of this hip, yet paradoxically established artist. His oeuvre begins with *September, Wut—eine Reise (September, Rage—A Journey)* (1981–83), wherein a twenty-year-old sets off to Goethe's destination of Italy to discover, like his predecessor, both homoerotic pleasures and the realm of art.[6] Brynntrup cites Goethe: "I haven't undertaken these marvellous travels in order to deceive myself, but rather to discover myself through the external." His oeuvre then ends with a return to mock autobiography (thus still inspired by Goethe's play between poetry and truth) in his plans for *Expositus*, a rehearsing of (the filmmaker's life through) his films.

The list of his works in between is long. His recent short, *Loverfilm: an uncontrolled dispersion of information* (1996), runs through a deadpan year-by-year, month-by-month countdown of his former (and fictional?) lovers, his journal and camera not so much jolting his memory as acting in its stead. Other films play off of and into the ability of the camera to reproduce and in so doing distort the image: in addition to *Handfest* and *Herzsofort. Setzung* these include *Stummfilm für Gehörlose (Silent Movie for Deaf People)* (1984), *Höllensimulation: frei nach Platos Höhlengleichnis (Simulation of Hell: Loosely Based on Plato's Parable of the Cave)* (1987), *Die Statik der Eselsbrücken (Engineering Memory Bridges)* (1990), *Tabu I–IV* (1988), and *Tabu V* (1998; one of Brynntrup's latest accolades has been the New York Film Academy Award at the 1998 Berlinale for this film). Likewise toying with the problematic of the simulacrum, but this time via transvestism, are the vignettes *Narziss und Echo (Narcissus and Echo)* (1989), *Liebe, Eifersucht und Rache (Love, Jealousy and Revenge)* (1991), and *Plötzlich und Unerwartet—eine Déjà Revue (Sudden and Un-*

Figure 29. Michael Brynntrup. Photo by Jürgen Baldiga. Courtesy of Michael Brynntrup.

expected) (1993). These projects of Brynntrup's inventive imagination are full of lyrical whimsy as well as masterful disguise.

Brynntrup playfully copies, too, the life of Christ. As its title alone suggests, *Jesus—Der Film* (*Jesus—The Film*) (1985–86) is a blasphemous, at times hilarious, at times banal film. Lasting 125 minutes and billed as "monumental," this omnibus super-8 production was organized by Brynntrup, who from section to section stars in the lead role, and contains contributions by, among others, Anarchistische Gummizelle, the German slasher director Jörg Buttgereit (whose *Nekromantik I* and *II* and *The Death King* have found an American cult following), the experimental directors Birgit and Wilhelm Hein, and filmmakers and photographers from East Berlin. The more deadpan moments of *Jesus—Der Film* include Christ's baptism in the backseat of a Soviet Lada as the rain pours down outside. When John the Baptist asks, "Is the rain from you?", Jesus answers, "No, it's from my father," to which his sidekick replies, "No kidding! [Sag, was!]." As is typical for Brynntrup, the film reflects back on its own medium, depicting miracles as trick photography: the bread, taken from the body of Christ, is produced by Brynntrup eating in reverse motion, and bread popping out of a toaster is played back repeatedly in

197

the reenactment of the miracle at Cana. From a Catholic family, Brynntrup frequently borrows from Christian iconography. In fact, the trailer to *Jesus— Der Film* is entitled *Veronika (vera ikon)* (1987), punning on the veiled screen reproduction of Christ's image. Brynntrup's baroque, allegorical fascination with death and its requisites (skeletons, skulls, funerals, graveyards) can also be witnessed in *Testamento memori* (1986), the *Totentanz (Death Dances)* series (1988),[7] *Kain und Abel—Eine Moritat (Cain and Abel—A Moral)* (1994), and *Plötzlich und Unerwartet*. Greek mythology also serves as a foundation on which Brynntrup launches his interrogation of the simulacrum and the mise-en-abyme of endless copies. Both *Orpheus—der Tragödie erster Theil (Orpheus— First Part of the Tragedy)* (1983–84) and *Narziss und Echo* reenact Rococo meta-morphoses of Ovid's tales, as well as of Cocteau and Greenaway. In addition, Brynntrup consistently dismantles the barriers between genres and media, raising questions. Are his films educational, documentary, autobiographical, or pornographic? Do they resemble silent comedies, animation, or move-mented collections of still-life photos?

Perhaps the best film for one to work through such an entanglement is *Statik der Eselsbrücken (Engineering Memory Bridges)*, a twenty-one-minute piece paradigmatic for a postmodern leveling of differences between original and simulacrum, authenticity and parody, depth and surface, text and image. After the initial disclaimer that actions and characters are fictitious and all re-semblence to persons living or dead is purely coincidental, Brynntrup appears holding up a false hand and wearing a striped bathing cap, while he elaborates to the camera: "even I look completely different." At times Brynntrup dons a blond dustmop reminiscent of Warhol, and in the sections where he applauds himself with shouts of "Bravo" he puts on an immense Baroque wig. Clearly this rendition of selfhoods is ironically executed, albeit with delicate humor, never heavy-handedly. In voice-over Brynntrup narrates his curriculum vitae, starting with his birth in 1959 which is simultaneously a death, his identical twin being stillborn, a loss that seems to haunt Brynntrup's preoccupation with doubling and demise. Brynntrup skimpily rehearses various stages in his life—among others, a trip to Italy, schooling, a jaw operation, the date of conception and funding for *Statik*—while offering no visual glimpses of his past. In *Tabu I–IV*, this recapitulation is conducted via shots of pages from Brynntrup's diaries, while voices read simultaneously from it, making its con-tent incomprehensible. In *Statik* the *Lebenslauf* (German for curriculum vitae) is rendered literally as an image of Brynntrup in a bathing suit running on the spot, that is, not getting anywhere, a loudspeaker in hand. Again, Brynntrup performs the course of his life, teasing our curiosity, yet, as the loudspeaker ironically comments, proclaiming very little. Moreover, the image swims due to the double projection onto an opaque glass of both the positively and neg-atively developed film.[8] In a slip of the tongue, Brynntrup correctly gauges the effect of this coy evasiveness on his viewers, his "sehr genervtes Pub-likum," or "dear unnerved audience."

As in other works, Brynntrup plays with the leader countdown and the clapper (in *Aide Mémoire* [1995] he turns his butt to the camera and smacks it), pointing out the arbitrariness of beginnings. In fact, the rhythm of *Statik* seems to be that of renewed false starts, a series of tests that perpetually re-commence. The *Eselsbrücken*, the memory bridges that are supposed to trig-ger recollection, are indeed static, ushering in dead ends—unless, of course, their function resides in the impish verbal and visual punning that character-izes this film. The tests (synchronicity, focus, vision, genetics, AIDS), an-nounced, as in a silent film, in handwritten intertitles, are a series of extended prolegomena; the focus test and vision test ironically comment on our "blind spot" (another intertitle) or our "optical disillusion" (the subtitle, playing on the German word for illusion, *Täuschung*). Like the beginnings of his films, the endings too are halting. *Tabu I–IV* stutters to its end, as the voice-over re-peats "this film could end this way or that": in fact, the film constantly alludes to the displacement staged by the words "now," "here," "previously," and "subsequently," their enunciation already belying what they signify.[9] In *Plötz-lich und Unerwartet* Udo Kier shuts a door after saying goodbye to the cam-era, signaling the abrupt end to a mazelike plot that loops around itself, so that the order of events remains opaque (we see the same event from three different perspectives but they seem to occur sequentially).[10] In *Statik* the ending is likewise self-conscious, as a hand comes to cover the lens of the camera.

Hands are everywhere in Brynntrup's films: as the date and copyright ap-pear in the penultimate shot of *Statik*, Brynntrup signs his name—the sig-nature (*Unterschrift*) always executed by hand (*Handschrift*). The scribbled intertitles also attest to the intervention of the hand, a metonym for bodily presence, as if Brynntrup were trying to intervene against the mechanisms of technical reproduction. Each finger, of course, has its own, very different print. And each palm traces a unique lifeline (Brynntrup has a woman read-ing his aloud in the film). But when Brynntrup repeatedly reproduces his fin-gerprint on the page, photographs it, and enlarges it, or in *Handfest* photo-copies his hands and displays their negatives and X-rays, he suggests that the singularity of the signature dissolves. When, in this film, he takes a shard from a broken mirror to slit his wrist, he again intimates via this minute ges-ture that self-reflection is an act of suicide, always killing off the self it reflects upon: now the hand is turned against itself, as the German phrase "Hand an

199

sich legen," "to lay hands on oneself," implies. The fact that the mirror is broken likewise signifies the imperfection of specularity.

Because each scribbling ends up being just as ephemeral as the other images in Brynntrup's fast-paced film, he then tries to write on the body. A little skeleton is tattooed on his arm, but does this "*Tät*owierung" reveal "Iden-*tität*," as his wordplay might desire? Is this epidermal inscribing a successful attempt at marking individuality, now expressed not by reference to one's interiority but on the exterior of one's skin? Does the tattoo signify that writing which cannot be erased? But even the tattoo etched into the skin was first traced from a former drawing onto Brynntrup's arm. It too marks the temporal succession of the copy and punctuates additional deterritorializing alterations to Brynntrup's appearance. His body becomes again the surface, the screen on which to project other pictures, a process that he takes to prodigious heights in *Herzsofort*, where he alters and superimposes images of himself at dizzying speeds. At such a tempo, the act of viewing becomes one of forgetting rather than recording the transformations of the visage. And if written or photographic language cannot stay or define the self, neither can the spoken word. The subject only stammers its signification in the translingual pun of "me, me" in the name "Michael" (from *Handfest*) or "ei, ei" (meaning "egg" or designating an exclamation of surprise, but which sounds like the English "I, I"). It is no wonder, then, that Brynntrup here creates, in the self-descriptive words of the film, an "anatomy of phantoms," the skeletal drawings and fleeting doubly projected and negatively developed shots of himself that flicker and dissolve across the screen: the phantoms thereby gain their own "autonomy."

Whether it be through a visual or verbal excerpt from his diaries, a cinematic album of (imagined?) former lovers, a matter-of-fact voiced-over curriculum vitae, or his manifold incarnations before the camera, Michael Brynntrup performs himself in a kind of drag. Dressed as Aunt Ida in *Liebe, Eifersucht und Rache* he actually looks convincingly disguised. A distinctly queer impetus lies behind this deconstruction of systems of identity, especially regarding the belief in scripted or imagistic self-representability.[11] The flauntingly shameless liturgy of partners in *Loverfilm* erodes norms of individuality and authenticity, and not only in terms of heterosexuality. In the gay community, the coming-out narrative presupposes the final attainment of a transparent, sincere relationship between self and society; in addition, the narrative of endless sexual exploits pretends to shock by virtue of its similar claims to veracity. Brynntrup ridicules all these autobiographical conventions in *Loverfilm* by frequently substituting clips from old super-8 porn films for actual shots of his lovers, thwarting the spectator's prurient desire to see the "truth" of his sex life. Moreover, he turns the tables on the spectator by inviting him or her to leave the room before he or she is party to invading another's privacy: he thereby holds a mirror up to the audience in which he displays its voyeuristic investment. Given such mischieviousness, it would be too simple to interpret Brynntrup's self-reflexivity as egoistic or exhibitionist. He instead disrupts narcissistic pleasures and fantasies via inventive alienation techniques. Nor can his role-playing automatically be dubbed subversive or transgressive; though it is tempting, it would be another self-gratifying narcissistic fantasy on the part of both Brynntrup and his critic. The reproductive medium for this artist always allegorically betokens, rather, a mechanized self-erasure or death.[12] Brynntrup's postmodern self is offered up in almost sacrificial exposure to the cinematic apparatus, especially to the latter's computerized editing capacities.

Part of Brynntrup's drag is to stage his body as strange to itself. This move is most clearly illustrated when he sets the camera before his bed at night in *Statik*, displaying the sleeping body as it can never see itself, with all its restless twitches. Although one might assume that the camera stands in here for the eye, gratifying an otherwise unfulfillable autoscopic desire, Brynntrup's body, laid bare, actually becomes vulnerable and exposed, like that of a child or even an embryo. Indeed, for all his defiance, Brynntrup appears shy before the camera, like someone who realizes that his physique and visage are still an enigma. It is insofar as Brynntrup renders this body strange to itself, and situates the ego outside itself, that he speaks truthfully. He eschews thereby any false or deceptive sense of authenticity. In other words, the filmmaker recognizes, as did Lacan, the méconnaissance latent in specularity. Moreover, his body surfaces throughout as the supplement or disruption to his written and spoken commentaries, not vice versa, for his self-images never explicate or illustrate the verbal text: the body appears in its inexplicable surplus. Failed attempts to read homosexuality from the body also preserve its secrets and its unmanageability. In *Statik*, in the film's sole mention of homosexuality, Brynntrup parodies pseudo-scientific, biological explanations for homosexuality by citing a theory that, according to tests on rats, prenatal stress could be its cause. He thereby presents his gayness as viewed by others from the outside, and thus refuses to respond to societal expectations that gays should confess their sexuality or that a public coming out belongs in even the mock autobiographical mode.

Brynntrup's importance as a gay director lies precisely in this twisting of habitual associations. His exploration of the simulacrum, for instance, is brilliantly queer when one considers its transvestite dimensions. Marjorie Garber writes, "the subversive secret of transvestism [is] that the body is not the

201

ground, but the figure," an insight that leads her to observe that "the transvestite effect . . . underlies representation itself" (374). Transvestism, of which Brynntrup makes prodigous use in his films, complicates the dynamics between original and copy. Taking imitation to profane heights, Brynntrup even has the male character Abel (from *Kain und Abel*), played by Ichgola Androgyn, give birth to a baby (doll) out of his anus. Here all recourse to notions of biology and gender specificity is abandoned. In *Plötzlich und Unerwartet*— a film replete with tangled repetitions—Ichgola Androgyn (who played the grown Charlotte von Mahlsdorf in Rosa von Praunheim's *Ich bin meine eigene Frau*) further displays his versatility by taking on three separate roles, unrecognizable as the same actor. I would now like to turn to three of Brynntrup's more recent films where issues of transvestism and gay sexuality are more prominent—*Liebe, Eifersucht und Rache, Narziss und Echo*, and *Aide Mémoire*.

BeV StroganoV masterfully performs two gender roles in *Liebe, Eifersucht und Rache*—as butch-boy Georg in tight shorts and leather wristbands and as femme fatale Inge—on either ends of a phone line. Although Inge spreads her legs wide in the initial shots to show an endowed crotch (to the sound of a tape breaking), BeV StroganoV is hardly reidentifiable as starring in *both* roles. Transvestism is thus involved in the same optical deception as the filmic medium itself, which links this short to Brynntrup's entire oeuvre. The fact that Brynntrup also cross-dresses as Inge's Aunt Ida (a female Id?) points to the filmmaker as illusionist. The phone exchange metatextually comments on blindness itself: because she cannot see what is happening at the other end of the receiver, Inge stares dumbfounded into her phone. Georg, in the meantime, is being lusciously fellated by the bartender, played by the photographer Jürgen Baldiga (see the later discussion of *Aide Mémoire*). Before this interruption, though, Georg's and Inge's stilted conversation illustrates the incompatibility of optical and auditory messages (hence the tape breaking); language, not just visuality, deceives.

The couple discuss the banal topic of the problems of enjoying foreign films, given their subtitles. But even the communication between the two is impaired. When Inge asks Georg to clarify a phrase, he disrespectfully asks if her hearing is poor, an accusation retorted back to him, in this series of doublings, later in the film. Since *Liebe, Eifersucht und Rache* itself is a lesson in translation ("German for Germans"), Inge and Georg—to fit their outlandish roles—enunciate exaggeratedly, and their dialog is translated with English subtitles. At one point, when they are listing foreign languages, the subtitles go awry and ridiculously deviate from their German original (in conclusion, the German word "Ende" is likewise mistranslated as "Happy End"). Like the gender roles BeV StroganoV plays, language, too, is stilted, artificial, and misleading. This hilarious German language lesson about how to conduct phone conversations thus parodies its pretended goal, the facilitation of communication. As if to underscore this dialectic between sound and image, the camera homes in alternately on Georg's mouth and then Inge's. Yet despite the similar teeth, the voices are so different that one does not want to believe this double drag.

In the end, although the penis, signifier of sexual difference, is uncovered once Georg's shorts are unzipped, it also disappears into Baldiga's mouth and is further obscured by the credits. This veiling raises the questions: What does one see, after all, at the end? What does the penis reveal? And by extension what does pornography divulge? *All You Can Eat* (1993), Brynntrup's mock pornographic film, showing a succession of porn clips, suggests that the answers to these questions are the same: very little. Also playing on orality, this film edits out any hard-core scenes and only depicts, to a boringly repetitive beat, faces of guys in sexual ecstasy: there is little meat here to eat. Pornography, Brynntrup seems to suggest, does not offer "the real thing." Nor, for that matter, do the iterations and mimicry of *Liebe, Eifersucht und Rache*,[13] which, though, is much more honest about its deceptions.

Such reflection on transvestite, representational artifice and on the "différance" latent in repetition can also be observed in *Narziss und Echo*. Marjorie Garber writes of "the power of the transvestite as that spectral other who exists only in representation—not a representation of male or of female, but of, precisely, itself: its own phantom or ghost" (373). Set in a nineteenth-century neo-Baroque palace and shot on black-and-white stock, *Narziss und Echo* evokes the past with its phantoms. Echo is played by Tima die Göttliche, wearing plastic fruit tucked into her low-cut gown, while Narcissus and his servants are androgynously garbed in wigs, lace collars, and tights. Echo's entourage also includes cross-dressers. This transvestite mirroring whereby the gender double both reproduces and slightly alters its counterpart is the key to unraveling this "film in the form of a riddle" (*Rätselfilm*). Brynntrup defines his allegorical genre at the start (allegorical in the sense that the meaning is delayed): "The film's content must be deduced from the film's formal structure." The piece begins and ends with Echo admiring herself in front of a mirror, this narcissism alone heralding the role reversals and doublings between herself and Narcissus. When the latter arrives to declare his love, Echo shuns him, at which point Narcissus smashes a statue from its pedestal. Following the narrative's binary logic, he himself then turns into stone, a metaphor for shunned love. We first see his statue when, next spring, Echo goes out of the confines of her palace and its mirror, searching for her lover and intoning his name. In a shot over the statue's shoulder, we see Nar-

Figure 30.   *Narziss und Echo* (1989). Courtesy of Michael Brynntrup.

cissus's face come alive in the mirror he is holding. As the statue begins to speak, Echo restates the ends of his phrases, through the repetition shockingly altering their meaning. For instance, when Narcissus shuns her with the words, "you think I would give myself to you!", she echoes in total self-abandonment, "I would give myself to you!" Whereas the statue comes to life and walks, Echo now falls down prostrate on the stairs, unable to move and barely able to stutter. And whereas earlier Narcissus, the lover, wanted to devour her hand in his mouth, now his words are placed on her lips. Narcissus's twin servants mock the maiden in derisive chanting of their master's words. In fact, hardly any snippet of dialog is not reiterated and reworked in this film. If Echo begins the film by counting "he loves me, he loves me not," in the end it is Narcissus's voice who chimes "I love me, I love me not." The smashed statuette becomes the champagne glass the forlorn Echo knocks from the same pedestal in the film's final shot.[14] With the (looking) glass now shattered, the film comes to its close. As Birgit Hein perceptively writes about one conclusion one can draw from this enigmatic work, "one cannot come together in union [*sich vereinen*] with a mirror image" ("Michael Brynntrup," 32). The beauty of *Narziss und Echo*, however, lies not in any fixed meaning one can derive from it but in its delicate Rococo asymmetries.

Allusions to phone sex, the impossibility of loving relations, intimations of pornography, as well as Brynntrup's death cult (with its hints of necrophilia), all point to the filmmaker's indirect evocation of the consequences of the AIDS epidemic. The question arises as to why he would tangentially address this complex issue. It is conceivable that Rosa von Praunheim's stridency and visibility, along with the rejection he has garnered among many German gays, has acted as a damper on other filmmakers (exceptions would be Wieland Speck's safe-sex videos and short *Zimmer 303* [1991],[15] Jochen Hick's *Via Appia* [1990], or Matthias Müller's private mourning in *Aus der Ferne* [*The Memo Book*] [1989], and *Pensão Globo* [1997]).[16] Another explication would be Brynntrup's avoidance of narrative film with its proclivity for personal histories as well as his eschewing of circumscribed themes in favor of experimental visual play. The situation is different, however, in his tribute to the photographer Jürgen Baldiga, who died of AIDS at the age of thirty-three.

Aide Mémoire, a sixteen-minute short, is decidedly not a documentary about Baldiga's life and work. Twice Brynntrup visits his friend, who is sick with AIDS, to ask a few informal questions and to get him on tape. This "Gay Document for Remembering" ("Schwules Gedächtnisprotokoll"), as Brynntrup subtitles the film, is full of gaps: it reproduces few of Baldiga's photographs and mentions only a couple of dates from his life, one of which is his death in December 1993. This reticence, even omission, makes the photographer's life seem all the more transient and the loss that much more poignant. Some of the footage appears at first glance to be trivial: Baldiga holds small objects from his belongings up to the camera—a minute hand of Fatima, a promotional lighter from a funeral home, a couple of removed teeth, even an old used condom—tiny, insignificant relics that the camera, however, appreciatively captures as tokens from everyday life. Although Baldiga admits that every time he looks at himself in the mirror he can see the progression of his illness and that he is conscious of dying every second of the day, Brynntrup asks about his first and then most recent sexual experience, recording for the gay protocol their laughter and affirmation of life. He registers, too, the horrendous verbal abuse to which he himself was subjected by a woman outside his apartment in a reminder that, even in a supposedly tolerant Berlin (and not just in Baldiga's hometown of Essen) homophobia has a public face.

When Baldiga reflects on his photographic art, parallels to Brynntrup's purpose in making this film come to mind. In stark, probing black-and-white photos, Baldiga captured the sufferings of PWAs and therewith the facts of the disease. Yet he also speaks about trying to show the dignity and liveliness that his subjects valiantly maintained, taking care not to sensationalize their situation. Brynntrup imitates these photos by freezing the frame and converting Baldiga's image into a black-and-white still. Through his photography, Baldiga says, he wanted both to hold on to his friends (though he admits he still loses them) and to leave a trace behind, something that will live on after death. *Aide Mémoire* shows in its brevity how vital yet fleeting this record is. Daringly, in the wordplay of its title, the film suggests that AIDS itself assists memory, that the fact of death helps to preserve a part of life. The juxtaposition with Baldiga implies that Brynntrup, too, hopes that death cannot take his friend away—he remains on film. Yet in its modesty the film intimates that this is only a hope, not an accomplishment. The memory does live on after the film is over, and the film has intensified the memory.

Throughout the interviews Baldiga is beautifully alert, smiling, and soft-spoken. The camera affectionately captures a close-up of his mouth. In truth, it is the voice that makes the cinematic art different from the photographic one. And it is a voice which is never shrill: taking his friend as a model, Brynntrup refuses to sensationalize his passing, nor does he play up the pathos of the loss—before the film ends with the words "it merely expires [es verblüht nur]"), the open coffin and tombstone are only momentarily shown. Shots of a hurdy-gurdy man playing in a Berlin courtyard also help provide an optimistic tone. Most important, the calm, low-keyed interviews reaffirm the presence and will of a friend with AIDS as well as the persistence of his sexuality and desires.

Insofar as Brynntrup also records himself with Baldiga and does not hide behind the camera, his own involvement in the other's life is not erased: another memory he avers is that he was an integral part of this life. In the broader view of Brynntrup's oeuvre, such a detail also serves as a reminder that despite Brynntrup's constant deconstruction of systems of identity, the presence of his own body, often naked, declares its facticity and distinctiveness. Even when masked as Aunt Ida, the actor is still immediately recognizable as Michael Brynntrup. In allegory, the clarity of the image remains despite all indirect signification. Here in Brynntrup's films, although he presents himself in drag, his palpability as engaged artist and unique person can still be felt.

Matthias Müller

Although melancholy tinges the charm of *Narziss und Echo* and the softness of Baldiga's voice in *Aide Mémoire*, Michael Brynntrup's ghoulish fascination with skulls and cemeteries seems to operate as an antidote to depression; his excessive, flamboyant indulgence in Gothic memorabilia, by forthrightly conjuring up death, exorcises it. By contrast, Matthias Müller's oeuvre, with its indirect signification, is drenched in melancholic beauty. His montage creates an emptiness around fleeting representations that incessantly dissolve into one another. The frequent use of the film negative, scratched or bleached celluloid, sepia tints, and double projection lend a haunting, worn quality to his works. Müller's postmodern bricolage of found footage, often from the fifties and sixties of his childhood, is also nostalgic. Müller's cinematic discourse is preeminently allegorical, not merely for the poetic elusiveness of its imagery but for its reference to temporality, to the source of its repertoire in the past, and to the dislocation, even forlornness of the isolated image in the present. Removed from their origin, Müller's images harken back to it wistfully; and, although the loss is irretrievable, beauty consoles. His is a cinema that reflects on itself—on cinema as mourning.

Born in 1961 in Bielefeld, Matthias Müller first studied in his home town before moving to Braunschweig to receive his master's degree in 1991 under the guidance of Birgit Hein and Gerhard Büttenbender.[17] Since then he has returned to Bielefeld, from whence he has organized avant-garde film events worldwide. In 1985 he cofounded, with Christiane Heuwinkel and Maija-Lene Rettig, Alte Kinder (literally, old children), which, as Mike Hoolboom describes it, is "a self-styled distribution organ that would tirelessly arrange tours, catalogues and speaking engagements" ("Scattering Stars," 81). Given the marginalized status of experimental filmmaking, such co-operative ventures are indispensable for visibility as well as mutual encouragement, as can also be seen in the group of young lesbian directors from Berlin (Percillier, Besilly, Zoller, Jordan, Kull) whose collaborative work has produced the stunning repertoire of predominantly animated shorts discussed in the next chapter. Matthias Müller has also collaborated on almost all his projects with the Berlin composer Dirk Schaefer, their longstanding joint efforts resulting in the haunting symbiosis of image and music. Schaefer has also served as sound producer for works by Brynntrup and Schillinger, testifying again to the underground links that, despite the obvious diversity of these filmmakers, unite them as a significant cinematic phenomenon.

Compared to symphonies despite their brevity, the lyric works of Matthias Müller echo those of Jean Genet, Kenneth Anger, Bruce Conner, Derek Jarman, and David Lynch. They have gained award after award, with both *Home Stories* (1990) and his latest film *Pensão Globo* (1997) taking the first prize of the Association of German Film Critics; *Alpsee* (*Nightmare Sea*) (1994), *Aus der Ferne* (*The Memo Book*) (1989), and again *Pensão Globo* winning prizes at the Oberhausen International Short Film Festival, and the latter also acquiring "special mention" in Locarno at the fiftieth anniversary of their international gathering. In addition his oeuvre includes *Continental Breakfast* (1985), *Final Cut* (1986), *Epilog* (1987), *The Flamethrowers* (1988–90, a collective film by Owen O'Toole, Alte Kinder, and Schmelzdahin), *Sleepy Haven* (1993), and *Scattering Stars* (1994). I shall focus first on his two reflections on mourning, *Aus der Ferne* (*The Memo Book*) and *Pensão Globo*, films that portray an estranged self-awareness in the aftermath of AIDS-related illness and death. I will cover more briefly important shorts lying between these landmarks, *Sleepy Haven, Home Stories,* and *Alpsee.*

Mike Hoolboom, the Toronto independent filmmaker and critic (as well as voice-over in *Pensão Globo*), introduces *Aus der Ferne* (*The Memo Book*) (1989, 27 min.) as "Müller's lyric opus, a compendium of a decade's work in super-8. It gathers his rigorous compositions and exquisite framings and summons them in the service of a resolutely first person cinema. Occasioned by a former lover's death of AIDS, *Aus der Ferne* is suffused with images of mourning and melancholy, haunted throughout by a keen sense of the maker's own mortality" ("Scattering Stars," 84). Not knowing the background to the film, and given that the clues are so sparse, it would be difficult to decipher that its incentive was the death of a lover from AIDS. Only the beginning hints in such a direction: hands gather up memorabilia (including a "Memo-Book" notepad), a voice intones "Death had come to a young man," and an avalanche of ice and snow, together with falling human figures, announces a catastrophe. Only one piece of footage, Müller's friend under a chandelier, suggests a snippet from a home movie lovingly retrieved, while a clip of two tuxedoed men dancing from an old film rebroadcast on television (followed by the caption "The End") makes the same-sex relation (and its termination) briefly explicit. Moreover, unless one had seen Müller, it would be impossible to know that the figure at whom he repeatedly turns the camera is himself (in close-ups of his hands, eyes, bare feet, and illumined, probing face), and hence that the film is also a reflection on the precariousness of his own body and his fear of disease.[18]

It would be too easy to attribute this oblique signification to Müller's preponderant lyricism or to appeal to the film's experimental status. Furthermore, it would be misleading to assume that Müller's images are private, that they hold memories too esoteric or disjointed to impart to others. Instead (quite the opposite of this personal expression theory), signification occurs here from a distance, "aus der Ferne," as if the loss of one's lover were too great to be named directly and a compilation of footage with him in it a sacrilege, for film can never act as his substitute. This *Memo Book* is not an assemblage of past activities recorded on film to trigger recollections, as usually occurs when one photographs or videotapes friends or family. Such a cinema would be a paltry surrogate for the act of memory, disguising and displacing its arduous task that never merely reproduces events in the mind. Instead, Müller renders the process of reminiscence and mourning in the form of the film itself. If he alters images through tinting, bleaching, filters, focus, extreme close-ups, slow motion, and unconventional angles, so that they sometimes become unrecognizable, then he mimics the movement of the unconscious or, as Freud describes it, the rapid displacements and condensations of the dreamwork. An intriguing example of such displacement is the scintillating close-ups of the chandelier prisms and then their incessant tingling on the soundtrack, shifting attention from the young man below them but invoking his absence all the more intently through auditory, fetishistic memory.

In various ways, *Aus der Ferne* is a film on the process of remembrance, concerned less with its imperfection than its transience. The images on Müller's screen flicker, fade, and dissolve into others, like memories. Schaefer's soundtrack matches the bricolage of found material and likewise relies on unpredictable, serendipitous links that evoke the involuntary nature of memory. Moreover, some sounds can be clearly identified while others cannot, a difference that reproduces the unevenness of recollection.[19] The gorgeous sepia tinting, too, suggests a faded, melancholic world brought only momentarily back to life. A flashlight illuminates merely part of the frame. Human figures appear as Expressionistic shadows. Cracks and scratches are left from the developing process, as if to signify that the recording is marred. Müller thereby seems to suggest that in bereavement one can register life only intermittently and in fragments.

This hand-developing is also an attempt to leave one's physical, tangible, yet ultimately opaque trace on the film, and works like the close-ups of Müller's body or his writing of the words, "I am filming this writing," which is echoed on the soundtrack. For despite their mutability, his images seem like imprints of a corporeality, remnants of what Lacan called "the Real," the repressed or abjected which resists systematization into the symbolic order. Hands pry a body open to reveal a beating heart and fingers probe a wound letting blood flow, again as if to signify the grasping for physical memory. Müller wanders through woods and a botanical garden, the jungle of branches evoking an entanglement of arteries and veins. Via rephotography shots are layered, pointing to the temporal process of their construction. The soundtrack too is an overlapping of recordings (sometimes of a voice, speaking words that are occasionally comprehensible), which lend a spatial thickness to this temporal art. In both cases, the metaphor for memory as a kind of palimpsest is conjured. The bits and pieces of the montage are elegiac and yet palpable, as if all that fell before one's eyes could possess the aura of a memento, of the Lacanian *objet a*. On the one hand, then, Müller's haunting, mysterious images intimate a depressing act of signification: in the absence of the beloved, objects are deprived of their legibility and color. Hence Müller films debris and various objets trouvés partially lit. On the other hand, though, *Aus der Ferne* presents an avalanche of radiant images, as if to compensate for their mutability. Cut loose from a narrative sequence and thrust into a montage, they seem all the more immediate and corporeal. This jubilant overabundance of images seems to want to refute the loss of the beloved. In the exchange, the erotics of physical skin is transferred to the erotics of the screen: indeed, Müller can make close-ups of plants evoke human flesh. The film thus stages a tension between the plenitude of meaning and dearth of it—between manic affirmation of the sign and depression at its brevity and mutability.

These extremes are also suggested by Müller's gorgeous play of light and shadow. Light often shines searingly into a darkened space, past silhouettes, grilles, and shutters, as if it wanted to burn through the celluloid itself. Indeed, Müller seems to want, like an alchemist, to marry fire with the recurring images of water in this film; his alchemy resides as well in his experimenting with emulsions in the film processing, turning the screen into shimmering gold or translucent jewels. This transformative process also gives rise to a renewal. If earlier in the short Müller films himself in his room, looking longingly out of a window, at the end his face is illumined as he rides a train. The submersion in memory (to evoke the metaphor of water once again) functions like a salutary baptism bringing the filmmaker back into life and out into the open—or is it an initiation through fire, through the light he perceives via the camera? Indeed, this eulogy to his friend is best described as a lyric affirmation of cinema's potential to articulate life's transient, scintillating beauty, even in its abject moments. It reminds one strongly of Derek Jarman's poignant *Glitterbug* (1994), a late work that compiles former super-8 footage in glistening, melancholic golden hues.

In *Aus der Ferne*, memory casts its sepia-colored shadow over the present. *Pensão Globo*, by contrast, is a film that mourns former lovers but that also reflects on the present as hollowed out in dread of AIDS and death. For the spectator and filmmaker, the present is the time of preemptive mourning for an anticipated bereavement, turning it already into a place of irretrievable loss. Although Müller himself is HIV-negative, his work shows an extraordinary empathy with the AIDS-anguished body and spirit; indeed, as the speaker in *Pensão Globo* says, "I can't sleep alone. I bring them all with me, the ones who came before." One's body resonates with the sufferings of others, wrenching it from itself; thus through the conceit used throughout of staggered double projection which creates a doppelgänger of the central figure,

Müller intimates both this disassociation from oneself as well as a haunting by other men. The voice-over itself is a bricolage, echoing passages from Derek Jarman, Hervé Guibert, and other AIDS diaries.

The story that *Pensão Globo* presents through image and voice-over (spoken by the HIV-positive Hoolboom) is that of a man in his thirties fighting dropping blood counts, who, needing to get away, ends up at a small hotel, the Pensão Globo, in Lisbon. The objects in his room—the bed, a red lamp, a fan, the radiator, and a closet door that opens itself—all seem, as in David Lynch's universe, to possess a thereness of their own, in mocking opposition to the man's transitoriness and restlessness. He wanders through the labyrinthine city, up and down steps and along walls. He loses his bearings, as we hear his echoing footsteps, marking his remaining time. His uprootedness (a card from the Rosedale clinic indicates that his home is in Toronto) is a metaphor for both mental and physical displacement from self. The voice-over interior monologue, in its nonsynchronicity, likewise betokens a disconnectedness from the body. Caught between reflections on his recent experiences at the AIDS clinic and a longing for death ("wondering when it will happen and hoping every day it will") the man is dislocated furthermore in time, his lonely present emptied of significance. To the same effect, his meditations on the past and future (the voice-over) are set in counterpoint to his figure roaming city streets or holed up in his red room. The thoughts that run through his mind themselves relate to temporality and his fragility: he envisages becoming a child again (as we see a negative of a mother feeding a child, an image pulsing to the sound of a heartbeat, as if heard in the womb); he feels old all at once; he watches plants grow, realizing he cannot help things changing; and, as noted, he is haunted by "the ones who came before." The voice-over itself is ghostlike. One wonders where its owner is now, as we, along with the speaker, anticipate him being overwhelmed by disease. The ending suggests an open-ended closure, as the bed that was being made at the start has its sheets removed; the shutters are closed again.

Müller's enthralling extended use of double projection, slow motion, filters, and various focuses concretizes the speaker's words, "sometimes it's like I'm already gone, become a ghost of myself." We simultaneously see an image and its double of a second ago (again pointing to temporal deferral), a technique of both pulsating beauty and sadness. Müller will also repeat a gesture several times in quick succession, as when the man curls up naked like a fetus, or at the close when he pulls his robe across his body, the crisp wrapping sound amplified. The spectral double also seems to take its inspiration from the X-ray to which the sick body is coldly subjected. The metaphor of doubling is executed on various levels, almost imperceptibly, due to the film's

211

lyric montage. Snatches of the voice-over are echoed; it then rehearses word for word a televised account of a hospital visit; the speaker notes that he stops looking in the mirror, because it's "not you anymore, it's the sickness." This last example particularly emphasizes the anamorphic disjuncture between self and its reflected image, while despairing of ever retrieving a whole body. The doppelgänger appears as a man in white shirt and pants (the color red dominates the rest of the film, especially in the sacrificial images of the bed, blood, and wine). The lead character follows this apparition down the streets, perhaps in desire, perhaps longing for death. The two are never shown together in the same frame; instead the editing cuts back and forth between them, suggesting that this angel of death is a hallucination of the dying man (we only hear one set of footsteps). The white figure leads the dying man into a botanical garden, whose cacti refer back to similar images in *Aus der Ferne* and evoke not only an illegible writing carved into their flesh but also the stubble of a man's cheek. Hands then slowly stroke the naked male body and member, as in the reveries from *Aus der Ferne* and *Sleepy Haven*, showing the indubitable perseverance of desire and strength. This time, however, the fantasy is short-lived. It cuts to a blackout followed by the man drawing his robe like a shroud around his body.

Through these uncanny doubles Müller reminds one that cinema itself is ghostly, its screen haunted by images recorded from the past and reproduced deceptively as present. *Pensão Globo* thereby stages the temporal disjuncture that the image signifies and consequently displays the purposefully allegorical dimensions to Müller's work: notwithstanding their intense beauty, his images appear as mere shadows, specters of that to which they refer. Through the movemented double exposure and the visual blur it occasions, moreover, it becomes impossible to see the man's face clearly: the film is a poignant testimony to our irrecuperable loss of once-familiar faces and bodies.

Sleepy Haven also uses dissolves, the negative, double projection, montage of images, tinting (here in blues and blacks), as well as gay sexuality. These characteristics put it into a cycle together with *Aus der Ferne* and *Pensão Globo*. If the bed framing the beginning and end of *Pensão Globo* suggests, among other things, dream and sleep, here too Müller probes the movement of the unconscious in its oneiric, erotic fantasies. Blue is the color of the sea, but it is also the color of Romanticism, whose phantoms of desire haunt this reverie. Images flow by to the sound of a scratched record, lapping waves, and the monotonous crescendo and decrescendo of a repeated string of music that matches the fade-ins and fade-outs. Ships heave at the dock, anchors drop into water, dripping ropes tug at chains, and naked sailors sleep in their berths, tossing and turning to the rhythm of their ships. The montage inti-

Figure 31. *Sleepy Haven* (1993). Courtesy of Matthias Müller.

mates that, as in Genet's *Un chant d'amour*, each man is (in) the dream of the other. As Mike Hoolboom, Müller's most eloquent critic, further suggests, "asleep, the body offers itself up to the gaze of its beholder, the film's day-dream structure suggesting that their minds are elsewhere, drifted far from these emptied tissues and ligaments, the better to offer themselves as vehicles of fantasy and projection. It is in the very absence of their activity that they may be reconfigured in Müller's homo-erotic reveries, these sleepers granted a common dream of fraternity" ("Scattering Stars," 86).

As in *Aus der Ferne*, the medium itself imparts an erotic palpability: the image pulses in flashes and phosphorescent blues and is drowned in bubbles. Light and shadows move in syncopation across the frame like waves. The re-peated cadence of the fade to black is lulling, as if the drowsy eyelid were closing and reopening. The entire film seems to want to induce a trancelike state. Enhanced by Schaefer's lulling music, the appearance and disappear-ance of the image mimics the rhythms of the body—a palm opening, noc-turnal tossings, the heartbeat, and breath. Through the processing the im-ages often seem submerged, as if trying to rise unsuccessfully to the surface of consciousness. Their logic of progression is associative: a tightrope walker balances over a waterfall; fabric, rigging, and chains break apart; hands tug at a fraying cord; fingers dig into cracked, dry earth and then rub against skin, exploring its surface as well as the taut muscles underneath. This is a film that sonically searches out subaquatic connections. Buried or sunken, too, is any clear narrative or meaning in Müller's elliptic montage. He only reflects on this shrouded signification through the allegory of a book submerged under water, whose leaves are opened by the ebb and flow. A typed page momentarily surfaces, and single words—"whirl," "sway," "plunge"—can be briefly made out. The voice-over reads a text pieced together from Joseph Conrad and Herman Melville, but the remontage, as in *Pensão Globo*, makes the sources unrecognizable. Moreover, this spoken text is drowned out by the layered soundtrack of music and waves. The word is thus acoustically as well as optically submerged, dissolved, and concealed. As the film crescendos to its close, tension mounts sexually to cracking, splitting noises and the increased tempo of images of naked bodies, including a tattoo of a penis. Finally, foghorns announce an orgasmic release.

In conclusion, I want to mention two other important shorts by Müller that, like the trio already discussed, are haunting, ghostly, though each differently so. *Home Stories* is a brilliant exercise in the assemblage of found footage.[20] Here Müller aligns similar clips from 1950s Hollywood cinema with such actresses as Lana Turner, Grace Kelly, and Doris Day to reconstruct and deconstruct the narrative that traps women in the dread and claustrophobia of the uncanny home. Dirk Schaefer's soundtrack likewise plunders 1950s films to heighten the suspense. Mirroring each other endlessly, these women wake up in the middle of the night to an unexpected noise, switch on lights, run down hallways, and slam doors, trying to escape from an unknown terror. No countershots reveal the source of their fear, but the expert editing with the cut on motion makes them seem to be reacting, as Robert Cagle puts it, "to 'herself'" (i.e. to representations of femininity). The female agent within the narrative attempts to flee, but finds no route of escape. She becomes literally inscribed, not only within the web of the spectatorial gaze . . . but also within the network of the gazes of other women within the narrative, and within the materialized 'conventions' of Hollywood narrative."

Cagle also broaches the camp sensibility in *Home Stories*—in its borrowing of melodramatic, histrionic, mannerized female performance and in "Müller's choice to 'detour' his voice, as a gay man, through representations of femininity," whereby his own exposure of the entrapment of Hollywood conventions is motivated by his own marginalization in the hegemonic culture. One could add that the pastiche itself, the citation and re-presenting of mass cultural material, is camp as well as pop. Müller here reminds his viewer of the uncanniness (*das Unheimliche*) which lurks behind every (camp) appropriation insofar as an element of inanimate mechanization underlies each repetition.

Uncanny and bordering on camp in its self-conscious, Lynchesque stilt-edness is Müller's 1994 film, *Alpsee*. It too recreates an early sixties lifestyle, not through found footage but through the decor, costume, and Technicolor gloss of its reenactment. A boy lives with his mother inside their home, where her daily routine—ironing, making a pie, dusting—seems by virtue of its speechlessness and montage-induced disconnectedness to become more and more surreal or uncanny. Something well known (the home, *das Heimliche*) secretively (*heimlich*) hides something, in Freud's familiar formulation. Despite the seemingly innocuous gestures of household life, a dark, unmanageable world seems to want to erupt from it. At one point it literally does: in a stunning image, the milk the mother pours for her son overflows the glass onto the table, the floor, and eventually down the hall in an endless stream. This uncontrolled secretion, pure white, is disturbingly connected to the enigmatic maternal body. The sparse decor of the home, the primary color scheme, and high key lighting all emphasize the preternatural clarity of the image in *Alpsee*. As in allegory, the sharp definition of the image belies its opaque, brooding signification. The pristine look of this film thus gives rise to its confusing, nightmarish quality, borne out by its name: the German word for "nightmare" is *Alptraum*.

Claudia Schillinger

Born in the same year as Michael Brynntrup, 1959, Schillinger creates, as he does, films that force the viewer to think through and piece together the logic of their enigmatic images. And with Matthias Müller she shares a passion for the lyric, erotic procession of montage. Her 16mm work comprises *Fatale Femme* (1985, 11 min.), *Dreams of a Virgin* (1986, 14 min.), *Das wahre Wesen einer Frau* (*The True Being of a Woman*) (1987, 13 min.), *Between* (1989, 10 min.), *In No Sense* (1992, 10 min.), and *Hermes* (1995, 25 min.). This last short moves into the documentary genre while rhythmically intersplicing it with poetic black-and-white camerawork that recalls her earlier pieces. As its subtitle, *Begegnung mit einem Mann, der Jungen liebt* (*Encounter with a Man Who Loves Boys*), indicates, *Hermes* approaches the controversial issue of pedophilia but from the perspective of a "meeting" between the filmmaker and her subject. In this work, despite its documentary format, Schillinger continues in the vein that marks her earlier oeuvre, a visually rich exploration of sexuality that does not shrink from explicitness, while maintaining a warm sensitivity or empathy for the bodies she is photographing. As with most of the directors discussed in this chapter, Schillinger puts herself in front of the camera,

215

neither to indulge in a public act of introspection nor (as with Brynntrup or Percillier and Besilly) to consciously perform a role, including an impersonated selfhood. Since the credits do not match actor onto role, or in the case of *Between* even indicate that Schillinger plays a part, her presence is quietly disguised; hence recognizing her does not constitute for the spectator a facile solving of the cinematic puzzle, as if her films were a secret, à-clef self-revelation. What Schillinger's presence does signify, however, is a reluctance to make the naked female body the object of an invasive, exterior gaze; she forestalls this objectification by locating herself in front of the camera, crisscrossing the conventional binary association of the active, directorial eye and passive, female screen body. Her move bespeaks honesty, insofar as she puts her own body (not another's) at stake in representation.

Given the general paucity of sexual imagery made by women of women, Schillinger's work is unique and attractive (the explicitly lesbian work of Barbara Hammer comes to mind as an exception). As a woman director moving in the realm of taboo representations of the female body, she wrestles it from its male, pornographic domain and reclaims it for the purpose of female erotic fantasies. To categorize the eroticized nudes in Schillinger's films as either representing her own sexual being *or* as objects of a lesbian or bisexual desire would be reductive of the resonant ambiguity Schillinger introduces between identification with and longing for another woman's body. By putting herself on the screen, she demonstrates the closeness to a body presented as other. Suddenly, for the female spectator as for Schillinger, one's own physical form with its curves and shadows becomes visually apprehendable and yet, at the same time, belongs to another, to the woman in the film, who in her nakedness erotically captivates. In *Dreams of a Virgin* this passage from mirroring to desire appears when toward the end of the film the doubly exposed flickering stills of the self (both played by Schillinger) begin to interact: the buoyant, dancing woman in the white dress begins to caress the superimposed image of her static somber doppelgänger in black.

This split between identification and a visual correlative—even a serialized disembodiment—of the self characterizes the process of fantasy as Laplanche described it. To recapitulate, Laplanche maintains that the subject "cannot be assigned any fixed place in [fantasy]. . . . As a result, the subject, although always present in the fantasy, may be so in a desubjectivized form, that is to say, in the very syntax of the sequence in question." "In fantasy the subject does not pursue the object or its sign: he appears caught up himself in the sequence of images" (17). Because of the hallucinatory nature of Schillinger's work (at least before *Hermes*), the spectator is "caught up . . . in the sequence of images" and "cannot be assigned any fixed place." Are her dreamlike images to be registered as part of the spectator's fantasy or are they to be attributed to a person in the film, and would the spectator then identify with this person? Given the very structure of fantasy, according to Laplanche, can these distinctions even be upheld? In any case, whether the body is imagined as the viewer's own or that of another woman, Schillinger's pornographic daydreams are as seductive as they are daring.

"My film is about fantasy, about the expression of a language which shows my fantasy" (63): with these words Schillinger announces her allegorization of fantasy in *Between*. The film begins in color with a woman wearing a red-and-black lace chemise lying in the grass. Among the various shots of her is one that reveals a dildo in her hand (fabricated by Schillinger for the film). What follows is a slowly paced but then increasingly quicker succession of black-and-white images that progress from hands groping along the shadow of a heavy chain, to a female torso with breasts bound flat, a frontal torso shot of a naked woman with a strapped-on dildo, and a woman, again naked, who is slicking back her hair, looking directly into the camera. As Birgit Hein points out, these images conceivably belong to the initial woman as her masturbatory fantasies ("'Das Wahre Wesen,'" 150). The camera cuts back to this woman daydreaming but places her in other settings—lying on a bed, masturbating while leaning up against a tree, or, in the final sequence, in a public toilet. These various locales seem to suggest other scenarios where she can let her erotic fantasies run free (but, as Hein points out, always taking on the same form [151]). The black-and-white episodes (all filmed against a black backdrop) are joined by close-up shots from various angles of hands tugging ever more aggressively at a woman's exposed genitals, a male reclining torso shot above the pelvis, a woman's waist with unzipped leather pants from which the dildo peeps, and a woman entering from behind with the strapped-on dildo a figure whose gender is indeterminate. These are visions that shift, as it were, at the blink of an eye. Intermittently the heavy rhythms of Prince start up on the soundtrack and just as quickly again give way to silence.

Because all the black-and-white shots, apart from that of the woman combing her hair, are framed without the head, the identity of the players remains anonymous and to a certain degree interchangeable. Birgit Hein maintains that there are only two actors in the fantasy—a man and a woman (Claudia Schillinger herself) (149). The filmmaker herself says that there are **217** two women in *Between* (63). And Ulrike Zimmerman casts the film as a kind of temporal mise-en-abyme: "The perspective is that of a woman who remembers herself, who also thinks back on herself as fantasizing" (89). The relationship *between* the woman in the chemise and the woman combing her

Figure 32. *Between* (1989). Courtesy of Claudia Schillinger.

hair is key in this ambiguity: are they the same person, but separated by an interval of time (as Zimmerman suggests)? Do they share the same fantasies? Is the one desirous of the other? What, too, is the relationship of the woman in color (also, incidentally, occasionally shot in black and white) to the other female images—that of identification, desire, or a shifting between the two?[21] The dildo and its use (what lies *between* one's legs) also suggests not so much an indecision as a plurality of sexual positions. It could, as Hein remarks, signify that the woman assumes an active, "male," powerful role, with her partner being the dominated man. Another possibility would be a lesbian one, with the prone partner being a woman; the strapping down of the breasts also recalls butch iconology. In addition, the fantasy could be a bisexual one, allowing room for both prospects and for the stunningly queer image of the possession and display of a multitude of eroticized body parts—penis, breasts, and vulva. As Schillinger elucidates in an interview: "Perhaps it's a bit like a puzzle. You take an ass, and breasts and cunt, and dildo and you combine them as you want. . . . I have a fascination with these fragments and to combine them [sic] into new forms" (63). Insofar as part of the woman's fantasy is to be looked at, the spectator is reminded of his/her own scopophilic position. Conversely, via the woman looking directly into the camera, as if she were our own mirror image, we are guided into taking the masturbatory fantasies as our own. Schillinger seduces her spectator into imagining bisexual and transgendered possibilities. As she observes, "in my film you can recognize a part of your own fantasies, it's not showing you in such a direct way [as in pornography] that it kills your own" (65). The very brevity of the short, experimental form allows for this array of queer dreams and desires.

Preparing the way for *Hermes*, her most important work to date, Schillinger's next film, *In No Sense*, likewise moves in the realm of taboo sexuality—that of a young girl. Again the sequence of images stages a daydream recollection, here of an adult woman reflecting back on childhood memories as she lounges with her partner on a bed, while the afternoon sun comes streaming into her room. The long duration of the shots from an immobile camera particularly suggests a reverie. The title puns on the word "innocence," yet also refers to the film itself and to childhood as an enigma. Although the settings are more realistic in this film, as if to suggest the intensity and precision of the memory/fantasy, the implications to be drawn from the silent images are not clear. A girl of about ten rides in a gymnastic pose on a horse, the slow motion capturing her spring and balance; in another shot she wildly rides a rocking horse; and in another she is rhythmically bounced up and down on her father's lap to a nursery rhyme. Another image shows her curling up next to the man in bed for an afternoon nap. Yet a further sequence in the montage depicts hands shaving off a woman's pubic hair, as if returning her to her girl's body, all the while insisting on the adult eroticism of the act. Another shot captures a woman naked on a bed with someone else's hand stretched into her crotch. In both frames, the camera refuses to pan to divulge the sexual identity of the partner, a hesitancy that links this film to the queer indeterminability of Schillinger's previous film while presaging the topic of unconventional sexuality in the next.

The queerness of *Hermes* lies not only in its explicitly gay subject matter, but in the filmmaker's fascination as a woman for male pedophilic attraction and the way in which she attempts to define the affinity between herself and the pedophile Hermes. Queer, too, is how she unnervingly challenges normative, heterosexual assumptions about parents' sensual closeness to their children, asking us through her montage to compare Hermes to a mother's physical play with her baby boy. Conceivably, in order to avoid the immediate categorization of the pedophile as male homosexual, the terms "gay" and "homosexual" are absent from the film, except in reference to the fear Hermes's parents have of him converting their other sons to homosexuality. Yet despite Schillinger's efforts to make a film that resists societal categories and conventions regarding unorthodox sexualities—labeled separately as gay, maternal, or juvenile—the film has been repeatedly rejected by gay and lesbian as well as feminist festivals. *Hermes* has never been screened in the United States, though it was screened once in Canada, and was only seen once in Germany, at a documentary film festival in Munich. In itself, this reception history exposes and condemns the entrenched strictures governing sexuality, even in feminist filmmaking, which initially inspired Schillinger to reclaim the female body for visual representation. In *Hermes* she specifically portrays maternal sexual desires, a step obviously too far in advance of her times.

The 25-minute piece begins with an over-the-shoulder shot of the director watching the film we are about to see, a mise-en-abyme that indicates the inextricable involvement of the spectator, right from the start, in this provocative topic; Schillinger's pose is one that we copy. To the same effect, while displaying photos from Hermes's possession, she shoots the hands that hold them, again mimicking the view we would see, as if we were handling the pictures ourselves: the hands are extensions of our arms. The film then ends with a photo of Schillinger as a bright-eyed nine-year-old looking into the camera; earlier, while examining photos of the Hermes family, her off-screen voice mentions how she must have looked similarly unabashedly into the camera when she was at his inquisitive age. Further cementing her ties to Hermes, she muses off-camera about whether she is charmed by him as a man and, rather queerly, whether he could be attracted to the boyishness in her. Indeed, she poses for a still shot in the position of one of the naked boys Hermes had photographed, while her voice-over queries: "Was there a way for me to relate to him? He asked me what it was about our conversation that interested me. There was something I was able to share with him, but I didn't yet know what it was." Schillinger therewith links empathy with allure, indirectly encouraging her audience to understand Hermes through a recognition of shared desires rather than through distanced critique. The spectator too is confronted with the erotic photos Hermes has taken, even one of a boy with erect penis, and is thereby forced to probe his/her own appreciation of their beauty. Thus, like the androgynous voice from the Kelly Family singing during the credits "Don't be afraid, I'll show the way," Schillinger guides the spectator gently into this sensitive topic, though clearly the "I" of the song also ventriloquizes for Hermes as self-appointed initiator of youth into the not-always-brightly-lit realms of sexuality.

The interview is reproduced word for word with an actor taking Hermes's part; the photos, however, are original and belong to him. Hermes charms with his smile and articulateness. He is also reflective and pensive, saying, for instance, that he has acted according to his own inner moral code, while also acknowledging that he has made serious mistakes by relying on his intuition. Many of his admissions are incendiary: He wants to help the pre-pubescent boys he encounters live out their sexuality, letting most of the initiative come from them. Although refusing the anal intercourse one or the other requests, he prefers to nibble at their penises, whose sensitivity, he claims, is incomparably greater than that of a grown man. Even their warm breath, Hermes confesses, gives him an orgasm. Although he criticizes the power structure between parent and child, remembering the threats of his own mother to withhold love, he at first naively speaks as if he could separate sex and power. He then, in the course of speaking, reveals that he reenacts the manipulative tactics of his mother with these youths, although he falls short of realizing the damning implication of his words—that his relationships with boys are not as innocent as he would like (us) to believe. By condemning his mother for always knowing what was good and bad for him and how he was to feel, he implies that she did not let him explore his own boundaries sufficiently. These limits between adult and child are ones that later in life Hermes is still struggling to determine.

Other comments reveal an equal degree of naiveté and utopianism: that in a different society he would be a teacher of eroticism, that the boy in him comes alive once among his young friends, and that his provocations would prompt his parents to an admission of love, although they have accused him

221

of being worse than a murderer and have denied him access to his brothers, with whom, Hermes intimates, he also shared sexual experiences. Hermes's self-absorption is most evident in his ultimate fantasy—that of being taken back across the barrier that puberty marks, a fantasy that romanticizes away the anxieties of childhood. Paradoxically, although they jar, such statements also seduce, if only for their unorthodoxy and openness in a sexually repressive Western society. Caught between acceptance and condemnation of Hermes, the spectator resembles the boy on the unicycle shown in a repeatedly inserted sequence: the boy cycles around the actor playing Hermes, eyeing him and pedaling back and forth to keep his balance.

Potentially more scandalous than even Hermes's statements is the context in which Schillinger places them. She cuts repeatedly to super-8, black-and-white scenes of a naked mother and three-year-old son, showing the aggressivity and initiation of the latter before his gentle, acquiescing mother. The baby asks to be slapped and tickled; he looks down at his little erect penis and proudly announces *"Pimmel"* (dick); and he spanks his mother hard on her bare bottom. The soft focus, slow motion, and unusual angles poeticize their relationship, granting us an aesthetic pleasure that hides the more suspect voyeuristic one of being privy to this intimacy, which includes that of the woman's voluptuous body. Despite the fact that such scenes are taboo in cinema, the general assumption would be that such closeness between mother and son is natural. The juxtaposition to Hermes's story asks one to consider how his physical tenderness to boys might be similar. On the one hand, Hermes's own memories of frequent cuddlings as a child raise the additional issue of how his upbringing might have influenced his pedophilic tendencies, for he himself intimates at such a connection while stopping short of analyzing it. On the other hand, the way in which the mother lets her son act out his aggressivity suggests that she is allowing him to experiment more in exploring relationships than Hermes's mother did. Moreover, the film indirectly poses the question of the extent to which Hermes's longing for closeness to boys acts as compensation for his currently severed ties to his family. Most of all, the use of black-and-white stock (also in the photos) evokes a nostalgia for a lost past, the paradise of tenuous, fleeting, uninhibited childhood.

The nude photos, in particular, seem suspended in time and separated from their narrative context and purpose, about which one can only speculate. Were they used, for instance, for Hermes's sexual pleasure? And what is their status as pornography vis-à-vis the spectator? Unlike the unorthodox scenes with the mother, these photos of naked boys lying vulnerably on a bed or, in one case, jubilantly posing with erect penis do evoke pornographic conventions. Schillinger does not sensationalize them, however, nor does she

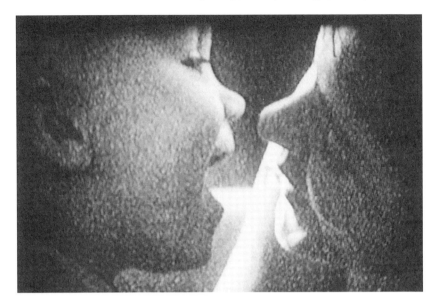

Figure 33. *Hermes* (1995). Courtesy of Claudia Schillinger.

make the spectator feel guilty for the pleasure she offers in reproducing them. The frankness of the boys suggests that they are aware of their attractive bodies and the visual delight they provoke. Yet, at the same time, insofar as these photos have captured a transient moment of boyhood on the cusp of puberty, they are melancholic and meditative.

The ellipses in *Hermes*, generated by the montage of differently recorded photos and footage, play a part in making it so disturbing.[22] The title itself suggests a montage of associations: Hermes as the messenger between heaven (of childhood) and the mundane world (of adulthood); the god of thieves, liars, and voyagers; and the father of the hermaphrodite. The title is a shorthand for multiple readings of the film. What remains most elliptical and enigmatic in Schillinger's works, however, is the naked body itself—captured in still frames, at unconventional angles, and in the provocative shadows of black-and-white stock. Schillinger arrests the body in gestures and fetishized fragments; it is a body that unites with the grainy, almost tactile photographic material, dissolving into it.[23] Schillinger thus visualizes a transition *between* skin and celluloid. If Hermes speaks of the necessity of reading the language of the body (*Körpersprache lesen*), then in Schillinger's works allegory appears with its most enigmatic countenance—for how is one to read the silent, intermittent, yet warmly palpable speech of the body/film?

223

Hans A. Scheirl and Ursula Pürrer

Among the filmmakers discussed in this book, the only one who self-identifies as transgender is Hans A. Scheirl (or as she has penned her name to earlier works, Angela Hans Scheirl). Hans is one of the individuals featured in Jewels Barker's *St. Pelagius The Penitent* (1998), a thirteen-minute short that interviews f2ms and commemorates, as the film points out, one of the many transgendered saints. In the film Hans Scheirl speaks of taking her first testosterone shot for her fortieth birthday and speculating that if she has spent her first forty years as a woman, he might spend the last forty as a man. In an interactive email interview published in *Rundbrief Film* in 1996, Scheirl writes to B. Fluid: "I identify myself as boy, dragking, transvestite, and transgender. Insect. That's the truly new word: insect" ("Interview," 492) and "I also identify myself as cyborg" (489). In this chapter's last section, I want to retrace the ways in which Scheirl, together with Ursula Pürrer, test how they can manipulate their bodies as objects on screen, using the cinematic apparatus as a technology for perverting representation. From the early super-8 home movies they made together to their lesbian cult film *Rote Ohren fetzen durch Asche* (*Flaming Ears*) (1991) and Scheirl's *Dandy Dust* (1998)—which he describes as a "cyber-cinema for the trans-X patriarchal fin-de-millennium" (489)—Scheirl and Pürrer explore cinema's potential as a hermaphroditic, cyborgesque medium. Highly experimental and vigorously antirealist, Scheirl's and Pürrer's art is particularly challenging in its abstraction, despite its concrete, even orgiastic, visual allure. Because it is so difficult to access, I want first to show where their work ends up—Scheirl's *Dandy Dust*—and then use this film as a lens through which to analyze their early essays in super-8. I will extend this analysis to their feature-length *Rote Ohren*, trying to map out continuities in their diverse and exploratory counterculture production.

The bizarreness of *Dandy Dust* was heralded in 1995 in *Dandy Dust: The Super-8 Trailer*. The trailer genre is disjointed, fragmentary, and highly fetishistic. Standing as a part to the whole of a film, it is essentially metonymic, with the goal of visually seducing through tantalizing glimpses. Playing upon this elliptical signification and orgasmic structure, Scheirl makes a trailer that offers a peep at the neo-gothic horrors of his transgender futuristic film. The ninety-four-minute feature, however, itself reads like an extended trailer. The editing is fast-paced, the bricolage shattering, and the plot barely discernible. Scheirl skips between stop-motion animation and cartoonlike real characters, shots of gooey fluids and the grainy empty screen, visions of futuristic technologies and eighteenth-century courtly decadence, and characters sporting bared breasts and those parading dildos. This plethora stems in part from the various influences that inform Scheirl's work—"techno, body-art, splatter, and comix culture (Tsui Hark, Shinja Tsukamoto, Valie Export, Kurt Kren, King Hu, Sam Raimi, etc. etc.)" (489). *Dandy Dust* recalls the post-apocalyptic look of *Blade Runner*, the horror film, the no-budget movie, together with the ellipticism of the avant-garde, experimental short. Depicting debris and waste of all sorts, Scheirl gives new meaning to the genre of trash.

This conglomeration matches the hermaphroditic characters Scheirl sets on the screen, "shape-shifters with comix qualities" (490). "I borrow methods from the underground films and B-pictures, as far as identity transformation [*Identitätenverun/mformung*] goes. Practically speaking, the figures are dragking, dragqueen, and the WHOLE wild family, including animals and planets. High camp mythology!" (490). The confusion between he/she/it becomes s/hit in this splatter-cinema. The deviant subjects that Scheirl invents include Dandy's mother, Super-Mother Cyniborg XVII, Duchess of Loft & Spire, who wears sixteen-inch heels and a bishop's miter. She has pointed claw fingers and one long arm reaching to the ground and navigates the spacecraft Mothership. Aided by Dandy's unborn twin sisters, who work as body-part collectors for her, Cyniborg stitches back together deceased ancestors. In her drive to protect and propagate the family, she grotesquely parodies maternity. Dandy's father is the English aristocrat landowner Sir Sidore, whose hard-on in his breeches is always in view and whose horniness is channeled toward his son. Exaggerated, his phallic potency is both parodic and horrific.

The film begins with its protagonist crash-landing on 3075, a "cybernetic planet/creature/city. Its humanoid inhabitants exchange bodily fluids with the city and each other inside the bladder of the planet" (director's notes). Here the notion of postmodern fluid identity goes to the limit with the tubular hookup to others' bodily fluids: "They communicate via chemical reactions and electronic mini-rhythms = sexual trembling." Turning the mirror stage into the simulacrum stage, Dandy himself is replicated in later reincarnations, including Dust and Mummy, his bandaged afterlife persona. In the perverse familial ties governing the action, Dandy is thus both his Mummy and, by one letter, his Daddy. Played by Scheirl looking amazingly young as a boy, Dandy takes the passive role in gay anal sex and awakens with Spider Cunt Boy attached to his genitals, a shape-shifting android-spider with huge labia for a torso. The name of the actor playing Spider Cunt Boy, Svar Simpson, is gender-indeterminate, as are Tre Temperilli (as Sir Sidore) and Hans

Figure 34. *Dandy Dust* (1998), Suzie Krueger as Cyniborg. Courtesy of
Hans A. Scheirl.

Scheirl himself. Referring to the enjoyment he derives from the pronoun confusion his identity causes, Scheirl says that "the linguistic tangle [*Sprachengewirr*] is huge and we recognize the potential for its celebration" (492). Not content to disrupt the human/machine binary via the cyborg, Scheirl thus also trespasses the boundaries between male and female.[24] Through its heterogeneous, hybrid characters, *Dandy Dust* proclaims a sublime disarray; its very discourse is compiled like a hermaphroditic, gender-confusing body.

Dandy Dust borrows from the allegorical, epic structure of the psychomachia that one finds, for instance, in *Pilgrim's Progress* or *Gulliver's Travels*.[25] Dandy flies backward and forward in time, trying to re-member his past; however, in this cyborgesque universe (read: cyber-space), the parts do not add up to a whole of a selfhood. The more Dandy reexperiences his former lives, the more opaque the links become. As the narrator mumbles: "sometimes when we know too much, we forget everything." In an interview Scheirl announces, "The main character was a being with twelve different identities, seven of which were played by me" (Graham Jones, 69). Given this multitude of personalities, it would be moot to search for a subjectivity, will, or individuality in this comix-inspired protagonist; character, as Scheirl states in the director's notes, is solely the product of "special effect."[26] These notes further elucidate Scheirl's project with regards to how his cinema reconstructs the "self": "My goal is to create my own visual language to express the hysteric state of the technologically extended human at the fin-de-millennium . . . mirrored by other cybernetic systems, the cyborg realizes that 'self'-creation lies at h fingertips. A cyborg's life is *experimental* always."

Literalizing the notion of "trans" in transgender, Scheirl sees his characters as traveling through the dimension of "Hindurch" (or "across") in a picaresque series of adventures. Novel, however, is that the body itself is traveled through. Scheirl maps out space and time onto parts of the body, that is, planets and spaceships are connected to various members and organs of the body. He elaborates: "One of the time/places is the 'planet of blood and swelling.' On this planet Dandy spends part of his/her youth: with the father in a country house. . . . The sky is at the same time the macro-surface in the father's intestines/colon. The scenes are lit by a slide projection of an electron-microscopic image of the blood vessels in the intestines" ("Interview," 491). This turning inside-out of the body—to peer pornographically inside it— marks an attempt to make it signify. But it remains illegible. So too the gender-deterritorialized body resists being appointed meaning: it frustrates the symbolic order whose matrices (although still present in the Freudian, familial structure) suddenly no longer function conventionally. Instead, the metamorphosed body marks sheer physical, material, and freakish presence. It is

227

also extremely eroticized, game for all varieties of sexual encounters, as one sees in the f2ms miming a gay orgy. Rejected by the social order, transgender signifies the repressed of society, its obscene hidden side. Insofar as it represents the abject, it leads in Scheirl to the exploration of other, similarly taboo realms: he recasts childhood as incestuous and queer and the Oedipal struggle as anally situated. He summarizes the plot as a "fight against a genealogically obsessed family" (director's notes), and indeed ruthlessly satirizes the idealized view of the family as nurturing and natural.

Other images of amorphous horror and anamorphotic transgression are bodies that squirt blood, semen, vomit, and piss. Dandy voraciously stuffs fruit down his pants and squishes it so that it stains his breeches. Playing upon the paranoiac fears of contamination through bodily fluids, skin and clothing are splattered so that the insides become exteriorized. Similarly, plastic props of cunts and penises are stuck on. In his "Manifesto for the Dada of the Cyborg-Embrio," Scheirl speaks of "gadget & tube sex, immense variety of transformer genitals" and advocates that one "terminate production of countless useless machines and build useful fucking attachments: chrome-dildo-machines, rubbermuscles that grow in reaction to guttural noises, toys (baby, motorbike, boxer, bull) remote controlled by fingers and other bodyparts working from the surface into the insides with relentless motorstrength" (52). In Scheirl's film, this techno body becomes monstrous, prosthetic and comic, as organs and limbs become independent, disintegrate into dust, or circulate in the outer-space traffic in body parts. Scheirl thus brilliantly contrasts cyborgesque artificiality with corporeal softness and porosity. He insists that in cyberspace one cannot depart from the flesh, while not letting us forget that gore, too, is a special effect.

If the body is reliant on cinema to show it, then it is also subservient to the apparatus, to be transformed and fetishized by it. Feminist film theorists from Laura Mulvey on have unpacked the patriarchal ideology of the cinematic apparatus; Scheirl, by contrast, explores its emancipatory, utopic potential. Cinema can drag, in other words, resignify the body, making it transgender, cyborgesque, or golemlike. It can accomplish this goal through transsex casting, gender-confusing costuming and makeup, and an editing that not only eroticizes body parts but also fetishizes grotesque protuberances and inner organs. In *Dandy Dust* artificiality is further emphasized through theatrical stage sets, animation, colored tints, double projection, and echoes of Expressionist cinematic style. Thus, if the cinematic apparatus is theorized as the sum of technological effects, then the body portrayed in it, too, is a compilation of effects. As an object for hermaphroditic bricolage and anamorphotic distortion, the body can be scopically toyed with.

Yet cinema not only plays with the body but for Scheirl actually becomes the body. "The protagonist in *Dandy Dust* is the film grain and the TV static [*Fernsehrauschen*]" (Scheirl in an interview with Braidt, 38). What is so fascinating about Scheirl's universe is the way in which he thinks through transgender in order to extrapolate a new, somatically conceptualized filmic language. He speaks of his "goal of developing a cinematic language that liquefies the hierarchies of the body: blood speaks through the light projection, skin through a certain flimmering of the film grain, the psyche in the ceremony of exaggeration and disguise—which to me means drag: parody, simulation" ("Interview," 492). Cinema itself is here hermaphroditically constructed—it is a compilation of lavish, metonymically successive details, perverse in a signification process that elides, fractures, and reassembles. On the one hand, this cinematic discourse interfaces with Net surfing: through unconventional editing techniques and camera angles Scheirl so disorients the viewer's sense of space that one has the impression that the image can transport one anywhere; one is everywhere at once in Dandy's chaotic virtual universe. On the other hand, this disjointedness also evokes the obscene, anarchic splaying open of the body. Manually handling and splicing celluloid on the cutting table, the Frankensteinian filmmaker operates like his creation Cyniborg. Fast-paced editing draws our attention to this cutting and reassemblage of the body/film—to the indifferentiation between body and cinema. Scheirl's project is no less than a reorganization of how we epistemologically perceive cinema via the perverse, transgendered body.

In its elliptical signification *Dandy Dust* relies heavily on allegorical effect. With spectacle emphasized over story, allegory's tendency to nonnarrative structure takes over. In the "cybernetic/interactive narrative," Scheirl describes, "first you collect materials, pictures, sounds, etc. of the film-to-be, then you trace movements and create links. The spectator is inspired by the ease with which the movie switches between dimensions/media/cinematographic languages/ in&out to do likewise & weaves h own stories" ("Manifesto," 55). This fast-paced switching ties into other allegorical effects: the gallery of bizarre figures and surrealistically isolated images, the visual parade of baroque excesses and memento mori, and dialogue that is only intermittently discernible, especially when the voices are electronically distorted. *Dandy Dust*'s power resides in this obscurity of its image repertoire, which, in Scheirl's post-apocalyptic universe, is beyond redemption or recuperation for the making of semantic order.

Insofar as allegory draws attention to its own iconographic status by hinting at meaning without divulging it, it attracts the eye to its surface. This exterior then becomes the place where ornament, artifice, and embellishment

229

collect, leading to what Maureen Quilligan calls the "absurdity of the surface" (28) in allegory. In an interview, Ursula Pürrer speaks of the "powerfulness of the exterior" ("Mächtigkeit des Außen," quoted in Blümlinger, 199). Her films, she says, relate to the classical feature film as comics do to the novel. In the underground world, out of which comics arise, fashion is everything, the exterior (*Außen*) constantly changing (Blümlinger, 199). Reading Scheirl's and Pürrer's films, then, means to focus on the externality of costume and gesture and on the theatricality of the body, which is now deployed as prop. This scopic fascination with enigmatic surface is what connects *Dandy Dust* back to the first films Scheirl and Pürrer made together. In fact, here skin literally serves as a surface upon which to paint, etch, and tattoo designs.[27]

Pürrer, alias Schi-zu, and Scheirl began making super-8 movies together in 1984 when they were both in Vienna. Like the gender hybridity of Scheirl and his characters, this collaborative work also signifies a negotiation of different identities coming together in a heterogeneous product. These shorts, executed between 1984 and 1986, exude an amazingly fresh intimacy and vitality. Referred to by the filmmakers as "home movies," they record actionistic performances in the directors' own living quarters, with added soundtracks of intermittent percussive sounds. They include *Super-8 Girl Games*, *Body-Building*, *Rhabarber und Zucker* (*Rhubarb and Sugar*), *Kampf und Kuss* (*Fight and Kiss*), *Gezacktes Rinnsal schleicht sich schamlos schenkelnässend an* (*Zigzagged Rivulet Sneaks Up Shamelessly, Wetting the Thighs*), *Im Garten der Gelben G.* (*In the Garden of the Yellow G.*), *Piss in Rosa* (*Piss in Pink*), *Ein Schlauchboot und Austern* (*Rubber Dinghy and Oysters*). These gemlike masterpieces ravish the eye with their brilliant colors. Quick cuts fetishize every frame. The body is adorned with shimmering fabrics, extravagant headdresses, flowers, and tattoos. Yet naked skin too appears as design. The shots that fetishize and isolate the body render it solitary and pensive in its unusual beauty; there is an incredible yearning in Scheirl's and Pürrer's work that extends even, despite its violence, to the melancholic *Dandy Dust*.

Already in *Super-8 Girl Games* Scheirl and Pürrer demonstrate their adeptness in fantasizing corporeal imaginaries. Facing each other, their bodies communicate whimsically, like comic-strip characters. Drawn onto the film, a dart bounces between their chests; swigglies join their mouths; one pours liquid from her armpits into the other's hands and squirts drops from her nose which the other then catches. Here the body is made to speak its own silly yet eroticized language. In *Body-Building*, the camera zooms in for a close-up and just as quickly backs away, showing Scheirl and Pürrer dancing. Quick takes reveal their breasts and the impression left on skin by a leather belt. In *Rhabarber und Zucker*, rhubarb is made into antlers and a tail. Pürrer shakes the leaves on a plant and then, imitating it, her head. As in a number of these pieces, Scheirl and Pürrer render the female body plantlike. In this hypermaterializing of the body—the body as plant, costume, paint— the human merges with the nonhuman, presaging *Dandy Dust*'s experimentation with the cyborg.

In *Kampf und Kuss* Scheirl and Pürrer resemble Japanese warriors engaged in ritualistic battle; through unusual angles, the camera fetishizes quick physical movements and exquisite articles of clothing, while fitful zooms produce a swirl of color and mimic the flow of scintillating veils. The film ends with drawings of the encounters, raising the questions: do the sketches distill the fight we just saw or was the latter patterned on the former; what comes first, art or action? The naked body, then, is used as costume in *Gezacktes Rinnsal*, where the pubis is shaved and painted and the skin peppered with needles. The body stages itself, as someone stands and urinates, creating the rivulet to which the title alludes. Liquid too are the female operatic voice and shimmering satin and lamé of *Im Garten der gelben G.* Women exchange bouquets of flowers that undulate like the body; peonies are squeezed as if they were breasts and stuffed into the mouth. Toenails become an appendage of design, here extended into long, red, dangling fabric. This focus on the sensuousness of objects and color stems from Pürrer's background in painting: she notes, "the movement is important to me. On the other hand, I really love the materiality of color and painting" (Blümlinger, 196). Further, "I work much more with images than with the story line or dialogues. From art history also comes the iconography: recurring objects, symbols. It's hard to define exactly, because I think all our films have a painterly quality which comes from the lighting and color. It's a question of materiality" (Blümlinger, 198).

This attention to visuality also characterizes three subsequent works—*Im Original Farbig (Originally Colored)* (1986) by Scheirl and Pürrer and *The Drift of Juicy* (1989) and *Das Aufbegehren oder das andere Begehren (The Revolt and the Desire)* (1991) by Pürrer alone. Marking a radical stylistic shift from the performance art of the home movies, these pieces experiment with reordering and challenging optic perception. *Im Original Farbig* confuses the eye with its miniature cardboard sets that mimic the look of architectural designs, computer games and electronic switchboards. Color and movement here bedazzle; through the isolation and abstraction of forms we "see color." Such snippets of written text call attention to how the film is "read" by the viewer. In *The Drift of Juicy* the screen is divided into various moving and overlapping frames, making it impossible to ascertain depth. Intricately constructed models are shot up close on super-8 and manipulated further on video: the segments seem like pieces of a puzzle that fit but never come together to form an entire picture. The soundtrack perplexes with its mechanistic noise. Yet despite this geometric and acoustic abstraction, the voice-over points out the sensuousness of perception: "Her glance caught the shapes. Her skin devoured these pictures." Innovative lighting renders the colors translucent and glowing. Using video techniques, Pürrer doubles herself on screen, fucking her look-alike with a dildo. The voice-over declares "It's tricky to be both," whereby Pürrer alludes to both the difficulty and deception of the maneuver, as well as the positions of filmmaker/voyeur and actress/exhibitionist that she assumes. She also offers her back up to an elaborate gothic tattoo of fish scales and devils' heads and to a Kafkaesque metal instrument that etches into the skin. Here again, as she points out in an interview, she underscores the iconographic function of the body: "In *The Drift of Juicy* the skin is tattooed, and what matters is the scratching forth of images. Perhaps one associates the procedure with pain because one sees blood, but it's more a question of the iconic" (Blümlinger, 201).[28] *Das Aufbegehren* also queeries perception, as unpunctuated sentences appear word by word on the screen, pointing to the temporality of the reading process and the instantaneity of their appearance. Various phrases comment on this fragmentation: "Irritatingly searching for a medium to express the simultaneity of spatial and temporal jumps" or "The concentrated gaze of the female fetishist experiences objects and movements in exactly defined excerpts." The body, too, as another phrase suggests, is split open (*aufgesplittert*). In this film about seriality, people are referred to as A or G[II] in their sexual relations with one another.

This deconstruction of eroticism and individuality also distinguishes the next film Scheirl and Pürrer made together (this time with Dietmar Schipek), the feature-length *Rote Ohren fetzen durch Asche* (*Flaming Ears*). Alienation and aggression determine the relations between women in this film that forecasts a futuristic dyke state as anarchistic and cruel. The very name of its city, Asche (Ashes), betokens bleakness, decay, and destructuring. Barely audible, a voice-over at the beginning of the film describes Asche as "an uncontrollable wild animal, always ready to pee into the face of death." Like the films discussed in the chapter "Lesbians Abroad," this sci-fi fantasy set in 2700 suggests that the lesbian breaks away from confines associated with the homeland and inhabits an elsewhere. Here the existence of an autonomous lesbian society is taken for granted.[29] In its punk anti-aesthetic, *Rote Ohren* parodies various masculine genres—film noir, spy thriller, terminator and cyborg films, and even the Western with its showdowns. It is a postmodern mélange of "horror-film and comic strip, trash movie and underground film, lesbian porn and fantasy film" (Schüttelkopf, "Blutig," 17), that combines

Figure 35. Filmmakers of *Rote Ohren fetzen durch Asche*, Scheirl, Pürrer, and Schipek. Courtesy of Women Make Movies.

lawlessness with sexual daring (the character played by Pürrer provocatively masturbates against a table). Like *Dandy Dust, Rote Ohren* depicts a theatricalized post-apocalyptic world filled with bizarre, repulsive characters, and like *Im Original Farbig* and *The Drift of Juicy* it plays with dinky toys, animation, and cardboard sets, here blown up to create a decaying cityscape. Announcing the theme of our next chapter, it stages the indetermination between the human and the inhuman that characterizes animation.

Rote Ohren repeatedly breaks narrative conventions and aesthetic norms. As Pürrer puts it, the story does not focus on one individual but on three female protagonists who are ranked equally; as a consequence, the narrative takes on the "form of a labyrinthine spiral" (Blümlinger, 202). The pretty but asexual femme, Spy, with long dark locks, becomes the cunning investigator of a pyromaniac plot. Its mastermind is the sexually voracious Volley (Ursula Pürrer), who is uneroticized, even when wearing only a harness, dildo, and pasties. The costumes are bizarre but hold little of the visual beauty evident in the wardrobes of Ottinger's films; in fact they proclaim lesbian fashion as an antifashion. Only the red-vinyl-clad, bald cyborg Nun (Angela Hans Scheirl) in this nearly exclusively female dystopia demonstrates any sign of gentleness as well as androgynous chic. Yet her robotlike character alienates too, especially in its appetite for rodents and snails. As Pürrer writes of her

233

cacti-like figures, "I stage women, no matter what the cliché or role, fundamentally with a total matter-of-factness [*Selbstverständlichkeit*]. Naturally I have my preferences: surrealistic figures, fighters, women engaged in sex, violence, power, . . . like in the comics [the woman] is defined through her own iconography" (Schüttelkopf, "Blutig," 18). The directors go beyond portraying sexuality as comprising a person's uniqueness or individuality: as Pürrer notes, their characters "step behind their sex" and, although female, are interchangeable stick figures (Blümlinger, 205).

Narratively, too, the film has a comic-book feel in the way that one frame succeeds the next. Pürrer speaks of the "roughness of the film" in the way the images are impertinently strung together and produced. According to her, this insolence is more aggressive than any individual theme (Blümlinger, 207). Contributing to the postmodern total lack of affect, the dialogue in *Rote Ohren* seems like interior monologues contiguously aligned; each character's words are a manneristic combination of deadpan irony and dadaistic self-engrossed lyricism. Alienation and artificiality also stem from the soundtrack having been added nine months after the shooting. With its radically discontinuous narrative lacking suspense and characters who repulse empathic identification or visual attraction, this film redefines a queer aesthetic as one that toughly pushes limits and transgresses boundaries. Additionally, its sudden cuts, frenetic hand-held camera movement, and long, static takes mock our desire for suture. As Ursula Pürrer speaks about her "experimental aesthetic" and "anarchistic tendency": "I've simply gotten used to working at the margins" (Schüttelkopf, "Blutig," 17).

"Through this confusion arises the freedom to look at things anew" (Blümlinger, 207). Although an intriguing experiment, ultimately *Rote Ohren* falls short of attaining this utopic vision that Pürrer speaks of. Given the length of the film, the constant disjointedness in image and narrative fails to sustain interest; the stilted acting and mise-en-scène erases the freshness that was evident in the director's early super-8 work; the dialogue, albeit lyrical in its minimalism, only intermittently makes sense. These are problems that also haunt *Dandy Dust*, although Scheirl's film does fare better in its vision of a hermaphroditic, somatically defined cinema and its more vibrant, fetishistic eroticism. The force of a queer cinema derives from its will to free one from the illegitimacy of the ruling symbolic order. Ideally, it would defy labels, pathologies, and moralities and demonstrate how uncontrollable the meaning generated by experimentation can be. *Rote Ohren* and *Dandy Dust*, however, illustrate how queer cinema can also border on a crisis in representation once its dissent tries to recode the discursive field on several fronts simultaneously. On the one hand, in *Dandy Dust*, the overload of images and trash ridiculousness begin to emit the impression of sheer noise: the film seems to mark a limit that the queer avant-garde has now reached. On the other hand, Scheirl does not pretend to work toward finality and perfection. He says in an interview that "the mistakes are a part of it, they definitely belong there" (Braidt, 36). In punk flourish, then, Scheirl celebrates an anti-aesthetic of rough edges. He therewith challenges other filmmakers to continue the experiment with low-tech, low-budget, multimedia productions.

Dyke Noir Animation

With ever-dwindling governmental subsidies for the arts and the lack of a tradition in private or corporate sponsorship, many filmmakers have had to turn to the short form, which they produce on the side, while earning their keep in the television industry or in teaching, where they have access to technical equipment. It is thus in the arena of the short experimental film that the most innovative cinematic work is being accomplished today in Germany. That a considerable amount of this work is being performed by gay and lesbian artists is not surprising—and not only because of the creative freedom unleashed from feeling "different from the rest" or, as one says in German, "vom anderen Ufer [from the other side]." The first major reason for this surge lies in the immense popularity of gay and lesbian film festivals. The global growth in the New Queer Cinema has had its impact in Germany insofar as it has given birth to festivals which provide a forum for native as well as foreign fare. Such events, not just in Berlin but in other middle-sized cities across the country, provide an immediate audience for German filmmakers. The Perlen 1997 gay and lesbian film festival in Hannover, for instance, devoted a special evening to the work of Percillier and Besilly. Plus, as the network of programmers for these festivals is wide-reaching, it is the norm that current German gay and lesbian films are shown to select, small audiences worldwide.

The second major reason for the growth and excellence in the German queer short is that gay and lesbian communities provide an additional common base for these filmmakers. In a medium where solo work is rare if not impossible, cooperation and contacts are vital. Located in Hamburg, bildwechsel has served since 1979 as a resource center, gathering place and archive for women (and unabashedly lesbians) in the audiovisual arts. Its sister project in Berlin, PELZE multimedia, was a similarly noncommercial space for lesbian art and culture from 1981 to the mid-1990s. In addition, although it sounds trite to say, there are probably more homosexual couples than heterosexual couples producing films together. The most salient example of such codirectorship is that of Monika Treut (one of the founders of bild-wechsel) and Elfi Mikesch on *Seduction: The Cruel Woman* (Mikesch has continued off and on as camerawoman for Treut as well as for Schroeter and Praunheim). The list of collaborations fans out broadly and, in fact, becomes too intricate to detail. But perhaps the most stunning example of joint effort is the oeuvre, primarily in the area of animation but by no means exclusively so, of a group of Berlin lesbian filmmakers that is comprised of Nathalie Percillier, Lily Besilly, Claudia Zoller, and Stefanie Jordan, with tangential connections from this core group out to Heidi Kull. Having studied together at Berlin film academies, where they formed a lesbian club, this group has screened their work collectively at various venues in Berlin, including on *Läsbisch-TV*. The power behind this group can be seen in the fact that the 1997 Berlinale gave prominent awards to two of their films: the Teddy Award for best gay or lesbian short to Percillier and Besilly's *Heldinnen der Liebe* and the Silver Bear for best short to Jordan, Zoller, and Stefanie Saghri's *Late at Night*. Stefanie Jordan did the camerawork for the former film, while Lily Besilly edited the latter; in fact, she has edited films for all of these others, as well as made and starred in (again together with her fellow filmmakers) her own films. In the course of this chapter I want to discuss various pieces by this group, as well as a few animated shorts by other lesbian directors. It remains to be seen whether it is pure coincidence that so many of these works have a distinctively "noir" ambience, playing on the detective and/or loner story in an urban setting "late at night."

This chapter can be seen in other ways as the continuation of the previous one. If the tradition of enigmatic, allegorical discourse in German cinema funnels into queer experimental film with its elliptical signification, then in animation, too, this tradition reaches a pinnacle. Animation can be theorized as a distillation or abstraction from real life, and as such its drawings approximate the reduction and abridgment that characterize allegorical signification. Ellipsis and minimalism are common to both, which does not mean that either dispenses with fantastical elaboration. On the contrary, a highly stylized look and self-conscious deviation from realism tend to be hallmarks of both, as is theatrical exaggeration. Given its split between signifier and signified, allegory transmits the impression of a kind of ventriloquism, a speaking from an elsewhere; animation, too, separates the body from the voice in its almost total reliance on the former (linking it to the silent film). Moreover, if allegory conjures up images of a still life, then animation literally takes as its material the inanimate. Although, as its name suggests, animation breathes life into its subject matter, it repeatedly calls attention to its stylization, mechanization, and artificiality.

237

To create the illusion of natural movement, the cartoonist paradoxically must make unnatural-looking drawings. For instance, exaggeration as well as follow-through are as crucial to depict as the action itself, a secret of the trade known as the sequence "anticipation—stretch—squash." Before a frog jumps, it crouches, its flight through the air is a long stretch, and when it lands, it looks like its body has squashed itself against the ground. This exaggeration, distortion, and even deformation link animation to allegorical mannerism, yet they can also be put to queer purposes. The conscious manipulation of the boundaries between natural and unnatural, especially when applied to societal gender and sexual norms, can be a rich field of exploration for queer animation. By pushing the limits of the customary and conventional, for instance, the lesbian animator can give power to her outlaw characters; they can partake of the cartoon hero's indestructibility. Moreover, as we know from Bugs Bunny's performance as Brünnhilde in *What's Opera, Doc?* (1957), animation thrives on drag. Although in this case, the rabbit's cross-dressing could be seen to function as a release for homophobic tensions (see Griffin), animation can also bitingly satirize or queer heteronormativity. As we shall see in conclusion, in Bärbel Neubauer's work what is seen as socially acceptable can be caricatured as grotesque: in performing stereotypically, cartoon characters make customary, habitual, heterosexual behavior appear perverse. Animation's presence in the space between fiction and reality, natural and unnatural, active and inanimate can deconstruct these oppositions to show up the fictionality of reality and to present normal life as an illusion.

Another appealing aspect of animation for the lesbian filmmaker is the license given to this form to frustrate the "laws of nature." For instance, a cartoon character sauntering off a cliff may not automatically fall, but keep on walking until he or she realizes what has occurred. Since animation does not have to conform to naturalism, the lesbian is free to determine her own rules in her own world. In this art, the impossible becomes possible. Feminist animation, such as Nicole van Goethem's Oscar-winning *A Greek Tragedy* (1983), has already explored such prospects: here three middle-aged women holding up a crumbling Greek temple finally liberate themselves from their centuries-long servitude and fly away. German lesbian animation, by contrast, does not even have to free the woman from conventions but sets her already in her own universe, where, for instance, she can appropriate and parody at will such traditionally male domains as the action film or comic book. Other conventions of animation, such as fairytale metamorphoses, disguises, and impersonations, can also be put to use to express the freedom and agency of the lesbian characters. In addition, techniques such as rotoscoping or the use of the blue box and video keyers can mix live-action and animation to further instigate a slippage between fantasy and life, between queerness and normalcy. Moreover, this cross-over between live action and animation can signify how the lesbian cartoon character too can traverse boundaries. Where the formalities of animation pose a particular challenge to the lesbian, however, is in its stock portrayal of gender difference; in other words, how can the female cartoon figure be portrayed without recourse to feminine-styled hair, clothing, and contours? Yet here too slippage in the form of gender indeterminability can be played upon productively.

Nathalie Percillier

In *Bloody Well Done* (1993–94), Nathalie Percillier, by breaking the "laws of nature" via animation also whimsically disrupts the conventions governing the action film, cartoon, and video game in her delightful amalgam of all these genres. She furthermore demonstrates the personal investment of a gay woman in animation by setting herself into the plot as its heroine. By filming herself in a blue box (the blue background becomes invisible in post-production), Percillier is able to superimpose her figure onto a colorful sketch of an apartment room. She wears a mid-calf yellow dress, gathered at the waist to clearly emphasize her gender, but also dons a bowler hat and ankle-length boots to match her masculine role as a hit man, who targets, ironically enough, those of the opposite sex. Parodically miming the stunt actor, she throws herself out her skyscraper window to fall down several stories, landing in the arms of her female chauffeur (Kerstin Schleppegrell), who passionately kisses her. They then zip around city corners in a car whose body, rear-view mirror, and windshield are all animated independently. Once dropped off at her assigned destination, the heroine pulls from her briefcase a Mixmaster beater that serves as a propeller to lift her above the city; a green spout from her handbag functions as a gun with which she targets unsuspecting men on the street, who disappear once hit. The floating Percillier, with a gleeful look of triumph in her eye, soon turns into a yellow video game figure zapping opponents and scoring points by the hundreds. A hillside transforms into a cord (of her beater?) that the cartoon character ascends to unplug. Her mission accomplished, the live Percillier reappears and returns to her apartment.

This metonymic train of association—a hillside becomes an electrical cord that becomes a staircase—demonstrates the whimsical fancy and freedom that govern this piece.[1] The use of a kitchen item as a means for flight is darling at the same time that its outrageousness pokes fun at the self-seriousness

Figure 36.   *Bloody Well Done* (1993–94), Nathalie Percillier. Courtesy of Nathalie Percillier.

of Hollywood action films where the guys do the killing. Percillier's revenge is thus not so much on the men she zaps (although her delight is unmistakable) as on the gendered assumptions of action films or video arcade games. This turning of the tables in a fantasy of revenge is also evident in her live-action film *Mein 37. Abenteuer* (*My 37th Adventure*) (1994–95) that plays with stereotypes at a lesbian bar. At the end, when one woman announces the approach of skinheads, the skinny butch wannabe volunteers to slip out the door (one assumes to be beaten up in a bizarre self-sacrifice); instead she returns victoriously, having knocked out all the punks, to the admiration of her red-headed femme.[2] Despite the tough-guy pose, the tone of Percillier's works is lighthearted and prankish. Instead of enacting a form of lesbian agency, through their capriciousness these scenarios poke fun at any self-important, pretentious claims to intervention. Furthermore, they are takeoffs on the irrational fear of the lesbian menace.

At the same time that Percillier parodies cinematic conventions, it is interesting to note how she borrows from animation to do so. Often the cartoon narrative centers on blowing the bad guy (the querulous Daffy Duck, the evil Boris and Natascha, or the mean Wile E. Coyote) to "smithereens." In Percillier, too, there is little stated motivation (though it is presupposed) to warrant the degree of violence. Her covert, underground activities are defiant gestures, hence tinged with a queer delight. Insofar as animation imaginatively fashions its own world, Percillier thematizes this act of creation in a heroine who sets her world right. To the same purpose, her earlier animated short, *Tapetengemüt* (*Tapestry Feeling*) (1991) depicts a woman pushing the stick lines of her room upright and ordering intruders to "stay back": animation is all about creating a special space. Most important, in *Bloody Well Done*, Percillier plays up animation's potential for breaking rules—though not only the law of gravity and the rule of cause and effect. Her target is rather animation's own patriarchal conventions, which cast men as the doers. The incorporation of live action into animation and the further slipping of the heroine into a video-game figure alludes to the deconstruction of the opposition between fantasy and reality: it is Hollywood's assumptions about masculinity that are the ultimate, dangerous fantasy—the fantasy that macho bravura should constitute reality. Percillier's role reversal is therefore not so much wishful thinking as the fanciful, satiric disclosure of this illusion.

Lily Besilly

Animation leaves manual traces, the signature of the artist as craftsman who puts long, lonely hours into creating mere seconds of footage. Due to this testimony of the hand, independent animation carries a certain potential for registering the individuality of its maker, whereas in conventional cinema the technologized apparatus of the camera, developing process, and projection intervenes while it mediates. The realism that animation forfeits is thus compensated for by a different kind of bodily immediacy. The question, then, of how the self is incorporated into, reflected upon, and distorted in animation is an intriguing one, especially because the genre is not one that tends toward autobiography or documentary. Much animation is abstract; conventionally, it tells the impersonal tale of cartoon characters who often are not even human; moreover, any drawing of oneself would reduce the live person to a few essential, caricaturing lines. Nonetheless, and however unhinged from reality it is, *Bloody Well Done* shows how the filmmaker places herself into the film and signifies the little stick figure as herself. Although this film in no way can be regarded as autobiographical, still it is an experiment for the filmmaker in fantasy role-playing. In *Heldinnen der Liebe*, too, Percillier along with Lily Besilly act out parts by "camping" as soldiers. Besilly's *Bernadette und Belfighor* (1993)

241

is similar to *Bloody Well Done* in that it combines real life with animation, yet also to *Heldinnen der Liebe* in that the filmmaker stars in the lead role as well as tells a story about imaginative role-playing. This work raises the issue of how the animator signifies herself and, by extension, signs herself as lesbian.

Facing the camera in a medium close-up and wearing a lavender vest, Lily Besilly recounts in *Bernadette und Belfighor* an episode from her childhood that occurred when she was in the second grade. At the bottom of the frame, little sketched characters appear like punctuating subtitles to illustrate her tale. She and her girlfriend would regularly meet at a construction site to play. One day her friend, who acts as the dominant one, determining their fantasies, suggests that they play at being princesses. The friend calls herself Princess Bernadette, and crowns Lily Princess Julia. Curiously, whereas Princess Bernadette suddenly appears at the bottom of the screen dressed in a long gown, the cartoon Princess Julia is still in shorts—in fact, she could not be distinguished from a boy were it not for the narrative. Trying to escape from Belfighor, a vampire who turns into a rat by day, the friend asserts that their only hope is to cut their palms with a knife and mix their blood so that it smells different, thereby fooling Belfighor. She proceeds to slice Lily's palm, enough so that blood flows, saving them from the vampire. As the two leave hand in hand, the sun shines and Lily recounts that, although her hand still hurt, she recalls the feeling of being truly happy. As cartoon characters holding hands, Bernadette has on a short green dress, while Lily is still clothed as a tomboy.

Animation is a genre that conjures up memories of childhood, through recollections of Disney or Warner Brothers cartoons or through the fairytale narrative it frequently tells. A reminder, though, that childhood has its dark sides are such animations as Karen Watson's *Daddy's Little Bit of Dresden China* (GB, 1988) or Marjut Rimminent and Christine Roche's *The Stain* (GB, 1991), where the account of incest is narrated in the tone of an adult reading aloud to a child. Using the animation technique of photokinesis (the shifting of layered cutouts to produce the illusion of movement on the screen), German director Suse Bohse likewise evokes the unspeakable, hushed crime of incest in her *Childhood—A Small Room* (1993). Here the collage form mirrors the struggle between memory and repression—layers of paper (which one hears being ripped) are peeled back, fingers try to cover up the torn pieces, and home photos are thrown down so quickly in visual squeeze that one can only register them subliminally. Snatches of phrases such as "in my fantasy I can't" or "I didn't know it" indirectly indicate the subject matter in this film, whose allegorical evasiveness matches the child's inability to understand and articulate what is happening to her.[3] *Bernadette und Belfighor* too calls for an adult allegorical interpretation of its tale, including its whimsical yet threatening fantasy of the vampire. Despite the dual level of narration (the vocal and visual), which would suggest a kind of exegetical commentary of one on the other, the lesbian subtext needs to be provided by the spectator.

Conceivably, one could watch *Bernadette und Belfighor* and not see it as a lesbian film, a distinct possibility in many of the animated shorts discussed in this chapter. (*Bloody Well Done* provides an exception in that it makes explicit two women kissing.) For the lesbian viewer, however, the cartoon figure of Lily as tomboy clearly provides the key, were the tale of a secret blood bond between two girls also not to point in such a direction. By extension, the fiction of the vampire could be seen as a displaced anxiety about being in a dangerous relationship with a girl, especially a friend who leads one in and out of an exciting fantasy. The finale, where Lily triumphs by walking out happy, hand in hand with her closest friend, gives affirmation to this redemption of a childhood memory for who she is now as a woman loving other women. It is thus the visual split between the adult on-screen narrator and the drawings that look as if they were executed by a child that signifies the allegorical gap that necessitates a lesbian reading, or even a covert or camp reading. In other words, what Besilly leaves unstated but ironically implied by the space between her tale and the woman in lavender needs to be filled in by the viewer. What is fascinating about the animated allegories of *Bernadette und Belfighor*, *The Stain*, and *Daddy's Little Bit of Dresden China* is that they derive their suggestiveness by recounting a story from the perspective of a child who cannot fathom the sexual implications of the events befalling her.

Although Lily Besilly herself appears on the screen in *Bernadette und Belfighor* and narrates an event from her past, her story is about role-playing and involves the depiction of herself as a cartoon character. Another of her films, *Jessesmaria* (1993), codirected with Stefanie Jordan, plays on this discrepancy between self-exposure and distancing; here she plays Christ, a sacrilegious *imitatio* not only because Besilly indulges in starring as the ultimate icon, but also because Christ is a lesbian with banded breasts. The film is a music video of sorts, using the beat of Depeche Mode's *Personal Jesus* to accentuate the cuts, beginning with a succession of stills of the crucifix and moving on to short scenes of a winking Besilly as Christ and of Jordan as Mary, who gets her head shaved punk and bares her breasts for the delight of a queer Jesus. If one compares the iconoclastic role-playing of this film and *Bloody Well Done*, where the main parts are acted by the director and hence mark a self-inscription into the film, with a number of American lesbian films that deal with self-performance, a major difference comes to light. Whether it be Tami Gold's *Juggling Gender* (1992), Alisa Lebow's *Outlaw* (1994) on Leslie Feinberg, or Sadie Benning's and Cheryl Dunye's films, the American productions are concerned with the expression of individuality and agency through the performance. In Besilly and Percillier's work, including *Heldinnen der Liebe*, however, although the directors star in their films, their goal is not to signify their uniqueness, idiosyncrasy, or personal strength, but the opposite, to move away from the self, with the emphasis shifted to the ironically assumed role.[4] Even in *Me and Mrs. Jones*, to take another example of a variation on the music video from this group of directors, where Stefanie Jordan and Claudia Zoller feature themselves as lovers, the black-and-white stylishness of the film overpowers the sense of it as a personal document. Risking the dangers that accompany such generalizations, one could say that this very different way of inscribing oneself into a film makes the German gay (for instance, Michael Brynntrup) and lesbian short appear much less documentary-based than its American equivalent, a dissimilarity which could be attributed to the strong tradition of American gay and lesbian identity politics that has stressed the assertion of the individual, his or her rights, and, consequently, the narrative of coming out and assuming a gay or lesbian identity.[5] Even *Bernadette und Belfighor*, which recollects a childhood memory and hence implies a narrative reaching into the present, does not name lesbian identity but subtly plays on the gaps between narration and animation, past and present, telling and interpreting.

Ulrike Zimmermann

Ulrike Zimmermann's films include *Die erregte Frau in der Videothek* (*The Excited Woman in the Video Store*) (1990), *Venus 220 Volt* (1991), and *Der letzte Schrei* (*The Last Scream*) (1993). She has collaborated with Jochen Hick, Mara Mattuschka, and Scheirl and Pürrer. Although most of her work contains no element of animation, pieces such as *Free Fucking* (1985), her filming of a live performance by Krista Beinstein, and *Touristinnen* (1986), a mermaid-meets-butch rhapsody by the sea, display a keen interest in lesbian role-playing. Her 1992 short *Showdown mit Gemi* continues this interest and uses the animation technique of rotoscoping to combine, like *Bloody Well Done*, live action and cartoon in a parody of the Western, detective, and action genres. *Showdown mit Gemi* is a compilation of found footage from various older Hollywood films showing sequences of men in various dangerous, bravura situations—shooting, falling off horses, talking tough, and so on. Superimposed over these men are the thick outlines of a female cartoon character. The animation

Figure 37. *Showdown mit Gemi* (1992). Courtesy of Ulrike Zimmermann.

is retraced from a reenactment by Mimi Minus (the screen name for Mara Mattuschka, herself a filmmaker who occasionally uses animation.[6] "Gemi" stands for "Die GEdachte MItspielerin" (the fantasized female player), an athletic accomplice who shaves her head bald and wears a g-string and a tight top that draws huge circles around her breasts. She is resurrected in each film snippet as a ghost who gleefully outdoes the men in her exuberance, indestructibility, and, given her costume, sex appeal. Indeed, she proudly shows the superiority of the cartoon character over the live-action hero by partaking of the true invincibility of the former: men only aspire to be cartoon characters. With the words, "the world never cared about me, so now I go around as an evil spirit [*Bösewicht*]," Gemi, in Mattuschka's husky part-Bulgarian, part-Viennese accent, points out the negligence of Hollywood (the world) vis-à-vis active female roles and announces the revenge that now motivates her. Like Percillier, Zimmermann ironizes the ridiculous imaginary roles assigned the Hollywood hero by outperforming him. In addition, the superimposition of Gemi onto the screen stands for the empowering fantasy of cross-gender identification the female viewer might secretly hold (see Mulvey, 33). It is comical to see the psychoanalytically informed theory of specularity rendered in a cartoon character. In its parody, *Showdown mit Gemi* joins the other works discussed in this chapter that rewrite the "dick" genre to form the impressive body of German dyke noir animation.

245

Heidi Kull

Film noir is known for its echoes of German Expressionist cinema and its mysterious shadows. Much of the contemporary noir animation discussed in this chapter also harks back to this period, beginning with Percillier's first attempt at direct animation, *Abgrundgeschichte (Story of the Abyss)* (1989), an enigmatic black-and-white piece with a gender-ambiguous stick figure, played to piano music which itself recalls the silent era. The cityscape backdrop that Percillier uses, like the one in Neubauer's *Zwischen Tier und Schatten (Between Animal and Shadow)*, evokes impersonal tenement housing and belongs to both the noir and the Expressionist urban look. *Late at Night* recalls street scenes from Ernst Ludwig Kirchner, and summons up the stark electric tension of works by the other artists in the Berlin group Die Brücke. But the film that most alludes to Expressionist art, especially to the sharp black-and-white contrasts and angularity of its woodcuts, is Heidi Kull's stunning *Geliebte Mörderin (Beloved Murderer)* (1992), subtitled *Ein Film Noir*, that won first prize at the Frauenfilmfestival Mörderinnen in Vienna in 1992.

Even Kull's first exercise in animation, *Nacht zum 29.4. (The Night of 4/29)* (1991), in which a voice-over tells a dream about returning to her decrepit house that is about to be demolished, is uncanny and sinister in its use of black and white. The self is represented as a hooded, catatonic figure that barely moves and looks more like a ghost than a human being. Tension mounts as she reflects on how and if to mercifully kill the cat that belongs to the house. Despite a minimal use of animation (the film reads more like a comic book), the scratchy drawings impart a sense of unease, nervous haste, and even destruction.

In *Geliebte Mörderin*, too, it is a haunting voice-over that breathes life into Kull's stark, still drawings. Even though the movement here is minimal as well—eyes blink, a finger pulls a trigger on a gun—the haggard, bony look of Kull's punk women is so beautiful that the image cannot stay long enough on the screen for the eye to enjoy it. The voice-over presents the lengthy address of a contract killer to her victim with whom she has fallen in love. We see a letter being typed, but the address itself—a kind of inner monologue of the writer (or is it the beloved reading it?)—is spoken. A throaty voice-over begins: "You'll find this letter on me after you have killed me. A bullet from your 38 will be stuck in my body or maybe in my chest, and you will have looked at me one last time before my death. Or in my back, then I would have closed my eyes and turned around so that it wouldn't be more difficult than it already must have been for you." The murder plan has gone awry and the hitman becomes the target, not only of a revolver but of her own fatal at-

Figure 38.   Geliebte Mörderin (1992). Courtesy of Heidi Kull.

traction. Hunting down her prey means searching out the woman in whose picture she has become obsessed. The letter addressed to the "beloved murderer" is both a confession of love and a warning for its recipient to flee. *Geliebte Mörderin* echoes the reversals of the Hollywood production turned lesbian cult classic, *Black Widow* (Bob Rafelson 1987), where Debra Winger plays a detective tracking down a murderess (Theresa Russell), only to become oddly attracted to her.

The "I" and "You" in this haunting monologue become uncanny doubles of each other,[7] a symmetry that spells out the closeness and the danger of lesbian attraction. This doubling is intimated in the enigmatic line from the song that accompanies the last images: as one of the women flees down the highway (is she the beloved and is she a murderer?), a voice sings "I change my name into another one." As in the genre to which it belongs, questions of epistemology, identity, and truth reside at the heart of this film noir. The deception lies not so much between the two women as in the situation in which they live: "Each one of us believed to be the only one to know the truth, the whole truth. There never had actually been a contract." References to the "I-You" dichotomy are replaced by "We-They": the two lovers seem to have been set up by hostile others to think that they needed to kill each other: "They didn't trust neither of us anymore. They wanted to see us fight or fail. We had become far too strong, too obstinate. Our doubts had made us suspect." The multiple ambiguities caused by the personal pronouns (to whom does "they" refer?) turn this film noir into a dark, enigmatic allegory. The letter addressed to the beloved murderer leaves out precise references as if it needed to speak in code; at the same time it intimates that gay women are able to read between the lines to decipher the allegory. Having become "far too strong, too obstinate," and by loving whom they shouldn't, these women threaten social norms. The speaker fears that "they would have gotten rid of us and with us of all doubts about our person." The "contract" (that is, the unstated assumptions) of heterosexuality kills; it aims to eradicate what the speaker calls "the true contract," the consent between the two women.[8]

For the most part Kull's androgynous, comic-strip women are depicted alone, though once as a pair, standing apart from each other, as if to emphasize the loneliness of this "lover's discourse," to invoke Roland Barthes's term for the interior monologue of the person in love. Repeatedly the drawings show ink running over them or shadowy fingers caressing the image. The blotting recalls the Rorschach test where ink is folded to create a doubled image that invites different readings. In fact, the typed letter is blackened over in places, yet a closer look reveals the silhouette of a woman's face. At other times, striated black lines run over the image of the woman, suggesting imprisonment, or a flashlight flickers over her image. The cartoon can be presented slanted or in one case turning around, evoking the image of the spiral staircase that occurred earlier in the film.

True to the mirroring between the "I" and "You," it is impossible to identify which woman is the "beloved murderer" or if the woman fleeing in the car is the writer or the addressee. The visuals themselves could represent the schematic memory of past events that goes through the writer's mind as she types at her desk or of her anticipating the "beloved murderer" shooting her. The sketches of a young woman also evoke the picture that each carries under her coat to identify her victim. The voice we hear could belong to either woman—to the one as she writes or the other as she reads. In no way, however, does Kull attempt to consecutively illustrate stations from the voice-over's narrative. Rather, the stark black-and-white animation gives a sense of the empty, dark space surrounding the protagonists. The closing image of the highway cloverleaf—of the labyrinth of the journey—echoes the earlier sketch of a spiral staircase and of the dizzying movement in which each lonely lover is entrapped. *Geliebte Mörderin* thus illustrates how animation works in tandem with allegory—in the sparse, shorthand signification, the elusive sketch that places its actors in an empty space, and in the multiple meaning that the cartoon, as ellipsis, invokes. In addition, *Geliebte Mörderin* relies on the semiotic structure of allegory—on its play between confession and concealment, truth and stealth, and on the secretive image (the picture pocketed in the coat) that strangely captivates.

Stefanie Jordan and Claudia Zoller

In various ways lesbian animation continues the trope of the lesbian abroad. In *Bloody Well Done* she takes to the skies; in *Showdown* she migrates from one film to the next; in *Geliebte Mörderin* and Bärbel Neubauer's *Sonderangebot* (*On Sale*) she is driving off into the distance. As animation is all about the movement of images, it is no wonder that the animated dyke is nomadic. *Late at Night* (1997) offers another twist on the lesbian abroad: here she is a stranger in her own city, a nocturnal flaneuse who paces the streets once the walls of her apartment become constraining. The solitary hero of the classic film noir becomes in this exquisite short the female loner, whose selfhood depends on her isolation and independence. She belongs to the urban night; indeed, by the end of the film she glows like the flickering lights from streetlamps. In *Crude* (1996), Stefanie Jordan's short on the leather crowd's Folsom Street Fair in San Francisco, or in Claudia Zoller's *Me and Mrs. Jones* (1994), where she and Jordan star as lovers, the lesbian is out in the open, to look and be looked at. In these films she claims the city streets as her own.

Cassandra Wilson's *Children of the Night* provided the synchrone music for *Late at Night* (the music to which the film action was made). Zoller, Jordan, and Saghri began by shooting a woman walking to the beat of the song.[9] Using the technique of rotoscopy but without the subsequent aid of a computer, they transferred the action to cels, transforming it unrecognizably in the process. Paradoxically, although this procedure takes live action and reduces it to single frames shot in succession, what actually happens in the course of the film is the opposite: the figure comes dynamically alive, surrounded not only by her long, whisking cloak but by a whole-body halo of light that flames up in emanation as she strides. Both the cape and the flare snap and

249

Figure 39.   Late at Night (1997). Courtesy of Stefanie Jordan, Stefanie Saghri, and Claudia Zoller.

spark around her. In addition, her body performs the music, capturing the movement and rhythm of Wilson's jazz. In this metamorphosis, the woman becomes the center of the nocturnal world: she does not so much turn corners as the city streets themselves swivel around her at expressionistic angles. Consequently, the night too is brought to life.

What, then, makes this film so successful is that it is about animation itself. At its most basic level, the story shows a woman going out to walk at night, but this very motion in its simplicity renders the essence of animation. As graphic motion, animation makes actions happen. Norman Mc-Laren has defined it as "not the art of drawings-that-move, but rather the art of movements-that-are-drawn" (quoted in Solomon, 11). *Late at Night* is sheer kineticism. Part of its consummateness, strangely enough, stems from its imperfections. Unlike Disney animation, here the sweep of the individual brushstroke is evident. In drawing and coloring each cel separately, rather than utilizing a technically more precise computer, the animators (who took two years to complete the project) introduce deviations that result in the film's flickering, almost incendiary look. In other words, it is not the isolated drawing of each frame that endows the film with movement but the differences between them. The electrifying quality of the film arises by virtue of this interstice between frames, where the movement originates. This particular example of animation illustrates what Brophy has claimed for the entire art: it demonstrates "the act of filming not as 'bringing something to life' but as 'film itself coming to life'" (Brophy, 105).

The process of making the film is also reflected in its thematic. The final result is a copy (or rather, multitudinous frame-by-frame copies on cels) of the live-action cinematic copy of a woman walking. This doubling then occurs literally as the music crescendos to the words, "until I find someone who is just like me, searching for some company" when the protagonist turns to see a replica of herself. A bath of glowing blue shifting to gold envelops them together against the black backdrop. If Wilson sings "I walk the shadows of the night," then this walking shadow encounters an uncanny phantom of herself. Is she a doppelgänger, as in one of E. T. A. Hoffmann's night pieces, who disappears as suddenly as she is recognized? Or is this "someone just like me" a possible lesbian lover, someone whom the protagonist desires when she discovers her in the night? Although this question cannot be answered, it also asks what allows one to read *Late at Night* as a lesbian film.

Two of its makers, as already indicated, are lesbian and have made films where their sexual orientation is explicit.[10] This fact, however, designates *Late at Night* as lesbian as shakily as the moment when the doubles meet. Where the film can be seen as queer, though, is in the androgyny of the protagonist, whose assertive stride (which calls attention to her pants and boots) and nocturnal prowling are markedly antifeminine. Her androgynous looks match Wilson's deep, masculine voice. Just as *Late at Night* springs to life in the interstices *between* the frames, so too the seductiveness of its protagonist lies in her gender in*between*ism. As a creature of the night, she resembles the other gender-ambiguous characters from Expressionist cinema—Nosferatu and Cesare—as well as the figures from *Bernadette und Belfighor, Geliebte Mörderin*, and *Froschkönige (Frog Kings)*. This last film by Jenni Tietze (1995) is a nightmarish, sexually scary twist on noir animation and the fairy tale. A naked figure with nipples, wearing red high heels and a crewcut, has her gender signified by her jagged line of labia. Inadvertently, like a child, she drops her hamburger down a street gutter to a giant frog that lives inside. An even larger frog captures her in what looks like an inflated condom, out of which he sucks her, using his tongue as a straw. Again, as in *The Stain, Daddy's Little Bit of Dresden China*, and *Childhood—A Small Room*, child abuse is obliquely signified. Eventually the girl is able to kill the frog, after which the police commissar arrives on the scene to investigate the murder case (from her point of view, an act of self-defense). The uncurvy body of the protagonist, her cropped hair, and the daringness with which her sex is portrayed mark a

251

protest against how women are conventionally portrayed in the cartoon. Her angular kinkiness indeed gives her a queer edge, perhaps, as the other examples also suggest, the way the lesbian is now to be signified in animation if her makers revolt against the copout of the tell-tale same-sex kiss.

The 1990s vogue for the androgynous-butch-punk is played up in this noir genre, enhanced by the leanness or starkness required in the animated drawing (if it is not an expensive Disney production). For it is the singular gaunt and lanky "look" of these women that enlivens them, although, paradoxically, this same "look" turns them into a picture, an inanimate object to be gazed upon. In *Late at Night* it is the gestures—the stride, the flick of a wrist throwing away a cigarette—as well as the swish of the cloak (especially in the dramatic finale that casts the protagonist as a glamorous rival to the caped crusader) that make the woman come alive. And yet, insofar as such stylization is manneristic, it invokes something frozen and dead, recalling the stasis that preceded the animation. The fascination with animation thus borrows from totemism; the art signifies the hypnotizing confusion between the human and the inhuman, the living and the dead. In that respect, animation reminds one of the same indecision governing all fashion, especially when captured in striking poses by the camera. Perhaps it is not surprising that the ravishing *Late at Night* was made by the directors of *Crude* and *Me and Mrs. Jones*, stylish takes on the music video with its players' bodies caressed by the camera, arrested at fetishizing angles, and highlighted by Besilly's rhythmic sense of editing.

Bärbel Neubauer

Bärbel Neubauer does not belong to the youngish Berlin group just discussed (apart from having taught animation for women at PELZE) but is one of Germany's most established animators, whose work is screened worldwide. Most of her work is abstract, for which she composes her own music. But when her animation is narrative, it is biting in its satire, mocking the unreflecting, automatic behavior of both straights and gays.

In *Zwei beste Freundinnen* (*Two Best Girl Friends*) (1990), a couple of women meet at a café. In heavy Bavarian dialect,[11] the one talks nonstop (except for puffs on her cigarette) about the men in her life to her so-called best friend, who sits impassively across from her, suffocated by clouds of smoke. Only when the gabby one leaves to meet her new boyfriend does the silent one open her mouth—to order a beer. The round, bald heads of the women and simple lines drawn for mouth, nose, and eyes underscore the superficiality and stiltedness of their (non)conversation. Neubauer ironizes what supposedly bonds straight women and utilizes the animation devices of exaggeration and caricature to demonstrate that such bombastic behavior—talking compulsively and exclusively about men, ignoring the boredom and suffocation of her best friend—is regarded as normal, socially acceptable, even expected among women.

Neubauer does not exempt lesbian relationships from her satire either. In *Sonderangebot* (*On Sale*) (1988/90), a frowning, inflexible queen rejects all attempts to cheer her up (food, music, dogs, and so on); a king bringing flowers especially riles her, so that her curls bounce up and down, while a violin squeaks dissonantly on the minimal soundtrack. She only becomes happy when, while shopping, she picks up a test tube in which she can water and grow a double of herself (one can hardly think of a more sarcastic view of lesbian attraction). When her protegée, for whom she has tenderly cared, grows wings and ungratefully flies away, the queen mother in despair chops up the throne and burns it, causing her whole house to go up in flames. The women meet again on the highway (of life) but the first queen shrinks in the car to nothingness: her once arrogant ego has dwindled, and the woman she has nurtured moves on alone. Neubauer here thinks through her medium: she recounts the very process of animation, of bringing something to life.

The allegory is even more indirect, but, for all that, more sardonic in her likewise black-and-white *Zwischen Tier und Schatten* (*Between Animal and Shadow*) (1986), a major contribution to the genre of noir animation. Here Neubauer borrows from the formulaic detective story, following its narrative conventions until the end, when she suddenly subverts them. A police commissar is on the track of a serial killer but never seems able to catch him. While cuts to the female victims suddenly introduce unfocused, blurred live action, suggesting a ghostly yet natural presence, the other characters are animated by their halved bodies moving separately—first the top half and then the bottom half advances—giving them a comic, wooden look. By the conclusion their actions prove to be truly mechanical and rehearsed. The title itself suggests the cartoon characters' nonhuman existence somewhere between an animate creature and a shadow, and, indeed, the commissar has a twin brother from New York who follows him like a shadow, while the commissar himself shadows the killer. The chase is long and drawn out, as we see the three jerking along past dark apartment blocks in this stop-motion animation; just as it seems the killer is about to finish off his next victim and the commissar to break in on him, Neubauer cuts to the conclusion. The killer has fallen in love with his victim; the commissar has married Frau Meier, whom he bumped into on the stairs; and the brother has returned to his wife in New

Figure 40.   *Zwischen Tier und Schatten* (1986). Courtesy of Bärbel Neubauer.

York. All three couples are depicted in their respective beds. In Neubauer's deadpan, grotesque ending domestic bliss overrides the suspenseful, violent story, for all's well that ends well in marriage.

This caricature of heterosexuality therewith draws on animation's potential, given its liminal status between the truly lifelike and merely counterfeit, to deconstruct the binaries of spontaneous and conventional, natural and unnatural, normal and queer. Through the fabricated world of animation Neubauer reveals that what one considers to be elemental—marital life—is a device for closure and illusion.

Philip Brophy writes that animation "displays the potential (some grab it— some do not) for *forgetting* how to relate reality to film because of its overt and sometimes flagrant disregard for pictorial mimeticism and temporal logic; and it is only through such a forgetfulness that one could start to treat the cinema as an *incursion* or *irruption* of reality and not as an illusory recreation or simulation of reality" (69). If, following Brophy, we take the characteristics of animation discussed in this chapter to apply to the films discussed earlier in this book, definite affinities arise. Time and again, dyke noir animation questions presuppositions about what constitutes reality, normalcy, and nature (or what cinema presents as such) and, in so doing, interrogates heteronormativity. This *"irruption* of reality" stems from its queer spirit and links it to the works of Fassbinder, Rosa von Praunheim, Schroeter, Ottinger, Treut, Stock, Brynntrup, Scheirl, Pürrer, and others who dismantle via hyperbolic (cross-)gender performance a notion of cinema as mimesis. They disrupt the generally held belief that perception is simple and straightforward. Instead, reality for them is comprised of gesture, costume, ventriloquism, and masquerade. Indeed, the puppetlike characters in *In a Year of 13 Moons, Nicht der Homosexuelle ist pervers, Der Tod der Maria Malibran, Dorian Gray im Spiegel der Boulevardpresse*, and *Prinz in Hölleland* themselves uncannily resemble stiffly animated figures. Life, not just animation, is a simulation. Moreover, insofar as allegory is a sign abstracted from actuality, it calls into question what constitutes the latter, a disjunction that resembles the distillation operative in animation.

The entire issue of how to read queer sexuality is, of course, linked to this questioning of empirical visibility: in other words, can the "truth" of sexuality (similar to the meaning in allegory) be visually disclosed? As we have seen in the androgynous figures from Expressionist cinema to dyke noir animation, sexuality and gender refuse legibility and thereby ironically play upon the threat that homosexuality or, even more, bisexuality, pose—namely, that they might go undetected or unmarked in society. Such a cinema thus resists the surveillance and systematic codification of sexuality and desire in the optic register. Given its childlike, whimsical aura, animation is especially a realm where one does not expect sexuality, let alone lesbian sexuality, to be addressed—its presence thereby subverts the visual symbolic order. That this strong allegorical and queer tradition has arisen neither on the stage nor in literature indicates that cinema today can function as a particularly important *"incursion* or *irruption* of reality." The tradition these filmmakers form is no mere compilation of gay and lesbian German films but an encompassing vision of cinema as capable of queerly resignifying what a hegemonic society perceives as normalcy and hence as reality.

Epilogue

An Erotics of Transgression

Queer Cinema and Counterpolitics

Given that the word "queer," an English import, is not prevalent in Germany except in a few countercultural and marginalized academic circles, "queer" as deployed in my title is bound to raise controversy. None of the filmmakers discussed here set out to make "queer films"; nor do they adhere to one stylistic, aesthetic, or thematic category in their works—their filmmaking is instead individual and unique. Thus the rubric "queer" cannot mark an attempt to taxonomize or compartmentalize these filmmakers as a group, least of all a fashionable, conformist one. On the contrary, the authenticity of their productions testifies to the differences between them. If they incidentally share a common project, it is precisely a conspicuous erotic experimentation made palpable through a reorganization of the visual field. Their works captivate to the extent that they are novel and inimitable in their gender and libidinal expressions. They articulate an erotics of transgression.

Clearly, the filmmakers discussed here also do not set out to appeal to a firm, unified constituency that could be labeled queer. Often they do not even envisage their audience as primarily gay or lesbian. As Matthias Müller wrote me, "I do not have any specific community in mind when producing my films." Because of the alleged eccentricity of his work, "it has taken a long time to get considered by and exhibited at gay and lesbian festivals. It obviously gets a stronger appreciation at events outside this circuit." The spectatorship can also shift: Bärbel Neubauer, much of whose work involves abstract painted films with music, sees her audience worldwide as varied but nationally running mostly at gay and lesbian festivals. Despite this variegation, several of the young filmmakers discussed in the last two chapters have made such festivals possible and profited from them: as Nathalie Percillier says, "I was happy to start making films and videos with the onset of lesbian and gay festivals, so that I always had the privilege of an audience. I was very fortunate, since all my pieces had the chance to live their life and not to finish unseen on some shelf." Nuancing the current festival scene, Stefanie Jordan welcomes the fact that "gay and lesbian film festivals are finally including more work by lesbian and gay filmmakers that is not so explicitly gay in its content" (as in her animations *Mayday* and *Late at Night*) and that they have come to "show work that is promoting a queer outlook" (as in her *Crude*).

As Jordan's remarks imply, the word "queer" can cut two ways. On the one hand, it risks smudging the boundaries of gay and lesbian identity affiliation. Especially many women are wary that it might erase lesbian specificity. On the other hand, gays and lesbians do share a strategy of transgressive erotic representation. Hence *Crude* promotes "a queer outlook" because it provocatively portrays leather-strapped gay and lesbian bodies mingling at San Francisco's Folsom Street Fair. "Queer," then, works with a double definition, at times in consonance with "gay" and "lesbian," at times in contradiction. It can collapse distinctions between gay, lesbian, bisexual, and transgender, yet it does not deny their common allegiance to nonheterosexual pleasures. It partakes in the activism of gay and lesbian communities and furthers their concerns, yet also questions their identity politics. Jordan contextualizes this duality in terms of the divergent paths the gay and lesbian movements have historically traversed: "The separate evolution of the lesbian (as part of the feminist) and gay movements" meant that they did not "really challenge gender-based separatisms or sexisms (although both communities have eased up their gender boundaries to include more transgender people). Queer politics must address that missing link."

While accordingly not naming themselves queer, several of the artists discussed in this book fully ascribe to being gay or lesbian (and in so doing invoke these discrete histories); undeniably much of their disrupting, antinormative force comes from this positioning. When asked, Rosa von Praunheim told me that he was a gay filmmaker and did not see himself as belonging to a New Queer Cinema; and why would he want to shift allegiances after having been at the forefront of the gay movement in Germany throughout the last thirty years? Percillier similarly asserts her lesbian and feminist loyalties: referring to the screen/filmmaker personae she assumes with Lily Besilly, she declares that "the Heroines are not queer but good old lesbians who never questioned that. They have enough other problems. . . . The Heroines wear dresses and skirts." Yet the whimsy and experimentation of Percillier and Besilly's work prove that they do not merely include lesbians in a cinematic language that would otherwise remain unaltered. Percillier points to this discrepancy in their comic roles: "The Heroines are just struggling within society in a role which hasn't been allowed them. The audience notices that a woman doesn't fit there and laughs." Thus insofar as the films of "die Heldinnen" operate subversively, against the grain, or "verquer," they can also be called queer. Along with the other films treated in this book, they are incongruous, elastic, and protean in their gender play, which matches their inventive visual language.

In this context, "queer" does not function generically as a fixed identity category but rather as an evolving concept that plays itself out on an experimental field. This dissidence and unpredictability, then, align these films with what I would venture to call a counterpolitics. They counter discourses or ideologies that try to legislate sexual and gender behavior, whether these come from straight or gay communities. A queer filmmaking in turn deploys the technological apparatus to alter our perceptions, to render these representations complex and visually nonconformist. As David Teague writes: "The work of many queer filmmakers brings to light an analogous relationship between denaturalizing the cultural assumptions of heterosexuality and denaturalizing the seamless illusions of cinema through dislocating techniques. Queer filmmakers often employ radical form because the contents of their lives are already radicalized" (7). In conclusion I want to reevaluate this link between a countercultural engagement and queer filmmaking—to ask where the minefields lie in conceiving art in terms of solidarity and political message, in separating a "private" sexuality from a "public" voice, and in juxtaposing provocation with a desire for social acceptance. Lurking behind these questions is the tension just rehearsed between queer experimentation and a gay or lesbian identity politics. Although I cannot begin to adequately untangle such conceptually difficult issues, I do want to indicate how many of the filmmakers discussed in this book themselves articulate these dichotomies; I want to give them the final word. Where do they see the dangers for their films when they are faced with the pressing expectation to be activist as well as (or as opposed to) entertaining? In exploring the lines along which a queer cinema can respond to these dilemmas, I want to draw on the responses that I received from several filmmakers when I asked them to reflect on their art and its audience in terms of activism.[1]

At a time when pragmatism is valued over imagination and practicality over originality, there is also a pitting of public activism against art, social justice against "cultural justice." This term was coined by the American theorist Andrew Ross to challenge the view that "suggests that cultural politics is not *real*, or that it diverts our attention from the real issues—predominantly economic in nature—that inspire people's quest for justice. If ever there was a false dichotomy, both disabling and divisive, this is it" (3). If artists are not to have to fall into a supplicatory, defensive position (Matthias Müller rightly states that "Artistic work in general should not depend on a justification as social or political activism," while Hans Scheirl asserts that "Art is Art. It is autonomous and needs to be free from political and economic usage"), then one needs to deconstruct the crippling dichotomy Ross identifies. In other words, in terms of a queer cinema one needs to contemplate ways in which this art is political even when it is not overtly activist, not dismiss it when it is not, and recognize how antitransgressive even a call for political positioning might be.

One binary (related to the one between social and cultural justice) that particularly traps gay, lesbian, and transgendered persons is the separation of the political from the personal, public from private, visible from invisible. In capitalist Western societies, these groups are most accepted when they remain in private and do not go public with their desires. In the United States, this sequestering leads to the twisted reasoning behind the "don't ask, don't tell" ruling in the military. Privacy does not mean the right to be able to do in bed what you please; rather, it means that queers should stay in the closet. The private/public opposition creates not only the closet for homosexuals but also a political closet, an insidious boundary that dictates what can be politically efficacious in order to exorcise the socially disruptive. Queer cinema militates against this confining view of privacy. It pleads not for a right to privacy but the personal right and freedom to be vocal and visible in public. Its counterpolitical stance defiantly refuses both the closet and assimilation. As Chris Holmlund and Cynthia Fuchs write in their book on queer documentary, "To see and be seen is a matter not only of visual representation but also of social acceptance and political clout. Increasingly, queer media makers and queer critics also take up questions of communication and translation, reconsidering how speaking and naming, silence and suggestion, are expressed and experienced" (1–2).

It should be evident by now that I want to broaden the notion of politics beyond rights politics—that is, the advocacy of law and policy on sexual orientation discrimination in such areas as age of consent, adoption, or partnership. In fact, there is a latent tension in West European and North American gay and lesbian communities between the provocation of "queer" and the call for full and equal rights for gays and lesbians. For example, one might argue in favor of the legislation of equal partnership benefits on the basis that same-sex partner rights are equivalent to spousal rights: here the similarities to the traditional and programmed norms of the dominant, couple culture are acknowledged. "Queer," however, underscores an eccentricity from the norm and leads one to ask whether respect for difference rather than acknowledgment of similarity is key to a state of equality. I would argue that precisely this deviance makes a queer cinema crucial for gay, lesbian, and transgender rights in Europe today. As sexual outsiders and artists who re-

259

arrange how we visually perceive the world, the filmmakers discussed in this book are in a unique position to offer a vision for change.

Let me make myself clearer. Although there is no anti-discrimination legislation at the federal level in Germany and no legal recognition of same-sex partnerships and gay or lesbian-headed families, public opinion tends otherwise. In 1996 one poll revealed a majority of the German population in favor of same-sex marriages and a two-thirds majority in favor of antidiscrimination legislation. Thus the general level of acceptance of gays and lesbians is far greater in Germany than in the United States. Yet in the States the lack of tolerance (together with the absence of socialized medicine) has galvanized ACT UP; for its affront to society, the transgender movement, too, has been more visible and controversial in the States. Paradoxically, then, the general acceptance and assimilation of gays, lesbians, and trangendered individuals in Germany has had a certain closeting or invisibility effect (coupled with no legacy of civil rights activism and no Bill of Rights to which to appeal). If it is harder to exceed the limits of political and social determinism in Germany, then conceivably there is a special need for the radical libidinal images that a queer cinema can bring to life.

When I sent out an email request to various filmmakers with whom I had been in contact to comment on the relationship of their films to gay and lesbian activism, Rosa von Praunheim was the first to respond and immediately addressed these limits in the contemporary German gay community. "It's interesting to look back in my old age to thirty years of gay filmmaking. My message was to provoke my own people, to make them wake up and take action. I did that in 1971 with *It's Not the Homosexual Who Is Perverse but the Situation in Which He Lives*. I did that in 1976 with *Army of Lovers*, and I did that during the AIDS crisis with my 1985 AIDS-comedy *A Virus Knows No Morals*. I wanted to change gay people, to have them be more aware, and now the opposite has happened. Especially in Germany gay people seem passive and unpolitical ever since they got a piece of the cake. They are no better than heterosexuals."

Monika Treut has a similarly pessimistic view of what provocation can accomplish in Germany today, and she too shares Praunheim's drive to combat complacency: "Queer for me indeed means more than just having a so-called same-sex partner. It's also an opposition to corporate capitalism with all its values—procreation, family, to name a few. In Germany in the 1990s where television shows gay men fistfucking late at night, where lower-middle-class straight couples talk about their s/m sexual practices on daytime talk shows, and where an ex-militant squatter is the minister of foreign affairs, counterculture has almost ceased to exist. On a superficial level anything goes in this country, thus marginalizing groups off the political center even more than, let's say, in the United States." Treut's profound critique of German society is a cry for a space of fabulation carved out by a queer cinema, for a visual language that would go beyond the trivialization and sensationalism of mainstream representations of so-called deviant sexualities. In other words, when, as in the United States, transsexuals appear on daytime talk shows in Germany (their private lives made a display for heteronormative consumption), the personal-versus-public, them-versus-us dichotomy is reinforced rather than broken down. A different visual legitimacy, one that consciously reflects on the mechanisms of the spectacle and is critical of the tactics of silencing, is needed to counteract this dumbing down and fake acceptance of sexual and gender difference.

Treut and Praunheim are directors who have continually sought out new subject matter that would push the envelope of transgressive visibility and redraw borders. Rosa von Praunheim, for instance, is currently fighting against the criminalization of homosexuality in countries around the world by helping to plan an international queer exhibition in Berlin in 2001. As in Treut's *Gendernauts*, much of their work has been documentary, conducted in a matter-of-fact tone that puts gender and sexual outlaws in the public eye without sensationalizing them. Theirs is thus no breakdown of sexual taboos via blatant offensiveness. Rather, their dissent engages the viewer through the unpredictability of their aesthetic and formal inventiveness, even when this is an unexpected dispassionateness.

In other words, if issues of visibility versus invisibility lie at the heart of queer activism, then how the cinematic apparatus retools our vision matters tremendously. Along with Scheirl, Brynntrup, Melhus, and others, Treut and Praunheim show how cinema can be a device through which to resignify masculinity and femininity, the commodification of desires, entertainment values, the sex industry, even technologies of simulation and fantasies of the cyborg. Scheirl, for one, advocates pushing "beyond queer into 'cyborg.' Because the changes that are happening to us technologized beings are fast and enormous, there is big potential for people like queers, who were forced to be experimental and creative in their lives and form new communities, to realize individual autonomy and create a cyborg-humanism that is not based on abusive control mechanisms." Along with Brynntrup, Scheirl deploys the cinematic apparatus to demonstrate bodies in the making. Questioning identity affiliations, they define the gay, lesbian, or transgendered body as the site of virtuality, hybridity, and metamorphosis. For a number of the filmmakers discussed here, human sexuality does not express some natural essence (or that which dare not speak its name) but is a matter of (excessive) representation and assemblage. They alert us as well as to how the enigmatic and erratic glimpses produced by photography and editing arouse us, with the result that our ultimate desire is for a technology that allows us to fetishize and see anew. In other words, what is truly transgressive in their works is not so much the subject matter as the erotics of the medium they explore.

Michael Brynntrup, too, emphasizes medium over message in addressing how cinema can reframe our vision. In nuancing the alignment of art and political awareness, he warns that films should not set out to manipulate or coerce. For the same reason that he is suspicious of illusionist cinema, Brynntrup rejects "other forms of spectatorial manipulation, for example, polemicizing [*plakativ*] political films. My films don't have any clear 'message' (that could be—perhaps even better—expressed in words. My so-called 'puzzle' films are not there to be solved)." For Brynntrup, it is a question "not of vocal solidarity but quiet comprehension [*Ein-verständnis*], not of protest but of subversion." As he cleverly avows: "I believe not in provocation, scandal, and the cult of stars—but in obsession."

Obsession is a potent concept for an erotics of transgression, and by it Brynntrup refers not so much to his own manias (or only insofar as these are infectious) but to how his spectator must obsess in coming to terms with his "puzzle" films. Brynntrup would like his works to stimulate the viewer's own thoughts, so that once one realizes that interpretation is dependent on one's own standpoint, "the perspective is opened to possible views other than one's own." As Brynntrup suggests, a queer cinema encourages one to move outside oneself. Taking this idea further, one can say that exposure for the spectator also means expanding the range of one's familiarity with erotic representations, however controversially into such realms as pedophilia, pornography, unsafe sex, and sadomasochism. Indeed, here one is in the zone of obsession, where each spectator has to question his or her own engagement and stake in the representation, as such directors as Stock, Brynntrup, Schillinger, and Pürrer do when they display themselves on the screen, performing the risky act of involvement.

Spectatorship, moreover, is fundamentally the ground on which an experimental creativity and the reaffirmation of gay, lesbian, bisexual, or transgender identities meet. On the one hand, from Europride to Lesbian Week in Berlin, from gay and lesbian film festivals throughout Germany to the Berlinale and its Teddy Award for the best gay or lesbian film, queer films form the centerpiece for events that unite the community and build solidarity. Queer cinema empowers its audience as well as its makers. On the other hand and (as I have tried to argue), even more important from a counterpolitical stance, this cinema offers persuasive models for the *remaking* (as opposed to consolidation) of identities and desires. As Scheirl points out, "The strength of queer culture and politix is in the appropriation ('camp,' 'drag') and in the practice of experimental life-styles. That fluidity needs to be always on top of the agenda." Thus, queer cinema not only reinforces a gay, lesbian, bisexual, or transgender self-esteem and courage but also spurs imaginativeness. Scheirl theorizes further on the importance of the physical and topographical space of viewing for this self-reinvention and its participatory potential: "Cinema has a power that no other medium possesses: this pseudo-public space in the cinema theater, the shared experience, the trance effect deriving from the flicker of the projection. . . . I simply believe in the power of cult movies. Cult cinema implies a special audience, which does not mean it is an elitist form: it is open, because everybody can participate. It is also open because in most cities there are these playgrounds for people who are not happy with mainstream" (Braidt, 38). Indeed, rather than remaining passive, queer cult audiences respond viscerally to the images on screen. These visions imprint themselves on the body; one wants to fuse with the insurgent fantasies one sees. In provoking such a passionate, performative engagement from its viewer, this queer cinema is essentially activist.

Yet despite its utopian potential, queer spectatorship currently threatens its own life. I should like to end on a cautionary note—to contest and not merely celebrate viewing practices. A number of the directors I contacted were distressed by the market conditions for their work: gay and lesbian audiences as well as festival organizers, let alone a general public, repeatedly felt overly challenged by their innovation. The reception of Claudia Schillinger's *Hermes* is the most poignant case. Her sensitive (and visually sensual) probing of the eroticism between children and adults (including herself as a mother) was too radical for most venues. Despite the extreme gentleness of the piece, it has hardly been shown. Schillinger reflects back: "In the meantime I've become very tentative in my personal wish to be influential, politically speaking. I try to thematize what interests and moves me. . . . That I meet with resistance does not reside so much in the fact that I want to provoke but in that my feelings and thoughts lie mostly in opposition [*quer*] to society." Curators, she says, have blocked her access to audiences, who tend to be more receptive once they have actually seen the film.

Echoing Rosa von Praunheim's critique of the gay community's complacency and attributing it to what he calls "social backlash," Matthias Müller trenchantly points out: "Gay audiences want gay mainstream, a mere replacement of male/female by male/male parts. Boy-meets-boy instead of boy-meets-girl. Gay audiences strongly cling to established patterns of story-telling. And a lot of gay festivals mirror this. That is why I feel more welcome at places devoted to truly challenging films than at the amusement parks/marketing events gay festivals have turned into. We have an incredible social backlash going on." Hans Scheirl, too, criticizes "queer film festivals that have a hierarchy in their programming, where art gets called 'experimental' and comes last in the catalogue, so that people can safely stay away from the 'difficult' works." He consequently sees the need for a new cinematic typology: "The title 'gay and lesbian film festival' has reached a dead end. We must look to more creative and futuristic namings like: 'Mix Brazil: Film and Videofestival of Diverse Sexualities' (6! Brazilian cities) or 'Trannyfest: Transgender and Transgenre Film Festival' (San Francisco)." Along with the other filmmakers discussed in this book, then, Scheirl challenges the comfortable position from which we believe that our perception of gender and sexual binaries is correct and true. They deny that the realm of the visible must necessarily codify, inscribe, and delimit sexualities. Instead, by restructuring the optic field, these artists reframe our desires and transform our selves.

As Jörg Fockele summarizes in bold words of blithe longing: "I don't want to waste time watching *Girl Next Door Comes Out* or *Normal Boy Meets Normal Boy*—I am tired of it. If anything what I want to see on the queer screen is this: Outrageously queer characters who do totally abnormal things and make the audience wonder: Maybe 'normal' is not a good place to be for everybody! Maybe there is more to life than what I am used to! Maybe there is something else *I* want."

We cheer Jörg, all queer cinephiles, and their filmmakers on! Theirs is a project of cultural inventiveness, of cultural justice.

Reference Matter

Source Guide

The following sources are listed only as a guide and are not intended to be exhaustive.

Chapter 1. *Weimar Cinema*

As video copies for the cross-dressing films discussed here are not distributed, I can only suggest trying various archives in Germany, with the warning that it can be difficult to find out their exact holdings and unpredictable what films they will make available at any given time:

Bundesarchiv—Filmarchiv, Postfach 310667, 10636 Berlin. Tel.: 49-30-86811. Fax: 49-30-8681 310.
Stiftung Deutsche Kinemathek, Heerstraße 18–20, 14052 Berlin. Tel.: 49-30-300 903 0. Fax: 49-30-300 903 13.
Filmmuseum, St.-Jakobs-Platz 1, 80331 München. Tel.: 49-89-233 225 75. Fax: 49-89-233 239 31. The Filmmuseum has restored *Geschlecht in Fesseln*.
In the United States, *Der Geiger von Florenz* is housed at the Library of Congress, Motion Picture and TV Reading Room, Room 336, Madison Building, Washington, DC, 20540-4800. Tel.: 202-707-5840. Fax: 202-707-2371.
Ich möchte kein Mann sein and *Hamlet* are available at The George Eastman House, 900 East Avenue, Rochester, NY, 14607-2298. Tel.: 716-271-3361. Fax: 716-271-3970.

Chapter 2. *Zarah Leander*

Given Zarah Leander's continuing popularity, several of her films (*La Habanera, Zu neuen Ufern, Es war eine rauschende Ballnacht, Das Lied der Wüste, Damals,* and *Die große Liebe*) are available on videotape in Germany and also can be purchased or rented in the United States through The German Language Video Center, Division of Heidelberg Haus Imports, 7625 Pendleton Pike, Indianapolis, IN, 46226-5298. Tel.: 317-547-1257. Fax: 317-547-1263.

Chapter 3. *Rosa von Praunheim*

Several of Rosa von Praunheim's works are distributed by Facets Video, 1517 W. Fullerton Avenue, Chicago, IL, 60614. Tel.: 1-800-331-6197. Fax: 1-777-929-5437. Email: sales@facets.org. Web: <http://www.facets.org>. For the more difficult-to-find films, contact Rosa von Praunheim Filmproduktion, Konstanzer Straße 56, 10707 Berlin. Fax: 49-30-881 29 58.

Chapter 4. *Werner Schroeter*

Schroeter's films are notoriously difficult to locate. The Filmmuseum (see address above) has a good but not complete collection. *Der Rosenkönig* is available through Futura Film, Weltvertrieb im Filmverlag der Autoren, Rambergstraße 5, 80799 München. Tel.: 49-89-38 1700 30. Fax: 49-89-38 1700 20.

Chapter 5. *Ulrike Ottinger*

Madame X, Dorian Gray, Johanna d'Arc of Mongolia, and *Countdown* are available through Women Make Movies, 426 Broadway, 5th Floor, New York, NY, 10013. Tel.: 212-925-0606. Fax: 212-925-2052. Email: info@wmm.com. Otherwise contact Ulrike Ottinger Filmproduktion, Hasenheide 92, 10967 Berlin. Tel.: 49-30-692 93 94. Fax: 49-30-691 33 30.

Chapter 6. *Monika Treut*

In addition to being carried via Facets and other video distributors, Treut's films are available through First Run/Icarus Films, 153 Waverly Place, New York, NY, 10014. Tel.: 1-800-876-1710 or 212-727-1711. Fax: 212-255-7923. Email: mail.frif.com.

Chapter 7. *Michael Stock*

For *Prinz in Hölleland* contact Arne Höhne at Ventura Film, Rosenthaler Straße 38, 10178 Berlin. Tel.: 49-30-283 65 30. Fax: 49-30-283 65 33.

Chapter 8. *Michael Brynntrup*

Michael Brynntrup Filmproduktion, Hermannstraße 64, 12049 Berlin. Tel./Fax: 49-30-621 78 00. Email: brynntrup@mbcc.de. Web: <http://www.brynntrup.de>.

Matthias Müller

Canyon Cinema, 2325 Third Street, Suite 338, San Francisco, CA, 94107. Tel./Fax: 415-626-2255.

Matthias Müller, August-Bebel-Straße 104, 33602 Bielefeld. Tel./Fax: 49-521-17 83 67.

Claudia Schillinger

Claudia Schillinger, Winterfeldstraße 24, 10781 Berlin. Email: cschill777@aol.com.

Hans Scheirl and Ursula Pürrer

Much of their work is collected at bildwechsel (see below). *Flaming Ears* is distributed by Women Make Movies (see under Chapter 5). For *Dandy Dust*, contact the sales agent, Tom Abell. Tel.: 44-181-5337308. Email: peccadillo.pictures@virgin.net.

Further Sources

By far the best collection of lesbian films and videos (including for Scheirl and Pürrer and the animation discussed in Chapter 9) is bildwechsel, Kirchenallee 25, 20099 Hamburg. Tel.: 49-40-24 63 84. Fax: 49-40-24 68 56.

For the male filmmakers discussed:

For Jürgen Brüning's *He Is Bold* . . . , contact Marc Huestis at Outsider Productions. Tel./Fax: 415-863-0611.

Jörg Fockele, 114-116 E. 1st Street, Apt. 28, New York, NY, 10009. Tel./Fax: 212-598-0506. Email: jofock@yahoo.com.

Bjørn Melhus, Christinenstraße 29, 10119 Berlin. Fax: 49-30-441 90 71.

Chapter 9. *Nathalie Percillier and Lily Besilly*

Heldinnenfilm, Schönhauser Allee 152, 10435 Berlin. Tel./Fax: 49-30-449 62 96. Email: dieheldinnen@w4w.net.

Heidi Kull

Geliebte Mörderin (*Beloved Murderer*) and *Frau Berger und Ich* are distributed by Frameline, 346 9th Street, San Francisco, CA, 94103. Tel.: 415-703-8650. Fax: 415-861-1404.

Ulrike Zimmermann

MMM Filmproduktion, Kreuzweg 7, 20099 Hamburg. Fax: 49-40-24 53 69. Email: mmmfilm@compuserve.com.

Stefanie Jordan

Stefanie Jordan, Hochkischstraße 12, 10829 Berlin. Tel./Fax: 49-30-782 19 02. Email: s.jordan@berlin.snafu.de.

Claudia Zoller

Claudia Zoller, Schönhauser Allee 152, 10435 Berlin. Tel./Fax: 49-30-440 45 522. Email: frau.zoller@snafu.de

Bärbel Neubauer

Bärbel Neubauer Filmproduktion, Lindwurmstraße 207, 80337 München. Tel./Fax: 49-89-747 07 01.

Introduction

1. Rosa von Praunheim directly cites Weimar's queer sexualities in *Anita: Tänze des Lasters* (*Anita: Dances of Vice*) (1988) and in *Schwuler Mut: 100 Jahre Schwulenbewegung* (*Gay Courage: 100 Years of the Gay Movement in Germany and Beyond*) (1997). He is currently making a feature-length film on the sexologist from the period, Magnus Hirschfeld.

2. The only books that have appeared on the two (apart from Rosa von Praunheim's books on himself) are in the Hanser Film Reihe.

3. Lambert's *1 Berlin-Harlem* (1974), though, does boast a brilliantly famous cast, including not only Fassbinder but his actors Ingrid Caven, Günther Kaufmann, and Brigitte Mira, as well as the personalities von Praunheim brought to the screen—Tally Brown, Dietmar Kracht, and Evelyn Künneke.

4. When asked about belonging to a group of German directors whose work deals with gays and lesbians, such as von Praunheim, Schroeter, and Ottinger, Monika Treut responded: "I'm friends with all of them. . . . I think we are a group, whether we acknowledge this or not" (Gemünden, Kuzniar, and Phillips, 6). She also speaks of being influenced by such films as Fassbinder's *Satansbraten* (*Satan's Brew*) (1976) and Schroeter's *Eika Katappa* (1969).

5. For a good overview of the implications of the word "queer," see Annamarie Jagose's *Queer Theory: An Introduction*.

6. These suspicions are reflected in Antke Engel's essay, "Verqueeres Begehren."

7. Elizabeth Grosz compares "freak" to "queer" as "a term whose use may function as an act of defiance" (56).

8. For an incisive critique of such readings see D. A. Miller, Lee Edelmann, and Edward R. O'Neill.

9. Wherein lies the difference between camp and allegory? Whereas camp floats, allegory remains weighty and pensive. Most of the films discussed in this book, despite their sartorial playfulness, partake of allegory's seriousness.

10. Dyer notes: "Lesbian/gay culture has always been aware of surface, of the construction of appearance—as a perception of the straight world, as an ironic distance on it, as a strategy for survival within it. Surface and construction are valued

for their own sake within lesbian/gay culture, because we see what is at stake in them" (*Now You See It*, 284). These sentences follow Dyer's discussion of Ottinger's *Madame X* (1977) as anticipating what he calls a post-affirmation cinema in its awareness of surface.

11. Kurz writes of twentieth-century literary allegories that they are increasingly allusive, subversive, and self-ironic; their meaning is uncertain ("Es gibt keine Sicherheit der Bedeutungen, sondern Unsicherheiten," *Metapher, Allegorie, Symbol*, 55).

12. One may recall here how the term "queer" similarly opens an oxymoronic field between an abusive term and a self-nominating affirmation.

13. On Lambert see *Lambert Underground* by Stefan Menche and "The Films of Lothar Lambert" by Jeffrey Peck.

14. I do not want to underestimate, however, the importance of self-affirmation and self-representation for gays and lesbians. In this respect Richard Dyer has been the first to recognize the centrality of Weimar cinema and German auteurs in gay and lesbian cinema. See also the groundbreaking works on lesbian cinema by Stefanie Hetze and Andrea Weiss.

15. Wary of such narratives, Stefan Hayn, a filmmaker himself, offers an intriguing critique of the homogenizing, regulating, and commodifying effect of "gay cinema": "the 'gay film' as a genre [not only] mirrors the different variations of gay identity but, more importantly, in its function as a mass medium establishes and modernizes them in the first place. . . . Both realms—sexuality and aestheticization—are mediated via the 'gay filmmaker' as the model of contemporary (artistic) subjectivity" (71).

16. For a queer critique of such narratives see Scott Bravmann.

17. As one sees in the film *Anders als du und ich* where the homophobic parents of a boy, whom they suspect might be gay, go to criminal lengths to lead their son back to the "straight" and narrow path. They bribe an underage ward to seduce him and accuse the boy's teacher of pederasty.

18. See Chris Straayer's excellent essay on the restrictions of the coming-out narrative and how Monika Treut's *Die Jungfrauenmaschine* rewrites the genre.

19. With few exceptions (Dyer, LaValley), film scholars, the press, and the public at large have not recognized Fassbinder as a gay or bisexual filmmaker. See Rosa von Praunheim's condemnation of this lack of reception in "Schwul, pervers, kontrovers."

20. For example, see Julia Knight.

21. Two recent publications on German experimental film do not mention them, the 1997 issue of *Millennium Film Journal* and *Der deutsche Experimentalfilm der 90er Jahre* (*German Experimental Film of the 1990s*).

Chapter 1

1. For studies into this rich area of research see the collection *Eldorado* and *Goodbye to Berlin?* as well as works by Hacker, Klaus Müller, James Jones, Hekma, Fout, Steakley (*Homosexual Emancipation*), and Lautmann.

2. Waugh, in his history of pornography, in which these images are to be ranged, discusses the overlap between the emerging iconography of male athleticism of the Frei Körper Kultur (FKK) in the 1920s with that of the earlier photographic idol, the adolescent boy: "Though the adolescents at the center of Brand's fantasy world sometimes visually echoed the smooth androgynes of yore, their association with the Wandervögel and Socratic ideals of the Gemeinschaft was all but explicit" (403). For a cinematic combination of these two physical ideals see *Wege zu Kraft und Schönheit*, a film celebrating the athleticism of FKK as well as the aestheticism of languishing same-sex nudes in the setting of Greek temples. The producer Nikolaus Kaufmann was a member of Hirschfeld's committee. See Dyer's discussion (25) of this film in the context of what he calls a "male-identified gayness" as opposed to "inbetweenism," a polarity I am arguing may not have been so fixed and predictable.

3. It is curious that male-to-female transvestites dominated the supplements to the lesbian journals, until one realizes that the umbrella category of the third sex allowed for such affiliations.

4. In her book *Joyless Streets*, Patrice Petro discusses at length the androgynous, mannish fashion of the New Woman as the play of female masquerade, but not in terms of its lesbian signification. Clearly, the Bubi-style was fashionable; the overtones it carried for lesbianism must not be overlooked, however. On lesbian styles of the 1920s see the essays in *Eldorado*; Adèle Meyer, *Lila Nächte*; and Plötz, "Bubis und Damen." Moreover, Petro frequently deploys the term "female bisexuality," but only to designate female gender mobility. She does not open the concept up to sexual desire between women.

5. For more information on gay and lesbian Weimar culture see Adèle Meyer, *Goodbye to Berlin?*, and *Eldorado*.

6. Wolfgang Theis, by contrast, sees a gay man represented best in the extortionist, whom Schünzel plays with erotic lust in his eyes and gestures (22).

7. I am citing from Steakley's English manuscript but referencing its published German translation.

8. In addition to Steakley see the documents surrounding the controvesy about *Anders* in Belach.

9. With the exception of Dyer's work and Ruby Rich's article on *Mädchen in Uniform*, there is a disappointing tendency to downplay or even discourage gay readings, as when Herzer writes that a film like *Michael* would demand "schon sehr gewaltsame Interpretationsverfahren" to be seen as gay (*Goodbye*, 106) or when Steakley writes of *Mädchen* that "the lesbian quality is very much in the eye of the beholder" ("Film und Zensur," 29).

10. In his book *Monsters in the Closet*, on homosexuality and the horror film, Benshoff offers a different take: "Many of the German 'Schauerfilme' of the era explored gothic themes such as the homosexual creation of life (*The Golem*, filmed in 1914 and 1920), while others focused on homoerotic doubles and madness (*The Student of Prague* [1913], *The Picture of Dorian Gray* [1917], and perhaps most famously

The Cabinet of Dr. Caligari [1919])" (21). Benshoff also fascinatingly links the gender invert and the horror film: "Like the mad scientist of the Hollywood horror film, Ulrichs was interested in the effects of blood transfusion, and wondered in print whether or not exchanges of bodily fluids might make an Urning into a 'normal' man, and vice versa. . . . Also less well known is that towards the end of his career Ulrichs wrote an explicitly homosexual vampire story entitled 'Manor,' which was published in 1885" (18–19).

11. Alan was played by the openly gay actor Twardowsky, who later also took the role of the gay man who seduces the protagonist in *Geschlecht in Fesseln* (1928).

12. Other examples include *Aus eines Mannes Mädchenjahren* (1912), *Eine Nacht im Mädchenpensionat* (1913); *Fräulein Piccolo* (1915), *Fräulein Seifenschaum* (1915), and *Das fidele Gefängnis* (1917) (three early Lubitsch films); *Excellenz Unterrock* (1920), *Der Page vom Dalmasse Hotel* (1933), *Charleys Tante* (1934), *Abschiedswalzer* (1934, briefly in the character of Georges Sand), *Schwarzer Jäger Johanna* (1935), and *Capriccio* (1938). See also the following note. For introductory discussion of the transvestite film see Gramann and Schlüpmann as well as Rosi Kreische, "Lesbische Liebe im Film bis 1950" in *Eldorado*, 187–96, and Wolfgang Theis, "Verdrängung und Travestie: Das vage Bild der Homosexualität im deutschen Film (1917–1957)" also in *Eldorado*, 102–15.

13. Nielsen cross-dressed as well in *Jugend und Tollheit* (1913) and *Das Liebes ABC* (1916); Bergner in *Dona Juana* (1928). This list of lesbian idols is cited in Hacker, 259.

14. On Valentino see Dyer, "Less and More," 22, as well as Wolfgang Theis and Andreas Sternweiler, "Alltag im Kaiserreich und in der Weimarer Republik," in *Eldorado*, 48–73.

15. Heide Schlüpmann writes about this film that it is not the woman who is exposed by the male gaze but she who exposes him (88).

16. On flower symbolism see Hacker (200–202) and the volume edited by Adèle Meyer entitled *Lila Nächte* on the lesbian bar culture. The lesbian Hohenzollern Café even advertised its Lilac Days, where every guest was promised a nosegay of lilacs.

17. On the prevalence of literary depictions of the homosexual artist and his connection to Italy see Jones, "*We of the Third Sex.*"

18. The precursor to *Michael* is Mauritz Stiller's 1916 Swedish film *Vignarne* (*The Wings*), adapted from the 1906 novel *Mikael* by the gay Danish writer Herman Bang. While Stiller (the man who made Greta Garbo's career) depicts the sculptor Zoret flinging himself in the ecstasy of death upon the naked statue of Michael, Dryer shows him more outwardly declaring the redemptive experience of his selfless love for the ingrate boy Michael.

274

19. In "Less and More than Women and Men" (45–47), Dyer notices the eroticism in this scene as well as the artist's ambivalent attraction to Renée but stops short of unraveling these moments.

20. In *Charleys Tante* (1934), no less than four marriages at the close clamp down

on the third-sex threat that the m2f cross-dresser presents, whom one character calls "ein richtiges Mannweib" (a real she-man).

21. My thanks go to Eva Geulen for this insight.

22. It has recently been restored by the Filmmuseum in Munich.

23. In *Liebeskommando* (1932, directed by Géza von Bolvary) Lieutenant Lorenz (Gustav Fröhlich) gazes in extraordinary affection at his cadet (Dolly Haas) and even asks him, "If I'm harsh with you, don't you feel the special interest I take in you?" Lorenz's military correctness, even sadism, is a cover for his leanings toward boy-love. Occasionally, such attempts at disguising homoeroticism are rather clumsy. The tender scene when Lorenz looks in unobserved on his sleeping cadets, for instance, is attenuated by military music on the soundtrack. Dolly Haas, as a cross-dressing girl in the military academy for three (!) years is made to play an extra-macho role among her comrades in order to dispel the menace that a pansy would present (except when she mends their clothes, garnering disdain from Lorenz). Most important, though, throughout the film women and the military are contrasted, so that the latent threat of homosexuality is subsumed under the more obvious threat of femininity and thereby exorcised. Although in the last quarter of the film it remains ambiguous if Lorenz is amorous toward the cheeky boy or the girl, by the close, Dolly Haas's character is dressed in decidedly feminine, frilly attire.

24. Gramann and Schlüpmann note the lesbian potential between the heroine and Lady Ellinor but also how it is downplayed by the predominant innuendos of male homosexuality (88).

25. Lilian Harvey was, incidentally, herself lesbian.

26. Kaltenecker writes of Hermann Thimig's concluding performance, where, dressed as Viktoria, he trips on his dress and gallops clumsily across stage, that "the comic performance of femininity emphasizes the impossibility of a non-masculine identification" (114). I will grant that Thimig's character reifies masculinity, but I do take issue with Kaltenecker's feminist and unqueer thesis that this genre solidifies gender and sexual dichtomies.

27. For a comparison of the structures of cinema and dream/fantasy see Metz.

28. Continuing the debate on psychoanalysis and spectatorship but introducing lesbian pleasures is Rhona J. Berenstein.

29. Asta Nielsen's Hamlet is, by contrast, an example of unwilling transvestism, though one immaculately performed and sustained until death reveals the disguise. Here the female spectator could empathize or identify with the restrictions that gender places on Hamlet.

30. That these films still offer pleasure to gay and lesbian viewers today can be seen in Maria Schmidt's compilation video of clips from transvestite films, many from the Weimar period: *Tanten, Tunten, Kesse Väter: Travestie im Spielfilm* (1996). The video was conceived to accompany an exhibition of the same title at the gay museum in Berlin. See also the article by Sannwald.

31. Note that the gay and lesbian journals of the period were distinctly high-

brow and eschewed reviews of the popular cinematic medium, making it difficult to unearth such examples of fandom.

32. Jane Gaines writes about Greta Garbo in *Queen Christina*: "Adrian's designs fashion the full erotic continuum for Garbo. In conventional romantic cuts, she is heterosexual; in drag, mirroring Antonio's gestures and dress, she articulates male homosexuality; in her male dress courtship of the skirted Ebba, Garbo acts out a butch-femme lesbian fantasy" (45).

33. Chris Straayer warns: "When contemplating the continuing popularity of films with temporary transvestism, one must consider mass-audience pleasure, which I believe is grounded in the appeasement of basic contradictions without challenging sexual difference. These films offer a momentary, vicarious trespassing of society's accepted boundaries for gender and sexual behavior. Yet one can relax confidently in the orderly demarcations reconstituted by the films' endings" (42).

34. On f2m cross-dressing, Sandra M. Gilbert writes: "feminist modernist costume imagery is radically revisionary in a political as well as a literary sense, for it implies that no one, male or female, can or should be confined to a uni-form, a single form or self" (394).

Chapter 2

1. The song referred to is "Ich steh' im Regen" ("I stand in the rain") from *Zu neuen Ufern*.

2. Leander never had the figure, though, to be a pinup girl for the soldiers and was always photographed with plenty of concealing drapery and distracting jewelry.

3. The transvestite cabaret where straight couples, usually of an older generation, go slumming is a peculiar German phenomenon.

4. See Ascheid, Dölling, Koepnick, Lenssen, Rentschler (*Ministry of Illusion*), and Silberman. Although scholarship tends to be split between treatment of the Ufa Sierck and the emigré Sirk, Gertrud Koch's article bridges the gap in an article that criticizes his treatment of women.

5. There is one study on gay fandom, however, which does link it to issues of national identity in the wake of the Third Reich. Currid argues that the abject, monumental spectacle of Zarah Leander offers the queer subculture a means to destabilize a heteronormative "Vergangenheitsbewältigung" (a coming to terms with the past). While postulating a fascinating thesis, Currid pathologizes the gay fan for his attraction to Leander's "Abscheulichkeit" (loathsomeness) and to her motherliness, the invocation of which he deprecates as "peinlich und armselig, aber gewiß auch interessant" (embarrassing and pathetic, yet certainly interesting) (76).

6. See Petley, Halliday. Silberman also investigates the irony in *Zu neuen Ufern*.

7. See also my chapter on Werner Schroeter for further discussion of the queer voice.

8. In *Der Blaufuchs* (*The Blue Fox*) (1938) and *Gabriela* (1950) her marriage fetters her, while in *Es war eine rauschende Ballnacht*, she is again married to a man she doesn't

love while longing for another—ironically, Peter I. Tchaikovsky (here clearly not depicted as gay!).

9. On melodrama as a "text of muteness" where the body substitutes for what cannot be uttered, see Peter Brooks.

10. Johannes von Moltke also observes this model of looting or plagarism operative in the phenomenon of the diva: "The attributes of the diva, that is, the diva as attribute of an extensive fund for the construction of cultural and sexual identities . . . can be and has been plundered in all kinds of ways and with each subsequent plundering is newly pieced together [bestückt] and made richer" ("Die Diva," 219).

11. Some speculations: conceivably, Fassbinder would have felt forced to hedge his adulation of Douglas Sirk; or praise for Nazi box-office hits might have compromised his picture of Sirk as well as the implicit dichotomy he sets up between American popular culture and the pompous German bourgeois self-image (he ironically writes in *Anarchy of the Imagination* of young Sirk's attending movies in secret because he "was supposed to become a cultivated man in the great German tradition, humanistically educated" [77]). By all accounts, such an inclusion would have been a controversial move, for his camp attitude toward Sirk not might have gone over well when applied to Nazi cinema (too serious a subject to make fun of), although Fassbinder certainly otherwise never shied away from controversy. If Fassbinder felt that the earlier Sierck did not match his discussion of the later Sirk and that he was thus inappropriate for inclusion, we do not know. Yet the stilted plots and hopelessly ill-matched love relations that Fassbinder gleefully retraces from *Magnificent Obsession* and *Written on the Wind* could easily have been applied to *Zu neuen Ufern* and *La Habanera*, which in retrospect can be seen as staging cliched emotion and stereotypical characters ripe for a camp reception. On melodrama and camp, Hollywood Sirk, and Fassbinder, see von Moltke, "Camping in the Art Closet" (82), and Feil.

12. Sybille Schmitz, incidentally, had lesbian leanings and played George Sand—the pants role of a woman dressing as a man—in *Abschiedswalzer* (*Farewell Walz*) (1934). See the biography by Friedemann Beyer.

13. As a parallel, it is interesting that when from Stockholm in 1944 the news came that Leander had declared herself to be pro-Semitic, her name never again appeared in German newspapers and some attempt was made to pull her films from circulation. The sheer difficulty of such a task prevented the Reich's film chamber from doing so completely. See Seiler, *Ich bin eine Stimme*, 76–84.

14. Bathrick compares the plot of *Lili Marleen* to *Wunschkonzert* (50), while Elsaesser finds parallels to *Schlußakkord* (164).

15. Elsaesser similarly writes: "The utterly subjective death-wish expressed in the song stands in symmetrical relation to the historical death towards which its listeners are headed" (167).

16. For other views on camp in Fassbinder see Babuscio, Dyer, and Farber and Patterson.

277

17. All parenthetical page references are from the screenplay (*Querelle Filmbuch*).

18. This exchange of women substituting for intimacy between men occurs in Fassbinder's *Berlin Alexanderplatz* (1979–80).

19. Monika Treut, in her article on the men in *Querelle*, writes: "The 'studs' Nono, Mario, and Gil are so secure in their straight identities that they can fuck men without threatening their maleness—yet they would never consider themselves homosexuals" (69).

20. Nor is it linked to castration, which might be one reason Silverman does not deal with *Querelle* in *Male Subjectivity at the Margins*, where she studies dephallicization and male masochistic ecstasy in Fassbinder.

21. This deconstruction leads me to disagree with Dyer's conclusion that *Querelle* affirms the hetero/homo hierarchy: "[Querelle's] pleasure/humiliation can only be that if homosexual acts are accepted as indeed inferior and degrading in comparison to heterosexual ones. . . . The self is annihilated through the internalisation of heterosexual norms" (*Now You See It*, 96).

22. The page references are taken from the screenplay published in *October* 21 (1982): 5–50.

23. See Burgoyne: "In *Thirteen Moons* the quest for a metalanguage which will deliver the characters from the muteness of their surroundings embeds the film in a proliferation of texts by which the characters probe their lives for concealed metaphors. The status accorded these narratives turns the characters into 'story-telling epicenters'" (58).

24. I disagree with Burgoyne here: "Elvira hopes to rescue herself from the nebulous zone in which she is bereft of sexual identity and to be restored to the system of clear definitions and polar organization, and thereby to the society which rejects her" (56).

25. The very difficulty one faces in how to name Erwin or Elvira reflects these exclusive binary restrictions. By contrast, Saitz insists his name be spelled correctly, for he cannot tolerate ambiguity.

26. See also Elsaesser: "The 'I' . . . does not repress suffering, nor does it voice it directly, but 'ex-corporates' it: suffusing the film in ways the filmic discourse fails to contain, except by modulating sound effects, light, music, ambient noise into an almost abstract figuration, as in the scene of Elvira weeping in the video arcade" (213).

27. Fassbinder therewith breaks with the pattern Elsaesser delineates: "One is tempted to say that in Fassbinder's films all human relations, bodily contact, even social hierarchies, and most forms of communication and action manifest themselves (and ultimately regulate themselves) along the axis of seeing and being seen" (60).

28. For example, see Frieden: "No longer a male, she can no longer act as a desiring subject; not accepted as a female—and though she is the object of derision—she cannot serve as object of sexual desire. As non-subject and non-object, Elvira is trapped in a social and sexual purgatory" (54). I would agree, however, with Frieden's thesis that the ambiguity of Erwin/Elvira's sexual identity creates unease in the spectator.

29. Corrigan (*Cinema without Walls*) holds the contrary view that "Elvira is left with the realization that she didn't wish to become a woman: Elvira's mistake is to misread or misunderstand the language of sexual difference as one of simple and reversible opposition and to make her body a text on which those differences can be written as merely a different reading" (69–70). My reading thus also clashes with Corrigan's pessimistic conclusion that "*In a Year of 13 Moons* is a movie about textual madness, about textualities that lose their ability to naturalize and balance the materials of signification with a sense of meaning" (69).

30. See also Shaviro, who contextualizes Fassbinder's representation of gay sexuality in *Querelle* in terms of a postmodern fascination with the surface: "He refuses to provide 'positive images' of either gay or straight sex. On the contrary, he willfully aestheticizes the most troubling moments of his narrative, those when male sexuality is explicitly associated with power and domination, with violence, and with death" (159).

31. LaValley is referring to the articles "Schwul, pervers, kontrovers" by von Praunheim and "Reading Fassbinder's Sexual Politics" by Dyer.

32. Another Leander fan is Lothar Lambert (see Menche, 10–11). Transgender performance also characterizes his films, including *Drama in Blond* (1984), *In Hassliebe Lola* (1994), and *Und Gott erschuf das Make-Up* (1998), where Lambert himself plays the outgoing transvestite. He also assumes this role in three of Dagmar Beiersdorf's films, *Dirty Daughters* (1982), *Die Wolfsbraut* (*The Wolf's Bride*) (1984), and *Eine Tunte zum Dessert* (*A Queen for Dessert*) (1992). Typically Lambert's underground, no-budget productions portray shrill, scurrilous individuals who live in Berlin. Having gotten the short end in life, these characters try, through their outlandishness, to create some measure of freedom and escape for themselves. Although Lambert pokes fun at the banality of these attempts, he also has sympathy for his characters and their human foibles. In an interview with Jeffrey Peck, he modestly says, "I am not trying to make socially critical movies. I want to show reality as I see it, with irony" (232).

In *Hassliebe Lola* portrays Lambert as an aging gay transvestite cabaret artist whose performances sail beyond camp into trash. *Make-Up* is particularly interesting for how the entire film revolves around others watching the transvestitic spectacle. The film is a remake of *Was Sie nie über Frauen wissen wollten* (*What You Never Wanted to Know About Women*) (1991) but with transvestites instead of women living communally in a mock-therapy experiment. Lambert plays the therapist, Dr. Prinz, who cares for this house of the ill-adjusted (m2f except for one f2m). The tight living quarters turn the commune into a panopticon, and much of the comedy resides in the dour looks the residents give each other. The main character is a pudgy, shy mama's boy, Manfred, who eventually is made up by the salon artist René Koch to look like Divine. Jeffrey Peck writes: "All of Lambert's work seems to be a kind of 'coming out' story. This exposure is not just meant sexually, but a metaphor for everyone who is 'closeted' in life and just does not seem to fit" (229). This statement also is true of all the characters in *Make-Up*. Even Dr. Prinz starts to cross-dress in order to better observe his patients, and eventually moves in with them. Mocking the documentary convention of rolling final titles that skip ahead to "several months after," Lambert at the conclusion of his film tells how Dr. Prinz underwent a sex change and sold his story to the German TV channel RTL.

Chapter 3

1. See von Praunheim's tribute to her: "Erika from Würzburg: A Portrait of the Actress Magdalena Montezuma (1981)" in Rentschler, *West German Filmmakers on Film*, 179–82.

2. Von Praunheim's AIDS activism is all the more crucial when one considers that no other well-known German director has tackled the problem, other than Doris Dörrie, who has the black gay man in *Keiner liebt mich* (*Nobody Loves Me*) (1994) say he has a deadly disease, and qualify this by saying that it is not AIDS!

3. This connection is clearly not meant to discount the influence of John Waters, Jack Smith, Kenneth Anger, Andy Warhol, and Derek Jarman, among others, on the New Queer Cinema. Warhol and Smith are also important figures for Praunheim, as is documented in his *Underground and Emigrants* (1975).

4. See the articles on Rosa von Praunheim in the Berlin gay magazine *Magnus* 2.7 (1990): 25–35. Other references to this issue are in parentheses.

5. The title of the film, in its punning, displays this playfulness: it offers us a Neu(e) Rosa, a new take on the neurotic Rosa.

6. In *50 Jahre pervers*, for instance, he bemoans that he has rarely accomplished the compelling combination of political aggressivity and bizarre poetry that Wojnarowicz has in his performance art (362).

7. This was not the first instance: he had penned other articles on AIDS in 1988 in *Der Spiegel*, in 1989 in *TIP*, and in 1990 in *Die Tageszeitung*.

8. I am condensing the review of this reception from Dietrich Kuhlbrodt's section on this film in *Rosa von Praunheim*.

9. See Stümke for a representative personal response to the film (17–22 and 75–101), plus his documenting of how young gays responded to a screening in 1997 (22).

10. On the other hand, when I asked Rosa von Praunheim how he would make the film differently today, he replied that the problems are still the same: gays in Germany are too complacent, ghettoized, and unpolitical.

11. The word used in the English version; in the original German *Schwule* possessed a derogatory meaning that has subsequently worn off.

12. See Karla Jay and Allen Young's anthology *Out of the Closets: Voices of Gay Liberation*.

13. For a parallel discussion of "a subject who repeats and mimes the legitimating norms by which it itself has been degraded, a subject founded in the project of mastery that compels and disrupts its own repetitions," see Judith Butler's discussion of *Paris Is Burning* (*Bodies That Matter*, 131).

14. Charlotte has subsequently moved to Sweden. On her life there see the film *Charlotte in Schweden* by John Edward Heys and Matthias F. Küntzel (1998).

15. In fact, what she enacts in the scenario with Herbert and Jochen is not solely or most importantly a cross-gendered role but a gay man's sexual proclivities. Her choices are not just gender-related but sexual as well. Thus the cross-dressing does not function to obfuscate the divide between men and women but to multiply differences queerly. Here the exposed penis serves as a marker sustaining this difference, although in its soft, limp form it does not signify phallic power. A less conventional libidinal part object, the prone buttocks, is more frequently amorously pursued in this film.

Chapter 4

1. On Schroeter's gay attraction to Callas see Sieglohr's essays, where she reads this fascination via Wayne Koestenbaum's *The Queen's Throat*.

2. He has even made such unconventional documentaries as *Der lachende Stern / The Laughing Star* (1983), on the Marcos regime in the Philippines, and *Zum Beispiel Argentinien* (*Argentina, For Example*) (1986), on Galtieri's dictatorship.

3. As early as 1970, Feurich observed in a review in *Filmkritik* that Schroeter's "actors do not embody roles, because detachable, independent roles don't exist anymore . . . the images don't demand from the actors a change of identity but create them as phenomena of pure visual expression" (qtd. in *Werner Schroeter*, 32).

4. This image recalls the opening of Schroeter's earlier film *Eika Katappa*.

5. On the length of these shots see Sieglohr: "in *The Death of Maria Malibran* the average shot length is 36 sec in comparison to a Hollywood film made between 1964 and 1969 where it is only 6–7 sec" ("Excess Yearning," 202).

6. Sieglohr writes: "Paradoxically through exaggerating their 'femininity' the female performers denaturalize their biological gender. It is through this double take and turning round of 'femininity' and by rendering appearance as artificial, that they invoke the drag queen" ("Why Drag," 164).

7. They star together in the earlier films *Neurasia* (1968), *Argila* (1968), and *Eika Katappa* (1969). Carla Aulaulu was married for a time to Rosa von Praunheim.

8. Cf. Corrigan: "In so aggressively exhibiting its excess the representation serves ultimately to deflate itself, so that . . . the portrayal contains that excess only at the cost of admitting the inadequacy of the medium" ("Operatic Cinema," 52).

9. Montezuma also assumes an astonishing pants role as the hunchback court fool/father from Verdi's *Rigoletto* in *Eika Katappa*. And in *Salomé* she plays the role of Herodes who queerly stares at Salomé.

10. On the debates surrounding lesbian spectatorship see de Lauretis (*The Practice of Love*), Evans and Gamman, Traub, and Weiss ("A Queer Feeling").

11. Corrigan suggests this doubling of the female pose shows "the separate symbolic divisions of one woman." The focus on women, moreover, comes "as a passionate expression rebelling against a patriarchal history" ("Edge of History," 14).

12. Contrast this reading with Sieglohr's: "It could even be argued that the very composition of figures in a tableau keeps the spectator at a distance, refusing to integrate him/her into the space. A tableau perspective cuts out the scene in a manner that separates the viewer, staging it in front and apart. The point of view constructed for the spectator by the tableau is a subject exterior to what is represented" ("Excess Yearning," 203).

13. Cf. *Schwarze Engel* (*Black Angels*) (1984) where Magdalena Montezuma is paired with Ellen Umlauf, who confesses, "I had to think the whole time about her, how intensely her gaze penetrated me." A voice-over also chants: "The gaze of the other forms my body in its nakedness, lets it arise, modulates it, and brings it forth as it is—sees it as I will never see it."

14. Possibly a Schroeterian allusion to Novalis, in whose life and work "l'amour" and "la mort" (echoing in the title *Flocons d'or*) were also intertwined (see Courant, 9).

15. Sieglohr also psychoanalytically links female song in Schroeter to the nostalgic fantasy of recovering the maternal voice ("Why Drag," 186–91).

16. In *Flocons d'or* Montezuma is strangled by a pearl necklace.

17. Sieglohr writes: "From a psychoanalytic point of view therefore it would seem that Schroeter's deployment of music conveys the nostalgic pull towards non-differentiation, whilst the punitive trajectory of non-harmonisation, the never quite synchronized sound track (remembering that this is post–synchronized dubbing) notes the struggle for subjectivity which is precisely predicated on differentiation. . . . Incoherence becomes a means to convey the psychic toll which this regressive movement towards non-differentiation entails" ("Excess Yearning," 211–12).

18. Given this oscillation, Schroeter's fixation on Callas is itself significant: she is renowned equally for the magnificence of her renditions and the jarring imperfections of her later work, which, Schroeter states, do not diminish but enhance her "claim to total truthfulness" (qtd. in *Werner Schroeter*, 65).

19. Gary Indiana points out an important difference from silent films: "Most silent films approximate the close narrative detail that sound movies achieve effortlessly—only the talk is missing (ergo, intertitles). Schroeter's elliptical exposition aims at the spiritual essence of a chosen reality, minus the plodding details. There is only the dream" (50).

20. Dietrich Kuhlbrodt writes about Schroeter's films: "The foreign language is only a means among others to rediscover language as gesture" (qtd. in *Werner Schroeter*, 17).

21. In this respect, it is interesting that Schroeter regarded Callas to be an androgyne: like the Mona Lisa she could seem to be either a man or a woman (interview on *arte* on the twentieth anniversary of Callas's death).

22. For other recent queer readings of opera see Abel, Koestenbaum, Blackmer and Smith, and Brett and Thomas.

23. The German word for pink is *rosa*, the gay associations of which are evi-

denced in Holger Mischwitzky's pseudonym Rosa von Praunheim and in the pink triangle, *rosa Winkel*.

24. Rosa von Praunheim, who also repeatedly used her unfailing eye, said that she was a "white sorceress, a magician of light" (*50 Jahre pervers*, 145).

25. A scene with confusing mirror images likewise suggests an indistinguishability between mother and son. The viewer cannot tell which of the two is reflected in the mirror or which of the two stands outside it. They are both entrapped in the image they have of each other.

26. Gary Indiana has observed regarding the segment with Mario and Carlo in *Eika Katappa* that "Schroeter's tact on the subject of homosexuality may seem like reticence, but it is really designed to sidestep the limitations of the subject as subject" (48). What becomes interesting is what unconventional strategies Schroeter uses to bend these restrictions.

27. Schroeter, like Genet, feminizes and eroticizes his male characters by having them be the object of a voyeuristic gaze. Other echoes of Genet are the association of the criminal with flowers and the chiaroscurist lighting. See Gary Indiana, who wrote, in an essay published before *Der Rosenkönig* appeared: "Schroeter blurs dreams, hallucinations, and ostensible reality in ways that recall Genet's only film, *Un chant d'amour*" (48).

Chapter 5

1. In photographs taken by Holger Trülzsch in 1973 Lehndorff has been body-painted in male attire and mimics macho posturing (see Lehndorff and Trülzsch).

2. See particularly Fischetti, Hake, Hansen, Longfellow, Mayne, Silverman (*The Threshold of the Visible World*), Weiss, and White.

3. *Johanna d'Arc of Mongolia* explores such female-female adoration through the gaze: women's eyes repeatedly dwell appreciatively on other women.

4. For articles on *Dorian Gray* see Mueller, Trumpener, and Perlmutter.

5. Seyrig has a lesbian cult following, primarily for her lesbian vampire role in *Daughters of Darkness* (Harry Kumel, Belgium, 1970). Weiss writes in addition about her role as Lady Windermere in *Johanna d'Arc of Mongolia*: "In what must be one of the most subtle pick-ups in cinema history, Lady Windermere invites Giovanna back to share her first-class compartment" (133).

6. Cf. Longfellow: "While there is some temporal progression of narrative in *Johanna d'Arc* . . . , this temporal axis is clearly secondary to the critical space of spectacle and performance" (128). Mayne: "In *Ticket of No Return*, the sightseer's itinerary has a built-in refusal of linearity, and even its classic conclusion in death confounds rather than confirms the narrative of passage or initiation" (153).

7. Mueller notes the specularity between Dorian and Dr. Mabuse: "Both rely upon each other for the gratification of their narcissism. Dorian's spectatorial narcissism allows him to see his own reflection in everything and to continue to feel at the center of the universe, while Mabuse, the director, enjoys the thought of re-creating the universe in her own image" (187).

8. Trumpener observes: "in the mirror of post-modernity, even characters [including the media magnates from around the world] who literally embody new worlds of racial difference are at the same time nothing more than flatly familiar, two-dimensional exoticist tropes" (87–88).

9. Trumpener additionally notes: "Eyes only on the love story, in which he has cast himself as the male lead, Dorian Gray misses what we are able to see, the opera's applicability both to his own situation and to the overall political world of the film. In fact it should warn him of Mabuse's will to personal domination, her attempt to get control of his life, and of her will to global domination as well" (82). In the opera, Dr. Mabuse plays the role of the Grand Inquisitor.

10. Another allegorical threesome is the three virtues of journalism—independence, objectivity, and nonpartisanship—whom Dr. Mabuse encounters in her basement archives as naked old men.

11. On allusions to Wilde in *Bildnis einer Trinkerin* see Mayne, 146, and Hansen, 203.

12. Other lesbian elements in Ottinger include the iconography of lesbian s/m in *Madame X*, the lesbian bar in *Bildnis einer Trinkerin*, and the same-sex appreciative gazes in *Johanna d'Arc of Mongolia*. For articles that address lesbian readings of Ottinger see in particular Hake, Longfellow, Weiss, and White. Russo's comment pertains to several of her films as well: "Certainly, the gender-layering of *Freak Orlando* privileges lesbianism as style and bodily surface" (104).

13. See Lacan, *The Four Fundamental Concepts of Psycho-Analysis*.

14. On the cinematic use of the psychoanalytical term "secondary identification" see Metz, and on suture see Silverman (*Subject of Semiotics*).

15. For a summary and evaluation of various positions on female fetishism see Gamann and Makinen. On fetishism in Ottinger see Hake (197–98) and Hansen (198).

16. Longfellow sees in *Johanna d'Arc of Mongolia* the eroticism of sexual difference transposed onto racial and cultural difference, which in turn mediates lesbian desire; "here difference does not provoke anxiety—it is, precisely, the lure and the cause of desire" (135).

17. In addition Hake refers to the "seven models of femininity" in *Madame X* as "a veritable freak show" (92).

18. Trumpener sees *Dorian Gray* in line with several other films by West German directors which exposed the mechanisms of the right-wing media in the public sphere and reflected on the complicity of the cinematic apparatus (83–85).

Chapter 6

1. Knight criticizes the film: "The film tends to reinforce the dominant perception of heterosexuality as the 'norm' rather than offer lesbianism as a serious alternative. Having initially responded to her woman friend's sexual advances, Johanna then rejects and avoids her. The actual affair serves no narrative purpose and appears to have been included in the film only so that the option of lesbian sexuality could be rejected in favor of heterosexuality" (155).

2. See Allen on how "racial differences between Kotzebue and Roswitha, along with differences of gender/sexuality between 'butch' Kotzebue and 'femme' Roswitha, are interwoven in an attempt to reinforce racial privileges and hierarchies within contemporary western lesbian culture" (70).

3. Cf. Judith Butler: "there is no one femininity with which to identify, which is to say that femininity might itself offer an array of identificatory sites, as the proliferation of lesbian femme possibilities attests" (*Bodies That Matter*, 239).

4. See Konstanze Streese and Kerry Shea, "Who's Looking? Who's Laughing? Of Multicultural Mothers and Men in Percy Adlon's *Bagdad Café*."

5. On the performance artist Annie Sprinkle see the chapter on "The Seduction of Boundaries: Feminist Fluidity in Annie Sprinkle's Art/Life" by Chris Straayer in her *Deviant Eyes*. See as well Treut's own short, *Annie* (1989), presented in the collection *Female Misbehavior* (1992).

6. How well Lisa serves as an example of upward class mobility is debatable: she works back in the kitchen, while Vicky, the prettier woman with the sexy European accent, is brought out front to serve tables.

7. Gerd Gemünden points out that through such continual performativity, Treut deconstructs the natural/artificial, surface/depth, inner/outer divides. When Vicky thinks she can keep these realms separate and switch on performances at will (either to trick her father or in her auditions), she fails (188). Gemünden's chapter on Treut deals in depth with issues of gender performance and cultural identity in her work.

8. Here I am indebted to the distinctions Judith Butler draws in her discussion of gender performance in *Bodies That Matter*.

9. Another example of compulsory citationality of ethnic affiliation that is no less terrible for being performed occurs in the opening sequence, when Vicky, in a casting tryout, is being coached to act the "typical" German, that is, obnoxiously.

10. Again the character of Lisa is troubling for its latent racism: as Biddy Martin would notice, "the femme-butch couple [is] made visibly different by way of skin color" (115).

11. Cf. Chris Straayer's chapter "Coming Out in a New World: Monika Treut's *Virgin Machine*" in her *Deviant Eyes*: "Many scenes in *Virgin Machine* collapse male-female and hetero-homo dualities within the more accommodating category of inventive pleasure seekers" (38).

12. To quote Straayer again: "In San Francisco, Dorothee's mentors help release sexuality from predetermined truths. Concerned with initiation rather than with classification, *Virgin Machine* provides a coming-out story that is *ars erotica*. . . . Dorothee's coming out . . . exceeds the limitations of identity" (40). On multiple sexualities and what Marjorie Garber has called a "category crisis" see Judith Halberstam, "F2M: The Making of Female Masculinity."

13. Marcia Klotz claims that in the "straight space outside" of Treut's "queer haven," "abuse is real and . . . hierarchies of race and class continue to dominate people's lives" (75). Klotz can only offer this critique by not mentioning the Latino

presence in *My Father Is Coming* and by stating that Annie Sprinkle is not Jewish (74) (which she is!).

14. The Berlin film festival is the only major international film festival to bestow prizes for gay and lesbian films; hence the competition is rigorous and such an award prestigious. It speaks for the strength and prominence of Queer German Cinema that the idea for such awards originated at the Berlinale and that the German gay filmmaker Wieland Speck organizes the gala event. Parodying the Oscars or the Golden Bears, the award is a statue of a rather stupid-looking pudgy bear designed by the gay comic-strip artist Ralf König.

15. Les Reines Prochaines are not only musicians but active in the visual and performing arts as well. Their video artists include Muda Mathis and (formerly) Pipilotti Rist.

Chapter 8

1. "[Psychoanalysis] argues, rightly I think, that what is exteriorized or performed can only be understood through reference to what is barred from the signifier and from the domain of corporeal legibility" (*Bodies That Matter*, 234).

2. An example would be the collections *Boys Shorts I* and *II*, compilations of short films independently produced but assembled for broader marketing purposes and held up to be representative of the genre.

3. It should be noted that the granting of public funds in Germany does not entail the direct policing of homosexual content as in the United States. Indirectly, though, such subjects may not compete well with less controversial topics before funding agencies, especially if the public television stations are involved.

4. See the recent exhibition catalog of the Goethe Institute, *Der deutsche Experimentalfilm*, in which Brynntrup, Müller, and Melhus are mentioned.

5. New titles appear more rapidly than I have opportunity to see them: these include Sylke Enders's *Auszeit* (*Time Out*) (1997), Kerstin Ahlrichs's *1000 Ameisen* (*1000 Ants*) (1998), Martina Witte and Marion Wildhaber's *Ballheads* (1998), and Maas, Brettschneider, Scholz, and Hamelberg's *Geschlecht ist Geschlecht ist Geschlecht* (*Gender Is Gender Is Gender*) (1997).

6. On Goethe and homoeroticism see Kuzniar, ed., *Outing Goethe and His Age*.

7. See Hoolboom, "The Death Dances of Michael Brynntrup."

8. In her analysis of this film, Hallensleben writes: "[Brynntrup] is followed by his own shadow, printed together now with its own negative which lags just slightly behind, announcing a meancing figure of Death . . . Life is running on, death goes with it" (46).

9. Brynntrup cites from Hegel's *Phenomenology of the Spirit*: "Shown is the *Now*, this *Now*. The *Now*; it has already ceased to exist the moment it is shown; *the Now* that is, is other than that which is shown, . . . The Now, as it is shown to us, is '*ein gewesenes*' (something-that-has-been), and this is its truth." By projecting one image on top of another or by enlarging an image, altering it, and rephotographing it, Brynntrup makes one aware of the temporal process that one moment encapsulates.

10. This delayed ending is further complicated by the fact that Brynntrup is planning a labyrinthine interactive CD-ROM version.

11. I therefore am uncomfortable with such phrasing as "Making films is for [Brynntrup] a process of searching for his own identity" (Hein, "Michael Brynntrup," 31).

12. Brynntrup's stock repertoire of death images (skull, skeleton, etc.) likewise functions allegorically: they are empty vehicles signaling death as a terminus beyond which one cannot find meaning.

13. Even the musak by Dirk Schaefer (the composer for the complicated soundtracks to Matthias Müller's films) is heavily repetitive.

14. For a lengthier discussion of these doublings see Hein, "Michael Brynntrup," 32.

15. See also Speck's essay on making safe-sex videos entitled "Porno?"

16. See also the essay on AIDS films by Behm.

17. Müller, Brynntrup, Schillinger, and Melhus all studied under Hein in Braunschweig.

18. To indicate this vulnerability one set of images evokes a hospital bed and a brief clip from Lang's *Siegfried*, followed by a shot of a torso with a leaf on its back. These tell in seconds of the myth of the fallible body.

19. In a talk delivered at one of Müller's screenings, Schaefer noted: "In compilation, just as surprisingly as regularly, relations between the musical citation and image appeared that one had not counted on, that were not consciously planned, and nonetheless struck one as compelling, as an objective fact." "This oscillation between the poles 'undefinable noise' and 'overcoded sign' (= citation) is typical for my work."

20. Müller has toured with a found footage program, introducing and leading discussions on films by Peter Tscherkassky, Martin Arnold, and others.

21. Hein suggests that the sudden shift to black-and-white indicates that "she is coming closer to her fantasy world" ("'Das wahre Wesen,'" 150).

22. Mike Hoolboom gently criticizes one particular omission: "There remains the question of consent and power, and without the voices of his young amours, rendered here in a series of grainy snapshots, there is no way to accede to the filmer's single urgent request: to judge. And to judge fairly" ("Femme Fatale," 62).

23. Schillinger achieves this grain by "printing from TV, from video to super-8 film, then back to TV, to 16mm and so on, creating patterns through the generations of film" ("I'm Not Against Pornography," 63).

24. *Dandy Dust* thus disputes Anne Balsamo's findings on the cyborg: "As is often the case when seemingly stable boundaries are displaced by technological innovation (human/artificial, life/death, nature/culture), other boundaries are more vigilantly guarded. Indeed, the gendered boundary between male and female is one border that remains heavily guarded despite new technological ways to rewrite the physical body in the flesh" (9).

287

25. On the relation of psychomachia and allegory see the chapter here on Ottinger.

26. Grissemann sees the cardboard characters in *Rote Ohren* as metacinematic: "Film figures, as [*Rote Ohren*] signals, are phantoms, to be sure immortal ones, yet no more than 2-D illumined visions of the screen" (285).

27. Cf. Grissemann on *Rote Ohren*: "The surfaces are what count: the painted bodies and walls, the thousand tattoos, the mannerisms of an imagined fashion—all this . . . melts into a disturbing dance of signs. Untranslatable" (281–82).

28. Grissemann links the reference to liquids in the title *The Drift of Juicy* to the omnipresence of fluids in *Rote Ohren* (283). One could add the titles *Gezacktes Rinnsal* and *Piss in Rosa*; as we saw, *Dandy Dust* also oozes images of wetness.

29. Just as in their "home movies" Scheirl and Pürrer stage their own lives, so too in *Rote Ohren* nonprofessional actors "come from their own world [the Viennese lesbian scene] and act close to their own reality [*knapp an der eigenen Realität vorbeispielen*], in other words, their reality is used for film's story" (Pürrer, qtd. in Blümlinger, 202).

Chapter 9

1. Percillier's affinity for miniaturization can also be seen in two films she made with Kerstin Schleppegrell, *Gavotte* ([1991] where she dresses her cat and holds up her front paws to make her dance) and *Mein Frühstück mit Doris* (*My Breakfast with Doris*) ([1991] where live beetles are used in different dollhouse/bar settings to imitate the life of women).

2. See similar butch-femme bar fantasies in birgit durbahn's *Mit den besten Wünschen* (*With Best Wishes*) (1982), Katrin Barben's *Bar jeder Frau* (*The Bad Girl Bar*) (1992), and Sylke R. Meyer's *Rituale des Werbens* (*The Rites of Wooing*) (1995).

3. Claudia Zoller also uses such shorthand and suspense in an animated commercial spot made for UNICEF against child abuse (1994).

4. Lesbian role-playing is also the theme of the Swiss director Katrin Barben's *Casting* (1995), where sadomasochistic positions (between an older woman director and a young aspiring actress auditioning for a role) are dizzyingly interchanged, with the consequence that reality and performance cannot be distinguished. Percillier's *Sensations As If* (1992) also plays with assuming different personae; she cuts faces of women, including notable lesbians, out of old photos and substitutes her own for them.

5. Another salient American example would be Marlon Riggs's work and the documentary made about his life, *I Shall Not Be Removed* (1997).

6. On Mara Mattuschka's films see the article by Klippel. She also starred in Brynntrup's *Plötzlich und Unerwartet*.

7. The proliferation of doubles in the films discussed here—*Late at Night, Sonderangebot, Zwischen Tier und Schatten*, (self-doubling in) *Bernadette und Belfighor*, (mirrored diptych in) *Zartes Reh* (*Delicate Deer*)—suggests a self-reflection on the animation process as frame-by-frame repetition with slight alteration and on animation as an art that necessarily and hence consciously simulates.

8. Kull's other animated film, *Ich und Frau Berger* (1991), likewise tells of a

covert affair—between a married older woman and her punkish young girlfriend. In ballade-style, the narrator sings of how she knocks on her lover's door, addressing her as Frau Berger so the neighbors won't suspect anything. On weekends Frau Berger sits at home knitting while her husband reads the paper, whereas during the week the two go out together. Frau Berger's sexuality is wonderfully evoked through her crooked smile, heavily lidded, slowly blinking eyes, and the strange eroticism of her naked cartoon body. Kull's *Malamut: Ein Erotik-Clip* (1993), edited by Lily Besilly, also portrays an unconventional relationship, erotically revealing skin next to fur under strobe lighting. The dog's coat and eyes are sensually inviting. A husky female voice sings "You are such a wild girl and I want to get close to you and I want to feel you."

9. Jordan and Zoller, who have worked independently as lesbian directors, came together with Stefanie Saghri to compose *Late at Night*.

10. They are also authors of other animated shorts, but these have no lesbian thematic: *May Day* (1995) by Jordan and *Zartes Reh* (1992) by Zoller. Jordan is currently working on a film on a dyke firefighter in San Francisco.

11. Many special thanks to birgit durbahn from bildwechsel for introducing me to Neubauer's films and for helping me understand the Bavarian dialect as well as the allegorical import of Neubauer's tales.

Epilogue

1. All the filmmakers responded in English, except for Schillinger and Brynntrup, whose remarks I have translated.

Abel, Sam. *Opera in the Flesh: Sexuality in Operatic Performance.* Boulder, Colo.: Westview, 1996.

Allen, Louise. "*Salmonberries:* Consuming kd lang." *Immortal, Invisible: Lesbians and the Moving Image.* Ed. Tamsin Wilton. London: Routledge, 1995. 70–84.

Ascheid, Antje. "A Sierckian Double Image: The Narration of Zarah Leander as a National Socialist Star." *Film Criticism* 23 (1999): 46–73.

Babuscio, Jack. "Camp and the Gay Sensibility." *Camp Grounds: Style and Homosexuality.* Ed. David Bergman. Amherst: University of Massachusetts Press, 1993. 19–38.

Baer, Harry. *Schlafen kann ich, wenn ich tot bin: Das atemlose Leben des Rainer Werner Fassbinder.* Cologne: Kiepenheuer & Witsch, 1982.

Balsamo, Anne. *Technologies of the Gendered Body: Reading Cyborg Women.* Durham, N.C.: Duke University Press, 1996.

Bathrick, David. "Inscribing History, Prohibiting and Producing Desire: Fassbinder's *Lili Marleen.*" *New German Critique* 63 (1994): 35–53.

Behm, Thomas. "Und das Thema geht weiter. . . . 10 Jahre Filme zum Thema Aids." *Rundbrief Film* 3 (1995): 198–200.

Belach, Helga, and Wolfgang Jacobsen, eds. *Richard Oswald: Regisseur und Produzent.* Munich: Edition text und kritik, 1990.

Benjamin, Walter. *Ursprung des deutschen Trauerspiels.* Frankfurt: Suhrkamp, 1978.

Benshoff, Harry M. *Monsters in the Closet: Homosexuality and the Horror Film.* Manchester: Manchester University Press, 1997.

Berenstein, Rhona J. "Spectatorship as Drag: The Act of Viewing and Classic Horror Cinema." *Viewing Positions: Ways of Seeing Films.* Ed. Linda Williams. New Brunswick, N.J.: Rutgers University Press, 1995. 231–69.

Bergstrom, Janet. "Sexuality at a Loss: The Films of F. W. Murnau." *Poetics Today* 6:1–2 (1985): 185–203.

Beyer, Friedemann. *Schöner als der Tod: Das Leben der Sybille Schmitz.* Munich: Belleville, 1998.

Blackmer, Corinne E., and Patricia Juliana Smith, ed. *En Travesti: Women, Gender Subversion, Opera.* New York: Columbia University Press, 1995.

Blümlinger, Christa. "Schi-Zu, das wilde Medien-Tier: Ursula Pürrer und ihre Filme." *Gegenschuss: 16 Regisseure aus Österreich.* Ed. Peter Illetschko. Vienna: Wespennest, 1995. 193–208.

Braidt, Andrea. "The Stuff That Gender Is Made Of: *Dandy Dust* by Austro-British Filmmaker Hans Scheirl aka Angela H. Scheirl." *Blimp-Film Magazine* 39 (1998): 34–40.

Bravmann, Scott. "Postmodernism and Queer Identities." *Queer Theory / Sociology.* Ed. Steven Seidman. Oxford: Blackwell, 1996. 333–61.

Brett, Philip E. W., and Gary C. Thomas, eds. *Queering the Pitch: The New Gay and Lesbian Musicology.* New York: Routledge, 1993.

Brooks, Peter. *The Melodramatic Imagination: Balzac, Henry James, Melodrama, and the Mode of Excess.* New York: Columbia University Press, 1985.

Brophy, Philip. "The Animation of Sound." *The Illusion of Life: Essays on Animation.* Ed. Alan Cholodenko. Sydney: Power Institute of the Fine Arts, 1991. 67–112.

Burgoyne, Robert. "Narrative and Sexual Excess." *October* 21 (1982): 51–61.

Butler, Judith. *Bodies That Matter: On the Discursive Limits of "Sex."* New York: Routledge, 1993.

———. "Imitation and Gender Insubordination." *Inside/Out: Lesbian Theories, Gay Theories.* Ed. Diana Fuss. New York: Routledge, 1991. 13–31.

———. "Performative Acts and Gender Constitution: An Essay in Phenomenology and Feminist Theory." *Performing Feminisms: Feminist Critical Theory and Theatre.* Ed. Sue-Ellen Case. Baltimore: Johns Hopkins University Press, 1990. 270–82.

Cagle, Robert. "The Mechanical Reproduction of Melodrama: *Home Stores* and Gender Critique." Unpublished.

Castle, Terry. "In Praise of Brigitte Fassbaender: Reflections on Diva-Worship." Blackmer and Smith, *En Travesti.* 20–58.

Clément, Catherine. *Opera, or the Undoing of Women.* Trans. Betsy Wing. Minneapolis: University of Minnesota Press, 1988.

Corrigan, Timothy. *A Cinema Without Walls: Movies and Culture after Vietnam.* New Brunswick, N. J.: Rutgers University Press, 1991.

———. "On the Edge of History: The Radiant Spectacle of Werner Schroeter." *Film Quarterly* 37 (1984): 6–18.

———. "Werner Schroeter's Operatic Cinema." *Discourse* 3 (1981): 46–59.

Courant, Gérard. *Werner Schroeter.* Paris: Goethe Institute / La Cinémathèque Française, 1982.

Crimp, Douglas. "Fassbinder, Franz, Fox, Elvira, Erwin, Arnim, and All the Others." *October* 21 (1982): 63–81.

Currid, Brian. "'Es war so wunderbar!': Zarah Leander, ihre schwulen Fans und die Gegenöffentlichkeit der Erinnerung." *Montage/av* 7.1 (1998): 57–94.

De Lauretis, Teresa. "Film and the Visible." *How Do I Look?: Queer Film and Video.* Ed. Bad Object Choices. Seattle: Bay Press, 1991. 223–76.

———. "On the Subject of Fantasy." *Feminisms in the Cinema.* Ed. Laura Pietropaolo and Ada Testaferri. Bloomington: Indiana University Press, 1995. 63–85.

———. "Rethinking Women's Cinema: Aesthetics and Feminist Theory." *Issues in Feminist Film Criticism.* Ed. Patricia Erens. Bloomington: Indiana University Press, 1990. 288–308.

———. *The Practice of Love: Lesbian Sexuality and Perverse Desire.* Indianapolis: Indiana University Press, 1994.

De Man, Paul. *Allegories of Reading.* New Haven: Yale University Press, 1979.

———. "Pascal's Allegory of Persuasion." *Allegory and Representation.* Ed. Stephen Greenblatt. Baltimore: Johns Hopkins University Press, 1981. 1–25.

———. "The Rhetoric of Temporality." *Blindness and Insight: Essays in the Rhetoric of Contemporary Criticism.* 2d ed. Minneapolis: University of Minnesota Press, 1983. 187–228.

Der deutsche Experimentalfilm der 90er Jahre (The German Experimental Film of the 1990s). Munich: Goethe Institute, 1996.

Doane, Mary Ann. "Film and the Masquerade: Theorizing the Female Spectator." *Issues in Feminist Film Criticism.* Ed. Patricia Erens. Bloomington: Indiana University Press, 1990. 41–57.

Dölling, Irene, ed. *Filmfrauen—Zeitzeichen.* Vol. 1. *Diva.* Potsdam: Universität Potsdam, 1997.

Doty, Alexander. "There's Something Queer Here." *Out in Culture: Gay, Lesbian, and Queer Essays in Popular Culture.* Ed. Corey Creekmur and Alexander Doty. Durham, N.C.: Duke University Press, 1995. 71–90.

Dyer, Richard. "Less and More than Women and Men: Lesbian and Gay Cinema in Weimar Germany." *New German Critique* 51 (1990): 5–60.

———. *Now You See It: Studies on Lesbian and Gay Film.* London: Routledge, 1990.

———. "Reading Fassbinder's Sexual Politics." *Fassbinder.* Ed. Tony Rayns. London: British Film Institute, 1976. 54–64.

———. *The Matter of Images: Essay on Representations.* New York: Routledge, 1993.

Edelman, Lee. *Homographesis: Essays in Gay Literary and Cultural Theory.* New York: Routledge, 1994.

Eldorado: Homosexuelle Frauen und Männer in Berlin 1850–1950. Geschichte, Alltag und Kultur. Berlin: Hentrich, 1992.

Eloesser, Arthur. *Elisabeth Bergner.* Berlin: Williams, 1927.

Elsaesser, Thomas. *Fassbinder's Germany: History, Identity, Subject.* Amsterdam: Amsterdam University Press, 1996.

Engel, Antke. "Verqueeres Begehren." *Grenzen lesbischer Identitäten: Aufsätze.* Ed. Sabine Hark. Berlin: Querverlag, 1996.

Evans, Caroline, and Lorraine Gamann. "The Gaze Revisited, or, Reviewing Queer Viewing." *A Queer Romance: Lesbians, Gay Men and Popular Culture.* Ed. Paul Burston and Colin Richardson. New York: Routledge, 1995. 12–56.

Farber, Manny, and Patricia Patterson. "Fassbinder." *Film Comment* 11.6 (1975): 5–7.

293

Fassbinder, Rainer Werner. "In a Year of Thirteen Moons." *October* 21 (1982): 5–50.

———. *Querelle: Filmbuch*. Munich: Schirmer/Mosel, 1982.

———. *The Anarchy of the Imagination: Interviews, Essays, Notes*. Ed. Michael Töteberg and Leo Lensing. Trans. Krishna Winston. Baltimore: Johns Hopkins University Press, 1992.

Feil, Ken. "Ambiguous Sirk-Camp-Stances: Gay Camp and the 1950s Melodramas of Douglas Sirk." *Spectator* 15 (1994): 30–49.

Fineman, Joel. "The Structure of Allegorical Desire." *Allegory and Representation*. Ed. Stephen Greenblatt. Baltimore: Johns Hopkins University Press, 1981. 26–60.

Fischer, Lothar. *Tanz zwischen Rausch und Tod: Anita Berber 1918–1928 in Berlin*. Berlin: Haude & Spener, 1996.

Fischetti, Renate. "*Écriture féminine* in the New German Cinema: Ulrike Ottinger's *Portrait of a Woman Drinker*." *Women in German Yearbook* 4 (1988): 47–67.

Fletcher, Angus. *Allegory: The Theory of a Symbolic Mode*. Ithaca, New York: Cornell University Press, 1964.

Fout, John C. "Sexual Politics in Wilhelmine Germany: The Male Gender Crisis, Moral Purity, and Homophobia." *Forbidden History: The State, Society, and the Regulation of Sexuality in Modern Europe*. Ed. John Fout. University of Chicago Press, 1992. 361–90.

Freud, Sigmund. "Three Essays on the Theory of Sexuality." *The Standard Edition of the Complete Psychological Works*. Ed. James Strachey. London: Hogarth, 1953. 7: 125–243.

Frieden, Sandra. "In the Margins of Identity: Fassbinder's *In a Year of 13 Moons*." *Gender and German Cinema: Feminist Interventions*. Ed. Sandra Frieden et al. Vol. 1. Providence: Berg, 1993. 51–58.

Gaines, Jane. "The Queen Christina Tie-Ups: Convergence of Show Window and Screen." *Quarterly Review of Film and Video* 11 (1989): 35–60.

Gamman, Lorraine, and Merja Makinen. *Female Fetishism*. New York: New York University Press, 1994.

Garafola, Lynn. "The Travesty Dancer in Nineteenth-Century Ballet." *Crossing the Stage: Controversies on Cross-Dressing*. New York: Routledge, 1993. 96–106.

Garber, Marjorie. *Vested Interests: Cross-Dressing and Cultural Anxiety*. New York: Routledge, 1992.

Gemünden, Gerd. *Framed Visions: Popular Culture, Americanization, and the Contemporary German and Austrian Imagination*. Ann Arbor: University of Michigan Press, 1998.

———, Alice Kuzniar, and Klaus Phillips. "From *Taboo Parlor* to Porn and Passing: An Interview with Monika Treut." *Film Quarterly* 50 (1997): 2–12.

Gilbert, Sandra M. "Costumes of the Mind: Transvestism as Metaphor in Modern Literature." *Critical Inquiry* 7 (1980): 391–417.

Goldman, Ruth. "Who Is That *Queer* Queer? Exploring Norms around Sexuality, Race, and Class in Queer Theory." *Queer Studies: A Lesbian, Gay, Bisexual, and*

Transgender Anthology. Ed. Brett Beemyn and Mickey Eliason. New York: New York University Press, 1996. 169–82.

Goodbye to Berlin? 100 Jahre Schwulenbewegung. Berlin: Rosa Winkel, 1997.

Gramann, Karola and Heide Schlüpmann. "Unnatürliche Akte: Die Inszenierung der Lesbischen im Film." *Lust und Elend: Das erotische Kino*. Munich: Bucher, 1981. 70–93.

Griffen, Sean. "Pronoun Trouble: The 'Queerness' of Animation." *Spectator: USC Journal of Film and Television Criticism* 15 (1994): 94–109.

Grissemann, Stefan. "Die aquarellierten Androiden: Bemerkungen zu *Rote Ohren fetzen durch Asche* von Angela Hans Scheirl, Dietmar Schipek und Ursula Pürrer." *Der neue österreichische Film*. Ed. Gottfried Schlemmer. Vienna: Wespennest, 1996. 275–85.

Grosz, Elizabeth. "Intolerable Ambiguity: Freaks as/at the Limit." *Freakery: Cultural Spectacles of the Extraordinary Body*. Ed. Rosemarie Garland Thomson. New York: New York University Press, 1996. 55–66.

Hacker, Hanna. *Frauen und Freundinnen: Studien zur "weiblichen Homosexualität" am Beispiel Österreich 1870–1938*. Weinheim and Basel: Beltz, 1987.

Hake, Sabine. "'Gold, Love, Adventure': The Postmodern Piracy of *Madame X*." *Discourse* 11 (1988–89): 88–110.

Halberstam, Judith. "F2M: The Making of Female Masculinity," *The Lesbian Postmodern*. Ed. Laura Doan. New York: Columbia University Press, 1994: 210–28.

Hallensleben, Silvia. "*Die Statik der Eselsbrücken*: An Experiment in Experimental Film." *Millennium Film Journal* 30–31 (1997): 43–47.

Halliday, Jon. "Notes on Sirk's German Films." *Douglas Sirk*. Ed. Laura Mulvey and Jon Halliday. Edinburgh: Edinburgh Film Festival, 1972. 15–22.

Hansen, Miriam. "Visual Pleasure, Fetishism, and the Problem of Feminine/Feminist Discourse: Ulrike Ottinger's *Ticket of No Return*." *Gender and German Cinema: Feminist Interventions. Vol. 1*. Ed. Sandra Frieden. Providence: Berg, 1993. 189–204.

Hanson, Ellis. "Undead." *Inside/Out: Lesbian Theories, Gay Theories*. Ed. Diana Fuss. New York: Routledge, 1991. 324–40.

Hayn, Stefan. "Anmerkungen zur Kategorie 'Schwulenfilm'." *Rundbrief Film* (1995): 65–75.

Hekma, Gert. "'A Female Soul in a Male Body': Sexual Inversion as Gender Inversion in Nineteenth-Century Sexology." *Third Sex, Third Gender: Beyond Sexual Dimorphism in Culture and History*. Ed. Gilbert Herdt. New York: Zone, 1994. 213–39.

Hein, Birgit. "'Das wahre Wesen einer Frau': Die Filme von Claudia Schillinger." *Blaue Wunder: Neue Filme und Videos von Frauen 1984 bis 1994*. Ed. Eva Hohenberger and Karin Jurschick. Hamburg: Argument, 1994. 145–57.

———. "Michael Brynntrup." *Journal Film* 1 (1991): 31–32.

Hetze, Stefanie. *Happy-End für wen? Kino und lesbische Frauen*. Frankfurt: tende, 1986.

295

Works Cited

Hirschfeld, Magnus. *Berlins Drittes Geschlecht*. Berlin: Rosa Winkel, 1991.

———. *Von Einst bis Jetzt: Geschichte einer homosexuellen Bewegung 1897–1922*. Ed. Manfred Herzer and James Steakley. Berlin: Rosa Winkel, 1986.

Holmlund, Chris, and Cynthia Fuch, eds. *Between the Sheets, In the Streets: Queer, Lesbian, Gay Documentary*. Minneapolis: University of Minnesota Press, 1997.

Hoolboom, Mike. "Femme Fatale: The Films of Claudia Schillinger." *Millennium Film Journal* 30–31 (1997): 59–62.

———. "Scattering Stars: The Films of Matthias Müller." *Millennium Film Journal* 30–31 (1997): 81–88.

———. "*The Death Dances* of Michael Brynntrup." *Millennium Film Journal* 30–31 (1997): 39–42.

Indiana, Gary. "Scattered Picture: The Movies of Werner Schroeter." *Artforum* 20 (March, 1982): 46–51.

Jagose, Annamarie. *Queer Theory: An Introduction*. New York: New York University Press, 1996.

Jay, Karla, and Allen Young. *Out of the Closets: Voices of Gay Liberation*. N.p.: Douglas, 1972.

Jones, James W. *"We of the Third Sex": Literary Representations of Homosexuality in Wilhelmine Germany*. New York: Lang, 1990.

Jones, Graham, interviewer. *Talking Pictures: Interviews with Contemporary British Film-makers*. Ed. Lucy Johnson. London: British Film Institute, 1997. 68–71.

Kaltenecker, Siegfried. *Spie(ge)lformen: Männlichkeit und Differenz im Kino*. Basel: Stroemfeld, 1996.

Klippel, Heike. "Starring: Mimi Minus. Die Kurzfilme von Mara Mattuschka." *Blaue Wunder: Neue Filme und Videos von Frauen 1984 bis 1994*. Ed. Eva Hohenberg and Karin Jurschick. Hamburg: Argument, 1994. 124–44.

Klotz, Marcia. "The Queer and Unqueer Spaces of Monika Treut's Films." *Triangulated Visions: Women in Recent German Cinema*. Ed. Ingeborg Majer O'Sickey and Ingeborg von Zadow. Albany: SUNY Press, 1998. 65–77.

Knight, Julia. *Women and the New German Cinema*. New York: Verso, 1992.

Koch, Gertrud. "Von Detlef Sierck zu Douglas Sirk." *Frauen und Film* 44/45 (1988): 109–29.

Koepnick, Lutz. "En-gendering Mass Culture: The Case of Zarah Leander." *Gender and Germanness: Cultural Productions of Nation*. Ed. Patricia Herminghouse and Magda Mueller. Providence: Berghahn, 1997. 161–75.

———. "Sirk and the Culture Industry: *Zu neuen Ufern* and *The First Legion*." *Film Criticism* 23 (1999): 94–121.

Koestenbaum, Wayne. *The Queen's Throat: Opera, Homosexuality, and the Mystery of Desire*. New York: Poseidon, 1993.

Kurz, Gerhard. *Metapher, Allegorie, Symbol*. 2d ed. Göttingen: Vandenhoeck & Ruprecht, 1988.

Kuzniar, Alice, ed. *Outing Goethe and His Age*. Stanford: Stanford University Press, 1996.

Lacan, Jacques. *Feminine Sexuality: Jacques Lacan and the "Ecole freudienne."* Ed. Juliet Mitchell and Jacqueline Rose. New York: Norton, 1985.

———. *The Four Fundamental Concepts of Psycho-Analysis.* Trans. Alan Sheridan. New York: Norton, 1981.

Läufer, Elisabeth. *Skeptiker des Lichts: Douglas Sirk und seine Filme.* Frankfurt: Fischer, 1987.

Laplanche, Jean, and J.-B. Pontalis. "Fantasy and the Origins of Sexuality." *International Journal of Psycho-Analysis* 49 (1968): 1–18.

Lautmann, Rüdiger, and Angela Taeger. *Männerliebe im alten Deutschland: Sozialgeschichtliche Abhandlungen.* Berlin: Rosa Winkel, 1992.

LaValley, Al. "The Gay Liberation of Rainer Werner Fassbinder: Male Subjectivity, Male Bodies, Male Lovers." *New German Critique* 63 (1994): 109–37.

Leander, Zarah. *Es war so wunderbar! Mein Leben.* Hamburg: Hoffmann & Campe, 1973.

Lehndorff, Vera, and Holger Trülzsch. *"Veruschka" Trans-figurations.* Intro. Susan Sontag. Boston: Little, Brown, 1986.

Lenssen, Claudia. *Blaue Augen, Blauer Fleck: Kino im Wandel von der Diva zum Girlie.* Berlin: Parthas, 1997.

Lewis, Reina, and Katrina Rolley. "Ad(dressing) the Dyke: Lesbian Looks and Lesbian Looking." *Outlooks: Lesbian and Gay Sexualities and Visual Cultures.* Ed. Peter Horne and Reina Lewis. New York: Routledge, 1996. 178–90.

Longfellow, Brenda. "Lesbian phantasy and the Other woman in Ottinger's *Johanna d'Arc of Mongolia.*" *Screen* 34 (1993): 124–36.

Mahlsdorf, Charlotte von. *Ich bin meine eigene Frau: Ein Leben.* Berlin: diá, 1992.

Martin, Biddy. "Sexualities Without Genders and Other Queer Utopias." *Diacritics* 24 (1994): 104–21.

Mayne, Judith. *The Woman at the Keyhole: Feminism and Women's Cinema.* Bloomington: Indiana University Press, 1990.

Menche, Stefan. *Lambert Underground: 20 Filme von Lothar Lambert, Berlin 1971–1991.* Berlin: Metro, 1992.

Metz, Christian. *The Imaginary Signifier: Psychoanalysis and the Cinema.* Bloomington: Indiana University Press, 1982.

Meyer, Adèle. *Lila Nächte: Die Damenklubs im Berlin der Zwanziger Jahre.* Berlin: Edition Lit. europe, 1994.

Meyer, Moe. "Introduction: Reclaiming the Discourse of Camp." *The Politics and Poetics of Camp.* Ed. Moe Meyer. London: Routledge, 1994. 1–22.

———. "Unveiling the Word: Science and Narrative in Transsexual Striptease." *Gender in Performance: The Presentation of Difference in the Performing Arts.* Ed. Laurence Senelick. Hanover: University Press of New England, 1992. 68–85.

Miller, D. A. "Anal *Rope.*" *Inside/Out: Lesbian Theories, Gay Theories.* Ed. Diana Fuss. New York: Routledge, 1991. 119–41.

Moltke, Johannes von. "Camping in the Art Closet: The Politics of Camp and Nation in German Film." *New German Critique* 63 (1994): 77–106.

297

Works Cited

———. "Die Diva *oder* Körper von Gewicht." *FFK 8: Dokumentation des 8. Film-und Fernsehwissenschaftlichen Kolloquiums an der Universität Hildesheim, Oktober 1995.* Ed. Johannes von Moltke et al. Hildesheim: Universität Hildesheim, 1996. 217–26.

Moreau, Jeanne. "My Encounter with the Unknown Dancer." *Rainer Werner Fassbinder.* Ed. Laurence Kardish. New York: MoMa, 1997. 99–101.

Müller, Klaus. *Aber in meinem Herzen sprach eine Stimme so laut: Homosexuelle Autobiographien und medizinische Pathographien im neunzehnten Jahrhundert.* Berlin: Rosa Winkel, 1991.

Müller, Matthias. "The Cinema of Difference." *Millennium Film Journal* 30–31 (1997): 3–6.

Mueller, Roswitha. "The Mirror and the Vamp." *New German Critique* 34 (1985): 176–93.

Mulvey, Laura. *Visual and Other Pleasures.* London: Macmillan, 1989.

Murphy, Richard. "Carnival Desire and the Sideshow of Fantasy: Dream, Duplicity and Representational Instability in *The Cabinet of Dr. Caligari.*" *Germanic Review* 66 (1991): 48–56.

Nägele, Rainer. *Theater, Theory, Speculation: Walter Benjamin and the Scenes of Modernity.* Baltimore: Johns Hopkins University Press, 1991.

O'Neill, Edward R. "*Poison*-ous Queers: Violence and Social Order." *Spectator* 15 (1994): 8–29.

Owens, Craig. "The Allegorical Impulse: Toward a Theory of Postmodernism." *Art after Modernism: Rethinking Representation.* Ed. Brian Wallis. New York: New Museum of Contemporary Art, 1984. 203–35.

Peck, Jeffrey M. "The Films of Lothar Lambert." *Gender and German Cinema: Feminist Interventions.* Vol. 1. Ed. Sandra Frieden et al. Providence: Berg, 1993. 225–39.

Perlmutter, Ruth. "German Grotesque: Two Films by Sander and Ottinger." *Gender and German Cinema: Feminist Interventions. Vol. 1.* Ed. Sandra Frieden et. al. Providence: Berg, 1993. 167–78.

Petley, Julian. "Sirk in Germany." *Sight and Sound* 57 (1987–88): 58–61.

Petro, Patrice. *Joyless Streets: Women and Melodramatic Representation in Weimar Germany.* Princeton: Princeton University Press, 1989.

Plötz, Kirsten. "Bubis und Damen: Die zwanziger Jahre." *Butch Femme: Eine erotische Kultur.* Ed. Stephanie Kuhnen. Berlin: Querverlag, 1997. 35–47.

Praunheim, Rosa von. *Army of Lovers.* London: Gay Men's Press, 1980.

———. "Die Baßamsel singt nicht mehr." *Der Spiegel* 27 (1981): 158–59.

———. *50 Jahre pervers: Die sentimentalen Memoiren von Rosa von Praunheim.* Cologne: Kiepenheuer & Witsch, 1993.

———. *Sex und Karriere.* Munich: Rogner & Bernhard, 1976.

———. "Schwul, pervers, kontrovers." *Berliner Zeitung* 10 June 1992.

Quilligan, Maureen. *The Language of Allegory: Defining the Genre.* Ithaca, N.Y.: Cornell University Press, 1979.

Raab, Kurt, and Karsten Peters. *Die Sehnsucht des Rainer Werner Fassbinder*. Munich: Bertelsmann, 1982.

Rentschler, Eric. *The Ministry of Illusion: Nazi Cinema and Its Afterlife*. Harvard University Press, 1996.

———, ed. *West German Filmmakers on Film: Visions and Voices*. New York: Holmes and Meier, 1988.

Rich, B. Ruby. "*Mädchen in Uniform*: From Repressive Tolerance to Erotic Liberation." *Re-Vision*. Ed. Mary Ann Doane. Los Angeles: University Publications of America, 1984. 100–30.

Rosa von Praunheim. Munich: Hanser, 1984.

Ross, Andrew. *Real Love: In Pursuit of Cultural Justice*. New York: New York University Press, 1998.

Russo, Mary. *The Female Grotesque: Risk, Excess, and Modernity*. New York: Routledge, 1994.

Sanders-Brahms, Helma. "Zarah." *Das Dunkle zwischen den Bildern*. Frankfurt: Verlag der Autoren, 1992. 57–64.

Sannwald, Daniela. "Nobody Is Perfect: Maria Schmidts Travestie-Video *Tanten, Tunten, Kesse Väter*." *Rundbrief Film* 6 (1996): 357–59.

Scheirl, Hans A. "Ein interaktives e-mail Interview." *Rundbrief Film* 8 (1996): 489–92.

———. "Manifesto for the Dada of the Cyborg-Embrio." *The Eight Technologies of Otherness*. Ed. Sue Golding. London: Routledge, 1997. 45–57.

Schillinger, Claudia. "I'm Not Against Pornography: An Interview." *The Independent Eye* Special Issue on "Germany: Over the Wall" (Spring 1990): 61–65.

Schlüpmann, Heide. "*Ich möchte kein Mann sein*: Ernst Lubitsch, Sigmund Freud und die frühe deutsche Komödie." *KINtop* 1 (1992).

Schüttelkopf, Elke. "Blutig ist die Revolution der Liebe." *Rundbrief Film: Filme in lesbisch-schwulem Kontext* 1 (June 1995): 15–18.

———. "'Da zeigt sich Wirklichkeit auf eine ganz besondere Weise': Ein Porträt der Videokünstlerinnen Ilse Gassinger und Anna Steininger." *Blaue Wunder: Neue Filme und Videos von Frauen 1984 bis 1994*. Ed. Eva Hohenberger and Karin Jurschick. Hamburg: Argument, 1994. 84–123.

Sedgwick, Eve. *Epistemology of the Closet*. Berkeley: University of California Press, 1990.

———. *Tendencies*. Durham, N.C.: Duke University Press, 1993.

Seiler, Paul. *Ein Mythos lebt: Zarah Leander*. Berlin: n. p., 1991.

———. *Zarah Diva: Das Porträt eines Stars*. Berlin: Albino, 1985.

———. *Zarah Leander: Ein Kultbuch*. Hamburg: Rowohlt, 1985.

———. *Zarah Leander. Ich bin eine Stimme*. Berlin: Ullstein, 1997.

Shaviro, Steven. *The Cinematic Body*. Minneapolis: University of Minnesota Press, 1993.

Sieglohr, Ulrike. "Excess Yearning: The Operatic in Werner Schroeter's Cinema."

299

A Night at the Opera: Media Representations of Opera. Ed. Jeremy Tambling. London: Libbey, 1994. 195–217.

———. "Why Drag the Diva Into It? Werner Schroeter's Gay Representation of Femininity." *Triangulated Visions: Women in Recent German Cinema.* Ed. Ingeborg Majer O'Sickey and Ingeborg von Zadow. Albany: SUNY Press, 1998. 163–72.

Sikov, Ed. "Querelle." *Cineaste* 8.1 (1983): 40–42.

Silberman, Marc. "Zarah Leander in the Colonies." *Medien/Kultur: Schnittstellen zwischen Medienwissenschaft, Medienpraxis und gesellschaftlicher Kommunikation.* Ed. Knut Hickethier and Siegfried Zielinski. Berlin: Spiess, 1991. 247–53.

Silverman, Kaja. *Male Subjectivity at the Margins.* New York: Routledge, 1992.

———. *The Subject of Semiotics.* New York: Oxford University Press, 1983.

———. *The Threshold of the Visible World.* New York: Routledge, 1996.

Skinner, Jody. *Warme Brüder. Kesse Väter: Lexikon mit Ausdrücken für Lesben, Schwule und Homosexualität.* Essen: Blaue Eule, 1997.

Solomon, Charles, ed. *The Art of the Animated Image.* Los Angeles: The American Film Institute, 1987.

Sontag, Susan. "Notes on Camp." *A Susan Sontag Reader.* New York: Vintage Books, 1983. 105–19.

Speck, Wieland. "Porno?" *Queer Looks: Perspectives on Lesbian and Gay Film and Video.* Ed. Martha Gever, John Greyson, and Pratibha Parmar. New York: Routledge, 1993. 348–54.

Spoto, Donald. *Blue Angel: The Life of Marlene Dietrich.* New York: Doubleday, 1992.

Steakley, James D. "Film und Zensur in der Weimarer Republik: Der Fall *Anders als die Andern.*" *Capri: Zeitschrift für schwule Geschichte* 21 (1996): 2–33.

———. *The Homosexual Emancipation Movement in Germany.* New York: Arno, 1975.

Straayer, Chris. *Deviant Eyes, Deviant Bodies: Sexual Re-Orientations in Film and Video.* New York: Columbia University Press, 1996.

Streese, Konstanze, and Kerry Shea. "Who's Looking? Who's Laughing? Of Multicultural Mothers and Men in Percy Adlon's *Bagdad Café.*" *Women in German Yearbook* 8 (1992): 179–97.

Stümke, Hans-Georg. *Älter werden wir umsonst: Schwules Leben jenseits der Dreißig. Erfahrungen, Interviews, Berichte.* Berlin: Rosa Winkel, 1998.

Teague, David. "Trash and Vaudeville." Honors Thesis. University of North Carolina, Chapel Hill. 1998.

Teskey, Gordon. *Allegory and Violence.* Ithaca, N.Y.: Cornell University Press, 1996.

Theis, Wolfgang. "Schünzels Requisiten: Zum Beispiel: die Handschuhe." *Reinhold Schünzel.* Ed. Jörg Schöning. Munich: edition text und kritik, 1989. 21–24.

Traub, Valerie. "The Ambiguities of 'Lesbian' Viewing Pleasure: The (Dis)articulations of *Black Widow.*" *Body Guards: The Cultural Politics of Gender Ambiguity.* Ed. Julia Epstein and Kristina Straub. New York: Routledge, 1991. 305–28.

Treut, Monika. "Man to Man." *Sight and Sound* 4.5 (1994): 69.

Ulrike Ottinger: Texte und Dokumente. Special Issue of *Kinemathek* 86 (1995).

Waugh, Thomas. *Hard to Imagine: Gay Male Eroticism in Photography and Film from Their Beginnings to Stonewall*. New York: Columbia University Press, 1996.

Weiss, Andrea. "A Queer Feeling When I Look at You": Hollywood Stars and Lesbian Spectatorship in the 1980s." *Multiple Voices in Feminist Film Criticism*. Ed. Diane Carson, Linda Dittmar, and Janice Welsch. Minneapolis: University of Minnesota Press, 1994. 330–42.

———. *Vampires and Violets: Lesbians in the Cinema*. London: Jonathan Cape, 1992.

Wellbery, David E. *The Specular Moment: Goethe's Early Lyric and the Beginnings of Romanticism*. Stanford: Stanford University Press, 1996.

Wenders, Wim. *Emotion Pictures*. Frankfurt: Verlag der Autoren, 1986.

Werner Schroeter. Munich: Hanser, 1980.

White, Patricia. "Madame X of the China Seas: A Study of Ulrike Ottinger's Film." *Screen* 28 (1987): 80–95.

Williams, Linda. *Hard Core: Power, Pleasure, and the Frenzy of the Visible*. Berkeley: University of California Press, 1989.

Wood, Elizabeth. "Sapphonics." Brett and Thomas, *Queering the Pitch*. 27–66.

Zimmermann, Ulrike. "*Between*—Verhüllung und Verfremdung: Inszenierung sexueller Phantasien neurer Experimentalfilme von Frauen." *Junge Kunst der 9oer*. Braunschweig: HbK Braunschweig, 1993. 89.

Žižek, Slavoj. *The Metastases of Enjoyment: Six Essays on Woman and Causality*. London: Verso, 1994.

———. *The Sublime Object of Ideology*. London: Verso, 1989.

Zweig, Stefan. *Die Welt von Gestern: Erinnerungen eines Europäers*. Berlin: Aufbau, 1981.

Index

In this index an "f" after a number indicates a separate reference on the next page, and an "ff" indicates separate references on the next two pages. A continuous discussion over two or more pages is indicated by a span of page numbers, e.g., "57–59." *Passim* is used for a cluster of references in close but not consecutive sequence.

Index

Index

O'Toole, Owen, 208
Ottinger, Ulrike, 3ff, 12, 14, 19, 88f, 91,
101, 114, 138–59, 195, 233, 255, 271n,
283f; *Berlinfieber*, 139; *Bildnis einer
Trinkerin (Ticket of No Return)*, 140, 142,
150f, 157, 283f; *Countdown*, 139; *Dorian
Gray im Spiegel der Boulevardpresse*, 4f, 8,
11, 19, 42, 139–56; *Freak Orlando*, 7, 112,
140ff, 150, 154f; *Johanna d'Arc of Mongolia*, 140f, 157, 283f; *Madame X—Eine
absolute Herrscherin*, 139–42, 151, 153f,
157, 284n; *Superbia—Der Stolz*, 140
Owens, Craig, 1, 9, 13f

Pabst, G. W.: *Pandoras Büchse*, 2, 30
Palermo oder Wolfsburg, see Schroeter,
Werner
Pandoras Büchse, see Pabst, G. W.
Paragraph 175, 18, 59, 92
Paris is Burning, 153, 280f
pederasty, pedophilia, 114, 215, 220
PELZE, 236, 252
Pensão Globo, see Müller, Matthias
Percillier, Nathalie, 3, 172, 207, 216,
236–45 *passim*, 256f, 288n; *Abgrund-
geschichte*, 246; *Bloody Well Done*, 239–44,
249; *Heldinnen der Liebe*, 160, 170ff, 237,
241f, 244; *Mein 37. Abenteuer*, 191, 240;
Tapetengemüt, 241
Petersen, Kristian, 191
Petersen, Wolfgang, 15
Petro, Patrice, 273n
Piss in Rosa, see Scheirl, Hans Angela
Plötzlich und Unerwartet—eine Déjà Revue,
see Brynntup, Michael
Pontalis, J. B., see Laplanche, Jean, and
J. B. Pontalis
pornography, 166ff, 176, 198, 227, 232,
287n; in Brynntrup, 14, 198, 203, 205,
262; in Praunheim, 93, 97, 101, 107; in
Schillinger, 216–22 *passim*, 262
Porzner, Hucky, 191
Positiv, see Praunheim, Rosa von
Postmodernism, 9, 12, 69, 149, 163, 169,
179, 198, 201, 207, 225, 234
Praunheim, Rosa von, 43, 88–115, 154,
160–63, 168–74 *passim*, 195, 205, 255–63

passim, 271n, 280f, 283n; *50 Jahre pervers*,
91, 280n; *Affengeil: Eine Reise durch Lottis
Leben*, 89, 103; *Anita: Tänze des Lasters*,
21, 89, 108, 163, 271n; *Armee der Liebenden oder Aufstand der Perversen*, 89ff, 260;
Die Bettwurst, 89, 96, 102, 108; *The Einstein of Sex: The Life and Work of Dr. Magnus Hirschfeld*, 88; *Feuer unterm Arsch*, 89,
91; *Grotesk-Burlesk-Pittoresk*, 88; *The History of Homosexuality from Stonehenge to
Stonewall and Beyond*, 88; *Horror Vacui*, 21,
88f, 102; *Ich bin ein Antistar*, 89; *Ich bin
meine eigene Frau*, 89, 93, 103–11, 163,
202; on Leander, Zarah, 57–66 *passim*;
Leidenschaften, 88; *Macbeth*, 88; *Neurosia*,
14, 91, 103, 108, 111f; and New German
Cinema directors, 1–5, 7, 16, 19, 74, 86ff,
113ff, 127, 137, 154, 272n; *Nicht der Homosexuelle ist pervers, sondern die Situation,
in der er lebt (Schwulenfilm)*, 4, 7, 13, 18,
89, 92–103, 111f, 115, 255, 260; *Positiv*,
89–92; *Samuel Beckett*, 88; *Schweigen =
Tod*, 89–92, 103; *Schwestern der Revolution*,
88; *Schwuler Mut—100 Jahre Schwulenbewegung*, 89, 172, 271n; *Stadt der verlorenen
Seelen*, 89, 108, 111; *Ein Virus kennt keine
Moral*, 88ff, 260; *Von Rosa von Praunheim*,
88; *Tagebuch in Rosa*, 88; *Überleben in New
York*, 93, 160, 169, 172; *Underground and
Emigrants*, 280n; *Unsere Leichen leben noch*,
89; *Vor Transsexuellen wird gewarnt*, 87, 89,
193
Prince (singer), 217
psychomachia, 139, 227
Pürrer, Ursula (Schi-zu), 3, 5, 14, 138,
187f, 195, 224, 230–34, 244, 255, 262;
Das Aufbegehren oder das andere Begehren,
231f; *The Drift of Juicy*, 231ff, 288n.
See also under Scheirl, Hans Angela:
collaborations with Ursula Pürrer

queer: defined, 5–8, 53, 99, 173, 256f, 260
Queer German Cinema, 3ff, 8ff, 13f, 17ff,
88, 161, 180
Quilligan, Maureen, 12, 230

Raab, Kurt, 74

Index

Library of Congress Cataloging-in-Publication Data

Kuzniar, Alice A.
  The queer German cinema / Alice A. Kuzniar.
    p. cm.
  Includes bibliographical references and index.
  ISBN 0-8047-3748-7 (alk. paper) — ISBN 0-8047-3995-1
(pbk. : alk. paper)
    1. Homosexuality in motion pictures. 2. Motion pictures—
Germany. I. Title.
PN1995.9H55 K89 2000
791.43'653—dc21   00-020494

⊗ This book is printed on acid-free, recycled paper.

Original printing 2000

Last figure below indicates year of this printing:
09 08 07 06 05 04 03 02 01 00

Designed by Janet Wood
Typeset by James P. Brommer in 9.75/13 Janson and
Franklin Gothic display